Reading Racism and the Criminal Justice System

Edited by
David Baker

Canadian Scholars' Press Inc. Toronto 1994

Reading Racism and the Criminal Justice System

First published in 1994 by
Canadian Scholars' Press Inc.
180 Bloor St. W., Ste. 402
Toronto, Ontario
M5S 2V6

Canadian Cataloguing in Publication Data

Main entry under title:
Reading Racism and the Criminal Justice System
Includes bibliographical references.
ISBN 1-55130-038-9

1. Criminal Justice, Administration of. 2. Racism.
3. Blacks - Civil rights. I. Baker, David (David Noel).

K5001.Z9R4 1994 342'.0873 C94-930128-0

Page design and layout by Brad Horning, Toronto

Printed and bound in Canada

To Claudette, Mandisa and Nichole.

Acknowledgements

I remain deeply indebted to several people on whom demands were made during the entire course of this endeavor. Firstly, I would like to thank the contributors, some of the leading scholars in the area, for bringing theoretically and methodologically challenging perspectives to this venture. I would like to thank the office staff of York University Sociology Department; Audrey, Myrna, Jackie, Pat, Ursula and Silvia. To them, I extend my appreciation.

Further, I am indebted to a number of colleagues and friends for the inspiration afforded during the preparation of this book. To Leyland Gudge, Kevin R.E. McCormick, Ken Panaram, Kathy Orban, Dr. James Hodgson, for their input in shaping of the text. And to the many students at York University who provided me with comments at several stages of this collection. I would like to thank Dr. Jack Wayne for undertaking to publish this work. Pamela Hamilton, your professionalism served as an inspiration.

This work would never have been made possible without the support of Dr. Livy Visano. Again, thanks for your guidance. Finally, I would like to thank my family for the ongoing encouragement and unconditional support through these times.

Table of Contents

Foreword

Leyland Gudge
Director, St. Clair Community Youth Services of Metropolitan Toronto

Complexity has always been synonymous with the justice system. However, in a simplistic sense this complex system is integrally rooted in our day-to-day community life. It is through the historic existence and development of neighborhoods and communities that policing traditions over the years were forged and shaped. Our jurors are drawn from the community. It is in the hustle and bustle of community life that our lawyers and later judges first nurture and experience the development of their professional practices. Also, it is the accepted levels of community standards that shape law-making and the manner of its application by the courts. Ultimately, we envisage a justice system that is and should remain accountable to the community-at-large. Progressively, our everyday community life and its citizenry are having a significant impact on the ever-increasing size, functions and complexity of our justice system. Despite this seminal communal characteristic of our justice system, our communities seemed locked in a relentless conflict with the agents and agencies of our justice system. Likewise, the incomprehensibility regarding the way our justice system works seems to increase in direct proportion to the system's growth and complexity. It is against this backdrop that race, as a similarly seminal and integral phenomenon of everyday community life, has progressively become a disconcerting, if not conflicting, issue within the justice system, its agents and agencies.

Moments in history, race has been a defining quality of communities, where in designated geographical areas, people of either similar or different ethnic backgrounds, values, beliefs and languages live and interact in pursuing their individual and/or group needs and interests. Anthropology and history would have taught us that all races of humans have established and implemented laws, institutions and systems of justice. However, throughout the same course of history, some race groups have experienced unceasing forms of oppressive, brutal, inhumane and unfair treatment by agents and agencies representative of the same or other race groups that purported to mete out a system of justice that was undeniably based on prejudicial, discriminatory and unfair practices. Let me make it clear that I am not talking simply about a system of justice that is relative to any particular ethnic, cultural and religious beliefs and values. Rather, I speak about a system of justice that is designed and developed by representatives of any dominant race group and where justice is interpreted and dispensed based on systemic and personal racist beliefs and practices of those representatives of that dominant race group.

Our world history, and particularly Euro-American history, is replete with documented accounts of the experiences of racial oppression shared by racial minority groups. Today, in many major metropolitan world centers, racial minority groups are experiencing a steadily escalating conflictual relationship with the criminal justice system, particularly policing. Despite such historic and lingering racial tyranny, there has been a dearth of literature on the subject of this conflicting duality of crime and race. Primarily, in the past twenty years, especially in the United States and Britain, some attempts have been made in producing a body of knowledge which speaks to the conflicts and inequities of the criminal justice system and its impact on the racial minority groups that it purports to serve. The customary focus of present-day literature is largely directed at police/racial minority relations, thus neglecting much-needed study and analyses of the other systemic areas of the criminal justice system. Historically oppressed groups have used the informal and sometimes underground methods of documenting and producing information material about their oppressive experiences with "the system." Though painfully real, many of these incidents and stories have not found and may never find expression in well-researched analytical studies which focus in a comprehensive way on how the various agencies and agents of the criminal justice system impact on racial minority groups.

Within contemporary literature on crime, law and policing the issue of race is reflected in scant fashion in a chapter or two. Likewise, within the walls of academic and professional studies of criminology, law, sociology and policing, this subject matter is neither comprehensively covered or integrally woven into the core curricula. Yet, and especially in some Euro-American major metropolitan centers of the U.K., the U.S., France and Canada, the criminal justice system in concert with other governmental bureaucracies prides itself in developing sophisticated race relations, cross-cultural and multicultural models designed to enhance the system's working relationship with racial minority groups. Without a fundamental and comprehensive body of knowledge that dualistically focuses on crime and race, efforts at combatting racism in the criminal justice system continue to ring hollow and remain selective and self-serving. Perhaps it is a further reflection of the notion of the dominant group utilizing its power in determining what kind of information is produced and made available about and to minority groups.

In Canada, any literature search on the dual topic of crime and race will disclose the abject paucity of such literary material in a country which prides itself as a multicultural society and which is also active in the vanguard of the international movements for human rights and justice. Canada's own historical accounts will have recorded the racist inequities suffered by its indigenous native peoples at the hands of Canada's criminal justice system. In recent times the Marshall Inquiry in Nova Scotia, the Aboriginal Justice Inquiry in Manitoba, the Caswey Report in Alberta and the Marcellus Francois Inquest Report in Montreal are all testimony to the existence of systemic racism in the Canadian criminal justice system. Together with the disproportionate number of Native Indians and Blacks involved day-to-day with the criminal justice system, those languishing in Canadian jails and others being fatally shot by police have moved governments to begin to seriously address the complaints, concerns and ongoing conflictual relationship between racial minorities and "the system." In the spring of 1993, the Ontario government established a Commission on Systemic Racism in the Ontario Criminal Justice System. One of the areas in which this Commission is mandated to examine and make recommendations is "the need for future studies into racism inherent in the law." There is no denying that if governments and the agencies and agents of the criminal justice system are to be taken seriously in their anti-racist initiatives, there must be an enhanced development in the body of knowledge which fundamentally serves to inform, mould and shape such anti-racist models, methodologies and practices. Literature on the dualistic issues of crime/law and race are not merely required for scholastic discourse. Rather, such literature is virtually necessary if citizens in society are to comprehend, preserve and promote the ideals of equality, fairness and justice on which "the system" is founded. Salient issues must be dealt with, e.g. the various symbolisms used by "the system" and what, if any, are their meaning and value to racial minority groups; systemic interdependency and its impact on minorities; the racial minority as victim; the meaning and validity of crime statistics by race; and accountability of "the system" relative to minority groups. A cursory look at some of these issues will underscore the need for greater understanding, awareness and knowledge at the community level.

For community groups, this book of essays provides a ray of focus on a number of the complex issues of crime and race which are at the front and center of current community discussions and debates. These essays should, at the least, whet the appetite and act as an impetus for action geared in further developing of much-needed studies, analyses and publication of literature on this growing, intertwined issues of crime and race. Communities of interests, e.g. race and ethnic groups, law enforcement and justice department officials, sociology research departments, etc., must seek to enhance the body of knowledge in this sorely neglected field of study — a field which has profound impact and effect on the everyday life of individuals in our community. In the meantime, the broad spectrum of community groups continue to believe in the principles of law and order and to hold out hope in the ability of the justice system to live up to its ideals and commitment to carry out its function in a fair and just manner towards all of humankind.

Editor's Introduction

Reading 'Racism' and Canadian Criminal Justice

David N. Baker

"They cannot represent themselves, they must be represented."
Karl Marx, *The Eighteenth Brumaire of Louis Bonaparte.*[1]

What importance does "racism" have as a meaningful category in the study of Canadian criminal justice and the shaping of the future? If we attempt to answer this question by examining the history of criminal justice and its criticism in Canada, our initial response would probably be "noting" or, at the very least, "noting explicitly." Indeed, until the past decade or so, in a subtle and sensitive way critics of Canadian criminal justice argued that, except for odd moments in the history of Canadian criminal justice, racism has not been brought to bear upon the study of the justice system, in any apparent way. An abundance of studies have been undertaken and many books, chapters, and articles have been written about *racism and criminal justice.* However, the way racism/crime is conceptualized remains a matter of choice of the various writers. Whether Britain, Canada or the United States is being engulfed by a wave of crime is debatable; but the nexus between Blacks and other racial minorities within the criminal justice system has been consistently overlooked. One has to be aware of a correlation between the condition of Blacks and the condition of other racial minorities in these nations. I had somewhat simplistically attributed the subordinate status of *other* groups to their historically oppressed economic situation. Clearly economics was the underlying element in racial subjugation in these metropoles. Under this premise I began to look into why specifically little has been written about *Blacks* and the Canadian criminal justice system. This motivated me to what will undoubtedly be considered a controversial deduction, insofar as it is based on a taboo topic: *racism.*

Whenever a serious crime of a violent nature — for example, a mugging, an assault or a rape — is discussed in private social circles, captured in the local newspaper headline, or is the subject of the nightly television news, the perpetrator who comes immediately to the public mind is a person of color. The stereotyped offender's race/ethnicity is usually modified depending upon the specific concentration of Native Canadians/Americans, Blacks, Hispanics or Asians in an area, but the abstraction/image persists that members of these subpopulations are more dangerous or criminal than the *Euro American*[2] majority group.

Whites typically stereotype — and often caricature — *others* who happen to be of a different skin color by, for example, viewing the classic rapist as a "black man," the representative opium user as a "yellow man," the "red man" as a drunken Indian, and each of these peoples of color, collectively and individually, as constituting the *crime problem.*

In sum, it is generally assumed that color plays a role in the determination of criminality, but existing research on this topic has not clearly demonstrated how or why this happens. Studies within Britain and U.S.A. focus primarily on Blacks and neglect other racial minorities. However, in the Canadian context the emphasis is on race relations and criminal justice. This body of literature is likewise singularly unhelpful to a study of racism and criminal justice, except peripherally here and there. Such literature is devoted to some administrative actions that involve either formal proceedings or judicial review. What it neglects is the percentage of actions that escapes both formal proceedings and judicial review.

Doing the research needed for a *developing* Canadian criminal justice may be compared with keeping in repair an old roof of an enormous building.[3] Canadian scholarly roof on this particular topic (racism and criminal justice) in its present condition, is strange to behold. But why?

My hope is that this collections of essays may induce some Canadian scholars who are crowding the rules end of the roof to direct their talents to the areas of racism and criminal justice that are urgently in need of repair. In reading this volume one has to keep in mind questions as to how frequent is differential treatment of racial minorities? In fact, who are these minorities? In what form does this differential treatment of blacks and other minorities manifest itself? And at what points in the system of criminal justice is differential treatment of minorities encountered? These and other questions are asked and some answers are provided by scholars to the left and right of the political spectrum.

Chapter Summaries

Various chapters focus on biases in criminal justice decision-making, from arrest to bail and sentencing decisions, the differential application of law and the economic factor. It is clear, according to Willhelm (1986) that the family thesis (e.g. feminization of poverty), the class analysis (e.g. Marxism), and the colonial model do not explain *The Economic Demise of Blacks in America.* Rather, it is capitalism divorced from black labor through computerized technology. The result: unemployment, the path to lower income, greater poverty, decreased education, higher crime and more racism. Robert

Staples (1987), looks at various reasons for the persistence of the black success myth advanced by whites who harbor gross misconceptions about the "progress" blacks have made towards equality.

The role of race in the imposition of death penalty has a long and controversial past. Radelet's (1989) archival research centers on the *Executions of Whites for Crimes against Blacks*. Special attention is paid to the status of the white defendant; the white defendant in some cases was already in trouble with authorities before he committed the crime against a Black. It is vital to note, as race is the most important, but not the only, status attribute in death sentencing. For Butler, Fukurai and Krooth (1991) racism is the institutional and individual bias in jury selection that includes various forms of structural conditions — privilege — that prevent full-community jury participation. Such structural conditions facilitate Anglo ideas of supremacy that set limits on the rights of black people and reduce their freedom to equally participate in judicial decision-making.

Patricia Williams' (1987) discussion looks at how the rhetoric of privatization in response to racial issues functions as the rationalizing agent of public unaccountability/irresponsibility. A sociolinguistic analysis of the language of jurors, lawyers and politicians is presented from three racially motivated violence cases in New York City. Racism or "spirit-murder," it is a argued, ought to be reconceptualized as a crime; as socially costly and physically obliterating as physical assault or robbery.

In "Discrimination Revisited," Bynum and Paternoster shed light on the backstage regions of criminal justice decision-making. They argue that while Native Americans are not more severely treated during sentencing, they are less likely to be paroled than the non-native American offender. To understand the present and future problems of racism and criminal justice, we need to understand the broader Canadian political agenda within which issues of racism exist. The same controversies that beset most economic and social policy-making in Canada also plague attempts in the fight against racism. At the core of any attempt to deal with this phenomenon is the conflict of Federal and Provincial interests and jurisdictions. Tom Fleming's (1993) thought-provoking article speaks to this dilemma. He also reminds us that the portrayal of oppressed peoples as criminals and their treatment as such by the criminal justice system is a tactic long employed by the dominant cultures. The 'law,' as Peter Fitzpatrick has so skillfully shown, is tied to a particular community which excludes those whom law would include through race relation legislation.

John Solomos and Tim Rackett (1991), reinforce a point often made, that if policy changes are not enacted to alleviate social injustice suffered by black people in Britain, tough policing will have to remain the order of the day. Eugene McLaughin (1991) addresses the issue of police accountability. Tony Jefferson (1991) reminds us that in order to produce an understanding of race and police work, it is necessary to unravel the complexities.

Complexities need to be unraveled through research. But, as Cyril Robinson (1985) notes, rather than helping people solve their everday problems, criminal justice research helps to mystify, obfuscate and complicate possible solutions. Racism of the sort described throughout this book will not disappear overnight. This will take a conscious effort on the part of society as we advance towards the twenty-first century. However

> [t]hose who believe that racial oppression is on its way out or can be readly eliminated in American life through reforms that guarantee greater equality in living standards and political participation, fail to reckon with the 'integrating'role that racism performs for the society and the depths to which it has penetrated the national culture (Blauner 1972).[4]

Such a conclusion does not provide a happy ending. But then, racism is not a happy story.

ENDNOTES

1. See R.C. Tucker (ed.), *The Marx-Engels Reader* (New York: W.W. Norton, 1976: 608).
2. See Coramae Richey Mann, *Unequal Justice: A Question of Color* (Bloomington: Indiana University Press, 1993), for the development of this concept.
3. See K.C. Davis, *Discretionary Justice: A Preliminary Inquiry* (Baton Rouge: Louisianna State University Press, 1971). Highlight the point:

   > Only an occasional worker gives attention to the big holes, while the majority of workers swarm over the rules end, stopping or preventing slow leaks, and reinforcing at points where leaks seem impossible.... Not much is attempted except patchwork, and that is one reason the workers ignore the big holes, many of which call for structural changes requiring architectural imagination.

4. See R. Blauner, *Racial Oppression in America.* (New York: Harper and Row, 1972).

Chapter 1

Capitalism without Racism: Science or Fantasy?

William Sales Jr.

Introduction

Currently, one of the popular slogans on the left is that "black liberation is a struggle for socialism." This slogan emerges from the orthodox Marxist analysis of the causal relationship between capitalism and racism. Capitalism is here seen as the material basis upon which the attitudes, policies and practices of racism rest. According to this line of reasoning the establishment of the Triangular Slave Trade and the institution of chattel slavery in the western hemisphere represented a tremendous impulse toward the development of capitalism in western Europe and America.

The brutal oppression and exploitation of African and native American labor which accompanied this process of primitive accumulation had to be rationalized. Herein we have the genesis of racism, the pseudo-scientific ideology which assigns to those of non-European and especially African origin, traits of biological, intellectual and moral inferiority, and on this basis assigns a superior and dominating status to those of European and especially Teutonic origins. Moreover, capitalism did not merely produce one historic rationale for racism but continuously reproduces new rationales for racism as the development of the process of capital accumulation assigns new but subordinate roles to black labor.

While the form of this reproduction of racism has varied over time, its functional content has remained the same. Orthodox Marxists have identified racism as a particularly powerful mode of the strategy of "divide and rule." Racism in this regard would be defined as a particular type of false consciousness which inhibits the development of

* Originally published in *The Black Scholar*, 23-34 (March 1978).
Reprinted by permission of Black World Foundation.

class consciousness between the black and white segments of a single exploited working class. In addition, racism has allowed for the reaping of super-profits through the creation of a black super-exploited subproletariat. Lastly, racism has been the system's lightning rod, absorbing the displaced antagonism of Whites who themselves labor under class exploitation.

The orthodox Marxist analysis of racism does not go without challenge. As one might expect, the established protest and "civil rights" organizations either do not perceive the causal link between capitalism and racism or prefer to obfuscate it where it is perceived for nefarious and narrowly self-serving reasons. Certain forces in the black community with roots in cultural nationalism are also extremely hostile to the foregoing analysis of racism because it contradicts the various "devil theories" of white behavior upon which these forces hope to build their version of racial solidarity.

It should come as no surprise to students of the Movement that integrationism and certain varieties of black nationalism make common cause with the ruling class in mystifying the motive force of racism since both ideologies fundamentally represent the interests of a developing black petty bourgeoisie. While these forces may be anti-racist or anti-white, they are basically not anti-capitalist or pro-communist.

It might be surprising, however, to find that among the forces working for a fundamental socialist transformation of American society there are those who feel that the development of monopoly capitalism is undermining capitalism's need for racism. They feel that racism can be eliminated within the framework of the capitalist system. There are those on the left who assert that a scientific analysis of monopoly capitalism indicates strongly that there are economic forces at work which made the continuance of discrimination in the labor market irrational. Since such discrimination is the material basis for racism, they argue that developing monopoly capitalism is anti-racist.[1]

The implications of their analysis are several: first, that the anti-racist liberation struggle of black people does not at the same time have to be anti-capitalist because racism can be resolved within the parameters of the capitalist system (black liberation therefore is not necessarily a struggle for socialism); second, that the multi-national corporation is an ally in the struggle against racism; and third, that the demise of the material basis of racism, job discrimination in the labor market, will hasten the emergence of a unified class-conscious proletariat in the United States and in so doing bring closer the socialist revolution.

The opinions of these friendly forces are important because we may assume they were arrived at through a conscious attempt to be scientific (in the Marxist sense of the term) and with the express purpose of furthering the struggles of all oppressed and exploited classes and peoples. Notwithstanding this, such a position must be closely scrutinized as to its accuracy.

In many respects, as shall be shown, this position objectively unites with much of the ruling class propaganda regarding the system's ability to resolve racial inequality and conflict. If it is in fact an accurate reflection of reality, then so be it. However if it is a fundamentally mistaken proposition, then it is extremely dangerous since it objectively clothes ruling class propaganda in the garb of Marx's scientific method. In this event no effort must be spared in friendly but firm criticism so as to forestall the emergence in our practice of the kind of opportunist errors such an incorrect analysis could give rise to.

It is the opinion of this author that racism cannot be eliminated within the frame of reference of capitalist social relations and therefore, that such a formulation is erroneous and dangerous. In addition, the complementary assertion that the mantle of racism will pass from the backs of blacks to some other unfortunate groups in America will be refuted in the course of this exposition.

The argument itself runs as follows. Monopoly capitalism requires a reserve army of the largest possible size in order to depress wages as low as possible while maximizing labor discipline. Today, under monopoly capitalism, such a "reserve army" must be composed of skilled and semi-skilled blue- and white-collar workers of average skill levels above that required in the jobs traditionally occupied by blacks. In other words, the demand for skilled labor has increased relative to that for unskilled labor as exemplified by such occupational categories as domestic workers, service workers and common laborers. The wage and job discrimination still with us, according to this argument, is an anachronistic remnant of an earlier form of capitalism. Thus to segregate blacks in the unskilled "dirty work" sector makes no economic sense, because the occupational structure of the reserve army under conditions of monopoly capitalism requires the upgrading of black labor and its complete integration into all occupational categories of the work force.

Proponents of this position feel that the corporate sector has taken positive steps to end job discrimination, especially the recent actions of construction companies. In addition, the pronouncements of corporate foundations such as Ford and Rockefeller document this commitment to end discrimination in the labor market. At the same time this shift in the labor force requirements of monopoly capitalism is seen as the material basis for the significant ruling class concessions to the militant struggle of blacks against the manifold forms of racism.

Lastly, the ruling class' decision to establish its military forces on a mercenary basis, thus tapping the large reserve army of teenage blacks, is seen as a major factor in the present anti-racist corporate stance. In sum, proponents of the foregoing position feel that the present anti-racist stance of the ruling class is motivated not by altruism but by their own self-interested recognition that racism and discrimination in the labor market are no longer profitable.

Before moving on to criticize the foregoing position, I must add to it a corollary formulated by Szymanski as a synthesis of the above and the orthodox Marxist position on race. He describes his synthesis in the following manner:

> Those that maintain that blacks are being integrated into the U.S. working class *are* correct. Economic discrimination against blacks is being undermined by the logic of capitalism, apparently for the reasons outlined. However, racism itself is not being eliminated. Here the proponents of the theory that capitalism requires racial discrimination must be supported. The problem with this theory as it is usually presented is that it is not historically specific. While it is true that capitalism necessarily generates racism, it is not true that blacks are the perpetual victims of that racism.[2]

It is important to note that Szymanski's "synthesis" accepts the premise that racism against blacks will disappear. He offers both historical, theoretical and statistical data to support this position. For that reason much of our criticism of the "withering away of racism" will be directed at his arguments. Moreover his position on a shift in the groups subjected to racism is open to serious question. Therefore our critique will include an analysis of what I think is both a misformulation and misapplication of the concept of racism. My criticism considers first the theoretical questions involved in Szymanski's arguments; secondly the statistical data he marshalls to support his conclusions; and lastly his historical understanding of racism and its relationship to capitalist development.

Theoretical Considerations

The assertion that monopoly capitalism requires the largest possible pool of homogeneous labor is based on the classical Marxist analysis appropriate to competitive capitalism. Capital accumulation is seen as depending upon the rate of profit which itself depends upon the rate of surplus value.[3]

The latter is seen as expanding with the downward pressure on wages created by an ever enlarging "reserve army of unemployed" but available workers. This reserve army comes into existence and expands in response to capitalism's tendency to increase machinery and labor-saving technology so as to maximize total surplus value. In addition, divisions of this reserve army can be thrown into new areas of production, thus depressing wages, increasing the rate of surplus value and profit and thus attracting capital to these new sectors. Ultimately this process produces a uniform and falling rate of profit throughout the economy (unless counteracting forces come into play).

The social relations of capitalist production are reproduced by the existence of a reserve army which maintains the tendency of wages toward subsistence and imposes labor discipline on those who hold jobs as a condition of their survival. If there were not a homogeneous reserve army of maximal, size the job security, wage level and autonomy of those workers with more skill would be enhanced, thus putting a downward pressure on the rate of surplus value. It is assumed that labor has absolute mobility — that is, the freedom to sell its labor power to the highest bidder in any labor market — for this assumption is basic to both the concept of surplus value and the reserve army of the unemployed. Theoretically, then, market forces push forward the process of capital accumulation and create the labor discipline so necessary to reproduce the class relations of capitalism.

These market forces, however, give rise to a contradictory tendency. Extraction of surplus value and the ever-increasing misery of workers that is attendant on the reserve army of the unemployed produces not only self-expanding value (i.e., capital) and labor discipline, it also generates its opposite, the struggle over the division of the working day, the struggle against an increase in the rate of surplus value, in a nutshell the class struggle. Thus the capitalist's problem is how to maximize profit while simultaneously minimizing the development of class consciousness. In attempting this the capitalist must become an active agent in structuring the labor force and the reserve army, for these market conditions do not materialize out of thin air. In the environment which confronts him, the capitalist finds historically both an absence of a homogeneous work force and the means for overcoming this drawback to capital accumulation.

The development of the detailed division of labor permits the capitalist over time to reduce the heterogeneous labor force he is initially faced with to a more homogeneous mass while he simultaneously garners increasing control over the labor process. Braverman has described this process quite well.

> Labor power has become a commodity. Its uses are no longer organized according to the needs and desires of those who sell it, but rather according to the needs of its purchasers who are primarily employers seeking to expand the value of their capital. And it is the special and permanent interest of these purchasers to cheapen this commodity. The most common mode of cheapening labor power is exemplified by the Babbage principle: break it up into its simplest elements. And, as the capitalist mode of production creates a working population suitable to its needs...[e]very step in the labor process is divorced, so far as possible, from special knowledge and training and reduced to simple labor.[4]

Another method by which the value of labor power is cheapened is through the super-exploitation of a portion of the labor force. This is based not on reducing the work force to a homogeneous mass but by exploiting aspects of its heterogeneity. Marx noted that "there enters into the determination of the value of labor power a historical and moral element" based on the fact that the workers' necessary wants, themselves, and the means of satisfying them are a product of historical development. This "historical and moral element" refers specifically to the "habits and degree of comfort" associated with the formation of the working class.[5]

Historically, the heterogeneity of the working class racially and culturally in the U.S. has resulted in no single concept of the subsistence wage but several subsistence wages depending on the position of different racial and cultural groups in the status hierarchy of the country. This then is the material basis upon which the super-exploitation of black labor has proceeded.

Super-exploitation is the situation which exists when labor power receives in wages less than the value of those commodities necessary to reproduce it. Between black and white labor it may be manifested in a differential wage rate for the same level of skill and same productivity. Another form of super-exploitation is the forcing of more skilled labor into jobs which require less skill — for this is but another way of raising the level of productivity above society's average for that occupation. Lastly, restricting the mobility, both geographical and occupational, of black labor relative to white labor "crowds" the available labor markets for blacks, creating a situation where labor is "coerced" into working for less than its value.[6]

All these examples have in common as super-exploitation the fact that the labor power-wage exchange is an unequal one resulting in an extra or super profit to the capitalist. This quality of super-exploitation, the unequal exchange in an environment of less than free labor, identifies it as a mechanism of the primitive accumulation of capital, one which emerged during the prehistory of capitalism but continues into the present.

The capitalist then maximizes the fund of surplus value by the foregoing two processes which have complementary and contradictory elements. To the extent that skilled labor still exists and can bid up its wage through black super-exploitation, the capitalist has a fund of extra surplus value otherwise unavailable with which he can increase the organic composition of capital and thus reduce his dependence on labor generally. He can invest a part of this extra fund of surplus value not only in labor-saving technology, but in technology which incorporates the skilled portions of the production process into automated machine operations, leaving to human labor machine tending or simple repetitive tasks. This advances the detailed division of labor.

Thus by super-exploiting black labor, the capitalist can hasten the reduction of white labor to homogeneous simple labor. On the other hand, as the process of homogenization of white labor to simple labor advances, so does the ability of the capitalist to further force down the wages of white labor by adding unskilled black labor to the available labor pool. If, however this unskilled black labor were truly integrated into a growing homogeneous pool of labor, that is integrated completely with no trace of super-exploitation, then the process of technological change producing homogeneous labor would slow down for want of the super-profits which are its basis. Whether it could be carried to its conclusion would depend on the capitalist's ability to extract super-profits from foreign populations or from an imported sub-proletariat. Since this possibility is most realizable in the Third World, the world of colored peoples, one would expect that rather than undermining racism, the need for the largest possible pool of homogeneous labor is based on a continuance of racism in some form.

At this point it appears that Szymanski's position has been borne out: that is, capitalism requires racism (for purposes of super-exploitation) but not necessarily in an anti-black form. However, a look at the modifications of this analysis necessitated by a shift from the framework of competitive to monopoly capitalism raises serious questions as to whether a shift in the occupational structure of black labor will result in a more homogeneous work force. In addition, it is not clear whether such a shift requires a corresponding alteration in the locus of racism.

The concentration of production, the centralization of decision-making and the tremendous expansion in the social character of production were affected by the monopoly capitalist's drive to achieve super-profits. Monopoly capitalism[7] aims at the highest profit but paradoxically adds nothing over and above competitive capitalism to the total value produced with a given level of capitalization. Super-profit in fact is realized by a restriction of output relative to productive capacity. Extra or super-profits are thereby realized by the oligopolies only to the extent that they can wrestle value from workers and non-monopoly capitalists. In fact, the bulk of extra profit is transferred to monopolies from the pool of surplus value in the competitive sector where relatively small-scale, low-wage, labor-intensive production takes place in an environment where the low level of capitalization allows for easy entry and thus precludes the stable combinations upon which monopolies are constructed.

Unlike competitive capitalism there is a hierarchy of profit rates positively related to the degree of monopolization in a particular industry or economic sector. What is interesting, however, is that this hierarchy of profit rates is supported to a significant degree by the wage structure of the competitive sector of the economy. Here the low level of capitalization retards the introduction of labor-saving technology and increasing the rate of surplus value is a necessary condition for survival. At the same time part of the surplus extracted supports the rate of profit structure in the monopoly sector. Moreover, monopoly prices apply double pressure to workers' wages in this sector.

First, the price of constant capital is above its value thus forcing the competitive capitalist to attempt to make up the difference by increasing the rate of surplus value. Second, the real wages of workers are reduced since monopoly prices raise the cost of the commodity equivalent of their labor power. As a consequence wages in the competitive sector are often lower than those of their labor power equivalent. Super-exploitation of the competitive sector labor force is the consequence. A disproportionate percentage of laborers in this sector are blacks and other Third World peoples and it is upon their backs and those of poor whites that the edifice of monopoly capitalism has been constructed.

On the other hand, the increasingly social character of production ushered in by monopoly capitalism has produced a rising labor militancy which reached its most developed form in the unionization of virtually the whole of the oligopoly's industrial labor force. Unionization has retarded the increase in the rate of surplus value in the monopoly sector (and in some areas retarded the entrance of blacks), but on the other hand has encouraged the kind of labor-saving and labor-simplifying technology mentioned above as well as the intensification of exploitation.

The super-exploitation of labor in the competitive sector and the labor-saving nature of technology in the monopolized sectors creates a marked tendency in monopoly capitalism toward underconsumption. Underconsumption exists when the productive capacity of society outstrips its capacity to consume. This tendency is attenuated through monopoly capitalism's creation of new areas of surplus value absorption, including the creation of a corps of unproductive consumers associated with the rising cost of selling and the expansion of the distributive system beyond socially necessary requirements. This reduces the rate of accumulation while increasing the rate of consumption.

The work force for these new unproductive sectors emerges from the reserve army created as increasing numbers of workers are thrown out of the older areas of monopolization, what is traditionally understood as the industrial proletariat. They emerge in those new sectors or older areas where labor-saving technology is more difficult to implement, establishing a wage level conducive to a rather high rate of profit and fueling the fires of expansion in these areas. In addition, some of these workers also are forced into the "crowded" labor market of the competitive industries, thus maintaining the downward pressure on wages there and assuring the continued existence of this sector. More and more members of the labor force are thus subjected to the wage relationship but the capitalist responds by more and more factioning wage earners. This process has been described by Francesca Freedman as follows:

> [A]s the objective conditions different groups of workers face become more alike, the need to divide them on an ideological basis becomes even more acute. As *objective* differences between workers decline, *subjective* divisions

> must be more frantically shored up by management, so that workers are kept from recognizing their essential unity as a class.... These divisions must *appear* ...both to capitalist and to workers...to arise naturally out of the technical requirements of production (regardless of the social formation to which they belong) or out of 'human nature.'
>
> Thus the emergence of new sectors of the economy...such as service and sales...with their characteristic work forces, the evolution of an occupational hierarchy within the working class, the apparent differentiation between mental and manual labor, productive and unproductive labor: all this becomes the objective basis for the increasingly subjective divisions of the working class characteristic of monopoly capitalism.[8]

The objective basis of these subjective divisions too often correlates with race to be merely an accident. This works itself out in the following manner: the process of the detailed division of labor and the subjugation of the labor process to total management control have made the traditional jobs of the industrial proletariat repetitive, dull, personally meaningless, devoid of thought and of control and thus of worker pride and commitment. The hot, dirty and dangerous jobs are still there, however. Together these jobs now conform to all of the parameters of the "nigger jobs" of yore. There has thus been a relative shift of white labor out of these areas into the newly emergent sales and distributive sectors characteristic of advanced monopoly capitalism.

Objectively pushed out by the relative decline of jobs in the traditional industrial proletariat, these workers are subjectively attracted by white-collar jobs and potentially "middle class" status in this new tertiary sector. The reevaluation of the traditional industrial jobs by all workers can be seen in the excessive rates of absenteeism, labor turnover, industrial sabotage, etc. Even though entry-level salaries and mean annual income in the lower reaches of these new sectors are often lower than their industrial counterparts, the mystique of the "white-collar" classification, its relative job security, safety and its placement by the capitalist in the occupational hierarchy leading to management positions and their correspondingly high incomes more than make up for the specter of a dull, tedious, dangerous, dead-end but higher hourly-wage-paying production job.

One should take note of the fact that many of these "new" workers are in the unproductive sector and thus are supported by the surplus value generated in the competitive and monopoly sectors disproportionately populated by black workers. A diminution in surplus value would reduce the standard of living of these unproductive workers and this fact establishes an objective basis for their susceptibility to viewing their interests as aligned with those of big business. The implications of this become evident if this dichotomy correlates with race.

The market mechanism which generates the material basis upon which these subjective divisions emerge along racial dimensions has been described by Baron and Hymer.

> [A] racially dual labor market means that there exists a primary metropolitan labor market in which firms recruit white workers and in which white workers

> look for jobs; side by side with the major market, there exists a smaller labor sector in which Negroes are recruited and in which Negroes look for employment. For each sector there are separate demand and supply forces determining the allocation of jobs to workers and workers to jobs. Over time, this dualism is characterized by a transfer of jobs from the white sector to the Negro sector as the economy develops and as the Negro labor force expands in absolute and relative numbers.
>
> The racial divisions in the...labor market are visible in many dimensions — by industry, by occupation, by geographic area, by firms, and by departments within firms.[9]

Thus occupational and job shifts in the black labor force are to be explained more accurately in terms of a secular shift in the constituent elements of the dual labor market just described. In this way, monopoly capitalism meets its labor force requirements while maintaining its discriminatory labor market posture toward blacks. It reproduces capitalist social relations by regenerating objectively different labor markets for black and white workers. In addition, increasing numbers of white workers become dependent on the surplus extracted from black productive workers. This result reproduces the subjective divisions which are evident in the lack of advanced class consciousness in the American working class.

In order to place the role of Third World immigrants in proper perspective, one must consider the structure of the reserve army of the unemployed. In so doing, we will see that Third World immigrant labor has not displaced blacks as the objects of racism but has joined them in this demeaning status. The significant gains blacks have made in the traditional jobs of the industrial proletariat are of a "one-shot" nature given the advanced state of the process of labor-saving technology in these areas. These industries are stagnant as a source of new jobs.

On the other hand, the "historical and moral factor" has developed to such a point that increasing numbers of blacks refuse to work at the traditional menial and unskilled production jobs in the service and competitive sector. They become part of the stagnant portion of the reserve army or become "*declassé*" as lumpen. No longer are they part of the active labor force. Survival is based on government transfer payments or on employment in the ghetto's irregular or criminal sectors.

Immigrant Third World labor then must be understood as part of the latent reserve army which is being tapped in the face of what amounts to a black boycott of servile and sweatshop labor. The black labor thus displaced is not readily absorbed into the productive sector of monopoly enterprises or into the growing white collar occupations but in fact most of it sinks lower and lower into the stagnant portion of the reserve army of the unemployed mentioned above.

We have now arrived at the following theoretical conclusions: monopoly capitalism has moved black labor disproportionately into the jobs of the industrial proletariat no longer palatable to whites now attracted to new jobs in the tertiary sector. This shift will not absorb anywhere near the potentially available supply of black labor. At the same time blacks are conducting what amounts to a boycott of traditional menial jobs in the competitive sector. For both reasons, more and more blacks from this sector are sinking into the stagnant portion of the reserve army rather than being absorbed into the industrial proletariat or other newer wage earning sectors.

Since monopoly capitalism depends in no small part on a viable competitive sector, immigrant Third World labor is filling the gap left by black drop-outs. These developments have caused the job and occupational structure of the dual labor market to shift. However, they have not done away with that dual labor market or objectively or subjectively produced a more homogeneous work force. Racism is then reproduced both in the labor market and the superstructure as a necessary rationale for this objective reality. The theoretical evidence then clearly indicates that monopoly capitalism does not erode racism against blacks and may even intensify it.

The Empirical Evidence

Apart from theoretical arguments, empirical data are mustered to support the contention that economic discrimination against black labor is disappearing. This evidence takes three forms: first, the purported development of an anti-racist stance within the giants of the corporate sector; second, the "volunteer army" and the need to placate its black members; third, the statistical trends in major industrial Standard Metropolitan Statistical Areas.* A logical interpretation of this data, however, seems to support the continuance of racism toward blacks rather than its demise.

Major corporations have in fact reversed the rather meager attempt made at the end of the '60s toward affirmative action. Ruling class researchers have described the real rather than the public relations behavior of the big corporations as follows:

> [F]irms in high wage industries will have poor performance in hiring minorities than other firms...and even under favorable conditions of steady labor force expansion, the 'affirmative action' phase will come to a halt on the basis of 'a shortage' of qualified applicants, but this 'shortage' a simply a reflection of the firms' refusal to place blacks into higher positions at higher wage rates.[10]

Of 247 major corporations, 201 had urban affairs programs by 1970. All, however, were lapsing only three years later amid labor surpluses and government apathy. Additionally, of 110 big companies, the predominant view was that "blacks weren't interested in jobs any longer."[11] This data would indicate that the supposed self-interested anti-racist big business stance is in part a myth motivated by a superficial attempt at cosmetics or government contract compliance. Governmental benign neglect and tokenism then have led to a reinforcement, not a reversal, of corporate racism.

The volunteer army concept is predicated on a continuance of racism, not its demise. Paradoxically, if economic concessions are required to those who supply monopoly capitalism's front line troops, then the material basis for blacks' willingness to enlist would be undermined. Grubbs and Landers take note of this in saying that

> [i]f the economic growth of the sixties had continued, the rising trend toward college attendance, especially among blacks, joined with the decreasing number

* This has been deleted for brevity.

> reaching military age annually, would undoubtedly have forced perpetuation of the draft. Worse still, it might have made it necessary to close loopholes and take the sons of the country club set. Now, however, presented with the stick of job scarcity and the carrot of training in the Army, almost half of all recruits are school dropouts and the Pentagon's only concern is that the services might become too black — a problem minimized by economic conditions that send a substantial number of whites along with blacks to the recruiting offices.[12]

The military requirements of monopoly capitalism will not lead or contribute to a demise of racism but on the contrary benefit from its continuance. Here some of our left intellectuals are making a reformist error more characteristic of the civil rights leadership, which refused to make Vietnam an issue because blacks supposedly have reaped lasting gains from their wholehearted participation in all of America's wars.

RACISM: AN ALTERNATIVE FORMULATION

While avoiding the well-documented pitfalls of the colonial model applied to the ghetto, we might say that the black community is analogous in some ways to the capitalist formations of the periphery. Transfers of value due to unequal exchange flow from the black community to the monopolists under conditions of informally coerced and unfree labor more characteristic of the pre-history of capitalism, the era of primitive accumulation, than of fully developed capitalism at the center. In this sense ghetto incomes may rise and the occupational structure of ghetto residents may change but this leads neither to cumulative and self-reinforcing development nor to a closing of the gap between the ghetto and the larger society.

In a very real sense, the development of the black community is blocked and while quantitative change occurs, qualitative change and thus true development do not occur. Samir Amin has developed this concept of "center" and "periphery" as follows.

> Whenever the capitalist mode of production enters into relations with precapitalist modes of production, and subjects these to itself, transfers of value take place from the precapitalist to the capitalist formations, as a result of the mechanisms of *primitive accumulation*. These mechanisms do not belong only to the prehistory of capitalism; they are contemporary as well. It is these forms of primitive accumulation, modified but persistent, to the advantage of the center, that form the domain of the theory of accumulation on a world scale.[13]

That aspects of this process are applicable by analogy to blacks can be seen from some of Amin's additional comments.

> True, with equal productivity, the proletariat at the center averages higher rewards than the workers in the periphery. But in order to fight against the law of the tendency for the rate of profit to fall at the center, capital imports labor from the periphery, which it pays at a lower rate (and assigns the least attractive kinds of work) and which it also uses to bring down wages in the metropolitan

> labor market. This importing of labor has assumed considerable dimensions: in Western Europe and in North America the increase in immigration from the periphery has increased annually since 1960 by a percentage ranging from 0.7 percent to 1.9 percent, depending on the countries and the years — in other words, at levels that are, on the average, much higher than the rates of growth of the national labor force; this contribution of labor power of immigrant origin also constitutes a hidden transfer of value from the periphery to the center, since the periphery has borne the cost of education and training this labor power.
>
> Analogous to this process is the mobilization of the internal colonial reserves, as with the proletarianizing of blacks in the United States, who have become the majority of the proletariat in a number of large industrial towns. The extreme form of this system is to be observed in the racialist states: South Africa, Rhodesia, Israel. Thus, the world system is increasingly mixing up together the masses it exploits, rendering the need for internationalism greater than ever. At the same time, of course, it makes use of this mixing process to stir up for its own advantage racialist and jingo moods among the white workers.[14]

However, for us who are members of the "peripheral" formations within the "center," the implications of this reality are quite different from colonial and neocolonial areas of the Third World. In their case, national liberation is a real alternative realizable if necessary through people's war. For blacks, the peripheral relationship can be overturned only with the defeat of capitalism in the center itself.

Conclusion

The position of some spokesmen of the left who believe that racism against blacks is losing its objective basis is incorrect. Monopoly capitalism reproduces the dual labor market even as it shifts the country's occupational structure. It is a detour from reality to assert that corporate capitalism's anti-racist stance in the job market is anything other than a public relations ploy. There is correspondingly little hard data to confirm this anti-racist stance. Similarly, recent newspaper reports buttress the argument presented above that the volunteer army will not spin-off anti-racist side effects. Although the militant struggle of blacks has won many battles, the war is far from over and co-optation of a few black demands should not be confused with implacable resistance to meeting the real needs of most blacks.

What is valid in the arguments criticized in this article is the fact that of all ethnic groups in the U.S., black people and others of the Third World confront monopoly capitalism directly in the process of producing surplus value. We are becoming the core of the industrial proletariat as larger numbers of white workers remain in the wage relationship but get more and more away from the actual production of the material wealth upon which U.S. society depends for survival. Herein is the material basis of racism and economism.

The errors of the left on the question of racism may stem from an over-zealous desire to call a racially unified class-conscious proletariat into existence on the basis of mechanistic applications of Marxian principles devoid of any real understanding of dialectics. This is the latest installment in the left's continuing difficulty with categorizing and analyzing the essence of racism. Sometimes the left's formulations on racism could more objectively be placed in the bourgeois stream of intellectual activity on this question. Szymanski's work on racism is certainly a case in point. At the same time, the left has been notably inept at confronting and defeating racism as it appears in the thoughts and actions of the white working class.

To designate racism merely as a particular form of false consciousness limits the analytic potential of the concept for explaining the racial component of intra-working-class fractioning. More exploration on the material basis of racism may allow us to elaborate on the roots of a phenomenon reproduced today out of the objectively different relationships that white and black workers have to the means of production, the former a working class of the center, the latter a working class of the periphery. It is the objective differences between center and periphery which explain the differential development of class consciousness which causes so many problems in the necessary struggle to unify the U.S. working class.

As the direct role of the state becomes even more manifest in extracting the surplus necessary to capital accumulation, market rationales for exploitation will yield to ideological mystifications. In U.S. society, where white workers are at present closer to the ruling class subjectively than they are to black workers, fascism and its attendant racist ideology may very well become an attractive alternative to the ruling class. In this sense, the immediate future might see a sublimation of class struggle in the guise of increased racial antagonism. While this will undoubtedly produce intense and bloody racial confrontations between black and white workers, it is more indicative of a ruling class rather than a working class crisis. For such clashes and their consequences might help to make clear to white workers that the common class interest they share with blacks is ultimately not based on their altruism but on overriding long-range material interests.

ENDNOTES

1. For a summary and the sources of this position see Al Szymanski, "Trends in Economic Discrimination Against Blacks in the U.S. Working Class," *The Review of Radical Political Economics*, vol. 7, no. 3 (Fall 1975), pp. 1-2.
2. *Ibid.*, p. 3.
3. For basic definitions of the Marxian value and profit concepts used in this section, see Paul Sweezy, "Surplus Value and Capitalism," chapter 4 of *The Theory of Capitalist Development* (New York: Monthly Review, 1968) pp. 56-74.
4. Harry Braverman, *Labor and Monopoly Capital: The Degradation of Work in the 20th Century* (New York: Monthly Review, 1975) p. 82.
5. Karl Marx, *Capital*, vol. 1 (New York: International Publishers, 1967) p. 171.

6. For a summary of the literature on "crowding" and coerced labor see Daniel Fusfeld, "Discrimination and Coerced Labor," chapter 5 of *The Basic Economics of the Urban Racial Crisis* (New York: Holt, Rinehart, Winston, 1973), pp. 60-74.

7. The following section draws freely from the theoretical material in chapter 15 of Sweezy, *op. cit.*, pp. 270-286.

8. Francesca Freedman, "The Internal Structure of the American Proletariat: A Marxist Analysis," *Socialist Revolution,* no. 26 (October-November 1975), p. 50.

9. Harold Baron and Bennett Hymer, "Institutional Racism in Urban Labor Markets," in Edwards, Reich and Weisskopp, *The Capitalist System: A Radical Analysis of American Society* (Englewood Cliffs: Prentice-Hall, 1972), pp. 298-299.

10. Duran Bell, "Occupational Discrimination as a Source of Income Differences: Lessons of the 1960s," *American Economic Review,* LXII (May 1972) p. 336, as quoted in Donald Grubbs and Clifford Landers, "Racism: From Irrational Anachronism to Functional Social Tradition," *The Review of Black Political Economy,* vol. 6, no. 1 (Fall 1975) p. 63.

11. Grubbs and Landers, p. 63.

12. *Ibid.*, p. 66.

13. Szymanski, "Trends," p. 6-18.

14. *Ibid.*, p. 8.

Chapter 2

The Economic Demise of Blacks in America: A Prelude to Genocide?

Sidney M. Willhelm
State University of New York at Buffalo

During the last full week of September 1985, NBC Nightly News (*New York Times*, 1985: A20) presented a daily account exploring "the growing debate over whether programs designed to help blacks have done as much harm as good." While giving coverage to the latest effort for placing responsibility upon the very blacks enduring a life of poverty — the "self-help" proclamation — its last presentation of the series posed the most significant point in the form of a question when NBC's newsperson Garritt Utley poignantly, yet casually, asked, "Is there a solution?" Even though this was the remarkable statement of the weekly "Special Segment" devoted to what is happening *to* blacks — rather than examining black/white relations — no one has recognized its extreme importance simply because few of us are prepared to perceive the actual fate for a black people suffering what is now considered a calamity. An NBC reporter responded to the grim life conditions among blacks by raising a question he could not answer, while the Report's own grim statistics elicit only slight responses from the thousands of people, including hundreds of social science scholars, who write and comment upon black/white relations.

The question posed by NBC News, raising doubt as to whether or not a "solution" can be found, reveals not only a profound sense of resignation but, more vitally, another step being taken by white America to replicate the past. In the same sense of today's exasperation concerning blacks, whites once asked *themselves*, in mid-nineteenth-century America, "What shall *we* do with the Indians?" (in Takaki, 1979: 175; emphasis added). In the pages of *The Nation* for 1867 where this question appears, the white author mandates that "[i]t is plain something must be done with the Indians, and that it must be

* Originally published in *Journal of Black Studies*, Vol. 17, No. 2: 201-254 (1987).
Reprinted by permission of Sage Publications, Inc.

something different from anything yet done." He proposed several options opened to *whites*: the natives could be "exterminated" or subdued to the "law and habits of industry." He favored the identical resolution whites now demand of blacks by declaring integration as "the easiest and cheapest as well as [the] only honorable way of securing peace" and, he insisted, "*[w]e* need only treat Indians like men, treat them as *we* do ourselves, putting on them the same responsibilities" to accomplish the integration (in Takaki, 1979: 175; emphasis added).

Walter Goodman's (1984: A14) *New York Times* 1984 interview with Kenneth Clark, whose studies were cited by the Supreme Court's 1954 decision to outlaw racial segregation in the nation's schools, depicts an individual who now "confesses that he has no new answers to the bleak and seemingly *intractable* situation" (emphasis added). "I believed in the 1950s," Clark stated during the interview, "that a significant percentage of Americans were looking for a way out of the morass of segregation.... It was wishful thinking." Where integration once seemed so patently obvious, there is now a very deep sense of doom; it is as though forces beyond human control foreclose the future in spite of the best intentions to narrow racial differences through integration. Felix G. Rohatyn (1985: E6), Chairman of New York City's Municipal Assistance Corporation, explains:

> The question is: Is it reversible? I'm not sure. I'm not sure that the pace of the technological and educational revolution isn't so rapid that it's almost impossible for the people who are getting left out to ever catch up. You get kind of an educational and cultural implosion, if you will. It's like getting caught in a vortex which keeps dragging you down farther and farther.

Because 60 percent of blacks, in contrast to only a quarter of whites, reside in cities, Robert F. Wagner, Jr. (1985: E6), former Deputy Mayor of New York City, concludes, "My sense is that increasingly American cities are becoming two cities — a city of people making it and a city of people not making it." Almost two decades earlier the National Advisory Commission on Civil Disorders (1968: 1), in what is commonly referred to as the Kerner Report, decisively predicted the emergence of "two societies:" "This is our basic conclusion. Our nation is moving toward two societies, one black, one white — separate and unequal."

These bleak assessments meet with vigorous rejection, for the eighties are joyfully contemplated as a decade for progress. Clarence M. Pendleton, Jr. (*New York Times*, 1984: A14), appointed by President Reagan to chair the U.S. Commission on Civil Rights, proclaimed, in November, 1984, that blacks were making "tremendous progress in literacy, economics, employment and housing" irrespective of "the black leadership's gloom and doom prophecy." Joel Dreyfuss (1984: E13), former executive editor of *black Enterprise* magazine and presently associate editor at *Fortune*, maintains that "1984 was a good year for black Americans." He dismisses the startling black unemployment statistics by writing, "the vast majority of black Americans work for a living," an observation that, given the present depression-level unemployment rate for blacks, ironically, would have been perfectly correct for disregarding joblessness in the midst of the 1930s depression; just as Robert Park (1913: 147), one of the nation's most famous sociologists, sustained the view of a "vigorous and pushing (black) middle class" at the turn of the century by noting that "one of the highest paid performers on the vaudeville stage today (i.e., 1913) is a colored man," Dreyfuss upholds "black achievement in 1984" by saying "Michael Jackson used his talents to shatter some of the most rigid racial barriers of the music industry;" he cites Reverend Jesse Jackson's presidential campaign to illustrate the "dramatic increase in black political participation" only to acknowledge in his own article that as a consequence the "Democratic Party officials responded by distancing themselves from their most loyal constituents (i.e., blacks) in the 1984 campaign." Optimists simply ignore the facts established within the Report as though the data do not exist.[1]

The factual presentation by the Report receives strong confirmation from other sources; recent investigations provide additional information to sustain the Report's own empirical findings. One of the most thorough has been published by the College Entrance Examination Board under the title, *Equality and Excellence* (1985). Like the Report, the Board's data reveal a pronounced deterioration in the living standards of blacks and, especially, relative to whites, so that the racial gap expands with the passage of time. Likewise, Denys Vaughn-Cooke (1985: 13) has composed a socioeconomic survey and voices a grim conclusion:

> It is interesting to note that from 1948 when unemployment statistics were first collected by race, black unemployment did not even approach 14 percent until 1981. This last recession of 1982 seems to be another nail in the coffin housing growing black/white employment differentials with blacks buried even deeper in this recovery period than they were before the recession started.

Thus there is ample information (see also Willhelm, 1983: ch. 2) to sustain the accuracy of the Report's own tabulations concerning the economic status of blacks at the midpoint of the 1980s. Optimists have yet to provide any comparable compilation of facts to marshall documentation for their pious declarations of progress.

Family Thesis Revisited

The Negro Family, a report published by the Office of Policy Planning and Research of the U.S. Department of Labor in 1965, addressed the economics of duress besetting blacks by the rather simplistic technique of focusing upon what it refers to as the "family structure;" by knowing what is happening to the kinship system, one simultaneously knows what is happening to blacks and, more important, why. Much to its credit, *The Negro Family* conceded the reality of a worsening life experience for blacks; it provided ample documentation to demonstrate the socioeconomic deterioration for the black minority and the greater socioeconomic disparities *vis-à-vis* whites. The Report, therefore, provides a current account of economic impoverishment increasing with each passing decade.

Written at a moment in history when black urban areas were in violent upheavals, *The Negro Family* (1956: 6) declared the breakdown within black families as the principal cause of poverty and social regression so vividly revealed by its empirical data:

> At the *center* of the tangle of pathology is *the* weakness of the family structure. Once or twice removed, it will be found to be *the principal source of most* of the aberrant, inadequate, or antisocial behavior that did not establish, but now serves to perpetuate the cycle of poverty and deprivation [emphasis added].

Family disintegration transforms, according to the approach, the very structure of family life; it initiates the collapse of the patriarchal kinship system and the emergence of the matriarchal family — which, in turn, brings in its wake such social pathologies as higher crime rates, increased rates of school dropouts, lower achievement aspirations, greater drug dependency, higher unemployment, and, subsequently, lower incomes that, thereafter, relegate more and more blacks to the ranks of poverty.

According to *The Negro Family*, from 1950 to 1960 the proportion of non-white women living with their husbands declined for all age groups; one-sixth more females were family heads at the end of the decade than at the beginning. Since the report's publication, black households headed by females have expanded from 28 percent for the 4.9 million black families in 1970 to 41 percent for the 6.4 million black families in 1982; during the same period, families maintained by married couples declined from 68 percent to 55 percent while the divorce rate more than doubled, going from 104 to 265 per 1,000. Unmarried women now head one-third of all black families. Thus the nuclear family parents only 42 percent of all black children while 49 percent reside with one parent, and eight percent live with neither (College Entrance Examination Board, 1985: 5). Of black births, 55 percent were to out-of-wedlock parents in 1979 in contrast to 38 percent in 1970; 83 percent of births to black teenagers came outside of marriage (Associated Press, 1981).

These trends in black family living appear also among whites as well. While the numbers are much smaller, nonetheless the rise over a period of time is substantial. Thus the percentage of white households headed by females rose by a third from 1970 to 1982, going from nine percent to 12 percent of all such families (College Entrance Examination Board, 1985: 5). From 1971 to 1981, divorces per 1,000 husband-wife white families grew from 48 to 100 (Associated Press, 1982: A11). Women headed only three percent of white families with children in 1950, then six percent in 1960, and 15 percent in 1983 (Noble, 1984: E20). In 1965, four percent of all white births were out of wedlock, and in 1976 it rose to 7.7 percent (Feinberg, 1978: 17). By the mid-eighties, it was commonplace for the mass media to portray the American family generally as a social system undergoing substantial changes. Thus *Time* (1985: 16) magazine wrote in its September 1985 issue that

> families with single heads grew by 69 percent from 1970 to 1983. One out of every five children, and more than half of all black children, lives in a one-parent household.

"Typical" is no longer an adjective that can describe the American household. Of all households, 40 percent consisted of husband, wife, and children 15 years ago; today that figure is 28.5 percent. The stereotypical nuclear family of mom, dad and two kids now accounts for only 11 percent of all households.

Now that family instability is declared for *all* families, it becomes fashionable to associate poverty as an affliction of female-head families; with declining poverty for the elderly as the foremost category of people beset by poverty, the "feminization of poverty" appears as the *cause célèbre* among specialists and by the media. While serving as Special Assistant Secretary of Labor within the administration of President Lyndon Johnson, Daniel Patrick Moynihan authored *The Negro Family* in 1965; 20 years later and an elected member of the U.S. Senate, he renewed his thesis in a series of lectures at Harvard University and declared the trend toward family disintegration to be a national feature that is substantially greater for blacks yet rapidly occurring among whites (Rosenbaum, 1985). Robert Pear (1983: A17) of the *New York Times*, under the headline "Poverty Data and Families," wrote, in 1983, of the Census Bureau's poverty statistics and family disruption:

> Over 15 years, changes in family composition have had profound effects on family income and poverty levels, outlasting year-to-year fluctuations in the economy. Families headed by women, unrelated people living together and individuals living alone account for a larger share of the population. Since these households tend to have lower incomes than families headed by couples, the poverty rate remains high, by historical standards, even though median family income...has risen for two straight years.

In a study investigating family status and personal income between 1971 and 1981, the Census Bureau (in Associated Press, 1982: A11) maintains that "overall, changes in family composition have accounted for 2,017,000 additional poor families." black family incomes were more depressed than for whites "since families maintained by women tend to have lower incomes than families maintained by men." In its otherwise excellent probe of socioeconomic data, the College Entrance Examination Board (1985: 5) explained that "Because households headed by females are substantially poorer than those headed by married couples, earning less than half as much on average,...children in these households are more likely to live in poverty." In July 1985, *Newsweek*'s (1985: 43) coverage on the American family stated that

> the financial demands of raising a family alone are creating what some see as a "new class of poor," particularly among women, who head nearly 90 percent of the nation's one-parent households. Single parenthood appears to be a major factor in what has been called "the feminization of poverty." ... According to a U.S. Commission on Civil Rights study, a staggering 54 percent of single-parent families were living below the poverty line in 1983, compared with 18 percent for all families with children. For families headed by females, the figure was 47.2 percent, compared with 19.7 percent for males. More than half of black families fall into poverty after a marital breakup — against a quarter of white families — explaining why 68.5 percent of black children in single-parent households are poor, versus 22 percent for all children in the United States.

From such accounts, poverty reflects the shifting character of family life; one enters the ranks of poverty because someone either fails to enter marriage, as in the case of an unwed mother, or leaves a marriage. "Among blacks," we are told, "the absence of a father at home has virtually become the norm.... Black leaders and social scientists now agree that the tide threatens to undo the black *economic* gains of decades" (Cummings, 1983b: 1). Now that family instability appears among whites, poverty for the general population is traced directly to the kinship system. "I want to make clear," Moynihan (Rosenbaum, 1985: 15) elaborated during an interview, "this is not a black issue. It's obviously worse there, but if you don't think it's bad in general, you're not going to get any remedial response."

Proponents of the family thesis for explaining poverty either turn to the "black community" or the federal government when proposing solutions. Moynihan, in his empirical study, *The Negro Family*, and in his Godkin lecture of 1985 at Harvard University, called upon the national government to initiate policy changes such as new legislation to reduce the tax obligations of low-income earners and to provide the kind of welfare assistance that strengthens the family structure as an American institution. William J. Haskins (1982: A19), director at the National Urban League, repudiates economic assistance from either the government or other sources such as foundations since both "will be useless unless black communities resolve to do something for themselves." The "burden of responsibility" rests upon the "black community;" racism is not so much a cause as it is a "crutch" that blacks must "throw away." blacks, Haskins argues, endure poverty because they lack the kind of ethics to create and sustain a nuclear family system; it is the moral responsibility of the middle-class black to educate the poverty-stricken black youth "off self-pity" and inspire the inner-city poor to assert "free will" in order to eradicate "the problem." Sheer self-determination instilled among the afflicted blacks will cause such blacks "to do something for themselves" in order to break the "syndrome of failure...aggravated by an already existing culture of poverty."

What advocates of the family thesis propound is that blacks are in a mess, and while they might have gotten that way because of racial oppression by whites, nonetheless, today, racial factors no longer matter since it is a specific quality of life among blacks, family disintegration, that they themselves bring about that explains economic deterioration for at least the past three decades. On the one hand, government that is not the cause can introduce definitive remedial programs and, on the other, poor blacks will experience socioeconomic gains by accepting the same kind of ethics practiced by the better-off blacks. Neither racism nor economic circumstances beyond the nuclear family enter into the explanation. Indeed, Moynihan himself concedes his lack of a comprehensive solution because, he claims, "We do not know the processes of social change well enough so as to be able confidently to affect them" (Rosenbaum, 1985: 15).

Adherents to the family explanation profess not just an ignorance of social change but also an intense reluctance to answer the numerous critics who have so effectively exposed the many shortcomings of the view. Years ago, the anthropologist Charles Valentine (1968) demolished the entire concept of a "culture of poverty" for explaining poverty; William Ryan (1971) articulated a devastating condemnation of the family thesis as an approach that blames the victim; and in a 1970 publication, I exposed weaknesses and dismissed the view as irrelevant. Subsequently, many individuals have noted the identical limitations as the previous critics — especially that the state of the black family offers no explanation because the fate of American family life itself reflects broad

Table 1
Proportion of Families by Race, Income Level, Female Head, and Metropolitan Residence, 1978

Subject	All Families (percent)	Female Heads (percent)	Families in Metropolitan Areas (percent)	Metropolitan Families with Female Heads (percent)
Black				
Under $4,000	15.9	80.3	71.1	85.1
$4,000 to $6,999	16.2	61.8	74.7	71.2
$7,000 to $10,999	18.3	46.2	74.8	50.7
$11,000 to $15,999	16.7	28.9	76.3	31.8
$16,000 to $24,999	19.2	15.3	82.7	15.4
$25,000 and over	13.4	7.7	88.5	7.6
White				
Under $4,000	4.3	42.1	53.3	50.2
$4,000 to $6,999	4.7	27.6	56.2	33.7
$7,000 to $10,999	12.7	19.5	57.7	21.9
$11,000 to $15,999	16.9	13.4	59.9	16.7
$16,000 to $24,999	28.8	7.2	66.0	8.5
$25,000 and over	29.5	2.9	75.4	1.1

Source: U.S. Bureau of the Census, *Current Population Reports, Consumer Income*, Series P-60, No. 123 (Washington, DC: Government Printing Office, 1980).

economic trends. And the most basic economic reality impinging upon the family is joblessness; with unemployment comes the transformation of the nuclear family, for as people lose their jobs, poverty rises and the lower one's income the greater is the likelihood of divorce, the death of a spouse, and the possibility of not marrying upon the appearance of pregnancy. Impeccable data vividly document just the opposite of what advocates of the family thesis proclaim: It is not family instability that gives rise to poverty, but rather it is poverty that gives rise to family disruption. Census Bureau (1980) data confirm this reversal of cause and effect; Table 1 strongly reveals that as income drops the percentage of female-headed families rises regardless of race, yet the rates are substantially higher for blacks in all income categories.

That it is a matter of joblessness rather than family structure is further demonstrated by data dealing with educational attainment and unemployment; as educational levels increase, the black-to-white unemployment ratio *rises*. Because higher educational achievement is associated with higher incomes, it is appropriate to infer that higher-income blacks have much higher percentages of female-headed families than whites of comparable incomes because they have, as Table 2 reveals, unemployment rates greater than whites of comparable incomes. Furthermore, Table 2 exposes what proponents of the family thesis so fervently repudiate, namely, the presence of racism in establishing a person's economic opportunity in the job market. If discrimination has now vanished, as

Table 2
Education and Unemployment by Race

		Unemployment Rate	
Education		Black	White
Elementary:	Eight years or less	17.3	12.0
High school:	One to three years	12.9	12.6
	Four years only	17.3	8.3
College:	One to three years	14.6	6.0
	Four years or more	8.9	2.6

Source: Ann McDougall Young, "Recent trends In higher education and labor force activity," *Monthly Labor Review*, February 1983, p. 40.

we are told it has, then how are we to account for the virtual four-to-one ratio at the very pinnacle of educational achievement according to race while remarkably lower ratios exist at the bottom of the educational scale? While some college educational accomplishment drops in half the unemployment rates for whites in contrast to the unemployment rates for white males with at least three years of high school, the identical comparison brings a reduction only of 16 percent for blacks. The unemployment rate for blacks with at least four years of college is half the unemployment rate for blacks with four years of high school, whereas the same contrast between whites brings about a 75 percent reduction. Thus joblessness brings the female-headed family to the fore, and joblessness itself reflects the persistence of racism in America.

Many other investigations confirm the transformation of the nation's kinship system away from the nuclear household as a consequence of unemployment. In a study conducted under the direction of Tom Joe and Peter Yu, released in April 1984 by the Center for the Study of Social Policy, the link between unemployment and family disruption has been associated. This investigation holds that female-headed families expanded as blacks dropped out of the labor force: while three-fourths of all black males worked in 1960, that number dropped to 55 percent during 1982 (Joe and Yu, 1984: 6). The study observes:

> These data on black men suggest that researchers may be treating the symptoms of poverty rather than the ailment.... At the very least, one can neither fully understand nor slow the growth of female-headed families without first assessing the deteriorating status of black unemployed men [p. 6].
>
> These data support a hypothesis that the erosion of the black family is not necessarily a mystical cultural trend but a palpable economic event. The boom in black families headed by women is not the simple result of the "welfare curse," pervasive and invidious discrimination, or changing sexual mores. Instead, the problem lies in an intricate economic and social dynamic [p. 10].

Thus the investigators found that

> graphing the percentage of black men out of the labor force or unemployed and the percentage of black families headed by women yields two roughly parallel lines.... In the last seven years alone, the number of black families headed by women has risen by 700,000 and the ranks of black men out of the labor force or unemployed has increased by the same number [pp. 8, 10].

James Turner (Noble, 1984: E20), director of the African Studies and Research Center at Cornell University, also challenges an intrinsic connection between poverty and sex: "The rise of impoverished female-headed households," he maintains, "is highly correlated with the disproportionately high rates of unemployment in the black community" among, particularly, young black maids. In a series of articles based upon interviews with three dozen black women who head households across the nation, Judith Cummings (1983b: 1) found that "the most common thread, one that ran through the lives of most of the women, was the inability of the fathers of their children to hold steady jobs." And in a most suggestive remark, Harriett Pipes McAdoo (Cummings, 1983a: 56), a Howard University sociologist, contemplates a possible connection between joblessness and unwed mothers:

> The tradition used to be that if a woman got pregnant, they were expected to get married, if not forced to get married, to supply income and a name for the child. But if the man has no job, there's no impetus for them to get married. Her parents would have three people to support instead of just two. The boy would become an additional burden on the family.

Of the 1.1 million pregnancies among teenagers per year only 17 percent are postmarital conceptions and a mere 10 percent become married following conception; 38 percent are terminated by abortion while the remaining 13 percent are miscarriages (Urban Institute in Associated Press, 1981: B11). During 1979, 55 percent, in contrast to 38 percent in 1970, of all black babies were born out of wedlock; the figures for whites, during the same time period, rose from 5.7 to 9.4. The increase in unemployment for black males matches the sharp increase in pregnant black women remaining single; while 26 percent of black pregnant teenagers married prior to giving birth in 1970, a mere eight percent did so by 1979.

Poverty expands among female single parents for *economic* reasons and not because of a "break-up" in family structure. As already noted, unwed black mothers do not establish a family by marrying an unemployed male. Likewise, divorce involves property settlements that clearly favor males and assure a drop in living standards for women, especially for women who gain child custody. Women generally, and divorced women specifically, experience considerable difficulty in obtaining well-paying jobs; for 1982, just 8.8 percent of white males 15 years and older were classified poor while 12.0 percent of white females, 23.8 percent of black males, and 35.8 percent of black females were so designated (Sparr, 1985: 13). Lenore J. Weitzman (1985) found that "divorced women and the minor children in their households experience a 73 percent decline in their standard of living in the first year after divorce while their former husbands experience a 42 percent rise" (in Youngblood, 1985: F4). Advocates of the family thesis have not explained this vivid female/male discrepancy, for if divorce causes poverty how is one to account for economic improvement among males and such an incredibly high loss among women? Clearly, it is the allocation of property and the lack of the same for the single woman that underlies the emergence of poverty rather than family status *per se.*

What does the Report inform us about the family thesis? Its message is straightforward: black income has dropped *regardless* of family life. Further, the loss in economic resourcefulness was greater for black households than white and among blacks the idealized husband-wife-children-centered family incurred the highest drop in disposable income. "*blacks,*" the Report itself emphasizes, "*were nearly twice as likely to have become poor since 1980 as other Americans were*" and the "hardest hit were black two-parent families in which one parent works and the other takes care of children." Were Moynihan and his followers correct in their prognosis, the "stable" black family should be the one to make economic gains. Instead, with the loss in purchasing power we should now anticipate a rise in divorce for the "average middle class black family;" the loss in income will place still greater strains in personal relations even within the nuclear household. Deterioration in economic terms generates the transformation of family life rather than the splintering of marital ties causing poverty.

The Class View

Some analysts refuse to seek explanation for the fate of blacks in a white America as somehow a mere reflection of a noneconomic force such as family structure. They are not so naive as to believe a materialistic society's economic viability is directly dependent upon sustaining marital vows when one is a parent or that property relations do not impinge upon family households within a society so dedicated to the creation and preservation of wealth as is surely the case for this nation. They are prepared to accept the reality of economic interests operating to the advantage of some individuals at the expense of others; people with wealth hold the power to manage and manipulate property that they might enhance their riches while others either stay in place or suffer economic losses. And this economic principle operates regardless of race; indeed, race itself is just another phenomenon to be manipulated to enrich still further the people of wealth. To act and to be able to act for one's property interest creates the dynamics of class relations; the interplay of class relations ordains the dynamics of race relations within a capitalist society such as America. Therefore, to account for what transpires between blacks and whites requires an accounting of property transactions associated with class interests. In short, to understand class relations is to understand race relations.[2] What, then, are the proponents of the class view expounding about class in explaining what is happening in relations between black and white? And how does the Report bear upon such views?

Marxists maintain that property interests virtually dictate social relations between black and white and they hold the upper class responsible for the system of race relations that exists at any moment in time; because the upper class possesses tremendous wealth in property holdings, its interests require the transformation of race relations as simply a tactic to exploit labor. Labor itself provides the sole source of value; only by manipulating labor is it possible for the owners of property to transfer wealth from the laboring class, which creates the wealth, and unto itself. Materialistic interests, not racism, motivate the ruling class, which just happens to be white, to extract still more wealth from blacks and by so doing drive still more blacks into the ranks of poverty. Capitalists first created and now sustain racial division as a more efficient strategy for exploiting the labor of all working people; racial distrust makes it so much easier to extract wealth disproportionately from black, in contrast to white, workers since the latter's hostility toward the former reduces resistance. The hatred of blacks by white workers divides the working class so that racial struggles prevail rather than class antagonism between labor and capital.

The Report contains considerable empirical confirmation of the Marxist orientation. The sharp decline in black income reveals the extraction of wealth; the rise in poverty demonstrates the impoverishment; the increasing disparity in black/white income to the advantage of the upper bracket, where capitalists abound, displays the dominance of property interests. The rise in the female-headed family is but a consequence of economic oppression since family structure reflects economic forces. The reductions in economic assistance by the federal government constitute domination by capital; government itself is under the jurisdiction of property holders and therefore acts to enhance the exploitation of labor. In short, blacks in America are experiencing severe economic deterioration because they must endure an economic system — capitalism — that requires an exploitation of labor to the benefit of capitalists.

However, while the Report contains much in support of the Marxist approach it simultaneously holds forth with data that stand in stark contradiction. Marxism simply cannot confront the indisputable facts concerning black unemployment. It is a perspective that treats labor as an exploitable commodity much as though it were a resource like coal, namely, something to be mined at the lowest possible cost to the mine owner. But what is involved when coal itself is no longer needed — when the demand vanishes? This is the very question intrinsic within the Report's data on the state of black unemployment. For while "black unemployment was 2.15 times greater than white unemployment when Reagan took office...today, black unemployment is 2.5 times greater than white unemployment." Indeed, as the Report notes, black joblessness rose during Reagan's first term in office, going from 14.4 percent to 16 percent. Marxism views unemployment as an inevitable feature about capitalism; workers must be thrown out of work during recessions and depressions and must then be available upon the return of prosperity to meet the greater demand for labor that subsequently develops. Capitalism must sustain a population upon which it draws during its boom phase of its cyclical economy and be able to cast aside any surplus labor upon the downward slide of the boom-bust cycle that haunts capitalism. This fluctuation in the need for labor explains, Marxists believe, the persistence of the incredibly high black unemployment rates noted in the Report. Thus, as acknowledged by the Report, the figures responded to a rebounding economy; when the recession "hit bottom" during November 1982, black unemployment went down 22 percent along with a 33 percent reduction for whites by August 1984. But what Marxists have not explained is the rise in the black/white unemployment *ratio*, going upward as it did, from 2.15 to 2.5 between 1980 and 1984, any more than they can explain why the two-to-one ratio emerged for the very first time as a post-World-War II phenomenon. What is it about capitalism for there to be a "need" to have an ever-increasing racial ratio at this point in history? Further, Marxists fail to offer any explanation for the persistence of depression-level unemployment rates for blacks during recessions and, more significantly, even during recovery and periods of prosperity. In other words, Marxists lack the analytical capacity to account for racial differentiation as evidenced by the unemployment ratio and have yet to explain the continuation of extremely high unemployment figures with the appearance and sustainment of economic expansion.

A much more telling limitation besetting Marxism is its total inability to explain what the Report refers to as "the extraordinary figures on long-term unemployment" among blacks. As in the case of unemployment, Marxists cannot explain either extended joblessness or the increasing black/white ratio as the numbers increased only 1.5 percent for whites from the beginning of 1981 through 1984 while they grew enormously — 72 percent — for blacks so that according to the Report, "over 30 percent of all the long-term unemployed in the U.S. now are black." Marxists could not proclaim the obvious conclusion drawn by the Report: "These sobering statistics provide further evidence of the degree to which the economic recovery is leaving blacks further behind than before." What is it about capitalism, if anything, so that today an economic upswing *excludes* blacks from employment, and in numbers greater than is the case for white workers, rather than necessitating hiring the "surplus" black worker? Is there an entirely new economic phenomenon that has come into existence since the 1950s so that blacks get expunged from the labor force even with the reemergence of prosperity? More cogently, can Marxists offer any insight into what the future will bring for those blacks being "left behind" in the depths of joblessness while capitalism flourishes? Is it just the economic greed for relentless profit taking by capitalists that causes, as the Report also observes, pronounced cuts in welfare generally and unemployment benefits specifically as black unemployment goes up? Still more to the point, will capitalists be content only to impoverish blacks whose labor can no longer be absorbed through economic expansion or will they resort to a solution to *dispose* of such people? Capitalists can — and will — raise such questions, for, unlike Marxists, they are fully cognizant of the transformation of the economy that brings in its wake a *permanent* surplus in black labor. Marxists, however do not offer replies to these questions.

Another economic orientation to race relations also emphasizes class differentiation as the basis for explaining black/white relations. It perceives sharp class divisions within both races. Among whites, capitalists have abandoned racism in favor of equality. Within the economic sphere, particularly in the attainment of jobs and education, they joined an alliance with the federal government to liquidate racism so that blacks will be judged regardless of color; the federal government pursues not only equality but also implements affirmative-action measures to promote occupational opportunities for blacks. Unimpeded by racial barriers of the past, blacks gain an equal footing with whites; freed from the bonds of segregation, they obtain the education, training, skills, and experience to compete for jobs without being exposed to discrimination. Consequently, many blacks have made substantial socioeconomic gains. Nonetheless, a large segment of black people, while no longer stigmatized by race, remain in the midst of poverty and even undergo still greater impoverishment. The widespread liquidation of discrimination fails to benefit blacks whose lack of education, training, and experience makes them marginal or irrelevant for occupational openings in a nation as technologically sophisticated as America. The modern mode of production, making its appearance during the fifties, leaves behind the poverty-stricken blacks portrayed in the Report. Blacks who are not "making it" in America fall behind whites not because of oppression predicated upon race, as in the past, but because they cannot compete effectively within the job market. The "impersonal" forces of the marketplace, in true Darwinian terms, impede economic accomplishments for the "disadvantaged" person regardless of color, and because proportionately more blacks than whites are so situated they are overly represented in the statistical presentation of poverty and loss income conveyed within the Report. William Wilson (1978: 120-121) explains this analysis as he has developed it:

> On the one hand, the relatively poorly trained blacks of the inner city...find themselves locked in the low-wage sector (operative, laborer, and service-workers jobs) where there is little opportunity for advancement and rates of job turnover are high. On the other hand, the more talented and highly educated blacks are experiencing unprecedented job opportunities in the corporate and government sectors because of the expansion of salaried white-collar positions and the pressures of demonstrated affirmative action by government and business.

While racism vanished in the economic sphere, it has not, according to Wilson, entirely evaporated. For it remains and, to some extent, flourishes in other areas of social discourse such as housing, urban politics, and local education. It persists for the very same reason it prevailed in the eras of segregation and slavery — the better-paid white workers, rather than the capitalists as argued by Marxists, hold an economic interest to discriminate in order to keep blacks from competing for their jobs. The corporate enterprise practices equality and the federal government mandates equality of economic opportunity, especially for employment, but racism prevails in America because of economic demands exerted by the higher-income white worker. Thus, in the modern era, Wilson (1978: 121) informs us, "racial strife has, in fact, shifted away from the economic sector. The traditional racial struggles for power and privilege are now concentrated in the socio-political order. The main actors are however basically the same as in the past — blacks and the white working class." Wilson perceives the "declining significance of racism" as the emergence of market forces determine the life chances for blacks exactly as they do for whites; racism persists only within the white working class that can no longer impose its will, as it did during both slavery and segregation, upon either business or the national government in behalf of white superiority.

Data within the Report contradict what would be anticipated by applying the "market force" explanation developed by Wilson. By entering the marketplace, we are being told, blacks escape the traditional white racism of yesteryears. Yet, if market forces determine people's life chances without regard to race, how is one to account for "blacks in every income strata, from the poorest to the most affluent" losing "ground" so as to have "less disposable income in 1984 than in 1980" while such "figures stand in sharp contrast to the findings for the white population" whose "top 60 percent...experienced income gains?" The Report found that "no other population group lost so heavily" as did blacks between 1980 and 1983. Further, and most telling, the "racial gap" expanded as the average family income for blacks dropped while it rose for whites, and blacks dipped further in poverty as 22 percent of Americans going into poverty were black even though blacks constitute only 12 percent of the nation's population. Since the loss of income cuts *across* class lines among blacks and income disparity expands on the basis of race, it simply is not feasible to contend that class differences have effectively substituted for race in determining the life chances of black people in this country. Proponents could suggest that the drop in black income is due to "modern" technology that has decimated the very types of jobs where blacks are concentrated, for example the automobile industry. But this effort to salvage the view would merely expose the impact of racism, for blacks have been "concentrated" in such occupations precisely because of discrimination. Furthermore, such an explanation to rescue the thesis would not account for the fact that, in the words of the Report, "*the average middle class black family has a lower standard of living in 1984 than in 1980, just as the average poor black family does.*" If Wilson's assertions were correct — that "more talented and highly educated blacks are experiencing unprecedented job opportunities...because of the expansion of salaried white-collar (i.e., middle-class) positions" within the economy — why would middle-income blacks experience a loss in income at all?

Advocates of the class analysis theory founded upon "market forces" must also subscribe to the myth of socioeconomic progress, if not for blacks as a collectivity then most assuredly at least for those "talented and highly educated" blacks flocking into the openings of an expanding white-collar economy. It never occurs to such writers that the "white" of the "white-collar" economy means exactly what it propounds — WHITE! Such advocates never bother just to glance at a set of statistics that has been readily available all along, namely, the proportional rate of unemployment on the basis of educational attainment by race and "class." The figures, presented earlier in this article, reveal a relentless racial differentiation irrespective of class lines, however the lower ranks for black and white are much more equal than are the upper educational categories where the ratio rises as high as four-to-one by race. Were the "market force" analysis correct, we would anticipate just the *opposite* — at least the two-to-one black/white ratio for the poorly educated where blacks are concentrated as a "working-class" population, and an equal unemployment rate for everyone with some college education. In the stead of "unprecedented job opportunities" for the "more talented and highly educated black," we discover "unprecedented" rates of unemployment for blacks relative to whites!

The "market force" perspective lauds the "equality" principle with unremitting praise, and credits, with equal acclamation, the initiative by corporations and the federal government to compel adherence to equality at least in the marketplace. The captains of industry were, according to Wilson, yielding to an awesome power of racist demands from their white workers as they practiced segregation in the workplace, while the government likewise acquiesced to the same racism so as not to upset the political disposition of white workers. Yet no analyst of the class view has ever expressed the slightest doubt about the validity of equality as a viable resolution to vanquish racism; it has been an article of unquestionable faith that the shift from segregation to the Great Equality Principle mandated by *the* Constitution guarantees at least the destruction of racism and a fair chance for economic opportunity. Yet how are they to reconcile the facts of economic deterioration presented within the Report with the undeniable reality that equality itself is being fulfilled on an unprecedented scale of accomplishment? That is, how can the supporters of "market force" analysis explain that as blacks become equal to whites they are simultaneously *less* like whites in terms of income, unemployment, poverty, family affiliation and so forth? A rather profound question has never entered into their deliberations: is equality itself a racist doctrine, perhaps even comparable to segregation, as well as the Constitution upon which it is predicated as the ultimate source for Supreme Authority of sanctioning equality? History is so conveniently overlooked, for there is no recalling that slaveholders once declared slavery to be beneficial to what would otherwise be a lazy, slovenly people, and, as with equality, the Supreme Court upheld Constitutional affirmation of slavery; that segregationists vigorously insisted racial separation would benefit both black and white; and that segregation itself, as with equality, received Constitutional endorsement from the Supreme Court — just as now advocates of equality give absolute loyalty, with Constitutionalized blessings from numerous rulings extended by the Supreme Court, that equality is *the* unquestionable goal for liquidating racism, providing on-par opportunities for blacks, and, indeed, to "save" the nation from the calamities of violent confrontation. Of course, if equality is intrinsically as racist as any other form of racism, then it would have to be conceded further that the capitalists, as asserted by Marxists, are indeed the racist vanguard who are in the forefront initiating changes in black/white relations out of some self-serving economic compunction rather than providers of economic opportunity unimpeded by racial considerations. No person of the class persuasion has been able to explain the reasons for shifting from segregation to equality at the point in time the transformation has come about. What suppressed adherence to equality, a principle declared within the very national Constitution that whites themselves composed, during slavery and during segregation?

Finally, the "market force" explanation offers no significant insight into the facts, cited by the Report, that "had Reagan Administration policies not been followed, average black disposable income would have been *up* slightly, rather than down;" that "one of the major factors accounting for this erosion in unemployment insurance coverage was a series of 1981 federal budget cuts;" or that "the budget and tax policies adopted since 1980 significantly reduced the incomes of low and moderate income families while greatly boosting the incomes of the most affluent." The Reagan administration, like the nation in general, enacts economic measures decisively detrimental to blacks and does so while declaring, as explained below, its full-hearted commitment to equality regardless of race. How, then, can "market-force" advocates convince us of a federal government committed to principles of equality that brings a "declining significance of racism" when racial differentiation is so apparent in America?

In sum, the Report's content cannot possibly be explained by any current theory that professes that class differences and/or processes can account for the fate of blacks in a white America; class is not race, and neither racism nor capitalism has vanished from the marketplace.

The Colonial Model

Oppression provides the key formulation for some writers in search of an explanation for white treatment of blacks.[3] It is a form of oppression that replicates the economic exploitation of Africa by Europeans. Just as European nations established African colonies, so too, white America perpetuates its colonial hegemony over blacks — and for the identical reason, namely, to exploit blacks so that whites might accumulate wealth in the form of profits. Africa's vast natural resources became the colonizer's very possessions, and a native people provided the labor resource so that an elite white European ruling class acquired tremendous riches out of both the environment and the black inhabitants. Likewise, whites in America seized vast territories in what would become a nation for white people but whose native peoples were decimated. A black labor force was imported to exploit a fertile soil with excellent climatic conditions to permit commercial crops such as tobacco and cotton so that a very small band of ruling whites could acquire tremendous wealth unto itself. Colonial elites imposed racism, not only to create what would, they hoped, become an impenetrable barrier to impede blacks from access to nature's domain for generating wealth, but also to control ambitious lower-class whites, since racism deflects class antagonisms away from the ruling whites and toward the subordinate blacks. All whites, although most were themselves economically exploited by the commanding elite within their own midst, remained superior simply because so many blacks remained their inferiors; white privilege, therefore, enhanced the accumulation of wealth for a limited number of whites but permitted advantages to all whites regardless of class position because blacks were denied employment opportunities, education, political rights, access to the courts, ownership of property, residential locations, association (especially through marriage with whites, which, of course, disallowed an avenue for acquisition of wealth) with whites and so forth. Under such circumstances, any subjected people would become poverty-stricken, powerless, destitute, ignorant, listless, docile inwardly and, at times, outwardly (such as through rebellions, riots, and other manifestations of violence), discontented and "unstable" in social relations (such as in regard to family life, customs, beliefs, and traditions). Racism, therefore, flourishes to vouchsafe economic prerogatives to all whites and great wealth to the tiny ruling white elite. While blacks vastly outnumber whites in Africa but have always been a minority within America, racism prevailed to further the economic interests of a white minority, namely, the capitalists. In both Africa and America, whites reassured themselves of the righteousness for the privileges they so openly denied to other humans, so much like themselves save for what they perceived to be racial distinctions, and were thereby able to exonerate themselves from any sense of wrong toward their fellow humans by articulating a conviction of Godly approval. They told one another and endeavored to convince the downtrodden black as well that the Almighty Himself blessed the domination of blacks by whites. Divine Grace absolved most whites of most doubts concerning most of their abuses of blacks for most of the time blacks remained in an outcast position.

The Colonial approach to black/white relations, like Marxism, combines racism and economics through materialistic connections and processes. As conceived by each of these two economic explanations, racism flows out of the economic needs of a select group of people, namely capitalists who happen to be white. Presented in this fashion, neither view accounts for what I refer to as the "Handlin question:" "Why should one group of people rather than another have been selected as the object of prejudice?" (Handlin, 1957: 50). That is, what explains the selection of color as the crucial criterion for choosing a victim if, originally, only economic concerns motivated whites? What explains the *initial* appearance if economics, rather than racial prejudices, truly account for race relations? Moreover, neither perspective explains the course of race-relations history between blacks and whites generally and, specifically, since the end of World War II when equality began to substitute for segregation as the expressed form of racial oppression.

There is much in the Report to confirm the Colonial approach. As in the case of Marxism, the vast economic deterioration conveyed by the Report is the *only* possible outcome because whites are intent upon exploiting black labor for profits. Further, the expanding racial gap sustains the Colonial analysis, for it reveals white domination over a black people; it reflects racism itself in that blacks, as a collectivity, are destined to be subdued by whites. The disintegration of the black family from the nuclear tradition is just another mark of oppression by white over black; the reductions in federal welfare programs reveal the determination of a white people to rule out the needs of a black people whose lives become increasingly desperate under the severe exploitive conditions so intrinsic to the business sphere.

Yet while there are considerable data sustaining the Colonial perspective, the most telling set of statistics offered by the Report undermines the validity of the Colonial theory. That is, the Colonial interpretation, as with Marxism, simply cannot address itself to the most fundamental quality about blacks in the postwar economy of a white America: the incredible increase in joblessness, not only absolutely but also relative to white unemployment rates. How it is possible for any theory purporting to explain what happens to blacks, under economic conditions controlled by white capitalists intent not only upon making economic gains for themselves by exploiting labor but also with a society that preserves racial privilege so advantageous to all whites regardless of class position, to account for massive black unemployment and *permanent* joblessness? Marxists, erroneously, contend unemployment fulfills specific economic needs of the moment — a slackening market demand for labor as during an economic downswing — while proponents of the Colonial explanation fail to provide *any* account for the disengagement of blacks from employment at such an accelerating rate as described within the Report. Thus Marxists would anticipate the eventuality of widespread unemployment even along racial lines since blacks would be the first to be thrown out of work, but the Colonial perspective ignores the matter altogether as though losing one's job were just another manifestation of whites oppressing blacks. Yet if such high unemployment was expressing a racial dimension of colonial rule, what is it about racism *per se* that brings such rampant removal of blacks and at this particular moment in history? Surely, it could not be because racism itself is more vicious today than it was 50 or 100 years ago; if such were indeed true, then it would be incumbent upon advocates of the colonial thesis to explain why this should be so. Until such an analysis is forthcoming, the Colonial model fails to provide an adequate interpretation of black/white relations now and for the foreseeable future. Furthermore, even though racism itself is a vital component of the approach, the Colonial orientation, as with Marxism, must intrinsically disregard any contemplation of genocide as a possible white resolve toward blacks; both these economic views call for an inevitable exploitation of black labor as the foremost reason for whites treating blacks so differently from the way whites treat one another and, therefore, the economic imperatives of a capitalist system will not tolerate the liquidation of a people whose labor is so essential to the well-being of a ruling white capitalist class.

The above survey and assessments demonstrate quite convincingly that current theories about black/white relations are either entirely erroneous, as in the case of the family thesis, or else fail to cover the full range of empirical data encompassed within the Report itself. The most glaring empirical discrepancy between the Report's content and the prevailing explanations for the fate of blacks in a white America is, as we have seen time and time again, between the alarmingly high unemployment rates and what each theory can inform us about the enormous increase. Further, and closely associated with joblessness, is the question of whether or not, in light of the equally rapid rise of long-term unemployment rates by race, blacks are being removed permanently from the job market of a capitalist society. If permanency is indeed the correct interpretation, then it is absolutely essential to incorporate this reality into any theory that purports to account for race relations in America. And any such theory must also offer an explanation for blacks becoming the initial victims of permanent unemployment just as blacks were chosen for enslavement by whites. Finally, any such theory must account for the very appearance of equality as *the* standard for reconstituting black/white relations in this moment in time, rather than in an earlier era, and why whites draw upon the Constitution to vouchsafe the integrity of equality as the sole basis for establishing a new racial format. After all, whites no longer rely upon Christianity to provide the sanctity of their treatment of blacks as was the case, for example, during the era of slavery. Yet, as in the instances of Marxism and Colonialism, any theory would have to acknowledge not just the forceful presence of racism, but also the vital impact of economics and how racism and economics rather than blacks and whites integrate with one another.

The Postindustrial Revolution and the Economics of Uselessness: The Technological View

For over a quarter of a century an extremely small group of writers has developed an entirely new school of thought in an attempt to explain black/white relations in America and, in so doing, to overcome the limitations of existing theories.[4] Such analysts have been ignored just as much as the economic demise of blacks itself has been so conspicuously ignored. Such denials, of course, go hand in hand; by disregarding the economic collapse of the black people it is a simple matter to disregard theories that expound the removal of blacks from the marketplace of employment. While citations to the published works of such writers are forthcoming, there is absolutely no engagement with the substantive ideas.

A distinct clustering of writers has articulated a view that considers economic values for establishing the direction and momentum of racism throughout American history. While racism emerged out of economic processes (Handlin, 1957; Willhelm, 1983: ch. 5), nonetheless, it now prevails as an autonomous quality about American society that makes its very own contribution to the nature of black/white relations independent of, yet within parameters set by, economic aspirations and opportunities that reflect property interests. The enhancement of property interests — wealth — motivates the introduction of new modes of technological production that, in turn, are implemented by reorganizing labor. In revamping labor to harmonize with the introduction of a new technology of production, black/white relations themselves are reassessed and in such a manner as to integrate into an efficient application of labor for meeting the specifications of any new technology of production.

To date, there have been three technological eras, and a specific system of race relations can be associated with each technological period. First came the preindustrial mode of production; slavery became the format for race relations, providing an essential supply of cheap labor for a southern agricultural economy heavily dependent upon producing tobacco and cotton. Blacks constituted property available for purchase as though a mere commodity. Whites could readily invoke a racism that kept blacks in bondage because substantial profits could be realized not only by exploiting black labor but by selling black bodies as well. With the appearance of industrialization midway in the nineteenth century, however, slavery threatened the property interests of northeastern capitalists; slavery could no longer be sustained as a vital labor supply in a market economy that the northeastern industrialists were determined to establish throughout the entire nation (Willhelm, 1983: ch. 5). Confronted by the South's uncompromising intent to perpetuate the racism of slavery that could no longer support slave-labor production, the nation entered into a civil war that eliminated slavery but not racism. Once the sectional issues were resolved by military destruction of the South, the regional agricultural economy vanished and an industrialized national economy emerged. Black/white relations necessarily altered in response to the shifting economics of industrialization. Just as the regional economic concerns became a national commitment, so too the North's very own regional system of race relations — segregation — became the standard for the entire nation. Thus the impetus for the industrial revolution in America and the appropriate kind of racism were northern in origin, and a defeated South could only accommodate. Segregation replaced slavery, an expression of racial superiority that would not interfere with the making of profits by the industrialists who had dislodged the planter's class as the focal point of power. In short, a new economic order with its new mode of production mandated a new system of race relations between black and white so as to enhance profits for a new power elite that seized control and established a national economy.

Today, a third technological era is in full swing that, as was true for the two others, will have its own sort of labor market so as to alter fundamentally black/white relations at least as revolutionary as the overthrow of slavery. The Age of the Computer is upon us, but unlike previous technological epochs, there is not so much a shift in demands within the labor market as much as there is the destruction of the labor market itself. For computer technology is a form of production explicitly designed to eliminate rather than transform labor. Many observers (Wilson, 1978) contemplate a continuation of a labor market; computer technology will replicate the impact of previous modes of production and merely transform the character of work. Thus observers perceive the shift from blue- to white-collar employment as the fundamental modification brought about by introducing the computer into the American economy. It is this basic feature that explains the economic deterioration of blacks; the black worker is unable to meet the labor specifications of the white-collar labor market that is the new economic imperative of the computer age. Consequently, blacks fall behind whites in ways noted by the Report and even get dislodged from employment because they have been unable to make the transition. Viewed in this fashion, blacks are designated as an "underclass"; they are people who cannot enter the labor market because they lack the new technical training so essential to the kinds of jobs generated by computer technology. By maintaining a transformation, rather than the decimation, of the workforce, it becomes possible to speak of the "declining significance of race" and to interpret the fate of blacks as a class phenomenon: those whose labor skills are no longer adequate to the technical requirements of an automated form of production experience severe economic hardships and become members of the underclass while individuals whose skills, talents, and knowledge are compatible with the kinds of labor needs for a computer technology can experience "unprecedented" job opportunities.

Instead of a transformation of work, work itself is being destroyed; while the labor that is drawn from the market is transformed, the need for labor is simultaneously being curtailed. That such is indeed the case is confirmed by the appearance of an unemployment rate that, for years now, does not officially drop much below seven percent and an ever-rising number of discouraged workers. Surplus labor is also being processed out of the marketplace by the millions of individuals turning to retirement. The huge expansion of college enrollment shrinks the labor force still further. The record level of part-time employment gives the imagery, rather than the substance, of record-high employment figures. And, most important of all for our purposes, the extremely high unemployment rate and the ever-rising number of permanently jobless blacks provide vivid documentation for the assertion that automation must necessarily disengage people from the work force (Willhelm, 1983: ch. 6).

An interpretation of automation as a mode of production that removes human involvement in production cannot refer to poverty-stricken blacks as members of an "underclass." When, however, automation is considered as a production technique that is no longer labor dependent, then the affected blacks lose not only their jobs but their class standing as well; they become not members of an underclass but *declassed* people. Just as it is not possible to speak of a class position for black slaves, likewise there can be no class standing for blacks who no longer enter the labor force.

Individuals with no class position cannot, obviously, exert prerogatives of class. Such persons have no standing in a society where class allocates a person's life chances.

Since class position establishes the individual's life opportunities, the loss of class by blacks accounts for blacks falling behind in their possessions and achievements predicated upon class. Indeed, is it possible for a declassed person to have a chance for life at all? When blacks were declassed entities during slavery, they were, nonetheless, economically valued because they remained in capitalism's market as *commodities.* Industrialization forced them out of the commodity and into the labor market. Today, automation pushes them out of the labor market altogether and into a declassed position that has absolutely no value in a capitalist society. Further, the fact that blacks possess virtually no property of their own can only mean that they have no economic resourcefulness. Therefore, they cannot enter the marketplace as consumers; without property holdings and with a rising rate of joblessness, blacks are increasingly denied access to the market, and with such options no longer available, blacks become dependent upon *legislative* rather than economic processes for survival. Forced out of the market, only the government, and especially the federal government, can provide material needs to blacks. In short, the economics of private enterprise introduces the new technology of automation that, in turn, diminishes the need for employment; blacks are the very first victims who, in search of alternatives, turned to the State to provide economic opportunity. As recipients of welfare benefits, blacks gain entry into the market as consumers. But, they do so only if legislation is enacted; the political apparatus of the State must act and make provisions rather than the economic processes, as in the case for whites, of private enterprise establishing their life chances. But what the Report clearly reveals is a growing reluctance on the part of the nation's political leaders to endorse the economic legislation so vital to black survival. Being such a minority and effectively denied political relevance by whites, blacks lack political resources comparable to their lack of economic resources; they can no more generate the political agenda for a nation of white people than they can generate economic opportunity within a corporate economy under the control of property interests held, obviously, by white people. In other words, blacks are hostages to a white America today just as surely as they were owned by a white America during slavery. They are not held in bondage as mere particles of ownership, but, nonetheless, their fate remains bound to the same kind of white people, namely people holding vast resources in the form of property. Just as whites acted out of property interests to keep blacks in slavery, today whites perform in accord with their property interests to eliminate the black person from the labor processes of production.

black removal from the economy and the ever-present reluctance to provide economic legislation beneficial to the dispossessed black take place without the slightest reference to racism. Blacks become, as evidenced by the Report, increasingly unlike whites as they are treated more and more like whites. Yet the economic disengagement of blacks is considered purely a technological phenomenon with no racial implication even though blacks are disproportionately affected by the economic consequences of introducing computerized production; likewise, government legislative decisions are mandated by fiscal necessities and the fulfillment of a public demand to cut out welfare programs in order to force people off welfare and to rid the government of wasteful spending. Again, as made apparent within the Report, the fact that blacks are disproportionately affected by welfare reductions supposedly does not establish the presence of racism even though whites are the decision-makers controlling the legislative process and blacks are the foremost victims. It is, however, a confrontation between divergent economic interests: to be economically viable, blacks must promote government programs for obtaining the necessities of life; property interests seek profits by implementing a form of technology, automation, which makes employment redundant and costly even when economic responsibility for supporting the unemployed is absorbed by the State. Such a confrontation, although decidedly economic in composition, is not a clash of class interests, for, as already noted, dispossessed blacks have been *declassed* and therefore cannot perform, even in conflict situations, in accord with class interests (as laid out by the Marxist perspective). Being "unfit" for labor, they cannot make the kinds of demands so traditionally expounded by a working class — more jobs, higher wages, better working conditions, and so forth. Furthermore, even though they are economically debilitated by a capitalist class, they do not have a class enemy in capitalists, for the very technology of production precludes capitalists from creating jobs. This, then, requires blacks to voice their demands and to direct their hostilities not toward capitalists but the State itself. When discontent is acted out by a declassed people assaulting the State, it is not possible to impose a class analysis to reach an understanding of the fate of a black people in a white America. Thus while social discord followed class lines so that confrontations focused upon working conditions being improved and was subsequently negotiated through the collective representation of working-class unions during the era of industrialization, the advent of the new technology of computer production initiates turmoil wherein the State apparatus confronts the demands of persons thrust into the economics of uselessness.

Just as the arrival of industrialization brought in its wake not only the transformation of labor but also the transformation of race relations, so too, will the economics of the new technology fundamentally alter black/white relations as it does away with labor. Although post-World-War-II America abandoned segregation for equality, racism itself has not been abandoned any more than racism vanished with the demise of slavery. For equality itself is simply a reformation of racism; it is white America's assertion so as to update black subjugation in light of the economics of automation; it has been tailored by property interests to meet the political prerequisites of a postindustrial technology. Just as segregation was a more economical form of white oppression to accommodate to the new economics of industrial production in order to be more effective in *exploiting* black labor, so today, equality is a more economical form than is segregation for whites to *exclude* blacks from the workforce so as to be able to accommodate to the new economics of automated production.

Equality is intrinsically racist (Willhelm, 1983: ch. 7) for at least two rather obvious reasons: (1) the assertion that blacks are to be treated *just like whites* requires that *white* standards and *white* conceptions about equality be *imposed upon blacks*; and (2) *blacks have neither been allowed to decide whether or not equality is to be the* basis for establishing black/white relations nor have they been permitted to contribute their very own conceptions in formulating the meaning of equality. Equality is Constitutionally imposed, a "right" that is provided regardless of race, yet no black was permitted to participate, either as a voter or participant, in the decision-making process when writing the very Constitution that provides the ultimate recourse for seeking redress. Conceived by whites and imposed by whites ruling over a Supreme Court that establishes white interpretations of a white Constitutional "safeguard" for a black people, equality yields no rights except as determined by white notions. And any thought or action that does not fall within standards endorsed by the equality principle is beyond the bounds of tolerance and acceptability of a white America.

Equality makes its appearance at this moment in history rather than at an earlier instant even though it has been expounded for hundreds of years because its application in the present involves no encouragement or redistribution of wealth into black hands. Had equality made its entry during the preindustrial era, blacks would have won their freedom from bondage at the expense of the white planter class; to lose slaves through equality would mean the loss of property for whites at a point in history when slavery was a rather profitable form of labor exploitation. Likewise, had equality appeared during the era of industrialization when segregation flourished, whites would have suffered economic losses beyond their level of acceptance, for black labor could not be exploited as severely and blacks would compete with whites in the labor market not only for comparable wages but for the very jobs held exclusively by white workers. Today, equality is enforced upon blacks by whites with a vengeful sense of righteousness precisely because there is no economic threat to whites irrespective of class. Equality does not extend to the point of redistributing *wealth* "regardless of color," and it *requires* blacks to compete with whites in the job market at a point in time when blacks are in no economic position to compete. Thus, under the banner of equality, neither property interests nor employment opportunity is threatened by judging blacks like any white would be judged. Why, therefore, discriminate when one can eliminate? Equality is as effective for separating the citizens of this nation by race as was accomplished under both slavery and segregation. And such effective racial separation can be accomplished without any reliance upon ideas of racial inferiority. Indeed, whites conscientiously adhere to equality because of the economic advantages it brings in the postindustrial economy; there is the economic imperative to be rid of people to accomplish production for profits, and, by relying upon equality, the economic costs of joblessness can be imposed more readily upon blacks than upon whites. While equality may indeed be seen as an "advance" in preference either to slavery or segregation, it brings, nonetheless, the kinds, in the cogent words of the legal scholar Derrick Bell (1980: 8) of "advances for blacks that result...from policies which were intended to, and had the effect of, serving the interests and convenience of whites rather than remedying racial injustices against blacks." Equality assures the promotion of white economic interests while giving equal assurance of imposing economic deterioration opon blacks without any hint on the part of whites to declare racial inferiority.

President Reagan asserted, "The truth is they aren't worse off than they were" as his response to the Democratic Party's accusation that blacks, the poor, and the handicapped have suffered during his first term in office (Rothberg, 1984: A10). While sounding positive declarations for his own administration, Reagan, in one of his radio interviews, suggested that some black leaders promote the creation of "two Americas, a black America and a white America;" black spokespeople, he proclaimed, ought to "focus more on what has been accomplished and less on creating an ill will" (*New York Times*, 1983: B8). Reagan, while blaming blacks, keeps blacks out of state employment: "12.2 percent of Mr. Carter's full-time professional appointments were black as against 4.1 percent now; 16.1 percent of the Carter Administration's Federal judicial appointments were black compared to 2.5 percent for Mr. Reagan. Of United States Attorneys appointed under Mr. Carter, 6.9 percent were black compared with 1.1 percent for Mr. Reagan" (Watson, 1985: A23).

The Reagan administration vigorously and uncompromisingly enforces a "race neutrality" ideology to cloak its discriminatory policies against blacks. Reagan's legal posturing for deprecating blacks is all too apparent. Time and again, the President repudiates any intent of bigotry or the slightest notion of racial discrimination. Before a dinner reception of the National black Republican Council on September 15, 1982, he explained,

> Well, usually I try to ignore personal attacks, but one charge I'll have to admit strikes at my heart every time I hear it. That's the suggestion that we Republicans are taking a less active approach to protecting the civil rights of all Americans. No matter how you slice it, that's all baloney.... There is no room in the Republican Party for bigots [in Hitchens, 1982: 358].

Reagan's attorney general, Edwin Meese, emphatically declares the Constitution is "colorblind" and all "public policy must be racially neutral" while repudiating any form of "race-conscious" remedies since "counting by race is a form of racism." Affirmative-action programs such as the establishment of numerical goals for hiring blacks stand in violation of the 14th Amendment's explicit guarantee of "equal protection of the laws for all citizens regardless of color" (Hitchens, 1982: 358).

Within a 30-page supplement for its 1986 budget, the Reagan administration boasted that it could assume credit for "substantial progress toward the colorblind society and it denounced past administrations for misconceiving civil rights laws to permit special treatment to blacks, women, and the handicapped" (Williams, 1985: A7). It is no surprise, then, that the Washington D.C. Council of Lawyers, a public interest organization, concluded that the Justice Department's civil rights division, under William Bradford Reynolds, "has seemingly gone out of its way to alienate minority groups" (Maitland, 1983: A18).

Scholars remain, for the most part, silent in regard to the socioeconomic demise of black people and oblivious to the white strategy so deliberately formulated by the Reagan administration that allows the enforcement of racism "free" of racial discrimination. By imposing equality standards predicated upon constitutional mandates such as the equality provision of the 14th Amendment, Reagan cloaks his brand of racism around the bodies of black people whose deteriorating economic realities prevent them from becoming equal to whites in a socioeconomic sense. Social relations along racial lines cannot possibly be eliminated while property relations remain so pronounced and become even more so by rigorous adherence to the principle of treating all people the same regardless of race, creed, or color. As Christopher Hitchens (1982: 358) observes, "Reagan's economic policy is not a racialist one. It demoralizes and damages *all* poor people regardless of color, creed or national origin. Its effect on black people will indeed be disproportionate." This is precisely the reason for upholding equality since it is a standard for judging black/white relations that assures disproportionate consequences because it does not call into question the prevailing distribution of property. Thus in the name of rejecting racism, Reaganites embrace the very bigotry they so fervently repudiate. They *know* the outcome — namely, the intensification of racial separation and the economic demise of a black people, and with this full realization they *demand* that the nation's courts enforce the 14th Amendment with uncompromising dedication to a "colorblind" interpretation.

It would be an error to believe that the "conservative trend" accounts for a "sudden reversal" of government policy from welfare programs and affirmative action as evidenced by the Reagan administration. The black fate is sealed into the dynamics in which it has been caught for centuries — the interaction between the economics of capitalism and white racism. The advent of a technological era transforms the interplay between economics and racism with the outcome being virtually certain and, hence, predictable. Throughout American history, racism exists within limits set by the economics of production; whites establish a form of racism that will not infringe upon the economic returns of their productive technology. In other words, as I have stated often in my various publications (Willhelm, 1970, 1983), racism expands to the limits of economic feasibility. When a new form of technology comes forth, racism does not vanish in the least but merely changes form to accommodate to the labor specifications of the new mode of production so as not to impede investment returns. Thus slavery ended when the ownership of human bodies became an economic liability. Emancipation was neither a humanitarian declaration nor a lessening of a tenacious racism but rather an economic imperative: whites altered their *manifestation* of a racism that was no longer affordable. Segregation emerged as the most pronounced manifestation of racism that could be economically practiced by whites during the era of industrialization. Then, with the appearance of computer technology beginning in the fifties and onward, equality provides *the* established standard for black/white relations and does so, as explained above, because it, too, is the affordable system of race relations now that neither black bodies nor black labor is necessary for the efficient operation of the nation's system of production.

Just as property interests *never* vary — the quest for profits remains persistent in America's history — so too, white racism *never* varies in its intensity but only in its outward manifestation. Thus equality is no less pernicious than either slavery or segregation; it is *still a racist formulation* that, as will be explained below, is actually more vicious than previous ones not because whites are more racist today than in the past but rather because economic circumstances permit a stronger racialist policy of conditional genocide. No better proof for this assertion could be offered than the empirical data contained in both the Report and in this very presentation; all the socioeconomic indicators reveal the indisputable reality that the two races are not only separate, so that it is now commonplace to speak of "two Americas," but are becoming even more unlike with the passing of each decade. The fact that there have never been any compelling economic forces to require the complete demolition of racial differences explains how it is possible for whites to invoke racism. I would go so as far to say, even though obviously no empirical confirmation would be possible to sustain the assertion, that even if economic circumstances precluded any *manifestation* of racism, racism itself still would not vanish as a fundamental white value but would rather simply be *repressed* in expression while remaining an internalized quality of whites.

In light of racism's tenacity and the claim made here that the form racism assumes is established by the economics of technological production and is therefore predictable, what system of race relations can we anticipate for the future with the appearance of the postindustrial era?

Before providing a response to the question, it is necessary to recall the present standing of blacks as argued in this article. The economics of automation, like its technological predecessors of preindustrial and industrial technology, introduces an entirely new system of race relations for the nation. Throughout the history of this country, progressive movements such as the Abolitionists, Socialists, Communists and even the standardbearers of Constitutional Democracy, intently and sincerely pressed for equality as the appropriate relationship and in so doing firmly believed that equality and integration were one and the same. This explains how Kenneth Clark could so valiantly believe America was committed uncompromisingly to integration as equality made its appearance through, especially, numerous Court decisions that eliminated the old segregationist regime. The expectation, however, cannot be fulfilled because equality does not destroy this country's racist heritage, since it does not impinge upon the distribution of property that makes racism economically viable for whites. Because the economics of the country remains unaffected by the shift from segregation to equality, racism flourishes rather than vanishes from the scene. Why should whites surrender their racism now that the economics of the computer age removes *all* white dependence upon black labor for gaining wealth? With no economic compulsion to do so, why should whites be expected to be more tolerant and accepting of blacks?

What the factual information in the Report unquestionably reveals as *the* most fundamental economic reality for blacks in America is that they are being *removed* from the labor market where they are immersed in the economics of exploitation and are entering into what I have referred to as the "economics of uselessness." With the passing of each decade, a larger percentage of the black population becomes, not members of an underclass but declassed individuals, because they are no longer needed for their labor so that the white economic elite of this nation might accumulate great wealth as they have always done but have done so by labor exploitation of all working people regardless of race.

That economic disengagement is the compelling reality is extremely apparent within the data on black males. While, for the mid-eighties, blacks generally had an official unemployment rate of about 15 percent, by 1982, 20 percent of the working-age (16-64) black men, some two million individuals, were entirely out of the labor force (Center for the Study of Social Policy, 1984: 6; Joe and Yu, 1984). This is three times the number for 1960 when almost three-fourths of all black men were employed in contrast to a mere 54 percent for 1982. "The picture," declares the Center for the Study of Social Policy (1984: 6) in April, 1984, "gets even worse. There are an estimated 925,000 working-age black men whose labor force status cannot be determined because they are missed in the Census. This 'undercount' in the Census is most severe among black men, amounting to more than 10 percent among working-age black men, compared to less than one percent for working-age white men." The elimination of the black male from the labor market becomes still more vivid in contrast to white males, for while "four million out of the 8.8 million working-age black men, or 46 percent, are without jobs" by being unemployed, discouraged, incarcerated or uncounted by the Census Bureau, in 1982 "78 percent of all working-age white men were employed" (p. 8). Thus for each white male unemployed, discouraged, or unaccounted for — 11 percent of the white work force — almost three working-age black men were in the same categories, that is, 30 percent of the black work force.

The future for a coming generation of blacks cannot possibly be a promising one; the economic calamity is something we can predict with virtual certainty by probing the data on black teenage joblessness. In March 1983, the unemployment rate for black teenagers stood at 45 percent in contrast to 23.2 percent for all 16- to 19-year-olds. As recently as 1979, the black teenage labor participation rate was 58 percent, but during 1982 it dropped to 36.6 percent. Economic disengagement of black teenagers, like their adult counterpart, can no longer be linked to the level of performance within the economy as a whole. "While the rates for white teen-agers," Janet L. Norwood (United Press International, 1983: A14) Commissioner of Labor Statistics, explains, "have continued to rise during nonrecessionary periods over the last ten years, the participation rate for black teenagers, particularly young black males, has tended downward."

What alternatives do blacks have as increasing numbers drop into the unemployable ranks? Their initial response took the form of a civil rights struggle; believing, as they did, that the shackles of racism in the form of segregation impeded their socioeconomic progress on terms comparable to whites, blacks engaged in *civil* strife without, for the most part, realizing the economic dimension of their confrontation. Faced with a discontented black mass, the federal government responded with legislation and judicial decisions that, basically, encompassed the civil rights demands. Federal programs, especially under the Johnson administration, expanded to offer, to a limited extent, economic opportunities through employment and welfare. While civil rights accomplishments demolished segregation through the establishment of equality, the economic responses were in essence palliatives to appease, at least temporarily, a highly violatile minority (Piven and Cloward, 1977). Following the presidency of Lyndon Johnson, the push for equality expanded while economic opportunities disintegrated. The impoverishment of blacks accelerated as the economics of uselessness became institutionalized. Blacks, having been pushed out of the agricultural economy by the arrival of highly mechanized machinery that now turns the soil and picks the crops, entered American cities at a point in time when automation made its appearance so that jobs would not be available. And now, the state economy, which once appeared as a promising alternative to removal from the private economy, rapidly evaporates and especially so under the Reagan terms in office by enforcing "race neutrality."

As *both* the private and state economies close out employment opportunities for a black people, the economy of crime enters as a viable alternative for an increasing number of black people. Already removed from the economy of capitalism and presently being pushed out of the public sector (in both the civilian and military spheres), blacks turn to crime for survival. With 143 people per 100,000 Americans behind bars in 1980, the highest rate since comprehensive records began in 1940, the nation boasts of the highest rate of imprisonment of any Western country and is behind only the Soviet Union and the Union of South Africa throughout the world (Martin, 1978: 100). The number of Americans in state and federal prisons leaped from 196,000 in 1973 to over 314,000 during 1981 — the sharpest rise in history (Lieber, 1981: 28). Blacks, needless to say, are far more likely to be incarcerated than whites and, over time, at an increasing rate. From 1973 to 1979, the number of whites imprisoned rose from 46.3 per 100,000 to 65.1 while it went from 368.0 to 544.1 for blacks. Although blacks made up 11 percent of the American population, in 1978 they accounted for 40 percent of federal inmates and, for 1979, 47.8 percent of state prison inmates. With blacks disproportionally restrained in prisons, white remains the color of their custodians: 97 percent of all prison administrators and 95 percent of all prison guards are white (Gary and Brown, 1975: 53).

Such statistics, reflecting, to some extent, expanding crime, convey, generally, a growing inclination among blacks to rely upon criminal activities as a livelihood, and, specifically, a higher likelihood of imprisonment as a result. Of imprisoned people, 31 percent were jobless for the month preceding arrest while 60 percent had an income of less than $6,000 for the year prior to arrest (Martin, 1978: 101). Clearly, then, crime is increasingly becoming an option for the impoverished people such that, in the words of Josh Martin (1978: 101), "our poor, blacks, unemployed and young are filling our jails." While the State rules out investment of its economic resources for economic opportunity, it continues to expand its investment in new prisons; during the seventies, 150 prisons were constructed while just for 1981 another 62 were opened (*Newsweek*, 1981: 54), while for the decade of the eighties another 726 new federal, state, and local prisons are anticipated (Carper and Naisbitt, 1980: E6). Nonetheless, even with such substantial growth in the number of new prisons, overcrowding has become an epidemic; while the number of prisoners climbed by 50 percent from 1972 to 1978, only 23,000 beds were added so that only one-third of the new inmates could be accommodated (*New York Times*, 1981: A17). Thus while blacks perceive criminal activity as a viable alternative to joblessness much more often than in the past, increased law enforcement and poor living conditions within prisons themselves assure the continuation of existing black impoverishment. The future cannot possibly be considered promising in light of the extraordinary fact, published by the President's Commission on Law Enforcement and Administration of Justice (1967: 216-228), that 90 percent of all black males will be arrested for at least one nontraffic offense during their lifetime!

To summarize, then, the black options in white America today, we find that as blacks get removed from private enterprise and the government simultaneously eliminates its employment and welfare programs, crime increasingly provides an option; whites retaliate as blacks resort to the underworld economy by throwing more blacks behind bars. Under such circumstances, what, then, will be the fate for the growing number of declassed blacks?

The "Indian fate" awaits a black people, for blacks will be forced to choose between a life of isolation upon a ghetto reservation under poverty as severe as for the Indian or, again, like the Indian, retaliate against whites through violent confrontations, such as in the sixties and seventies, and endure military reprisals of forceful repression. Racial separation means a white strategy of, in the words of Jean-Paul Sartre (1968), "conditional genocide:" blacks, either explicitly or implicitly, will come to realize that they will live a life of destitution upon their ghetto reservation under the condition imposed by whites that they remain "peaceful" (that is, passive) and that any violent assault by blacks upon whites will meet with extermination. Such an "understanding" came forth in regard to Indians in the nineteenth century and, whether recognized or not today, it reemerges in regard to blacks in the twentieth century.[5] In the nation's past, racial hostility by whites toward blacks was restrained by the economics of property interests; white animosity to the point of extermination could not come forth until whites no longer depend upon blacks as an exploitable source of labor. Just as the mid-nineteenth century marks a pronounced historical transformation of black/white relations — the shift from slavery to segregation — today, a mid-twentieth century America introduces another mode of production that assures the transformation of black/white relations from segregation to separation through conditional genocide that, obviously, threatens the very survival of blacks.

Several rather recent developments confirm the reality of "conditional genocide" in addition to the documentation contained in the Report and here in this article.

- In January 1986, Bill Moyers presented a special program, "The Vanishing black Family," over CBS television, a title conveying the destruction of blacks in America. This very day we so easily refer to a "vanishing black family" as a precursor to speaking of "the vanishing black American" just as only yesterday we spoke of "the vanishing Indian." A banished people whose family now vanishes will themselves soon be vanquished people.
- A recent book by George Parkin Grant, *English-Speaking Justice*, provides a profound exploration into the meaning of "justice" as conceived by Anglo-Americans. Grant (1985: 69) maintains that constitutional rights take priority over "any account of good" concerning human welfare. What happens, he asks, when "the stern demands of equal justice...sacrifice the right to existence of the inarticulate [i.e., for our subject at hand, Blacks] to the convenience of the articulate [i.e., the elite White property owners]? ... Once we have recognised what we can now will to create through our technology, why should we limit such creation by basing our systems of 'justice' on presuppositions which have been shown to be archaic by the very coming to be of technology?" (pp. 72, 80). Grant (p. 83) furnishes this reply as a reflection upon America's conception of justice:

> [T]echnological destiny has its own dynamic conveniences, which easily sweep away our tradition of justice, if the latter gets in the way. The "creative" in their corporations have been told for many generations that justice is only a convenience. In carrying out the dynamic convenience of technology, why should they not seek a "justice" which is congruent with those conveniences, and gradually sacrifice the principles of liberty and equality when they conflict with greater materialistic conveniences?

And with very obvious implications for the fate of blacks in America, Grant draws an ominous implication for the "excluded people:"

> It will be an equality which excludes liberal justice for those who are inconvenient to the "creative." It will exclude liberal justice from those who are too *weak* to enforce contracts — the imprisoned, the mentally unstable, the unborn, the aged, the defeated [i.e., black people] and sometimes even the morally unconforming [p. 84, emphasis added].

Grant takes note of a refusal of "modern thought" to reformulate the Anglo conception of equality into a justice that makes life possible and meaningful for an "excluded people" and reaches the identical conclusion — a "terrifying darkness" — that I have drawn in regard to black people:

> How, in modern thought, can we find *positive* answers to the questions: (i) what is it about human beings that makes liberty and equality their due? (ii) why is justice what we are fitted for, when it is not convenient for white property interests? Why is it our good? The inability of contractual liberals (or indeed Marxists) to answer these questions is the *terrifying darkness* which has fallen upon modern justice [p. 86, emphasis added].

Thus, a most recent analysis of the Anglo's concept of equal justice sets forth the identical conclusion as I have drawn for blacks in America even though Grant does not mention the topic of black/white relations in America a single time! An analysis, completely independent of my own as well as the topic of black/white relations, outlines the same general interpretation as my own analysis concerning the interplay between technology, economics, race relations and power: "the terrifying darkness which has fallen upon modern justice."

For over two decades I have contended the economic demise of black people, a conclusion that now receives still more support from the data contained in the Report. Although belatedly conceded, nonetheless, the persistence of impoverishment among blacks is more widely recognized today than when I first made such an assertion in the mid-sixties (Willhelm and Powell, 1964). Thus, for example, a study by the National Urban League (in Williams, 1986) over a 15-year period, released in January 1986, reaches the conclusion that blacks have "been left out of the nation's economic recovery" as evidenced by persistently high unemployment and expanding poverty such that blacks are now "verging on *permanent* exclusion from the nation's economic life" (emphasis added). To the best of my knowledge, I remain the only individual to insist that such an economic calamity means "conditional genocide." For there is no other possible outcome now that the Report makes plain the economic deterioration of all blacks regardless of class standing. While differences in opinion may prevail in regard to the specific economic reasons for the demise, the outcome — "terrifying darkness which has fallen upon modern justice" — simply cannot be challenged. It may very well be that economic processes other than, or in addition to, automation account for the Indian fate now besetting blacks, but the vanishing black behind the invisible wall of separation under conditional genocide is now beyond dispute.

Endnotes

1. For an academic voicing an optimistic conclusion, see Farley, 1984.
2. While sharp differences prevail among them, nonetheless, for a sample of a class approach to black/white relations, see: Nearing, 1929; Cox and Szymanski, 1948; Perlo, 1975; Bonacich, 1976; Winston, 1977; Geschwender, 1978; Goertzel, 1970. For additional citations and a more extended critical presentation of the class view, see my own recent work (Willhelm, 1983: ch. 3).
3. For writers voicing the Colonial view, see: Allen, 1970; Tabb, 1970; Blauner, 1972; Pinkney, 1976; Feagin, 1978. For additional citations and a more extended critical presentation of the Colonial thesis, see my own recent work (Willhelm, 1983: ch. 4).
4. One of the most significant and yet most ignored interpretation of black/white relations from a perspective of the economics of automation has been Martin Luther King, Jr. (1968). Although celebrated as the outstanding black leader of a civil rights movement, King's economic analysis remains completely unrecognized save for my own effort (Willhelm, 1979). While the economic analysis of postindustrial technology had a number of early adherents — Madhubuti (1978), Yett (1971), Patterson (1970) and Cleage (1968) — the perspective has all but faded except for my own publications. For references and a more complete development of my own view, see my *Who Needs the Negro?* (1970) and *Black in a White America* (1983).
5. For a more extensive discussion, see my books (Willhelm, 1970: ch. 8; 1983: ch. 7).

References

Allen, R. L. 1970. *Black Awakening in a Capitalist America.* Garden City: Doubleday Anchor.

Associated Press. 1981 "Births to the unwed found to have risen by 50 percent in 10 years." *New York Times.* 26 October: 1, B11.

.... 1982. "Rising poverty in '70s linked to jump in divorce." *Buffalo News.* 23 September: A11.

Bell, D. 1980. *Race, Racism and American Law.* Boston: Little, Brown.

Blauner, R. 1972. *Racial Oppression in America.* New York: Harper & Row.

Bonacich, E. 1976. "Advanced capitalism and Black/White relations in the United States: a split labor market interpretation." *American Sociological Review.* 41 (February): 34-51.

Carper, J. and J. Naisbitt. 1980. "More prison riots likely as public mood toughens." *Buffalo News.* 9 March: E6.

Center for the Study of Social Policy. 1984. *The "Flip-Side" of Black Families Headed by Women: The Economic Status of Black Men.* Washington: Author.

Cleage, A. B., Jr. 1968. *The Black Messiah.* New York: Sheed and Ward.

College Entrance Examination Board. 1985. *Equality and Excellence.* New York: College Board.

Commission on Law Enforcement and Administration of Justice. 1967. *Task Force Report: Science and Technology.* Washington: Government Printing Office.

Cox, O. C. 1948. *Caste, Class and Race.* Garden City: Doubleday.

Cummings, J. 1983a. "Breakup of Black family imperils gains of decades." *New York Times.* 20 November: 1, 56.

.... 1983b. "Heading a family: stories of 7 Black women." *New York Times.* 21 November: 1, B14.

Dreyfuss, J. 1984. "Why '84 should please Blacks." *New York Times.* 30 December: E13.

Farley, R. 1984. *Blacks and Whites: Narrowing the Gap?* Cambridge: Harvard University Press.

Feagin, J. R. 1978. *Racial and Ethnic Relations.* Englewood Cliffs: Prentice-Hall.

Feinberg, L. 1978. "Half of Blacks born in '76 illegitimate." *Buffalo Evening News.* 10 May: 17.

Gary, L. and L. P. Brown. 1975. *Crime and Its Impact on the Black Community.* Washington: Howard University Press.

Geschwender, J. 1978. *Racial Stratification in America.* Dubuque: Wm. C. Brown.

Goodman, W. 1984. "Dr. Kenneth B. Clark: bewilderment replaces 'wishful thinking' on race." *New York Times.* 27 December: A14.

Grant, G. P. 1985. *English-Speaking Justice.* Notre Dame: University of Notre Dame Press.

Handlin, O. 1957. *Race and Nationality in American Life.* Garden City: Doubleday.

Haskins, W. J. 1982. "A Black responsibility." *New York Times.* 4 October: A19.

Hitchens, C. 1982. "Minority report." *Nation.* 235 16 October: 358-359.

Joe, T. and P. Yu. 1984. "Black men, welfare and jobs." *New York Times.* 11May: A31.

King, M. L., Jr. 1968. *Where Do We Go From Here?* Boston: Beacon.

Lieber, J. 1981. "The American prison: a tinderbox." *New York Times Magazine.* 26 March: 26-30.

Madhubuti, H. R. 1978. *Enemies: The Clash of Races.* Chicago: Third World.

Maitland, L. 1983. "Bar group study finds 'retreat' on civil rights under Reagan." *New York Times.* 16 September: A18.

Martin, J. 1978. "Andrew Young is right." *Nation.* 227 5-12August: 99-101.

National Advisory Commission on Civil Disorders. 1968. *Report of the National Advisory Commission on Civil Disorders.* New York: Bantam.

Nearing, S. 1929. *Black America.* New York: Vanguard.

New York Times. 1981. "Study urges cutting populations in crowded prisons." 26 March: A17.

.... 1983. "Reagan said to 'berate' Blacks." 28 January: B8.

.... 1984. "Pendleton assails Black leadership." 21 November: A14.

.... 1985. "Advertisement." 23 September: A20.

Newsweek. 1985. "Playing both mother and father." 15 July: 42-43.

Noble, K. B. 1984. "Plight of Black family is studied anew." *New York Times.* 29 January: E20.

Park, R. E. 1913. "Negro home life and standards of living." *Annals.* 49 (September): 137-149.

Patterson, W. L. 1970. *We Charge Genocide.* New York: International.

Pear, R. 1983. "Poverty data and families." *New York Times* 29 September: A17.

Perlo, V. 1975. *Economics of Racism U.S.A.* New York: International.

Pinkney, A. 1976. *Red, Black, and Green.* New York: Cambridge University Press.

Piven, F. and R. A. Cloward. 1977. *Poor People's Movements.* New York: Pantheon.

Rohatyn, F. G. 1985. "Catching up." *New York Times.* 20 January: E6.

Rosenbaum, R. E. 1985. "Moynihan reassessing problems of families." *New York Times.* 7 April: 1, 15.

Rothberg, D. M. 1984. "Congress battle shaping up between Reagan, Democrats." *Buffalo News*. 8 November: A10.

Ryan, W. 1971. *Blaming the Victim*. New York: Vintage.

Sartre, J. P. 1968. *On Genocide*. Boston: Beacon.

Sparr, P. 1985. "Re-evaluating feminist economics." *Dollars and Sense*. 9 (September): 12-14.

Szymanski, A. J. and T. G. Goertzel. 1970. *Sociology: Class, Consciousness, and Contradictions*. New York: D. Van Nostrand.

Tabb, W. K. 1970. *The Political Economy of the Black Ghetto*. New York: W. W. Norton.

Takaki, R. T. 1979. *Iron Cages: Race and Culture in Nineteenth-Century America*. New York: Alfred A. Knopf.

Time. 1985. "Snapshot of a changing America." 2 September: 16-18.

United Press International. 1983. "Black teen-age job plight: lack of skill and hope." *New York Times*. 19 April: A14.

U.S. Bureau of the Census. 1980. *Current Population Reports, Consumer Income*. Series P-60, No. 123. Washington: Government Printing Office.

U.S. Department of Labor. 1965. *The Negro Family*. Washington: Government Printing Office.

Valentine, C. 1968. *Culture and Poverty*. Chicago: University of Chicago Press.

Vaughn-Cooke, D. 1985. "No recovery in the economic status in black America." *black Scholar*. (September/October): 2-13.

Wagner, R. F., Jr. 1985. "Suburban shift." *New York Times*. 20 January: E6.

Watson, D. L. 1985. "Four more years in the back of the bus?" *New York Times*. 9 January: A23.

Weitzman, L. 1985. *The Divorce Revolution*. New York: Free Press.

Willhelm, S. M. 1970. *Who Needs the Negro?* Cambridge: Schenkman.

.... 1979. "Martin Luther King, Jr. and the Black experience in America." *Journal of Black Studies*. 10 (September): 3-19.

.... 1983. *Black in a White America*. Cambridge: Schenkman.

Willhelm, S. M. and E. H. Powell. 1964. "Who needs the Negro?" *Society*. I (September-October): 3-6.

Williams, J. 1985. "U.S. 'restoring' anti-bias laws, report says." *Buffalo News*. 8 February: A7.

.... 1986. "Data show Blacks slicing income gap." *New York Times*. 2 February.

Wilson, W. J. 1978. *The Declining Significance of Race*. Chicago: University of Chicago Press.

Winston, H. 1977. *Class, Race, and Black Liberation*. New York: International.

Yett, S. 1971. *The Choice: The Issue of Black Survival in America*. New York: G. P. Putnam's Sons.

Young, A. M. 1983. "Recent trends in higher education and labor force activity." *Monthly Labor Review*. February: 39-41.

Youngblood, R. 1985. "No-fault divorce becomes economic boomerang." *Buffalo News*. 27 October: F4.

CHAPTER 3

BLACK MALE GENOCIDE: A FINAL SOLUTION TO THE RACE PROBLEM IN AMERICA

ROBERT STAPLES
UNIVERSITY OF CALIFORNIA

Throughout the ages, philosophers have wrestled with the concept of reality, how we construct it out of our own experiences and location in a particular society. When these perceptions of reality collide, that conflict often derives from the interests a group has in the definition of social reality.

At no time has there been such a gap in the interpretation of the black situation in the United States as exists in the decade of the 1980s. Despite increasing black deprivation, a noted white economist seriously writes, "The greatest irony of Reaganomics is that its most vociferous opposition has come from the two groups — women and blacks, who have benefited most from its policies."[1]

After citing figures which ostensibly show that, since 1982, blacks have far outstripped whites in employment gains, this economist claims that "the economics recovery of 1982-1986 has been mainly an 'affirmative action' job explosion, with white males badly trailing women and blacks, both male and female."[2]

The Gallup Poll's 1987 survey on the community's treatment of blacks shows that 64 percent of the nation's whites believe blacks are treated as well as whites and only three percent say blacks are treated badly. Conversely, 52 percent of blacks say they are treated badly or not very well.[3] The above survey did not measure the beliefs of a substantial number of whites who think blacks actually receive preferential treatment over whites.[4]

Since past years have revealed racial discrimination as the reason for the low status and discriminatory treatment of blacks, it seems practically an absurdity for a majority of whites to think that blacks have achieved equity with whites in the United States. While

---

* Originally published in *The Black Scholar*, Vol. 18, No. 3: 2-11 (May/June 1987).
Reprinted by permission of Black World Foundation.

all blacks — men, women and children — are burdened by the persistence of institutional racism, the situation of black men has deteriorated to the point of their being called an "endangered species."

"Endangered Species?"

Newsweek magazine began a cover story on black men with this statement, "Black men are six times as likely as white men to be murder victims. They are two and a half times as likely to be unemployed. They finish last in practically every socio-economic measure from infant mortality to life expectancy.... Black men in America seem almost an endangered species."[5]

Time magazine had largely reached the same conclusion when it wrote, "Perhaps as much as 50 percent of young black males in certain cities still find themselves cut off from the American mainstream. Unemployed and undereducated they seem unable and in some cases unwilling to fit into the broader society."[6]

If the white-controlled news magazines can make such apocalyptic claims about the status of black men in America, the alarm in the black community is considerably greater. According to Reverend Floyd Rose, a former president of the Toledo Chapter of the NAACP, "We have lost our children. When they get to high school age they are not in school, and they are not in jobs, they are on the streets. By the year 2000 it is estimated that 70 percent of all black men will be in jail, dead or on drugs or in the throes of alcoholism."[7]

Echoing the same concern, a black newspaper columnist quotes a black medical doctor as saying:

> "Judging by today's statistics, unless a cure is found for AIDS and unless black people stop taking drugs to the extent they are, we won't have to worry about integration or equality at all; we'll be extinct as a race in less than a century. We won't be around to celebrate the 200th anniversary of our own emancipation."[8]

Black Male Genocide

The statistics, as dismal as they are, would seem to substantiate both of the above statements. Among the problems confronting black men in the 1980s:

(1) While black men account for only six percent of the population in the United States, they make up half of its male prisoners in local, state and federal jails.

(2) The majority of the 20,000 Americans killed in crime-related incidents each year are black men.

(3) Over 35 percent of all black men in American cities are drug and alcohol abusers.

(4) Eighteen percent of black males drop out of high school.

(5) Twenty-five percent of the victims of AIDS are black men.

(6) Over 50 percent of black men under the age of 21 are unemployed.

(7) Forty-six percent of black men between the ages of 16-62 are not in the labor force.

(8) About 32 percent of black men have incomes below the officially defined poverty level.[9]

While there is no shortage of theories to explain the aforementioned statistical trends, ranging from change in the economy to the breakdown of the black family, two older theories seem most applicable to the understanding of what I will call black male genocide.

One of them is W.E.B. DuBois' prediction that the problem of the twentieth century would be the color line.[10] Whereas a combination of social and cultural forces have brought about a social movement for black liberation, other problems of color have resulted in national wars of liberation in Africa, Asia, Latin America and the Caribbean islands. Most important, the internationalization of the world's labor force has significant implications of color.

White Misconceptions

The other theory is that of Sam Yette as articulated in his book, *The Choice*. Yette predicted a choice between accommodation and extinction for the black population of the United States.[11] His prediction of genocide for the entire black population diverges from current trends, in that it is black men who are most vulnerable to the ravages of an unbridled and dying American capitalism. Accommodation may no longer be an option for most of them.

The statistics on black male progress belie the racial millennium perceived by a majority of the nation's whites. What accounts for this dichotomy in the two races' perceptions of the status of black Americans?

First, the development of a substantial and highly visible black middle class has led many whites to generalize about black "progress." On the basis of that premise, it is easy to reject the notion that there are any serious barriers to black achievement. Present inequities can be rationalized as reflecting the pathologies of the black underclass.

Secondly, the white male has experienced some downward mobility from his former monopoly on all high-paying jobs in U.S. society. Between 1979 and 1983, five million families headed by white males were added to the poverty rolls, for much the same reasons as black males dropped out of the labor force.[12]

The bulk of the new and lower-paying jobs created in the 1980s went to women and the international labor force. Yet, to a white working class person indoctrinated with racism, the natural tendency is to scapegoat blacks as a source of all white problems.

A member of the Ku Klux Klan noted that there are more Klansmen from the North now than there are from the South. He asserts, "Basically, they're from Illinois and Michigan, the northern industrial states. Most of them have lost their jobs. They blame it on the blacks. I don't know how they tie it in."[13]

Virulent Racist Attacks

The decline of industrial jobs and the shift to a service and information processing economy favored female workers, pushing black and white males out of the labor force. The Reagan Administration cleverly manipulated a propaganda campaign to convince white workers that they were being discriminated against in favor of blacks. The result has been an outpouring of violence against black men by working class white males.

Beginning with the shooting of four unarmed black male youths in New York City by Berhnard Goetz, there has been a plethora of racial incidents. These include:

- the beating of three black men by whites in the Howard Beach section of the borough of Queens in New York City, which led to the death of one of the victims;
- the order by a Louisiana sheriff that blacks passing through white neighborhoods be routinely stopped;
- the hazing of a black cadet at a Citadel Military Academy; and
- the taunting of blacks in marches at the time of the Martin Luther King holiday in 1987.[14]

The racial climate created by Ronald Reagan and his minions has led to an unprecedented number of attacks on blacks in white neighborhoods, college campuses and public streets. Racial slurs by public officials are becoming commonplace, lending some observers to claim, "It looks like open season on blacks."[15]

Racial Differences in Incomes

In reality what has happened in the last decade has been the enrichment of the wealthy and the impoverishment of lower income groups. While the income of the richest one-fifth of families increased by 14 percent in the last six years, the poorest one-fifth of families had their share of the total income of all families reduced by one-third.[16] It is apparent that most blacks are concentrated in the poorest one-fifth of all families, and the upper one-fifth is overwhelmingly white.

Income, however, is not the only measure of the racial difference in wealth. When other accumulated assets that can be converted into cash, such as stocks, bonds and property are included, the median wealth of white households is 12 times that of black households.[17] Although average income and poverty rates can be useful, they actually overstate the gains made by blacks and disguise the fact that 99 percent of the wealth in the US. is held by whites.

Along with Reagan policies that have created an upward transfer of wealth has come the internationalization of the work force. In the post-World War II era, the role of non-white nations has largely become that of reserve labor supply, previously designated for Third World peoples, women and lumpen in the U.S. The black labor force has been impacted in several ways by the internationalization of the working class.

Since World War II, the U.S. and some of its European allies have been busily engaged in maintaining non-white nations in a semi-colonial status. They have intervened in two wars of national liberation, Korea and Vietnam, in order to prop up American puppet states. Additionally, they have supported oligarchies in Latin American and Pacific Rim countries that have caused internal resistance movements and created massive dislocations of indigenous populations.

WAVES OF IMMIGRATION

American imperialism has given impetus to successive waves of immigration to the U.S. by collaborators in the colonial effort, such as Filipinos, Vietnamese, Cambodians, Cubans, Nicaraguans, Salvadorans and Chileans. Other immigrants are fleeing war-torn conditions in their countries and the harsh economic climate created by American-supported dictators in Third World nations.

These immigrants often take menial and low-paying jobs traditionally held by black Americans. Immigrants typically take the lowest-paying jobs as more established ethnic groups move up the economic ladder. After 400 years, black males have not moved up in large numbers and find themselves locked into the bottom of the socio-economic scale by the latest groups of immigrants.

While the victims and collaborators of American imperialism replace black male workers in the U.S., American capital chases the cheapest labor. Jobs in U.S corporations are exported to Third World nations in Pacific Rim and Caribbean countries. Exporting jobs to friendly Third World dictatorships serves a variety of purposes.

First, it has created a cheap pool of labor in U.S. puppet states such as the Philippines, Haiti, Mexico and Taiwan, labor that can be exploited by multinational corporations. American workers, after all, earn a guaranteed minimum wage, insist on occupational safety rules and belong to labor unions that call strikes to protest oppressive working conditions.

THIRD WORLD WORKERS

Workers in impoverished and debt-ridden Third World nations consider themselves lucky to acquire jobs at 70 cents per hour in unregulated plants. In such plants output quotas are often increased, hours lengthened, wages reduced, industrial pollutants ignored and nascent dissidents fired. *If* workers organize to protest such conditions, the army may be used to intimidate or terrorize them. The infusion of capital to such nations provides an illusion of prosperity, but in fact, it is inflationary and subject to immediate change.

This increasing practice of exporting jobs abroad provides graphic evidence to counter the notion that capitalism creates jobs for its native labor force.

Despite the growing problems of a displaced black male labor force, the image inculcated in white consciousness is that of a group that has succeeded in American society. Certainly the symbols and role models of black male success are abundant at the top levels of society, with black male Presidential candidates, mayors of large cities, astronauts, sports heroes, highly paid entertainers and more. To the unenlightened white public, there is not more evidence needed that the American dream applies to everybody willing to play by the rules and work hard.

The reality of black male achievement in the U.S. is that with the exception of entertainers and athletes, most black males in successful positions are examples of the most egregious tokenism, who possess little power that cannot be vetoed by a white male in a superior position. As Theodore Cross has noted:

> Almost without exception, black people in the United States are born into a state of powerlessness. Even when their professional, management, or business attainments are very great, individual blacks are seldom in a position where they are feared, obeyed, or greatly respected by whites.[18]

Economic Disenfranchisement

Beginning with economic power, black men are disenfranchised in the capitalists' own arena. Black businesses, largely owned by males, take in less than one percent of all U.S. business revenues.

For those who hope to make it to the upper echelons of the white corporate world, the statistics reflect the scant chances of their succeeding. Among senior executives of the nation's 1,000 largest companies are *four* black males.

Even the comparatively conservative group of blacks holding Masters of Business Administration (MBA) degrees attributes the Reagan Administration's attacks on affirmative action as a major reason for the low number. In one survey, 40 percent of black MBA's felt their company was reluctant to accept blacks, and 41 percent believed their company was patronizing to them.

Other surveys indicate their feelings have validity. A report revealed that not only are blacks underrepresented at senior corporate levels, they have lost ground within the past seven years. One corporate manager summed up the situation nicely with this assessment:

> Chief executives aren't picked because they have 15 years of this experience, 10 years of that. They're picked to fit into the group that's already there. And, just as it was 20 years ago, that group is primarily white and male.[19]

The paucity of black male executives is so pervasive that they play by rules peculiar to black men in a white world. Generally those rules are: (1) do not question the impact of the company policy on the recruitment and advancement of racial minorities and women; (2) insist that your company only insists on hard work and competency for upward mobility; (3) question the competency of blacks who have not made the normal progression to the higher ranks of management; and (4) avoid any intimate associations with white female employees.

Political Arena

Not only has playing by these unwritten rules failed to elicit the expected rewards for blacks in the corporate world, it has not worked very well in the political arena either.

One such attempt was that of William Lucas to become the nation's first elected black governor in Michigan. Running as a Republican who supported conventional Republican policies, Lucas only attracted 23 percent of the overwhelmingly Democratic black vote and 30 percent of the white vote. A post-election analysis indicated that 30 percent of the white Republicans crossed party lines to vote against Lucas.

As a political researcher summed it up, "Republicans didn't take into consideration that there are two sides to a racial question. Blacks voted their party and their interests. The blacks didn't fall for it, and the whites voted by race. They voted for the white male."[20]

The hypocrisy of the white position that achievement should be based on merit is the fact that it entraps blacks into playing by the formal rules while whites often employ the informal methods for getting ahead. Whites can use intra-company social and business relationships with white peers and superiors to gain advancement in their companies, whereas blacks rely heavily on educational credentials and performance of their job descriptions to attain the same and more elusive goals.

Racial Images

Even in the 1980s racial images shape the black male's access to upward mobility in the corporate structure. One black male, a designer in a print ship in Chicago, requested to go out and work in sales for his company. His supervisor's response was:

> You know, I really believe you could do some sales, and I'd like to work with you, but I think you're too big and too black, and you might intimidate our clients.[21]

Because the gap between aspirations and achievement is so great for even highly educated and high income black males, racial membership becomes burdensome for all but those who deny that it still has some significance in American society. Studies have shown that higher income and status are not a shield against heart disease for blacks as they appear to be for whites.[22]

Writing in the *New York Times Magazine*, former tennis superstar Arthur Ashe revealed:

> Early on I learned that white society would tolerate only so many of us in one group at any one time; only so many or none in some places — "nice Negro families" in a previously all-white suburban neighborhood; only so many in certain public schools; only so many in white colleges. When I got in any of these, I was supposed to feel lucky.[23]

Ashe goes on to say that middle income professional blacks pay a heavy price if beholden to the myth that success in America is independent of racial membership. Many of them, he observes, are barely able to tolerate the stress. Nearly all of them, he says, are hypertensive and some are even visiting psychiatrists.

Black Entertainers

Among the greatest contributors to the black success myth are black entertainers. Because they are paid huge sums of money, are very visible, and highly publicized, they serve as role models for blacks who seldom see or know of black successes in other fields. They are also a major source of black images for whites, who are unlikely to know members of the black underclass and come into contact mostly with the token blacks placed in highly visible positions.

In the three dominant media, television, movies and music, black males are extensively represented but limited in the roles they play. In both television and movies, black males are confined to comedies or assigned roles as sexually neutered sidekicks to white male actors.

Black women have fared even worse, either absent or given a limited range of roles such as household servant (usually obese and sassy) or degenerate prostitute.

In the music world, black male singers represent flamboyant and androgynous characters that do not symbolize the romantic fantasies of white female record buyers.

Circa the 1980s, black male media stars seem to have fallen into two character topologies. One is the larger than life caricature such as Mr. T., and the Refrigerator (William Perry), who can be merchandised and not taken seriously by the white public. Their female counterparts would be Whoopi Goldberg and Oprah Winfrey. Even the brilliant and angry black comedians such as Richard Pryor and Eddie Murphy have been reduced to playing stereotyped street-smart ghetto males with little or no involvement with a girlfriend, wife or children.

"Safe" Black Male

The other type is the "safe" black male, who represents no threat to the white supremacist system. The ultimate safe black male image is exemplified by Bill Cosby on television's "The Cosby Show." Cosby has made major contributions to black causes. Probably more whites are exposed to him as a positive black male model than anyone else in America.

Yet his television show portrays a black family that is the epitome of black middle class success, contrary to the reality of the daily lives of most black Americans. Perhaps because the program's Huxtable family is a paragon of family and economic stability, one has to question the popularity of the show at a time when a growing consensus is emerging that black males are an endangered species.

Certainly, black male dominance in sports has to be a bright spot in an otherwise bleak picture. A close look reveals that while black males are engaged in injury-producing sports that result in short, albeit lucrative careers, white have equally lucrative and greater longevity in sports such as golf, tennis and bowling which the more economically deprived black males seldom have the opportunity to play.

Even the dominance and progress of black men in the major sports (baseball, football and basketball) are diminished by the persistence of racial discrimination in media treatment of black athletes, segregation in football positions and the lack of opportunities for blacks as managers or in front office jobs in sports organizations. This last deficit was brought to public attention and controversy by a statement on a nationally televised program by Al Campanis, the general manager of the Los Angeles Dodgers.

Black Stereotypes

Campanis said that blacks lack the intellectual skills to be major league baseball managers and high level executives. While his statement implied acceptance of every stereotype about blacks, praising their physical abilities and displaying contempt for their mental abilities, his comments only reflected the tip of an iceberg. As sports columnist Glenn Dickey observed,

> [t]he color line has been broken on the field but it's still largely intact when it comes to managers and executives. There have been only three black managers. There are no black general managers. But that only hints at the problem, which is a system that virtually locks out blacks on all levels. At the top, the general manager hires people throughout the entire system. Whites hire whites. It's as simple as that.[24]

Since the black liberation movement was quieted by the imprisonment, assassination or co-optation of its leaders, and attempts at racial equality were channeled into the more easily controlled institutional forms (such as black politics and capitalism), segments of the white ruling class have gained the ideological initiative. Diverting attention away from challenges to racism and capitalism, the ruling class shifted the ideological focus to issues of reverse racism and the victim's culpability for his own plight.

Research studies and official pronouncements all encouraged the perception that the pathology of the black underclass — unemployment, crime, welfare dependency, family dissolution, the breakdown of social values — is attributable to race, not poverty. Not only are the victims of racism blamed for their poverty, white society projects social pathology on all black men and singles them out as indolent, violent and irresponsible. In reality, the negative behavior of black males is the specific consequence of their powerlessness and economic isolation.

Black Male Unemployment

The black male is blamed for his high rate of unemployment because he has failed to prepare himself to compete in a technological society. It is estimated that as many as 44 percent of all black males can be classified as functional illiterates (i.e., unable to read or comprehend complex written material).[25]

While such a high percentage of functionally illiterate males begs the question of why the public school system allows that many males to reach the tenth grade or graduate without marketable reading and writing skills, it is questionable that these black men are obsolete in a modern economy. After all, many of the jobs they could perform have been exported to countries which will employ non-English-speaking people who may be functionally illiterate in their native language.

Moreover, according to Clyde Taylor, a much lower level of literacy is needed for job performance in Third World countries than is demanded by the American occupational structure. Taylor cites evidence showing that in Third World countries, only mass education at the elementary level for 30-50 percent of the population is needed, far below the level of "functional illiteracy" experienced currently in the United States.[26]

Other students of the subject have claimed that black men have less incentive than white men to acquire an education since data show that the same amount of educational investment yields considerably less return in the form of superior occupational status or mobility to nonwhites than to whites.[27]

Products for Profit

Because the productive forces of U.S. capitalism are geared toward making products for profit, not social needs, the work that black males could perform has a low priority among the leaders of industry. Even the federal government is directing its resources toward a massive military buildup that will drain much of the capital needed for the reindustrialization of America's manufacturing stock.

As a result, black males are selected out of the labor force by the educational credentials needed to compete for jobs in our technological society. The jobs they could do without the credentials, such as rebuilding the infrastructure of the U.S. (dams, bridges, highways, etc.) have been relegated to a lower funding priority than the building of missiles and other objects of human destruction.

Under mature capitalism, the job most typically offered to uneducated and young black males is that of the minimum wage security guard, an occupation that entails protecting the property and person of affluent whites from other black males of the underclass.

American society appears to have made the decision to spend a hundred billion dollars a year more for protection against the underclass than to educate and provide them with jobs. As capitalism in America has declined in its ability to provide the white male worker with the unchallenged monopoly he once had on the highest paying jobs, best housing, education, women, etc., his overriding motive has shifted from productivity to the monopolization of positions and incomes.

White Male Dominance

Only in this way, the white male worker believes, can he achieve and maintain his privileged place in the social stratification scale. The dominance he hopes to reacquire will be through voting for a President who ostensibly represents this interest, the elaboration of even higher educational requirements and the articulation of the meritocracy myth.

This attempt to reassert while male supremacy is laid bare by the statistics that show black male educational levels are closer to their white male counterparts than 30 years ago, but their unemployment rate has risen from double to triple that of comparable white males during the same period. The college-educated black male is four times more likely to be unemployed than his white male peer.[28]

Institutional racism and economic marginality have forced black males to disproportionately experience the ravages of inner city life. Unlike black women with children, black men are not eligible for public welfare. Bereft of any income from legitimate sources, only a limited number of options are available to them.

Alternative Economy

According to a U.S. census report, 54 percent of black males 18-29 years old are living with their parents.[29] Some of them may find temporary shelter with a black woman who is eligible for public assistance (if no adult male is living with her). After those two options, all that is left is homelessness and public begging or participation in the underground economy.

Increasingly the sale of drugs to alienated and powerless young black men has produced an alternative economy which can provide high wages and self-esteem to young men denied both in mainstream America. With the lack of equally successful role models in the inner city, drug dealers often become heroes to ghetto youth.

A combination of the above named forces threatens to institutionally decimate much of the black male population. The public schools fail to provide them with marketable skills in today's economy, and increasing competition among a variety of cultural groups for the scarce jobs available places black males among the most vulnerable groups to unemployment status.

For those with no job, hence no income, commission of street crimes can lead to a lifelong career in prison. Those who survive by other means are still left with nothing meaningful to do in a society where money and work define masculinity. Instead, they will define their masculinity by siring children they cannot support, and defend their masculinity by a violent response to any slight or provocation.

Their time will be occupied by the use of alcohol and drugs to allow them to blot out the awareness of their superfluous existence in a country that devalues and fears them. The predictable consequences are fatherless families, black homicides that occur at a rate six times higher than among white men, early death from drug- and alcohol-related causes, AIDS and a life expectancy that is the shortest of all sex-race groups in the U.S.

White Settler Societies

This morbid situation is not unknown or unprecedented in the history of white settler societies. The American Indian is a prototype of a similar form of genocide in this country. Similar parallels can be found among the Maoris of New Zealand and the Aboriginals of Australia. All these groups had in common a forced coexistence in a white-dominated culture that had appropriated their land or their labor.

Because their conformity to Anglo-Saxon demands could not be elicited, American Indians, Maoris and Aboriginals were perceived as continuing threats to the existence of white rule. As the capacity of the economy to function without them occurred, they became excess baggage and a competitive threat to the privileges of white males.

For many black men, forced idleness and impotence have encouraged self-destruction created through the use of alcohol and drugs, fratricidal violence and suicide. The criticism of this behavior itself by black female authors like Michelle Wallace, Ntozaki Shange and Alice Walker constitutes part of a selective force of black male erosion, when it is not cognizant of the sociological problems affecting black men and women.

Let us be clear, however, that an epitaph for black men is premature. Many of them remain valuable commodities to American capitalism. As athletes they are 20th century gladiators without peers. In the entertainment world, they provide amusement and escape from reality for the white citizenry and role models for blacks. Indeed, entertainment may become the opiate of the 21st century.

War of Containment

If America is to avoid the specter of a nuclear holocaust, conventional warfare will require large numbers of black males to fight its wars of containment against the oppressed masses of Asia and Latin America. Certain sectors of the economy will still require black labor. Although new immigrants will accept the low paying, dirty jobs when they first come to the United States, they will not be content to stay in those positions for 400 years as black Americans have been forced to do. Thus, unless there is a constant flow of immigrants, the dirty work will still have to be dome by men of color.

Another scenario is possible. The contradictions of world capitalism are reaching a crisis point, and its ability to use racism to divide workers is at the point of diminishing returns. Disenfranchised white farmers and steel workers may discover their commonality with unemployed black teenagers in Harlem.

Decline of Capitalism

Already the white jobless of Europe are experiencing poverty and economic dislocation because of the declining ability of capitalism to provide them decent jobs. Even the welfare state, or its measure, will be unable to pacify members of the working class who will realize there is work to be done and wealth to be shared in a society not based on class rule.

Only the strange mixture of racism and sexism could have motivated American white workers to elect as President a man whose policy was to help the wealthy, claiming that the benefits would trickle down to the working class.

The competition for jobs among black and white and male and female workers may prolong the divisions in the working class somewhat longer than in Europe. But economic justice is an idea whose time must come. Black men may not only survive to participate in it. They may lead the struggle for it.

Endnotes

1. Warren T. Brookes, "An Affirmative Action Explosion in Employment," *San Francisco Chronicle*. 7 October 1986, p. 53.
2. *Ibid.*
3. George Gallup, Jr., "How Blacks, Whites View Blacks Treatment," *San Francisco Chronicle*. 19 February 1987, p. 9.
4. Joe Reichwein, "Whites on Blacks: Opportunities Plentiful," *The National Leader*. 17 February 1983, p. 12.

5. Sylvester Monroe, "Brothers," *Newsweek.* 23 March 1987, p. 55.

6. "A New Generation of Native Sons," *Time.* 1 December 1986, pp. 34-35.

7. John Herbers, "More Blacks Slip into Poverty," *San Francisco Chronicle.* 28 January 1987, p. 2 2 .

8. Stanley GT. Robertson, "Drugs, AIDS and Blacks: A Catastrophe," *Los Angeles Sentinel.* 2 April 1987, p. 6.

9. Cf. Robert Staples, *Black Masculinity: The Black Males' Role in American Society* (San Francisco: The Black Scholar Press, 1982). The actual figures were compiled from a number of sources and are for the year 1986.

10. W.E.B. DuBois, *The Souls of Black Folk* (Greenwich: Fawcett, 1961), p. v.

11. Samuel Yette, *The Choice: The Issue of Black Survival in America* (New York: Putnam, 1971).

12. Michael Harrington, "White, Male and Poor," *San Francisco Chronicle.* "This World," 15 March 1987, p. 19.

13. Dudley Clendinen, "Behind the Hatred," *San Francisco Sunday Examiner and Chronicle.* "This World," 8 February 1987, p. 4.

14. Gallup, *loc. cit.*

15. Manning Marable, "Open Season on Blacks — Again," *Los Angeles Sentinel.* 8 January 1987, p. A7.

16. Barbara Ehrenreich, "Two Americas: Are We Becoming a Nation of Haves and Havenots?" *San Francisco Sunday Examiner and Chronicle.* "This World," 23 November 1986, p. 9.

17. William O'Hare, "Wealth Data Puts Black-White Gap in Sharp Focus," *Focus.* August, 1986, p. 4.

18. Theodore Cross, *The Black Power Imperative* (New York: Faulkner, 1984), p. 36.

19. "Wall Street: Racism, Inc.," *Los Angeles Sentinel.* 4 September 1986, p. A7.

20. Remer Tyson, "Lucas' Race was Factor in Margin, Analysts Say," *Detroit Free Press.* 6 November 1986, p. 1.

21. The Oprah Winfrey Show. "Prejudice Against Black Men," 23 January 1987.

22. Black Doctors Have Higher Rate of Heart Disease," *Jet Magazine.* 13 April 1986, p. 36.

23. Arthur Ashe, "Now More Zero-Sum Game," *The New York Times Magazine.* 31 August 1986, p. 26.

24. Glenn Dickey, "What's Sad is Than Many Think Like Campanis," *San Francisco Chronicle.* 10 April 1987, p. 97.

25. Jonathan Kozol, *Illiteracy in America* (New York: Morrow, 1985).

26. Clyde Taylor, "The Politics of Illiteracy," Institute for the Study of Educational Policy, *Monitor* (Howard University). Vol. 7, Nos. 3-4, Special Education, 1983.

27. John Ogbu, *Minority Education and Caste* (New York: Academic Press, 1978).

28. "Rights Panel Reports White Males get the Jobs," *San Francisco Chronicle.* 24 November 1982, p. A5.

29. Paul C. Gick and Sung-Ling Lin, "More Young Adults are Living with Their Parents. Who Are They?" *Journal of Marriage and the Family.* 48 (February 1986), pp. 107-112.

CHAPTER 4

EXECUTIONS OF WHITES FOR CRIMES AGAINST BLACKS: EXCEPTIONS TO THE RULE?

MICHAEL L. RADELET
UNIVERSITY OF FLORIDA

Abstract: This article examines the relationship between status and law in general and race and the death penalty in particular. It focuses on cases in which whites have been executed for crimes against blacks. The goals of the article are to (1) determine the frequency of such cases, and (2) interpret the role of status characteristics (other than race) in explaining why the executions occurred. Records of 15,978 American executions were reviewed, and 30 relevant cases were identified. While the findings appear anomalous when race alone is used to explain death sentencing, the use of more general measures of status to explain such events supports sociological interpretations of the relation between law and status.

One of the most important issues studied by modern criminologists is the relationship between law, case processing and the status attributes of defendants and victims. This article examines this issue by viewing race as one measure of status and the death penalty as one aspect of law. We focus attention on one type of case: executions of white defendants for crimes committed against blacks. A first goal is to document the existence and frequency of such cases. A second goal is to see whether nonracial status characteristics can help explain why these executions occurred, since each execution is theoretically anomalous when race alone is used as an indicator of status. By examining the details of relevant cases, we will ask whether such executions constitute true exceptions to the more general pattern that the social statuses of defendants and victims are important determinants of who is selected for execution.

* Originally published in *The Sociological Quarterly*, Vol. 30, No. 4: 529-544 (1989).
Reprinted by permission of JAI Press, Inc.

BACKGROUND

American history is replete with examples of criminal cases in which final dispositions were (and are) explicitly determined by the race and/or social status of the defendant or victim. One storied example of the mild treatment given those who victimized minorities arose in the chambers of Judge Roy Bean in the 1880s. Bean's son, believing that he was being overcharged, murdered the Chinese proprietor of the local laundry. The son was tried by his father. Judge Bean opened the session by spending two hours reading the Texas statutes aloud to the courtroom spectators. He then closed the law book, and, dropping it on the bench, declared: "That's...the complete statutes of this here state from the Alamo on ahead, and there ain't a damned line in it nowheres that makes it illegal to kill a Chinaman. The defendant is discharged" (Botkin, 1944: 143).[1]

This and other case examples lead one to wonder if any whites have ever been executed for crimes against minorities. Statistical research adds to the conclusion that in understanding death sentencing, race matters. But this research, particularly that which examined sentencing patterns in the years before the death penalty was temporarily banned in 1972 (*Furman v. Georgia*, 408 U.S. 238), has been far from comprehensive (for reviews, see Bowers, 1984; Dike, 1982: 43-51; Gross and Mauro, 1984: 38-42; Kleck, 1981; Radelet and Vandiver, 1986).

One of the best early studies, conducted by Garfinkle with North Carolina data (1949), found that blacks who killed whites were treated more harshly than other homicide defendants. The clearest patterns of racial bias have been found in examinations of executions for rape (Wolfgang and Riedel, 1973). Of the 455 men executed for rape between 1930 and 1967, 89 percent were black. Overall, however, much of this pre-*Furman* research was conducted in the South, failed to consider the effects of prior criminal record and the independent and interactive effects of race of defendant *and* victim, and used methodologies that are amateurish by today's standards. Hence, their results are somewhat inconsistent (Kleck, 1981). In addition, the only major study that examined the economic status of the defendant, done in California, found that economic status, but not race, was associated with death sentencing (Judson, Pandell, Owens, McIntosh and Matschullat, 1969).

Research on racial disparities in the administration of the death penalty statutes passed in the wake of the *Furman* decision has been more sophisticated, and has examined the race of both defendants and victims. This body of work has consistently found that, given similar legal factors, the victim's race is a strong determinant of who is sentenced to death (e.g. Bowers, 1984; Gross and Mauro, 1984; Radelet, 1981; Radelet and Pierce, 1985). By any measure, the best of these studies, examining sentencing patterns in Georgia, was conducted by David Baldus and his colleagues (Baldus, Pulaski and Woodworth, 1986; Baldus, Woodworth and Pulaski, 1985). After examining over 2,000 Georgia homicides from the 1970s and controlling for some 230 variables, Baldus reached the disturbing conclusion that the odds of a death sentence for those charged with killing whites were still 4.3 times higher than the odds of a death sentence for defendants charged with killing blacks.[2]

Three general conclusions from this body of literature can be made: (1) the research showing strong race-of-defendant bias in death sentencing for rape is definitive; (2) the race-of-defendant effects in pre-*Furman* studies are modest and uneven; and (3) the post-*Furman* work has consistently found strong race-of-victim effects.

Applied to white-on-black crimes, these empirical findings would lead one to predict that the severity of societal reaction varies by defendant-victim racial combinations, with black-on-white expected to be most severe and white-on-black the least. No executions for white-on-black offenses are predicted, and any found are theoretically anomalous. Such executions support the theory only because their relative frequency is low.

This leads into our second question: if race is an important determining factor, how can we explain the existence of *any* executions of whites for crimes against blacks? As individual cases, each white-on-black execution stands as theoretically deviant. Being unanticipated and anomalous, each is a "datum which becomes the occasion for developing new theory or for extending an existing theory" (Merton, 1968: 158). Understanding them necessitates theoretical specification of what factors can explain the effects of defendant and victim races on case processing.

At a broad level of abstraction, Black postulates that law in stratified societies has a vertical direction. "Downward law is greater than upward law," according to Black (1976: 21). By this he means that upward crimes — crimes where the victim's status ranks above the offender's status — are treated as more serious than downward crimes, and punishment is more likely to have a downward than an upward direction. Consistent with this postulate, Farrell and Swigert (1978, 1986) found in their study of homicides that convictions were most severe for low status defendants who were suspected of killing high status victims, and that the defendant-victim racial combination had no significant effect on legal treatment. They argue that this pattern results from an interpretive process "wherein authorities come to rely on the social attributes of actors in arriving at determinations of culpability" (1986: 349). As Garfinkle states (1949: 376), "From the point that murder is 'recognized' until the case is finally disposed of, the offender is involved in a system of procedures of definition and redefinition of social identities and circumstances." Race is one of the attributes used in arriving at determinations of culpability, but only one, with overt discrimination subordinate in its explanatory ability (and theoretical centrality) to more encompassing status attributes of defendants and victims and imageries of the threat to prevailing power relationships.

Thus, while race is one measure of status (and alone it leads us to expect no relevant executions), it is not the only measure. If the measure of status is broadened to encompass such characteristics as class, occupation, economic value (for slaves), marginality, prior criminality and community integration, it may be that such executions are more theoretically consistent than they appear at first glance.

Since there have been so few white-on-black cases, researchers have virtually ignored them. For example, Garfinkle (1949: 380-381) says "We shall be unable to fulfill the task of interpreting [such] cases"; Gross and Mauro (1984: 71-72) report "there were too few cases in which white suspects killed black victims to permit meaningful comparisons"; LaFree (1980) simply excludes white-on-black assaults from his sample of rape cases. But these cases, given a broader conceptualization of status, can be examined to explore the hypothesis that, while first appearing to be theoretical anomalies, they in reality might fit the more general pattern that reactions to homicide are more severe when the victim is of higher status than the defendant.[3]

METHODOLOGY

The best single source of information on American executions is the extensive archive in Headland, Alabama, developed and maintained by Watt Espy.[4] To date, Espy has gathered information on 15,978 executions that have occurred in American jurisdictions since 1608 (see, e.g. Bowers, 1984: 395-523; Espy, 1980).[5]

Not all executions in American history are known. As with similar types of historical research, there is no way to determine how many executions occurred for which there are no records. Espy's best guess is that there may be as many as 7,000 executions that he does not yet know about, of which perhaps 90 percent have an extant trail that he or other researchers may someday be able to discover. If we assume that, because of their rarity, whites executed for crimes against blacks received more publicity and that the publicity always noted the relevant races, then Espy may very well have every such case in American history already included in his files.

For this research, the Espy archives were searched. These data were supplemented with additional information culled from contemporary local newspapers and published court decisions. The first leads on all cases, and about half the cited sources, were obtained from the Espy files.

FINDINGS

Frequency

Our first question concerns the frequency of executions for white-on-black crimes. The archive search identified 26 relevant cases, four of which involved two defendants.[6] These 30 cases represent .00188 of the 15,978 cases examined — about two-tenths of one percent of known American executions.[7] In other words, there has been one execution of a white for a crime against a black for every 533 recorded executions in American history.

It is possible that the reason executions for white-on-black crimes are so rare is that white-on-black crimes that might be interpreted as capital offenses have similarly been nearly non-existent. A precise estimate of the risk of execution for each racial combination (white-white, black-black, black-white and white-black) would require estimates not only of the number of executions per category, but also the number of capital or potentially capital crimes committed.[8] Although the data in the Espy archives allow us to construct the divisor for each category, it is not possible to estimate the needed dividends. Part of this problem stems from the way in which capital crimes have been defined. In Virginia in the 1830s, for example, there were five capital crimes for whites but 70 for black slaves. In 1848, Virginia passed a law that required the death penalty for blacks if convicted of any crime that was punishable by three or more years of imprisonment if committed by a white (Bowers, 1984: 139-140; see also, Higginbotham, 1978). Because blacks could not testify against whites in some states, it was almost impossible to prosecute whites for crimes against blacks (Merrill, 1976: 269). In short, the impossibility of assessing the risk of execution by race for capital offenses stems from the lack of reliable historical crime statistics, broken down by defendant's and victim's race. Given the history of well-documented and massive crimes against blacks by whites (e.g. Patterson, 1970), however, it would be preposterous to suggest that the frequency of such crimes is as low as the two-tenths of one percent figure shown here.

We now turn our attention to the characteristics of the relevant cases. Vignettes of each case, ordered by dates of execution, are presented in the Appendix. It will be seen that in some cases only minimal facts, in addition to the existence of the execution, are known. Even the most thoroughly documented cases are described only in a newspaper article or two and a published judicial decision, and these sources often accentuate the spectacular facts and fail to tell us the subtle, behind-the-headlines maneuvering that may have occurred at trial, appeal and clemency. While important gaps in the stories of all the cases remain, it is possible to make some inferences from the existing information.

Table 1 gives the jurisdictional and temporal distribution of the cases, plus information on the victim's sex. Eight of the cases come from outside the South (3 in New York, in 1829, 1877 and 1910, and one each in Connecticut in 1816, Kansas in 1944, Massachusetts

Table 1
Executions of Whites for Crimes Against Blacks by Jurisdiction and Victim's Sex

Jurisdiction	No. of Cases	Year and Victim's Sex
Alabama	2	1913(2)
Connecticut	1	1816
Georgia	2	1878; 1911*
Kansas	1	1944
Kentucky	1	1936
Louisiana	1	1752*
Massachusetts	1	1822
Mississippi	1	1890
Missouri	1	1876
New York	3	1829; 1877; 1910*
North Carolina	3	1820; 1880;* 1938
Ohio	1	1923
South Carolina	4	1853; 1854(2); 1880
Tennessee	3	1885; 1912(2)*
Texas	1	1854
Virginia	4	1739;* 1739(2); 1775
Total	30	

Note: *Female victim.

Table 2
Executions of Whites for Crimes Against Blacks by Era

Era	No. of Cases
1739-1800	5
1801-1833	4
1834-1866	4
1867-1900	7
1901-1933	7
1934-1944	3
Total	30

in 1822, Missouri in 1876 and Ohio in 1923). The remaining 22 cases (73.3 percent) come from the southern states. There are no apparent qualitative differences between the South and the non-South cases.

Each of the 30 cases involved the execution of a male. In seven cases (Case Nos. 1, 4, 18, 21, 22, 23 and 24), the victim of the crime was female (the last two culprits were codefendants who also killed a male). The remaining 23 defendants were all convicted of the murder of one male victim. The only person not convicted of murder, Pierre Dochenet (No. 4), had two female victims who were repeatedly stabbed and nearly killed. Interestingly, of the four cases that involved multiple victims (Nos. 4, 22, 23 and 24), all the victims were female, again with the latter two involving two girls and their father.

Table 2 classifies the cases by the date of execution. The earliest occurred in 1739, and the most recent was in 1944. Five cases occurred before 1800 and 10 others in this century. There is no pattern that indicates the cases were clustered in one decade or in one era; they appear scattered throughout the country's history.

The negligible frequency of these cases offers support for the theoretical model proposed above, though this support must be qualified. That only one of each 533 executions resulted from a white-on-black crime lends strong support to the model that links stratification and law in general and status and the death penalty in particular. But while the relatively low categorical frequency supports the model, each individual case is anomalous if race alone is used to predict sentencing, as the theory would predict none. We therefore turn our attention to the second question under study: the role of nonracial status attributes in explaining why these 30 executions occurred.

The Role of Nonracial Status Attributes

What about these cases can explain the anomalous event of executing a white for a crime against blacks? Surprisingly, the modal category of cases, with 10 entries, involves crimes that victimized slaves (Nos. 1, 2, 3, 4, 5, 7, 10, 11, 12 and 13). In two cases (Nos. 5 and 10), the culprit was the slave's owner. The data indicate that these two executions were intended to warn other slave owners to "treat their slaves with moderation," as occurrences of such brutality might have threatened the legitimacy of the institution of slavery. In the other cases, the crimes against the slaves can be interpreted as economic crimes, with the status of the victims a product of that of his or her owner.

According to our theoretical perspective, economic value is an indicator of status. Slaves are property, the wealth of someone else, and their rank should be measured accordingly (Black, 1976: 18). Consider, for example, the case of John Cobidge (No. 1), an indentured servant who killed a slave. As an indentured servant, Cobidge had little monetary value; he would be totally free as soon as his debt was paid. On the other hand, the slave he killed had an economic value for the master, as slaves were expensive to replace. In another case (No. 13), James Wilson killed a slave out of anger for the victim's affluent master. The economic value of slaves is underscored by the fact that when a slave was executed for criminal behavior, the state compensated the owner (not the victim's family) for the loss (Kay and Cary, 1976). Indeed, records of compensations are the best sources available for researchers to document slave executions.

Prior criminal record is another indicator of status. Seven of the remaining cases (Nos. 8, 15, 16, 18, 19, 28 and 30) involved defendants who had previous histories of serious troubles with the legal authorities. Two of the culprits (Nos. 8 and 16) were also alleged to have killed whites, although they were not, or could not (for lack of proof), be prosecuted for it. However, they could be, and were, prosecuted for murdering the black. Cases 8 and 15 involved a prison murder, and in Case 18, the defendant had a long record of previous criminality. The three remaining cases (Nos. 19, 28 and 30) involved defendants who had been previously sentenced to life imprisonment. It is probable that these seven were men who had totally exhausted their communities' tolerance, and whose histories made the authorities eager to accept any further criminality as justification for the harshest possible punishment.

In five of the remaining cases (Nos. 20, 23, 24, 25 and 26), the occupational status of the black victim clearly surpassed that of the white assailant. Two of these cases (Nos. 23 and 24) involved white men who killed their affluent employer, while two others (Nos. 25 and 26) involved the killing of a man who had accused one of the defendants of theft. In the other case (No. 20), a black testified against Mel Cheatham, a white gambler, in grand jury proceedings, and, after Cheatham was indicted, he killed the black man in revenge and to prevent further testimony.

Closely parallel to this category is a group with four cases (Nos. 14, 17, 21 and 27) in which the defendants were marginal members of the white community, perhaps being labeled as "white trash." "At every level of the legal process, a marginal person is more vulnerable to law" (Black, 1976: 55). Case 14 involved William Foster, who was described as, among other things, a "tramp." In Case 17, Thomas White was described as a "dissipated character" and "a hard drinker." Case 21 resulted in the execution of an Italian, Antonio Fornaro, who had lived with the female victim (and who barely spoke English). In Case 27, the defendant, a Greek, not only murdered a black but also assaulted and critically wounded a white police officer.[9] It may be that anti-Italian or anti-Greek prejudices contributed to the condemnation of the latter two defendants.

Of the four remaining cases (Nos. 6, 9, 22 and 29), the available evidence, although brief and sketchy, indicates that the heinousness of the crime itself may have been sufficiently powerful to cancel the effects of the victim's race. One of these cases (No. 22) involved a man convicted of killing two women (a mother and her daughter during a robbery), while a second (No. 9) involved a transient foreigner (British) who killed a mulatto. While further research may uncover evidence that the defendants in these cases were despised for other reasons, absent such information we conclude that in these four cases, the community reaction may reflect an unqualified disgust and contempt for the offender unmitigated by the fact of his or the victim's race.

Conclusions

The answers to both questions raised in this article lend strong support to the general theoretical model that uses status attributes of defendants and victims to explain case processing by the criminal justice system. Our first question concerned the prevalence of these anomalous cases. We are now able to say definitively that executions of whites for crimes against blacks have indeed occurred, that such executions have occurred mainly in the South, and that they have occurred more frequently than "common sense" might predict. However, the scandalous paucity of these cases, representing less than two-tenths of one percent of known executions, lends further support to the evidence that the death penalty in this country has been discriminatorily applied.

A second conclusion is derived from inspecting the known facts in the 30 cases. Do even these few cases represent true exceptions to the general rule that executions almost always involve lower status defendants who stand convicted for crimes against victims of higher status? The answer is no: they are not exceptions to the rule. The analysis shows that, even in these rare cases, it was not primarily outrage over the violated rights of the black victim or the inherent value of the victim's life that led to the condemnation. Ten of the cases involved murders of slaves, which were treated as economic crimes and offenses against the slaves' owners, or as threats to the legitimacy of the institution of slavery. In seven others, the defendant was already in deep trouble with the authorities for prior criminality before the murder which led to his condemnation. In five cases, the occupational status of the victim surpassed that of the defendant, and in four others the defendant's standing in the community was already quite marginal before the homicide. Thus, nearly all the cases were treated as economic crimes or involve defendants who were hated, had low status, or posed a threat or challenge to the white power structure. In only four cases does it appear that the heinousness of the crime itself operated as a primary factor in explaining the condemnation of its perpetrator, and even here it is possible that status factors not known today were instrumental in determining the outcome.

As Merton (1968) pointed out, analysis of deviant cases can be useful in extending existing theory. Executions of whites for crimes against blacks are deviant cases only if the defendant's and victim's race are the sole measures of status that are used to explain case processing. As Black (1976) has suggested and Farrell and Swigert (1978, 1986) have shown, this analysis supports the contention that race alone is not sufficient to explain the nuances of case outcome, and that more encompassing status measures are needed.

The data show that the criminal justice system deems the executioner's services warranted not simply for those who *do something*, but who also *are someone*. The homicide alone provides an insufficient explanation for the outcome; we also must consider the status attributes of the defendant and victim. In cases where the racial attributes alone would lead us to predict no execution, other status attributes may come into play to cancel out their expected effect. The capital crime may present a convenient excuse to rid the community of the deviant, but does not by itself explain why the community wanted to get rid of him. The crime is more a pretext than a cause for the hanging.

Both questions raised in this article have policy and practical lessons. The answer to our second question is that nonracial status differences between victims and defendants are apparent. The answer to our first question is that in death sentencing, race alone has crucial explanatory value; it is the most important, but not the only, status attribute. The relative absence of executions for white-on-black crimes adds further documentation to the sad legacy of racism that has plagued the death penalty throughout its history. Yet, just two years ago the U.S. Supreme Court rejected a challenge to Georgia death sentencing patterns which was based on strong statistical evidence of race-of-victim discrimination (Baldus, Woodworth and Pulaski, 1985; Baldus, Pulaski and Woodworth, 1986). In the majority justices' view, the statistical correlations failed to prove a specific intent to discriminate (*McCleskey v. Kemp*, 107 S. Ct. 1756 [1987]). But as Justice Brennan (joined by Justices Marshall, Blackmun and Stevens) wrote in dissent in the *McCleskey* case, "Warren McCleskey's evidence confronts us with the subtle and persistent influence of the past.... Nonetheless, we ignore him at our peril, for we remain imprisoned by the past as long as we deny its influence in the present" (107 S. Ct. 1794).

Appendix

Vignettes of Cases

1. November 23, 1739. Virginia. John Cobidge. An indentured servant, Cobidge was convicted of killing a black woman (a slave), with an axe, without any provocation. Source: *Virginia Gazette* (Williamsburg), 16-23 November 1739, p. 3: 1.

2-3. November 23, 1739. Virginia. Charles Quin and David White. Quin, an overseer, and White, an accessory, from Essex County, were hanged for the murder of a black slave belonging to Col. Vraxton "by whipping him to death in a most cruel and barbarous manner." Source: *William and Mary College Quarterly*, 8 (July 1899), pp. 35-36 (reprinting article from *Virginia Gazette*, 21 April 1775).

4. July, 1752. Louisiana. Pierre Antoine Dochenet. Convicted of attempted murder by repeatedly stabbing two female slaves with a bayonet. Source: *Cruzat*, 1938, pp. 567-573.

5. May 12,1775. Virginia. William Pitman. Convicted of beating his "negro boy" to death. "This man has justly incurred the penalties of the law, and we hear will certainly suffer, which ought to be a warning to others to treat their slaves with moderation." Source: *William*

and Mary College Quarterly, 8 (July 1899), p. 36 (reprinting article from *Virginia Gazette,* 21 April 1775).

6. June 6, 1816. Connecticut. Miner Babcock. Convicted of stabbing a free black man who lived with his (Babcock's) mother. According to Babcock, he stabbed the man after Babcock tried to break up a fight between him and his mother. Source: 1 *Conn.* 401 (1815); McDade, 1961: 18; Green, 1816.

7. November 10, 1820. North Carolina. Mason Scott. Convicted of the murder of a slave (male), "against the peace and dignity of the State." The defense was insanity. The victim was constantly referred to in the appeal as property, and one basis of appeal concerned a question of the identity of the victim's owner. Only three years previously, the N.C. Legislature had made the killing of a slave a capital offense and removed it from the protection of the benefit of clergy. Source: 8 *N.C.* 12 (1820).

8. April 25, 1822. Massachusetts. Samuel Green. Convicted of murdering a fellow prisoner who had revealed to the authorities Green's plans to escape. Green had a long prior record, including theft, robbery, assaults and counterfeiting; he had also attempted to kill his schoolmaster. After the murder, he would have killed another prisoner had he not been restrained by the authorities. Green also murdered a white man in Canada, although he was never prosecuted for it. As St. Clair wrote, "(F)rom his earliest childhood he showed...innate depravity.... Mischief was his whole study." His death sentence was "a fate he had a thousand times merited." Source: 17 *Mass.* 514; McDade, 1961: 116-117; St. Clair, 1834: 62-75.

9. May 28, 1829. New York. George Chapman. An Englishman and temporary resident of Geneva, N.Y., Chapman was convicted of killing a mulatto by splitting his head with four cuts of a spade while the victim was lying down. An estimated 10 to 15,000 spectators witnessed the execution. Source: *N.Y. Post,* 6 June 1829 2: 4; Correspondence from Seneca Falls (N.Y.) Historical Society to Michael L. Radelet (March 8, 1988).

10. January 14, 1853. South Carolina. L.A.J. Stubbs. Convicted of the murder of a slave (probably male). "(C)onvicted of the neglect of his duty as a master as of any other ingredient. In this point of view, the case speaks volumes in behalf of our laws enacted for the protection of our slave population and puts to blush thousands of the lies invented and propagated by Northern fanatics to disparage the institution of slavery." Source: *Southern Advocate* (Huntsville, Ala.), 2 February 1853.

11-12. March 3, 1854. South Carolina. William Blackledge and Thomas Motley. Convicted of murdering a slave. One of their slaves had absconded, and in their search for him, the defendants instead captured another runaway slave. The slave was tortured to death and his body was fed to the tracking dogs. Source: 7 *Richardson's Law Reports* (S.C.) 327 (1854); *N.Y. Times,* 19 November 1853 2: 6 and 22 March 1854 3: 2.

13. June 2, 1854. Texas. James Wilson (a.k.a. Rhode Wilson). Wilson had been on bad terms with a powerful white farmer, and had threatened to kill him on several occasions. One day Wilson arrived at the farm with the intention of carrying out the threats. The farmer was not home, so Wilson instead murdered the farmer's favorite slave (male). Source: Correspondence from Max K. Sniffin (Woodville, Tex.) to Michael L. Radelet (Nov. 25, 1987); Moseley, 1985: 107-109.

14. June 19, 1876. Missouri. William Foster. A tramp, Foster was convicted of killing a black traveling companion by shooting him in the back of the head. The man was murdered

so Foster could steal his watch. Said the St. Louis newspaper: Foster "was as common a specimen of the ordinary criminal as could be found, utterly incapable of telling or comprehending the truth, possessed of a sly cunning.... only capable in the use of a certain smart kind of Billingsgate that characterizes criminals of the lower order...." Source: *St. Louis Globe-Democrat*, 20 June 1876, p. 1: 3; 61 Mo. 549 (1876).

15. December 7, 1877. New York. John C. Collins (a.k.a. Harvey N. Thorpe). Convicted of killing another prisoner. Collins was sentenced to two years imprisonment for burglary in 1873, and to five years for another burglary in 1875. He and the victim frequently quarreled in prison before the murder. Source: *N.Y. Times*, 8 December 1877, p. 2: 3.

16. March 15, 1878. Georgia. Augustus J. Johnson. Convicted of killing a ferryman. At the gallows, before a crowd of 15,000, Johnson confessed to having killed four men. He was suspected of killing even more. He had previously escaped from an asylum after being found not guilty by reason of insanity for a rape. Johnson killed the ferryman in front of several witnesses, with no attempt to conceal it, because he hated blacks and believed the victim was moving the boat too slowly. Source: *Atlanta Constitution*, 16 March 1878, p. 1: 1; 59 Ga. 190 (1877).

17. May 14, 1880. South Carolina. Thomas White. White "had all his life borne the reputation of being a dissipated character and was a hard drinker." He spent the day of the murder continuously drinking. When a young black man (age 18-20) came to the door of the saloon and asked that White's drinking companion come outside to speak with him, White walked out of the bar and shot the man. There was no provocation. Though every member of the trial jury asked that White's life be spared, it was not. Source: *Charleston (S.C.) News and Courier*, 15 May 1880, p. 1: 3.

18. December 17, 1880. North Carolina. Daniel Keath. Convicted of raping and murdering an eleven-year-old girl. Keath was described as a horse thief, swindler, bigamist (with three wives), and rapist who drank heavily and had deserted from the Confederate Army. He had served a prior prison term in Kentucky. In January 1880 he assaulted the girl, and then put a pillow slip over her head and "beat out her brains with a large stone." Between four and five thousand people witnessed the execution, which occurred in Rutherford. Source: 83 *S.C.* 626 (1880); *Raleigh News and Observer*, 19 December 1880, p. 2: 5.

19. June 19, 1885. Tennessee. William Morrow. From a wealthy family, Morrow was convicted of killing a black youth in 1883 who had been employed by Morrow's brother. Morrow bound the victim and made him march to a cave, where he shot him and hid the body. Some 3,000 citizens signed petitions asking that the sentence be commuted to life. Morrow had murdered another black man in 1877 for which he and two companions were sentenced to life in 1884. Source: 82 *Tenn.* 475 (1884); *Nashville Banner*, 19 June 1885, p. 1: 2.

20. March 19, 1890. Mississippi. Mel J. Cheatham. Convicted of shooting a man (mulatto) in revenge for testimony the victim had given against him for gambling violations, and to stop him from future testimony. The victim, fearing for his life, had at first refused to testify, and for doing so was jailed. After the murder, the victim's body was weighted down and thrown into a river. There were two blacks on the jury. Source: 67 *Miss.* 335 (1890); Pittman, 1981.

21. June 21, 1910. New York. Antonio Fornaro (Italian). Electrocuted for murdering his mistress. The defendant, who could barely speak English, lived with the victim, and they

frequently quarreled about her activities with other men. Source: 91 *N.E.* 542 (1910); *N.Y. Times*, 22 June 1910, p. 9: 4.

22. November 27,1911. Georgia. A.J. O'Berry (a.k.a. James William Gatlin). Convicted of killing a woman and her thirteen-year-old daughter. The murder occurred in the course of a robbery. Source: *Atlanta Constitution*, 27 October 1911 5: 3; 27 November 1911 2: 6; 28 November 1911 3: 4.

23-24. July 26, 1912. Tennessee. John Bailey and George Shelton. Convicted of killing an affluent farmer and his two children. The men were employed as cotton-pickers by the victim; the motive was robbery. Shelton claimed that he had been told that it was not illegal to kill blacks. Source: *Nashville Tennessean*, 26 and 27 July 1912.

25-26. March 21, 1913. Alabama. Arthur Jones and William Watson. Convicted of killing a chicken farmer who earlier had accused Watson of stealing. Said the state Supreme Court in affirming Watson's conviction, "The evidence for the state tended strongly to show a deeply laid plot between defendant and his codefendants to take the life of deceased and the execution of the plot in cold blood and without any pretense of extenuation or justification." Jones's brother, Walter, was sentenced to life for his role in the crime. All three culprits confessed to other crimes, and indeed Walter was convicted for murdering a white and hanged just two weeks after his brother and Watson. Source: *Montgomery Advertiser*, 22 March and 5 April 1913; 181 *Ala.* 9 (1913); 181 *Ala.* 53 (1913).

27. December 7, 1923. Ohio. John Karayians (Greek). Convicted of murdering a black man; at the same time he critically wounded a white police officer by shooting him in his spinal column. While the jury was deliberating his fate, Karayians stabbed another prisoner three times who had testified against him. The deceased victim, a farmer, had sworn out a warrant against Karayians for stealing corn; it was while the officer was trying to arrest Karayians that the assault and murder occurred. Source: 1 *Ohio Law Abstracts,* 456 (1923); 108 *Ohio St.* 505 (1923); *Columbus Citizen*, 7 December 1923, p. 7: 1.

28. March 20, 1936. Kentucky. Erline Whitehead. Convicted of killing a man at the victim's home during an attempted holdup. Whitehead had served three prior terms in the penitentiary, and shortly before the crime had been paroled from a life sentence. Source: *Glascow (Ky.) Times*, 23 March 1936, p. 2: 1.

29. February 18, 1938. North Carolina. Milford Exum. Exum was convicted of killing an elderly basketmaker (male), anchoring his body and throwing it into a river. The murder occurred during a $4 robbery of the victim's home. A codefendant, Earl Sasser, was sentenced to life. Both men were drunk at the time of the crime. Source: 213 *N.C.* 16 (1938).

30. April 15, 1944. Kansas. Fred L. Brady. Convicted of killing a man during the course of an attempted robbery. Brady had served time for previous convictions in Arkansas, Missouri, Nebraska and Kansas, and his record of arrests began thirty years before the homicide. A previous life sentence had been commuted to twenty years. The victim was known to have frequently carried large sums of money; $1,700 was found on his body. Brady waited for several hours at the victim's home for the victim's appearance so he could commit the robbery. Source: 156 *Kan.* 831 (1943); *Topeka Daily Capital,* 15 April 1944 1: 8.

ACKNOWLEDGEMENTS

I would like to thank Ronald L. Akers, Hugo Adam Bedau, William J. Bowers and an anonymous reviewer for their helpful comments on earlier drafts, and Watt Espy for allowing access to his data archive.

ENDNOTES

1. There are, on the other hand, some documented exceptions to the general rule that whites received lenient treatment for crimes against blacks (see, e.g. Nash, 1970). An excellent example occurred in the family of former president Thomas Jefferson in Kentucky. In 1811, two of his nephews (sons of his wife's brother), Lilburne and Isham Lewis, gathered several slaves in a room and made them watch as the brothers stabbed and nearly decapitated a seventeen-year-old slave of Lilburne's. The victim, named George, had broken a water pitcher. After the murder, the slaves were ordered to cut up and burn the body (although the victim's partially incinerated head was later found as it was being eaten by a dog). Even the white citizens were appalled. Both men were indicted for the crime, and it appears likely that they would have been convicted and possibly executed. Before trial, however, Lilburne took his own life and Isham escaped from custody and fled the country (Merrill, 1976).

2. Records of the NAACP Legal Defense Fund indicate that 51 of the over 3,500 people who they know were sentenced to death between December 1972 and January 1989 (roughly 1.5 percent) were whites condemned for killing blacks. Perhaps the most famous (or infamous) is Henry Hays, sentenced to death in Alabama for lynching a young black man, Michael McDonald, in 1981. Mr. McDonald's mother later won a $7 million judgment against the United Klans of America for their role in encouraging the murder (Kornbluth, 1987).

3. More broadly, to allow for cases in which the statuses of the defendant and victim are more or less similar or they are unclear or unknown, this proposition can be reworded as predicting the most severe reactions in cases where the status of the defendant is not clearly higher than that of the victim(s).

4. The story of how Mr. Espy trained himself in research methodology and, usually at his own expense and without institutional support, spent the last 17 years chronicling information about executions, is remarkable (*New York Times*, 21 October 1987 8: 1).

5. A computer tape, listing selected variables from about 14,500 of these executions (although not race of victim), is available from the Inter-University Consortium for Political and Social Research at the University of Michigan.

6. Two additional cases were found in which relevant executions were scheduled, but no record could be found that confirmed they actually took place. In Adams County, Mississippi, Isaac Jones was condemned for murdering a slave; his conviction was affirmed and execution scheduled for July 27, 1821 (2 Miss. (Walker) 83 (1820)). In 1988 a reference librarian at the Adams County Library in Natchez checked all county historical books and contemporary newspapers, but could not confirm the execution occurred. Similarly, in Iredell County, North Carolina, John Hoover was condemned for

murdering a slave, and his conviction was affirmed on appeal (200 *N.C.* 500 (1839)). *The Raleigh Register* (27 March 1840) reported the execution was scheduled for May 15, 1840. However, after an extensive search in 1989, the reference librarians at the Iredell County Library (Statesville) were unable to confirm that the execution took place.

In at least one case, the authorities refused to execute a white man sentenced to death for killing a black. In 1850 in Pennsylvania, Alexander Hutchison (white) was condemned for murdering Nathaniel Edminston (black). Two governors refused to sign a death warrant. Finally, Hutchison simply walked away from the prison and was never heard from again (Teeters, 1963: 231).

7. The existence of 30 relevant cases is far more than even the most careful scholars have expected. In *An American Dilemma*, Gunnar Myrdal (1944: 1345, note 23) claimed that a 1936 North Carolina execution was the first example of a white being executed for a crime against a black. We can now see that other cases escaped his attention. The execution to which he referred actually occurred in 1938, and it was preceded by 21 other southern executions of whites for crimes against blacks.

8. The fact that the rate of black-on-white murder exceeds the rate of white-on-black murder can be explained by the population distribution in the U.S. (that is, a randomly picked murder victim would probably be white) and by the overrepresentation of blacks among offenders (O'Brien, 1987).

9. In a recent case, James Dupree Henry (black) was executed in Florida for murdering a black, an odd case because so few defendants are condemned today for crimes against blacks. But, like Karayians, Henry also assaulted a white police officer. Newspaper accounts of the crime devoted much more attention to the assault than to the murder (Radelet and Mello, 1986).

References

Baldus, D.C., C. Pulaski and G. Woodworth. 1986. "Arbitrariness and Discrimination in the Administration of the Death Penalty: A Challenge to State Supreme Courts." *Stetson Law Review.* 15: 133-261.

Baldus, D.C., G. Woodworth and C. Pulaski. 1985. "Monitoring and Evaluating Contemporary Death Sentencing Systems: Lessons From Georgia." *University of California-Davis Law Review*. 33: 1-74.

Black, D. 1976. *The Behavior of Law.* New York: Academic Press.

Botkin, B.A. 1944. *A Treasury of American Folklore.* New York: Crown Publishers.

Bowers, W.J., with G.L. Pierce and J.F. McDevitt. 1984. *Legal Homicide: Death as Punishment in America, 1864-1982.* Boston: Northeastern University Press.

Cruzat, H.H. 1938. "Records of the Superior Council of Louisiana." *The Louisiana Historical Quarterly*. 21: 567-573.

Dike, S.T. 1982. *Capital Punishment in the United States.* Hackensack: National Council on Crime and Delinquency.

Espy, W. 1980. "Capital Punishment and Deterrence: What the Statistics Cannot Show." *Crime and Delinquency*. 26: 537-544.

Farrell, R.A. and V.L. Swigert. 1978. "Legal Disposition of Inter-Group and Intra-Group Homicides." *The Sociological Quarterly*. 19: 565-576.

.... 1986. "Adjudication in Homicide: An Interpretive Analysis of the Effects of Defendant and Victim Social Characteristics." *Journal of Research in Crime and Delinquency*. 23: 349-369.

Garfinkle, H. 1949. "Research Note on Inter- and Intra-Racial Homicides." *Social Forces*. 27: 369-381.

Green, S. 1816. *The Life and Confession of Miner Babcock*. Printed privately by author and available from the American Antiquarian Society, Worcester, Massachusetts.

Gross, S.R. and R. Mauro. 1984. "Patterns of Death: An Analysis of Racial Disparities in Capital Sentencing and Homicide Victimization." *Stanford Law Review*. 37: 27-153.

Higginbotham, A.L., Jr. 1978. *In the Matter of Color: Race and the American Legal Process — The Colonial Period*. New York: Oxford University Press.

Judson, C.J., J.J. Pandell, J.B. Owens, J.L. McIntosh and D.L. Matschullat. 1969. "A Study of the California Jury in First-Degree Murder Cases." *Stanford Law Review*. 21: 1297-1437.

Kay, M.L.M. and L.L. Cary. 1976. "'The Planters Suffer Little or Nothing': North Carolina Compensations for Executed Slaves, 1748-1772." *Science and Society*. 40: 288-306.

Kleck, G. 1981. "Racial Discrimination in Criminal Sentencing: A Critical Evaluation of the Evidence with Additional Evidence on the Death Penalty." *American Sociological Review*. 46: 783-805.

Kornbluth, J. 1987. "The Woman Who Beat the Klan." *New York Times Magazine*. 1 November: 26-39.

LaFree, G. 1980. "The Effect of Sexual Stratification by Race on Official Reactions to Rape." *American Sociological Review*. 45: 842-854.

McDade, T.M. 1961. *The Annals of Murder*. Norman: University of Oklahoma Press.

Merrill, B. 1976. *Jefferson's Nephews: A Frontier Tragedy*. Princeton: Princeton University Press.

Merton. Robert K. 1968. *Social Theory and Social Structure*. New York: The Free Press.

Moseley, L. 1985. *Pioneer Days of Tyler County*. Tyler County: Tyler County Heritage Society.

Myrdal, G. 1944. *An American Dilemma*. New York: Harper and Brothers.

Nash, A.E.K. 1970. "A More Equitable Past? Southern Supreme Courts and the Protection of the Antebellum Negro." *North Carolina Law Review*. 48: 197-242.

O'Brien, R.M. 1987. "The Interracial Nature of Violent Crimes: A Reexamination." *American Journal of Sociology*. 92: 817-835.

Patterson, W.L. 1970. *We Charge Genocide*. New York: International Publishers.

Pittman, W.E., Jr. 1981. "The Mel Cheatham Affair: Interracial Murder in Mississippi in 1889." *Journal of Mississippi History*. 43: 127-133.

Radelet, M.L. 1981. "Racial Characteristics and the Imposition of the Death Penalty." *American Sociological Review*. 46: 918-927.

Radelet, M.L. and M. Mello. 1986. "Executing Those Who Kill Blacks: An 'Unusual Case' Study." *Mercer University Law Review*. 37: 911-925.

Radelet, M.L. and G.L. Pierce. 1985. "Race and Prosecutorial Discretion in Homicide Cases." *Law and Society Review*. 19: 587-621.

Radelet, M.L. and M. Vandiver. 1986. "Race and Capital Punishment: An Overview of the Issues." *Crime and Social Justice*. 25: 94-113.

St. Clair, H. 1834. *The United States Criminal Calendar.* Boston: Charles Gaylord.

Teeters, N.K. 1963. *Scaffold and Chair: A Compilation of Their Use in Pennsylvania, 1682-1962.* Philadelphia: Pennsylvania Prison Society.

Wolfgang, M. and M. Riedel. 1973. "Race, Judicial Discretion, and the Death Penalty." *Annals of the American Academy of Political and Social Science*. 407: 119-133.

Cases Cited

Cheatham v. *State*, 67 Miss. 335 (1890).

Commonwealth v. *Green*, 17 Mass. 514 (1822).

Furman v. *Georgia*, 408 U.S. 238 (1972).

Johnson v. *State*, 59 Ga. 190 (1877).

A. Jones v. *State*, 181 Ala. 9 (1913).

Karayians v. *State*, 1 Ohio Law Abstract 456 (1923).

McCleskey v. *Kemp*, 107 S. Ct. 1756 (1987).

Morrow et al. v. *State*, 82 Term. 475 (1884).

People v. *Fornaro*, 91 N.E. 542 (1910).

State v. *Babcock*, 1 Conn. 401 (1815).

State v. *Brady*, 156 Kan. 831 (1943).

State v. *Exum*, 213 N.C. 16 (1938).

State v. *Foster*, 61 Mo. 549 (1876).

State v. *Hoover*, 20 N.C. 500 (1839).

State v. *Jones*, 2 Miss. (Walker) 83 (1820).

State v. *Keath*, 83 S.C. 626 (1880).

State v. *Karayians*, 108 Ohio St. 505 (1923).

State v. *Motley and Blackledge*, 7 Rich. 327 (S.C., 1854).

State v. *Scott*, 8 N.C. 12 (1820).

Watson v. *State*, 181 Ala. 53 (1913).

Chapter 5

Where Did Black Jurors Go? A Theoretical Synthesis of Racial Disenfranchisement in the Jury System and Jury Selection

Hiroshi Fukurai
Edgar W. Butler
Richard Krooth
University of California

The jury system evolved as an essential ingredient of America's judicial framework. In recent years, however, frailties of the jury system in respect to its lack of fairness for women, blacks, Latinos and the poor have increasingly become the center of controversy. Federal law is clear that these groups have the right to participate in court as jurors, according to two key concepts: there must be a random selection of jurors, and it must be representative within specified geographic districts wherein a particular court convenes (U.S. 90th Congress House Report, 1968: Section 1961). The logic is that qualified residents of a given geographic domain should be part of the pool from which a jury is selected — on the basis of a chance-opportunity for each to serve on a jury panel. Recent U.S. Supreme Court decisions have held that any substantial violation of these basic requirements of representativeness in jury selection is a *prima facie* case of discrimination (Alker and Barnard, 1978; Fukurai and Butler, 1987; Fukurai, Butler and Krooth, 1991b; Horowitz, 1980).[1]

Challenges concerned with the underrepresentation of minorities have been brought claiming violation of the Sixth Amendment, which requires a representative jury selection from a fair cross-section of the community (Burns, 1987; Jalee, 1968).[2] Yet, the lack of a fair cross-section has been shown in a variety of cases. Careful research indicates that discrimination in jury selection procedures occurs by gender, age, race and socioeconomic status (Carp, 1982: 257-277; Chevigny, 1975: 157-172; Diamond, 1980: 85-117; Fukurai, Butler and Huebner-Dimitrius, 1987; Fukurai, Butler and Krooth, 1991a).[3]

In terms of the race of empanelled juries, however, the literature deals almost exclusively with the *surface* phenomenon of the lack of adequate black representation.

---

* Originally published in *Journal of Black Studies*, Vol. 22, No. 2: 196-215 (December 1991).
Reprinted by permission of Sage Publications, Inc.

Clearly more elaborate research on judicial disenfranchisement is needed to examine the social mechanisms that produce and maintain the subservient condition of black people, women and other U.S. citizens with Third World backgrounds. This is particularly important because there has been a paucity of research examining the impact of the social and structural mechanisms that historically have perpetuated the subordination of blacks in the jury system and jury selection.

The next section provides the theoretical synthesis to the problematic of judicial inequities in the jury system and jury selection by examining four specific determinants of disproportionate racial representation on juries: (a) racial discrimination in jury selection procedures; (b) socioeconomic barriers preventing full community participation by blacks and other racial minorities; (c) judicial discrimination that allows racially demarcated jury representation; and (d) institutional racism and bureaucratic discrimination in perpetuating judicial inequality. The reminder of this article, then, demonstrates that there still exists a racially demarcated jury system that systematically discriminates against blacks and their full jury participation.

Racial Discrimination in Jury Selection Procedures

Jury selection procedures have long-established effective mechanisms for racially demarcating jury participation. Here, then, are several of the legal mechanisms used to subjugate blacks. An example in ensuring underrepresentation of racial minorities is the use of registered voters' rolls (ROV) as source lists from which potential jurors are to be selected. ROV lists provide a legal mechanism effectively enforcing the 'rule of exclusion,' because minorities are less likely to register to vote, and thereby, jury pools consist primarily of Anglos (Butler, 1980; Fukurai and Butler, 1987; Fukurai, Butler and Krooth, 1991a).

Administration of qualification questionnaires also helps eliminate racial minorities from serving on juries. Psychological qualification examinations to select jurors in some counties in California have eliminated a large number of potential black jurors (Boags and Boags, 1971: 48-64).[4] Other subjective criteria and language requirements are also used to limit full community participation by eligible black jurors. There also are various different statutory qualifications at the state level to serve on juries. Those are:

1. mentally sound, 38 states
2. no conviction, 35 states
3. physically sound, 33 states
4. age, 30 states
5. ability to read, write and speak English, 27 states
6. prior jury service, 27 states
7. key-man characteristics, 26 states
8. resident or citizen of the state, 24 states
9. resident or qualified elector, 23 states
10. resident or citizen of the country, 22 states
11. U.S. citizen, 17 states
12. jury solicitation, 8 states.

(Benokraitis, 1975)

The important notion here is that some of these mandatory qualifications (1, 3 and 7) are subjective criteria. Past jury research has pointed out that, of the 11 southern states, ten require that a prospective juror be mentally sound, eight require physical soundness and eight states stipulate that prospective jurors have key-man qualifications of 'good character,' 'sound judgement' and 'intelligence' (Benokraitis, 1975: 38). California law similarly reiterates the subjective discretion by stating "the qualified jury list" shall include persons suitable and competent to serve on juries. In making such selection there shall be taken only the names of persons "who are in the possession of their natural faculties, who are of fair character and approved integrity and who are of sound judgment" (CA. 1981, Section 17.205 (a)). Those subjective criteria are used to impose a limit on black participation on juries. Because of a variety of selection criteria involving subjective qualifications, it is expected that greater disproportionate racial representation is found where jury commissioners and district clerks have substantial discretion regarding both the sources and methods of selection.

Personnel involved in the jury selection process, thus, play an important role in generating black underrepresentation on juries. For instance, the systematic selections by jury clerks has been found to be an important factor in maintaining disproportionate jury representation. In *Avery* v. *Georgia* (1953), the U.S. Supreme Court found that jury panels in Georgia were drawn from a jury box that contained county tax returns with names of prospective Anglo jurors printed on white tickets and names of potential black jurors printed on yellow tickets. Jury clerks consciously sought white jurors for trials, excluding potential black jurors from serving on juries.

Jury commissioners also played a crucial role in limiting full community participation of black jurors. Review of litigated cases by the Supreme Court has overwhelmingly revealed an implicit view of blacks as inferior, reaffirmed by the limitations imposed to manipulate the jury selection process. In *Akins* v. *Texas* (1954), testimony revealed that all three jury commissioners in Dallas County consciously sought only one black grand juror. Consequently, black participation on grand juries was severely limited. Further, in *Cassell* v. *Texas* (1950), the Court discovered evidence of systematic selection exercised by jury commissioners. The statements of jury commissioners revealed that they chose those they knew for grand jury service, and that they knew no eligible blacks in an county where blacks made up approximately one seventh of potentially eligible jurors. The systematic selection by jury commissioners was further compounded by the manipulation of selected black jurors to set a proportional limit on black jury participation. For instance, in *Smith* v. *Texas* (1940), the Court found that between 1931 and 1938, a list for grand jurors had 512 Anglos and only 18 blacks. Of them, 13 blacks were at the bottom of the list; only one was put among the first 12. Further, only five blacks took places in the grand jury room, and the same individual served in three separate instances. In the same period, 379 Anglos were allowed to serve as grand jurors.

The racial composition of the jury is also affected by lawyers using peremptory challenges in *voir dire* (Blauner, 1972). Because so many different persons are allowed to use individual discretion in deciding who should be excused and who should serve, the possibility of individual prejudice influencing excuses and exemptions is great (Van Dyke, 1977: 391). Some of the uncharted consequences may be corrected by recent U.S.

Supreme Court rulings (see *Batson* v. *Kentucky,* 1986), but eliminating peremptory challenges and replacing them with reasons for all challenges will still not guarantee that the parties challenging minorities will give the real reasons: racism, sexism, xenophobia and ageism.

Minorities have to operate within the framework of a racially oppressive institutional system. As a result, blacks and other racial minorities have learned to mistrust the fairness inherent in most Anglo-dominated institutions of power, such as law enforcement agencies and courts that make decisions via racially disproportionate juries (see *Batson* v. *Kentucky,* 1986; Van Dyke, 1977: 32). One dominant ideological underpinning suggests that criminality is inherent in minority groups, and they need to be controlled by the legal system (Cullen and Lind, 1980; Hepburn, 1978; Kramer, 1982). In modern phraseology, the "black community takes a permissive view of crime within its border. As a result, the black community is vulnerable to its own criminal element as well as to the criminal element of the white community" (*Yale Law Journal,* 1970: 534).

Crimes, criminals and the trials of those accused are also obviously linked. Those accused of crimes may defend themselves, but courts, judges and juries seem locked into legal structures handed down from a past of discrimination and racism. This past has in fact contoured the underrepresentation of minorities on jury panels in our time. And such racial prejudgment generates different outcomes in various trials. In at least one Black Panther murder trial, the contention was made that the race of the defendant itself predisposed certain jurors to a negative verdict (Rokeach and McLellan, 1970). Studies covering the psychology of juries provide numerous examples of racial prejudice impacting verdicts (*American Criminal Law Review,* 1980; Hans and Vidmar, 1986; Lipton, 1979; Starr and McCormick, 1985; Wishman, 1986).

A wall of hatred and noncommunication is put up between black and Anglo populations, despite — and because of — such ideological justifications and structured practices as underrepresentation of minority jurors (Kairys, Kadane and Lehoczky, 1977). Through their nonparticipation, however, racial minorities are forced to participate in strengthening the legitimation of Anglo-dominated judicial systems. And without such participation, racial supremacy is structurally reinforced by the dominant population, perpetuated by individual racism and the withdrawal of support by minorities. In fact, the large proportion of blacks who do not respond to jury qualification questionnaires or summonses have been classified as 'recalcitrants' and eliminated from subsequent jury selection procedures (Fukurai, 1985; Fukurai *et al.*, 1991b; Van Dyke, 1977).

Socioeconomic Barriers and Handicaps

The economic life of a disenfranchised people makes that of the colonizing people possible. If the disenfranchised must be moved physically to make the colonizers' labor system efficient, the stability of residence and life of the colonized can be disregarded. In the oppressive legal system set up in the United States, indentured servants and slaves were replaced by new sources of cheap labor, with unsteady migratory labor uprooting large segments of the black and other minority populations.

Obviously such labor market positions are closely related to residential mobility and affect jury representation by racial minorities. Since jury summonses and qualification questionnaires are generally sent by mail, one's labor market position as a migrant enhances the probability of being excluded from a jury pool, as those who move and fail to receive jury summonses (called undeliverables) or to return jury qualification questionnaires ('recalcitrants') cannot qualify for selection. In fact, such persons are systematically eliminated. Thereby a potential juror who has just entered the job market and/or is placed in a secondary labor market tends to be eliminated long before being called into the courthouse for jury service. Even those who make it into the courthouse are likely to be granted an excuse for reasons of economic hardship.

Two principal factors explain the high residential mobility among unskilled minority laborers. First, their position in the labor market involves low wages, seasonal work, and thus a high degree of occupational instability (Featherman and Hauser, 1978; Lipset and Bendix, 1959). Unstable job markets and economic shifts in production location and volume are conducive to a high level of geographic mobility in search of steady employment (Edward, Reich and Gordon, 1975; Gordon, 1972).

An internal labor market that calls up temporary or seasonal workers also makes sedentary life impossible for colonized labor. The migratory search for jobs is the lifebread of the nation's poorest, hence its blacks, other minorities with a Third World background and women. The high geographic mobility of racial minorities creates the largest segment of those who do not receive jury qualification questionnaires and who are thereby classified as undeliverables (Fukurai, 1985). Forcing jury commissioners to track down those undeliverables is rare, even though such follow-up is required by law (CA. 1981, Sec 13.204.3 (b)).

Those who must move often to find work are more likely to be renters than owners of a residence (see Butler and Kaiser, 1971; Butler *et al.*, 1969; Sabagh, Van Arsdol and Butler, 1969). Low residential ownership plays an important role in generating high incidences of residential mobility among blacks and other members of racial minorities.

The results are that youths, laborers with low income and education, and particularly blacks are mobile workers subject to systematic jury exclusion and thus are underrepresented on jury pools (Fukurai *et al.*, 1991a; Zeigler, 1978). For example, for a three-year interval, using national data, a study found that 48.0 percent of blacks moved, while 25.2 percent of Anglos moved (McAllister, Kaiser and Butler, 1971). During a one-year time period in Los Angeles County, 49.8 percent of the age group between 15 and 29 moved, while only 12.8 percent of those 60 and over moved. The mobile groups were predominantly members of racial minorities (Feagin, 1984; Fukurai *et al.*, 1991b; Van Arsdol, Maurice, Sabagh and Butler, 1968).

This is in contrast to prospective jurors who work in large companies and are more likely to be reimbursed for jury service. They usually have a greater chance of surviving the jury selection process, and, in the world of job-structured benefits, they are predominantly Anglos (Fukurai *et al.*, 1991b).

Judicial Discrimination against Black and Minority Jurors

In a racially demarcated society, oppressive institutions use restrained power and regimented administrations to benefit one group at the expense of others. The racially demarcated society can be based on overt violence, such as slavery, or on covert structures that brandish the symbols of freedom but establish conditions for subjugation. The institutions of the greatest legitimation of authority and discrimination are the systems of laws and courts.

Echoes of such institutionalized inequality in the United States today appear as four judicial dimensions that set limits on racial participation on juries. First, there is the 'blue ribbon jury,' which systematically and disproportionately excludes minorities. Second, juries of unusually small size undercut minority participation. Third, jurors may be empowered to enforce less than unanimous decisions, so that minority opinions can be disregarded, and fourth, in selecting jurors, the process of constructing gerrymandered judicial districts may systematically exclude minority-dominant neighborhoods but include majority-dominant areas.[5]

Under a blue ribbon system, special jurors are selected from the general panel based on perceived special qualifications to hear important and intricate cases. Narrowly qualified jurors present an insurmountable fairness problem. Jury studies indicate that homogeneous panels selected with certain criteria may be less adept at reaching reasonable verdicts than are the heterogeneous ones. The latter bring to the decision-making process a rich mix of points of view and life experiences, and they are more likely than the homogeneous jury to recognize and offset one another's biases (Van Dyke, 1977).

Although the blue ribbon jury has not met the "fair cross-section of community" criterion demanded by the Sixth Amendment (*Fay* v. *New York*, 1947), the Supreme Court has nevertheless given constitutional sanction to the practice. Blue ribbon juries are thereby still empowered to parade their constitutionality and give judicial justification to the systematic exclusion of racial minorities from juries (Mills, 1969: 338-339; *Yale Law Journal*, 1970).

Nor does the Constitution require a jury of 12; a state may use a jury of six in criminal trials, even when the sentence is as severe as life imprisonment, the U.S. Supreme Court declared in *Williams* v. *Florida* (1972). Numerous studies show that without an adequate theory of group dynamics, the Supreme Court was in error in assuming that there are no differences in the behavior of 12- and six-member juries (Kaye, 1980; Roper, 1980). The fact is that smaller juries have a greater propensity to be controlled by a dominant group or person. A change of verdict may sometimes be attributed to an authoritarian personality who can control and influence small groups more easily than large groups (Goffman, 1959; Hastie *et al.*, 1980). Distinct or authoritarian personality traits are often characterized by the dominant ideology that shapes perceptions and affects everyday interactions (Hans and Vidmar, 1986). Because the prevailing ideology is likely to reflect the dominant group in society, the minority's alternate view — once formulated — may be sidestepped by controlling participation in judicial decision-making processes or disregarding their opinions.

A clear pattern of racial discrimination is found in death penalty cases. Blacks are more likely to receive the death sentence than whites, particularly if the victim was white. In Florida, for example, if a black person killed a white person, the chances of receiving a death sentence were about one in five; if a white killed a white, the chances were about one in 20; if a black killed a black, the chances were about one in 167; and if a white killed a black, the probability of a death sentence was zero (Bowers and Pierce,

1980). When a large number of extraneous factors was controlled (e.g. crime severity, past criminal records and the number of charges), the basic pattern of racial discrimination remained. One explanation is simple racism; a white life is more valued than a black life. Another explanation is that whites are much more supportive of the death penalty than blacks, and the white community therefore may pressure the prosecutor to ask for the death penalty when a white victim is killed (Baldus, Pulaske and Woodsworth, 1983). Given the prevalence of white overrepresentation on juries and the impact on the jury decision-making process, a smaller size jury exhibits a greater propensity to be controlled by the dominant ideology reflected by white jurors.

Less than unanimous decisions also pose problems for racial minorities. In *Apodaca* v. *Oregon* (1972) and *Johnson* v. *Louisiana* (1972), the Court voted by a narrow margin not to apply the unanimity rule to state jury cases, concluding that the rule lacked constitutional authority.[6] Rejecting the previous pronouncements on unanimity requirements as inconclusive, the Supreme Court majority upheld verdicts in which the juries had voted 11-1, 10-2, and 9-3 for conviction. One study shows that the elimination of the unanimity rule favors the prosecution and increases the conviction rate (Kalven and Zeisel, 1966: 466). It is clear that relaxing the unanimity rule allows the opinions of racial minorities to be ignored and undermines the nature of justice and fairness in the judicial system. The new rule becomes especially problematic in cases of possible hung juries. In some capital punishment cases, for instance, the discrepant initial vote on the verdict, which eventually led to a final unanimous decision, was racially demarcated (*Harris* v. *People of California*, 1984).[7] Thus frequent incidents of racially disproportionate votes in deliberation can be used to empower the racial majority ideologically (Fukurai *et al.*, 1991b).

Racially demarcated points of view are found in cases involving interracial sex. A study found that white jurors were more likely to find a defendant culpable of rape when he was black and the victim was white than in other racial combinations. Blacks, on the other hand, were more likely to judge that a white defendant was culpable when the victim was black (Ugwuegbu, 1979). In a rape simulation study, black defendants were treated more harshly than white defendants (Feild, 1979). Further, race was a significant factor when the evidence was more clear-cut in favor of guilt or innocence. Less than unanimous votes, thus, become particularly problematic because relaxing the unanimity rule is likely to disregard votes by racial minorities. Racially demarcated votes in deliberation can be used to delete the power of racial minorities.

Another effective mechanism in maintaining the racially dominant judicial institution is the construction of gerrymandered judicial districts. How this has been done is an adventure in mental and legal gymnastics. To begin, it is known that vicinity requirements are an essential ingredient of the Sixth Amendment. As a prime example, the legislature in California long ago defined a judicial district in Los Angeles County as the area within a 20-mile radius of each courthouse. Early in the 1970s, the Los Angeles County Board of Supervisors adopted this rule because Los Angeles County had wide geographic boundaries. The Senate approved the bill, A.B. 1454, which added the 20-mile rule to the *California Code of Civil Procedure*. Research has demonstrated that in fact the 20-mile rule for judicial districts has not been followed. Rather, systematic inclusion and exclusion of certain neighborhoods has led to a significant underrepresentation of minority populations (Fukurai, *et al.*, 1991b). By regulating the degree of minority participation on jury panels, and thus ultimate judicial decision-making, the dominant population's control over the political and judicial apparatus creates an effective mechanism for gerrymandering geographic definitions of judicial districts. Particular neighborhoods with a high concentration of blacks and other racial minorities have simply been excluded from the defined boundary of judicial districts (Fukurai and Butler, 1987).

Institutional Discrimination: Subordinating Blacks

Numerous Supreme Court decisions have also perpetuated and legitimized the domination and racial supremacy of the majority in both judicial and political spheres. The very apparatus of law regulates racial participation, and Court decisions reify the dominant bureaucratic system, elevating the 'rule of law' while degrading rights of blacks. In *Carter* v. *Jury Commission of Greene County* (1970), for example, the petitioner claimed that the entire state apparatus — which included the county jury commissioners, their clerks, one local circuit judge and even the governor of Alabama — was in conspiracy in perpetuating racial inequality in jury selection. The appellant sought to establish three principles in the case:

> 1. A *declaration* that qualified blacks were systematically excluded from grand and petit juries in Greene County, making the Alabama statutes unconstitutional, and that the jury commissioner operated illegally through his deliberate segregation of a government agency.
> 2. A *permanent injunction* forbidding the systematic exclusion of blacks in juries, thereby requiring all eligible blacks to be placed on the jury roll.
> 3. An *order to vacate the appointment* of jury commissioners and to compel the Alabama governor to select new members without racial discrimination.

Further, *Turner* v. *Fouche* (1970), announced the same day as *Carter*, also argued the notion of institutional discrimination against potential black jurors. The petitioner alleged that the county board of education, which consisted of five freeholders, was selected by the grand jury, which in turn was drawn from a jury list selected by the six-member county jury commission. The commissioners were appointed by the judge of the state superior court for the circuit in the county. The problem here is that all board of education members were white, selected by all-white grand juries, which in turn had been selected by all-white jury commissioners. Because of racial oppression against blacks, the petitioner alleged that "the board of education had deprived the Negro school children of text books, facilities and other advantages" (*Turner* v. *Fouche*, 1970). The notion of a racially discriminatory judicial system is also reported elsewhere. In the Huey Newton trial, for instance, ethnographic research confirmed the notion of white supremacy in the criminal court system. The study notes that

> a black man like Huey Newton is tried under a system of law developed by white Western European jurists. He is confronted in the black ghetto by white police officers, then indicted by an all-white, or predominantly white, grand

jury, prosecuted by a team of all-white district attorneys, tried by a white judge, convicted by a predominantly white jury, and denied bail on appeal by white state appellate courts and a white federal judge. It is not simply the color of the principals that is at issue, but the more profound point that the various officials and processes in the system represent institutions that reflect and are responsive to values and interests of the white majority — a power structure and a community that benefit from keeping black people in "their place," namely, in the ghetto and without power.

(Blauner, 1972: 253)

Elsewhere we have documented the precise way in which this was done (Fukurai and Butler, 1987; Fukurai *et al.*, 1991b). Yet, this is only a single case, and further evidence of institutional racism is required of future investigators. In the view of those who feel they are oppressed, the judicial and legal structures are grounded upon Anglo supremacy and create the opportunity to maintain oppressive social conditions that — while gradually undergoing change awarding minorities some rights — continuously reproduce the subordination of blacks. The theoretical tenet of discrimination against blacks in the jury system and jury selection is summarized in Figure 1.

Figure 1:
Racial Disenfranchisement in the Jury System and Jury Selection

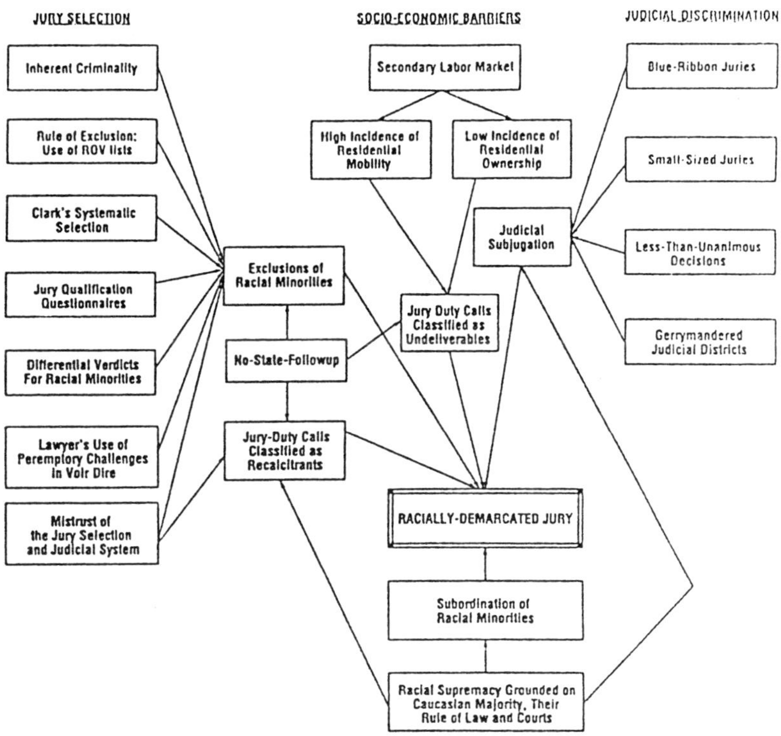

Conclusions

This article argued that the racially demarcated social system in the United States still exists in the form of oppressive legal and judicial structures that continuously reproduce, maintain and perpetuate the subordination of blacks. Historically they are discouraged, if not prevented, from full community participation in labor markets, political structures, courts and the judicial decision-making processes. Up until the last few decades, the jury-participation privilege was largely reserved to the Anglo majority.

Specific mechanisms still exist today and are used to sculpt systematically a racially demarcated jury. Potential sources of institutional biases in jury selection include various forms of structural and individual racism that prevent full community jury participation, thereby perpetuating and maintaining racially demarcated juries. Labor market characteristics also set limits on racial minorities, who are likely to be in secondary markets with a high degree of residential mobility, so that the call to jury service legally becomes "undeliverable" and they become "recalcitrants" who do not respond. As well, judicial discrimination points to various strategies that regulate the degree of minority participation on juries: the use of blue ribbon juries, a smaller-size jury, less than unanimous decisions and gerrymandered judicial districts.

Perhaps more important is the notion that the entire jury system and jury selection are grounded on Anglo-controlled institutions and structural ideas of supremacy. Only time will reveal if the United States can free itself of such powerful forces, which set limits on the rights of black people and curtail their freedom to participate equally in the judicial decision-making process. What can be said, though, is that until it overturns the past, such a society will be the target of those still unfree who view its courts and other institutions as chains to be broken, not to be shackled by.

Endnotes

1. For additional information, see Benokraitis, 1975; Butler *et al.*, 1991; Erlanger, 1970: 345-370; Fukurai *et al.*, 1987; *Iowa Law Review*, 1973: 401-419; *The Yale Law Journal,* 1970: 531-550.

2. Also see Cromer, 1910; Krooth, 1975, 1980; Lewis, 1984.

3. For additional information, see Alker, Hosticka and Mitchell, 1976: 9-41; Brady, 1983: 241-263; De Cani, 1974: 234-238; Finkelstein, 1976: 338-376; Heyns, 1979; Kairys,1972: 771-806; Kairys *et al.*, 1977: 776-827; Mills, 1969: 329-339; Morris, 1965; Roberts, 1939; Robinson, 1950: 73-78; Staples, 1975: 14-22; Summers, 1961: 35-42; U.S. 90th Congress Senate Report No. 891, 1967; U.S. 90th Congress House Report No. 1076, 1968; Whyte, 1956.

4. Research in Oakland found that 81.5 percent of blacks and 14.5 percent of Anglos failed to qualify as jurors; in central Los Angeles, 38 percent of blacks and 8.5 percent of Anglos failed the examination; and in Long Beach failure rates were 40 percent for blacks and 13 percent for Anglos.

5. The cumulative effect of institutional racism is crucial in eliminating racial groups during the jury selection process. For example, research in Maryland found substantial bias against those with less than 12 years of formal education. Because inequality in the quality and accessibility of education leads to fewer blacks finishing high school, and because most jurors are expected to have a high school education, many blacks are disqualified from jury lists.

6. Rulings in both *Johnson* v. *Louisiana* (1972) and *Apodaca* v. *Oregon* (1972) were by 5-4 votes.

7. Postverdict interviews revealed that the first vote on the penalty was 9-3 in favor of death. The three jurors who voted against the death penalty were black. The second vote resulted in a unanimous decision in favor of life without possibility of parole. Postverdict interviews also indicated that one black male juror walked into the deliberation room after hearing all the penalty phase evidence and said: "I'm not going to vote for the death penalty and no one is going to change my mind." Ultimately, the assertiveness of that one black juror, working his chemistry with the others, significantly affected their final verdict, changing the first vote of death to life without possibility of parole (for more detailed descriptions of the case, see Fukurai *et al.*, 1991b).

References

Akins v. *Texas*. 1954. 325 U.S. 398.

Alker, H.R. Jr. and J.J. Barnard. 1978. "Procedural and social biases in the jury selection process." *The Justice System Journal*. 3: 220-241.

Alker, H.R. Jr., C. Hosticka and M. Mitchell. 1976. "Jury selection as a biased social process." *The Law and Society Review*. 9: 9-41.

American Criminal Law Review. 1980. "'Grigsby v. Mabry:' a new look at death qualified juries." 18: 145-163.

Apodaca v. *Oregon*. 1972. 406 U.S. 404.

Avery v. Georgia. 1953. 345 U.S. 559.

Baldus, D., C. Pulaske and G. Woodsworth. 1983. "Judicial review of death sentences." *Journal of Criminal Law and Criminology*. 74: 661-753.

Batson v. *Kentucky*. 1986. 105 S. Ct. 1712.

Benokraitis, N. 1975. *Institutional racism: An empirical study of Blacks and jury selection process in ten Southern states*. Unpublished doctoral dissertation. Austin: University of Texas.

Berle, A. 1959. *Power without property: A new development in American political economy*. New York: Harcourt, Brace.

Blauner, R. 1972. *Racial oppression in America*. New York: Harper and Row.

Boags, C.D. and R.M Boags. 1971. "The misuse of a so-called psychological examination for the selection of jurors" in Thomas, C. (ed.), *Boys no more: A Black psychologist's view of community*. Beverly Hills: Glencoe.

Bowers, W. and G. Pierce. 1980. "Arbitrariness and discrimination under post-Furman capital statues." *Crime and Delinquency*. 26: 563-635.

Brady, J. 1983. "Fair and impartial railroad: The jury, the media, and political trials." *Journal of Criminal Justice*. 11: 241-263.

Burns, J.F. "After echoes of empire, countries are on edge." *New York Times*. 17 October 1987.

Butler, E.W. 1980. *Torrance Superior Court panels and population analysis*. University of California: Riverside.

Butler, E.W., S. Chapin, Jr., G.C. Henmens, E.J. Kaiser, M.A. Stegman and F.S. Weiss. 1969. *Moving behavior and residential choice: A national survey*. Washington: National Academy of Science.

Butler, E.W., H. Fukurai and J. Huebner-Dimitrius. 1991. *Anatomy of the McMartin case*. New Brunswick: Rutgers University Press.

Butler, E.W. and E.J. Kaiser. 1971. "Prediction of residential movement and spatial allocation." *Urban Affairs Quarterly*. 6: 477-494.

Carp, R.A. 1982. "Federal grand juries: How true a 'cross section' of the community." *The Justice System Journal*. 7: 257-277.

Carter v. *Jury Commission of Greene County*. 1970. 396 U.S. 332.

Cassell v. *Texas*. 1950. 339 U.S. 282.

Chevigny, P.G. 1975. "The Attica case: A successful jury challenge in northern city." *Criminal Law Bulletin*. 11: 157-172.

Cromer, E. 1910. *Ancient and modern imperialism*. New York: Longmans, Green.

Cullen, F.T. and B.G. Lind. 1980. "Crime as occupation." *Criminology*. 18: 399-410.

De Cani, J.S. 1974. "Statistical evidence in jury discrimination cases." *The Journal of Criminal Law and Criminology*. 65: 234-238.

Diamond, W.H. 1980. "Federal remedies for racial discrimination in grand jury selection." *Columbia Journal of Law and Social Problems*. 16: 85-117.

Edward, R., M. Reich and D. Gordon. 1975. *Labor market segmentation*. Lexington: D.C. Heath.

Erlanger, H.S. 1970. "Jury research in America." *Law and Society Review*. 5: 345-370.

Fay v. *New York*. 1947. 332 U.S. 261.

Feagin, J.R. 1984. *Racial and ethnic relations*. Englewood Cliffs: Prentice-Hall.

Featherman, D. and R. Hauser. 1978. *Opportunity and change*. New York: Academic Press.

Feild, H. 1979. "Rape trials and jurors' decisions: A psychological analysis of the effects of victim, defendant, and case characteristics." *Law and Human Behavior*. 3: 261-284.

Finkelstein, M.O. 1976. "The application of statistical decision theory to the jury discrimination cases." *Harvard Law Review*. 80: 338-376.

Fukurai, H. 1985. *Institutional racial inequality: A theoretical and empirical examination of the jury selection process*. Unpublished doctoral dissertation. Riverside: University of California.

Fukurai, H. and E.W. Butler. 1987. *Jury Selection: Institutionalized racial inequality*. Unpublished manuscript.

Fukurai, H., E.W. Butler and J. Huebner-Dimitrius. 1987. "Spatial and racism imbalances in voter registration and jury selection." *Sociology and Social Research*. 77: 33-38.

Fukurai, H., E.W. Butler and R. Krooth. 1991a. "A cross sectional jury representation or systematic jury representation? Simple random and cluster sampling strategies in jury selection." *Journal of Criminal Justice.* 19: 31-48.

.... 1991b. *Race and the jury: Racial disenfranchisement and the search for justice.* New York: Plenum.

Goffman, E. 1959. *The presentation of self in everyday life.* New York: Doubleday Anchor.

Hans, V. and N. Vidmar. 1986. *Judging the Jury.* New York: Plenum.

Hastie, R., S.D. Penrod and N. Pennington. 1980. *Inside the jury.* Cambridge: Harvard University Press.

Harris v. *People of California.* 1984. 36 Cal 3d. 16.

Hepburn, J.R. 1978. "Race and the decision to arrest: An analysis of warrants issued." *Journal of Research in Crime and Delinquency.* 15: 54-73.

Heyns, B. 1979. *1979 jury analysis.* No. A-344097. Los Angeles: Superior Court, County of Los Angeles.

Horowitz, I.A. 1980. "Jury selection: A comparison of two methods in several criminal cases." *Journal of Applied Social Psychology.* 10: 86-99.

Iowa Law Review. 1973. "'Jury-mandering:' Federal jury selection and the generation gap." 59: 401-419.

Jalee, P. 1968. *The pillage of the Third World.* New York: Monthly Review Press.

Johns, M.A. 1960. *American immigration.* Chicago: University of Chicago Press.

Johnson v. *Louisiana.* 1972. 406 U.S. 356.

Kairys, D. 1972. "Juror selection: The law, a mathematical method of analysis and a case study." *American Criminal Law Review.* 12: 771-806.

Kairys, D., J.B. Kadane and J.P. Lehoczky. 1977. "Jury representativeness: A mandate for multiple source lists." *California Law Review.* 65: 776-827.

Kalven, H. Jr. and H. Zeisel. 1966. *The American jury.* Boston: Little Brown.

Kaye, D. 1980. "And then there were twelve: Statistical reasoning, the supreme court and the size of the jury." *California Law Review.* 46: 461-474.

Kramer, R.C. 1982. "From 'habitual offenders' to career criminals." *Law and Human Behavior.* 6: 273-293.

Krooth, R. 1975. *Empire: A bicentennial appraisal.* Santa Barbara: Harvest.

.... 1980. *Arms and empire: Imperial patterns before World War II.* Santa Barbara: Harvest.

Lewis, G.C. 1984. "On the government of dependencies" in Lucas, C.P. (ed.). Oxford.

Lipset, J.M. and R. Bendix. 1959. *Social mobility in industrial society.* Berkeley: University of California Press.

Lipton, J.P. 1979. *Sociocultural and personality perspectives on jury behavior and decision making.* Unpublished dissertation. University of California.

McAllister, R.J., E.J. Kaiser and E.W. Butler. 1971. "Residential mobility of blacks and whites: A national longitudinal survey." *American Journal of Sociology.* 77: 445-456.

Mills, E.S. 1969. "A statistical profile of jurors in a United States district court." *Law and the Social Order.* 1: 329-339.

Morris, R. 1965. *Government and labor in early America.* New York: Harper and Row.

Roberts, G. 1939. *The Nazi: Claims to colonies.* London: John Murray.

Robinson, W.S. 1950. "Bias, probability and trial by jury." *American Sociological Review.* 15: 73-78.

Rokeach, M. and D.D. McLellan. 1970. "Dogmatism and the death penalty: A reinterpretation of the Duquesne poll data." *Duquesne Law Review.* 81: 125-129.

Roper, R.T. 1980. *The American profile poster: Who own what, who makes how much, who works where and who lives with whom.* New York: Pantheon.

Sabagh, G., M.P. Arsdol and E.W. Butler. 1969. "Some determinants of intra-metropolitan residential mobility: Conceptual considerations." *Social Forces.* 48: 88-98.

Smith v. *Texas.* 1940. 211, U.S. 128.

Staples, R. 1975. "White racism, black crime and American justice." *Phylon.* 36: 14-22.

Starr, V.H. and M. McCormick. 1985. *Jury selection.* Boston: Little Brown.

Summers, M.R. 1961. "A comparative study of the qualifications of state and federal jurors." *Wisconsin Bar Bulletin.* 34: 35-42.

Turner v. *Fouche.* 1970. 396, U.S. 346.

Ugwuegbu, D. 1979. "Racial and evidential factors in juror attributions of legal responsibility." *Journal of Experimental Social Psychology.* 15: 133-146.

U.S. 90th Congress Senate Report. 1967. No. 891. Washington: U.S. Government Printing House.

U.S. 90th Congress House Report. 1968. No. 1076. Washington: U.S. Government Printing House.

Van Arsdol, J. D. Maurice, G. Sabagh and E.W. Butler. 1968. "Retrospective and subsequent metropolitan residential mobility." *Demography.* 5: 249-267.

Van den Berghe, P.L. 1974. "Bringing beast back in." *American Sociological Review.* 39: 777-788.

Van Dyke, J.M. 1977. *Jury selection procedure.* Cambridge: Ballinger.

Whyte, W. 1956. *Organization man.* Garden City: Doubleday.

Williams v. *Florida.* 1972. 406, U.S. 356.

Wishman, S. 1986. *Anatomy of a jury.* New York: Times.

Yale Law Journal. 1970. "The case for Black juries." 79: 531-550.

Zeigler, D.H. 1978. "Young adults as a cognizable group in jury selection." *Michigan Law Review.* 76: 1045-1110.

CHAPTER 6

BLIND JUSTICE? THE IMPACT OF RACE ON THE JUVENILE JUSTICE PROCESS

JEFFREY FAGAN
ELLEN SLAUGHTER
ELIOT HARTSTONE
CENTER FOR LAW AND SOCIAL POLICY AT THE URSA INSTITUTE

Abstract: The increasing prevalence of minority youth in the juvenile justice system has renewed concerns over racial disparities in juvenile justice processing. Previous research has yielded ambiguous results, with findings complicated by methodological shortcomings, divergent research strategies and design artifacts. To resolve questions on the extent and source of racial disparities in juvenile justice processing, research is needed on the nature, location and magnitude of discrimination in the juvenile justice system. This study examines racial disparities in decision making at six points in the juvenile justice process, from apprehension through judicial commitment decisions. Samples of Anglo and minority youth were drawn at each point, controlling for offense security, other offense characteristics and extralegal factors in addition to race. The results show racial disparities at each point, with minorities consistently receiving harsher dispositions. Disparities took different forms at various stages of the process, usually for nonserious offenses. Race was a direct, indirect, and interactive influence at various decision points. Disparities were observed at other times only when controlling for other extralegal factors such as family status. The results suggest that the juvenile justice system reflects social and economic disparities endemic in other social domains. The correlates of delinquency in minority and predominantly Anglo populations are similar. Accordingly, base rate differences may be less important than societal reaction in explaining the overrepresentation of minorities in the juvenile justice process. The narrowing of social gaps may also reduce disparate perceptions of minorities in the juvenile justice system, and restore their population balance in delinquent populations.

* Originally published in *Crime and Delinquency*, Vol. 33, No. 2: 224-258 (April, 1987).
Reprinted by permission of Sage Publications, Inc.

A major issue facing juvenile justice practitioners across the United States is the involvement of minority youth in the juvenile justice system. As noted by Martin (1983: 2) Black youth make up approximately 12 percent - 17 percent of the country's youth population. However, "Black youth account for more than 50 percent of the nation's property crime arrests...[and represent] more than one-third of all [juvenile] offenses involving violence." Black youth are overrepresented in detention, correctional and shelter facilities as well. The 1985 Child in Custody census shows that 37 percent of all youth in these facilities were black (U.S. Department of Justice, 1985).

A continuing controversy surrounding the overrepresentation of minorities in the juvenile justice system is the base rates of offending by Anglo and minority youth. The empirical evidence is ambiguous and contradictory on whether minority or lower-class youth have differential offending rates, or whether minority youth commit a disproportionate share of crime. Regardless of the base rate question, several studies suggest that one factor contributing to minority overrepresentation in the juvenile justice system may be disparate and discriminatory treatment of minority youth. Although the extent of differential treatment revealed by research findings has varied by location, juvenile justice decision point and study methodology, the data suggest possible differential processing at each level of system decision making (police, prosecutorial, judicial, probation and corrections). Racial bias in the justice system is antithetical to the precepts of "equal protection" (Langan, 1985), and has been socially and legally rejected for over a century in this country. To resolve questions on the sources of minority overrepresentation in the justice system, and to correct disparities in processing, we must first determine the extent, nature and location of discrimination.

Race, Social Class and Delinquency

There is little consensus in the empirical literature on the relationship between race, class and delinquency. Conventional wisdom assumes (and research with official records shows) an inverse relationship between social class and criminality. Using self-reported delinquency, however, Tittle *et al.* (1978), Johnstone (1978), and Krohn and Massey (1980) all reject meaningful social class influences on delinquency. Others (Braithwaite, 1981; Elliott and Ageton, 1980; Elliott and Huizinga, 1983) argue to the contrary. However, few studies have disentangled race from social class to understand the independent contributions to delinquency. Eliott and Ageton (1980) found that class differences were more pronounced for serious and violent offenders, irrespective of race. However, these are minority opinions. Thornberry and Farnworth (1982) differentiated between social class and social status, and found that status and adult crime are indeed related, but not so for serious delinquency. Moreover, they found social status and race to be interactive with respect to criminality, with the relationship between status and crime strongest for adult blacks.

Whether minorities, and specifically blacks, have higher base rates of offending also is unresolved.[1] Serious and violent juvenile crime are primarily urban phenomena, with both prevalence and incidence rates increasing with urbanization (Laub, 1983; Sampson, 1986). Regardless of the measures of crime used, serious delinquency rates increase as the geographical focus approaches the inner city. These are the locales with the highest concentration of minorities, poverty, unemployment, high housing density and weak social institutions (schools, informal social controls). Aggregate studies consistently point toward the association between relative economic and ecological isolation and higher crime rates (Byrne and Sampson, 1986).

Analyses of individual offending rates based on official records show that minority adolescents living in inner-city neighborhoods are at greater risk for both general and serious delinquency than adolescents living in more affluent areas (Wolfgang *et al.*, 1972; Strasburg, 1984; Comer, 1985). However, self-report surveys disagree on race differences. Hindelang *et al.* (1981) found fewer differences in self-reported delinquency between Anglo and black youth in urban areas, whereas Elliott and Huizinga (1983) found that differences disappear when social class is controlled.

These associations raise a host of questions regarding the components of urbanism and their bearing on our general understanding of serious delinquency. The concentration of risk factors (specifically, poverty, unemployment and high concentrations of minority populations) leads to a confounding of urbanism, race, social class and crime. The concentration of serious delinquency in urban areas may be the result of urban form, the socialization processes that inevitably result from structural poverty in urban areas, the aggregate characteristics of individuals who cluster in urban areas, or the dynamic effects of these factors when they converge. Smith (1986) has already identified the effects of neighborhood context on police arrest decisions. The accumulation of a juvenile record, central to the debate on differential rates, appears to be a process that is differentiated by race, possibly accounting in part for the disproportionate minority representation in the juvenile justice system. Whether ethnicity and social class contribute to differential juvenile justice processes is an unresolved question caught in this complex web of questions.

RACE, CLASS AND JUVENILE JUSTICE

Research on race and social class discrimination in the juvenile justice process has yielded mixed results. Thornberry (1973), utilizing the Wolfgang birth cohort in Philadelphia, noted that both the police and the juvenile courts provided black offenders more severe dispositions than Anglo offenders. For example, Thornberry found that "remedial arrests" by police (no further action taken) were given to 79 percent of the Anglo youth as opposed to only 59 percent of the black youth. Further, 42 percent of the adjudicated black youth were sent to correctional institutions as opposed to only 24 percent of the Anglo offenders. Black youth adjudicated for crimes given a low severity score were institutionalized 39 percent of the time versus only 15 percent of the less severe Anglo offenders.

Ferdinand and Luchterhand (1970) further specified the relationship of ethnicity to police decision making. Police handling of more serious delinquent acts or youth with more extensive prior records was influenced by factors immediately relevant to the case. But if the delinquent act or youth's record was less serious, ethnicity was the most influential factor in the disposition. Dannefer and Schutt (1982) found race to be the most important predictor of police disposition. Black and Anglo ethnic status was highly correlated with court referral (in opposite directions). Hispanic status was not correlated with police action. Both Chused (1973) and Reed (1984) found that the police were more likely to detain black youth in detention facilities than Anglo youth, even when holding offense record was constant.

Reed (1984) found that, controlling simultaneously for type of instant offense, whether the youth was detained overnight, prior record, sex, age and race (black/Anglo), race retained a slight independent effect on whether a case was handled formally or informally by the court. Reed also found that black youth received more severe dispositions by the court, even when offense and prior record were controlled. Thomas and Cage (1977) and Datesman and Scarpitti (1977) found that within each offense category (felon, misdemeanor, status), blacks were more likely than Anglos to receive the most severe disposition; the same was true when the number of prior offenses was controlled. Lewis *et al.* (1980) found that in lower socioeconomic sectors of urban areas, violent, disturbed black youth were incarcerated, whereas oftentimes violent, disturbed Anglo youth were hospitalized.

Finally, McCarthy and Smith (1986) found that legal factors became distal influences on juvenile justice decision making as cases penetrated further into the system. Tracking a sample of (N=649) youth from referral through disposition, they found that discrimination builds as cases penetrate further into the system. Screening, detention, charging and adjudication decisions were directly and strongly influenced by legal factors, including severity of offense and prior record. But race and social class directly influenced dispositions, with minority youth receiving more severe dispositions.

Others have found no evidence of racial disparities in juvenile justice processing. Race was not a consistent factor in juvenile justice processing. Race was not a consistent factor in studies of preajudicatory (intake) detention (Sumner, 1970; Bortner *et al.*, 1985), though these studies did not adequately control for prior court referrals or severity of offense. Terry (1967a, 1967b), Cohen and Kleugel (1979) and Meade (1973) found no race effects in police detention decisions. Dispositional decisions also show contradictory race findings, with Bailey and Peterson (1981) and Arnold (1971) finding no contributions of ethnicity or social class to the juvenile justice process.

Thus the weight of evidence on racial disparity at individual decision points shows no clear trend. Ethnicity has only small, direct influences in the early stages of juvenile processing, once prior record and instant offense are controlled. However, several recent studies have examined juvenile justice as a process, where even small racial effects at the earliest decision points are amplified to larger and significant differences at later stages, where the consequences are more serious and potentially harsher. Farrell and Swigert (1978) and McCarthy and Smith (1986) examine the cumulative effects of individuals' prior offense histories. The earliest, most trivial biases (such as the decision to charge a minor felony instead of a misdemeanor, the accumulation of additional counts of an offense) can begin the process of building a prior record. The accumulation of arrests then results in a greater probability of referral to court, and in turn influences later decisions, especially dispositions. If the prior offense history itself is the product of differential decision making, then minor or nonsignificant racial differences are masked in their contributions to later decisions. Thus research on disparate decision making should look at both the cumulative processes as well as the decisions at each point, with adequate controls to assess these preceding effects.

Artifacts of Design and Measurement

The debate is clouded further by the methodological variation in the studies examining the relationship. For example, delinquency is measured at various times by official or self-reported offenses, prevalence or incidence estimates, discrete or overlapping and occasionally trivial items, summary scales of homogeneous behaviors that confound frequency with severity, typologies based on varying offense severity and frequency thresholds, and retrospective time frames that range from one month to several years. The few longitudinal studies on delinquent behavior either rely heavily on official records or use interview intervals that entertain recall problems. Sampling problems also complicate this area. For example, probability samples often overlook or undersample youth at the extremes of the behaviors of interest (Cernkovich *et al.*, 1985).

Moreover, the few "high-rate," serious, or violent offenders tend to be concentrated in urban areas, or at least in areas where the correlates of serious delinquency are highly concentrated (Fagan *et al.*, 1986). Institutional samples of adjudicated offenders yield biased estimates of the social class relationship, results of both restricted range problems and bias in the selection processes within the juvenile justice process, particularly in dispositional decisions (Reed, 1984; McCarthy and Smith, 1986).

The measurement of social class has also contributed to the ambiguity in the empirical literature, particularly with respect to minorities and crime. When social class is analyzed in studies of crime and delinquency, it tends to be conceptualized in one of two ways. First, when the relationship is examined using aggregate data, it is the social class of the social area, or its inequality from surrounding areas, that is studied. The rates of crime and delinquency in a given community, city, or other social area are analyzed in terms of the area's level of poverty or inequality of proportion of working-class households (see Carroll and Jackson, 1983; Sampson, 1986). Second, when the class-crime relationship is examined for individual rates of offending, differential social organization and social class are viewed as an attribute of the individual (that is, typically, his or her parent's occupational status). But the social status of an individual's social area may also have etiological relevance, as well as relevance in understanding differential sanctioning and enforcement. Thus middle-class minority youth from predominantly minority neighborhoods may be unaffected by socialization processes in the area, but their official delinquency status may be determined by aggregate processes of social status of the area. In short, the understanding of race and social class is tangled in a complex set of relationships that can be separated only by adequate controls (and samples) for both *area* and *individual* social status, and race. From there we can proceed to a more refined understanding of base rates of offending, base rates of sanctioning and subsequent disparities in juvenile justice responses.

The Research Problem

Despite growing empirical support for discrimination in juvenile justice decision making, the evidence remains ambiguous and contradictory regarding the impact of discriminatory extralegal factors on screening, detention, adjudication, and dispositional decisions. Yet the proportion of minority offenders in the juvenile justice system continues to increase. Accordingly, if discriminatory processes contribute to the overrepresentation of minorities, the factors that comprise discrimination must be isolated as a prelude to removing bias and reducing disparity.

Previous research has treated each decision point independently (Dannefer and Schutt, 1982) without controlling for the *cumulative* effects of race and other extralegal factors. Also, the criteria to establish discrimination have varied extensively. Finally, samples of heterogeneous referral or offender groups have further complicated analyses of possible interactions between offense-type crime severity and discriminatory factors. Research to examine discrimination must address these design issues.

This article analyses the impact of extralegal factors, especially race, on six decision points in the juvenile justice system: apprehension, detention, prosecutorial charging, adjudication, probation and dispositional decisions. Shortcomings in prior research on racial discrimination are addressed in several ways. First, samples include violent, serious and minor offenders. Second, adequate controls for legal factors (such as prior record) are introduced. Third, by sampling each decision, controls are introduced for prior effects of discrimination in earlier decisions. At the same time, this approach allows us to identify distinct sources of influence while retaining a perspective across a range of decisions (Liska and Tausig, 1979).

The criteria for discrimination are clearly set forth, and follow the recommendations of Cohen and Kluegel (1978: 172):

- the existence of a direct effect of race or class, such that non-Whites and/or lower-income groups received more severe dispositions, controlling for legal factors such as offense and prior record;
- the existence of interaction effects involving race or class with legal factors, such that lower-class and/or non-White juveniles receive more severe dispositions for the same category of legal factors; and
- the existence of indirect effects of race and/or class through other factors considered to be theoretypical in nature.

The research setting is a B-level metropolitan statistical area in a western state.[2] The selection of an urban locale avoids confounding urbanism with both delinquency rates (Laub, 1983) and police decision making (Smith, 1986).

Methods

Samples

Youth were selected for this study from 1983 records, and analyzed at six different decision making points in the juvenile justice process. This time frame ensured that most youth would have completed probation or juvenile corrections commitments by the end of the study. Recognizing that large numbers of youth "fall out" of the system at several processing points (for example, police and prosecutor dismissals), stratified random samples of youth were selected at four points in the system: police apprehension, petition filed, placed on probation and commitment to juvenile corrections. The samples were later supplemented at two additional decision points (referred to the prosecutor and judicial disposition) to ensure adequate cell sizes for analysis. Samples were also stratified according to offense type and ethnicity. Stratifying by ethnicity was required to allow for sufficient numbers of minority or Anglo youth to be selected in areas where simple random samples would have generated insufficient populations for meaningful analysis. Stratification by offense type assured sufficient numbers of violent and serious offenders in the sample. The definitions of violent, serious and other offenders conform to specific statutes in the state that target violent and serious offenders for harsher sanctions.[3]

Methods

Data were abstracted from juvenile justice system records. Information was recorded on actions taken by the police, the prosecutor's office, the juvenile court, the probation department, and the state juvenile correction agency. Control variables included demographic and offense history data and the nature of specific violent offenses (such as, use of weapon, extent of injury, and victim's age and sex).

Data for demographic characteristics were obtained primarily from police records, since many youth never moved beyond the stage of police apprehension. Prior offense history and details of police processing of the instant offense were also collected from police records for all samples. Charging information was collected from district attorney records or from diversion/probation files when prosecutor records were unavailable. Court processing data were collected directly from court files that contained summaries of findings and actions taken at each court hearing, as well as the original petitions, motions filed by counsel, predispositional reports and other reports and records relevant to the case. Data on prior petitions and adjudications were also obtained from the courts. Juvenile corrections data were obtained from a computerized data system that tracks movements of youth through the system, including institutional and community placements, prerelease and parole, and AWOLs.

Analysis

Analyses are simple two- and three-way contingency tables. Most tables are formatted to allow comparisons of minority to Anglo youth within offense types. Although social class and family backgrounds are not a concern of this study, these data are used primarily as control variables to locate possible interaction effects or indirect contributions of race through other factors with which race is highly correlated. Analyses examine system decisions at each sampling point comparing decision making by ethnicity within offense type.

Results

Offender and Offense Characteristics

Table 1 presents information on the characteristics of the youth in the police apprehension sample. Data are presented on the age, sex, family composition (intact/ not intact), and offense history (extent and severity) of the offender. With a few

Table 1
Characteristics of Youth Apprehended by Ethnicity within Offense Types (in percentages)

	Violent		Serious		Other	
	Anglo (N=34)	Minority (N=40)	Anglo (N=40)	Minority (N=40)	Anglo (N=40)	Minority (N=40)
Age at apprehension						
10-12	14.7	2.5	10.0	15.0	15.0	10.0
13-15	50.0	47.5	62.5	57.5	45.0	40.0
16-17	35.3	50.0	27.5	27.5	40.0	40.0
Sex						
Male	91.2	90.0	77.5	90.0	85.0	72.5
Female	8.8	10.0	22.5	10.0	15.0	27.5
Family status						
Intact	54.5	38.5	38.5	33.3	33.3	35.0
Not intact	45.5	61.5	61.5	66.7	66.7	65.0
Prior arrest history*						
None	61.8	20.0	60.0	27.5	67.5	27.5
1-2	20.6	17.5	25.0	22.5	25.0	27.5
3 or more	17.6	62.5	15.0	50.0	7.5	45.0
Arrest history (severity)						
None	61.8	20.0	60.0	27.5	67.5	27.5
Other	20.6	15.0	17.5	15.0	22.5	35.0
Serious	11.8	47.5	22.5	45.0	10.0	30.0
Violent	5.9	17.5	0.0	12.5	0.0	7.5

*p<.01 for all offense types.

exceptions, 40 percent or more violent or serious offenders were 16 or 17 years of age, and no more than 15 percent were under 12 years of age. Thus Anglo and minority youth in the police apprehension sample show no significant differences when contrasting age at the time of apprehension. Most (over 85 percent) of the study youth were males, and for both Anglo and minority offenders the percentage of females arrested increased for less severe crimes. Although this pattern emerged for both ethnic groups, it was more pronounced for minority youth. Most youth were from families without both parents.

The extent and severity of the offense history of the apprehended sample shows that minority youth typically possess more extensive and more severe offense histories than Anglo offenders. For example, 45.0 percent of the minority, and only 7.5 percent of the Anglo, "other" offenders were arrested three or more times prior to the instant

Table 2
Characteristics of Violent Offenses by Ethnicity (in percentages)

	Anglo (N = 30)	Minority (N = 40)
Weapon use*		
Gun	5.9	8.1
Other	41.2	73.0
None	52.9	18.9
Injury		
Injury/medical attention	31.3	37.9
Injury/no medical attention	28.1	34.5
No injury	40.6	27.6
Victim's sex		
Female	53.6	30.0
Male only	46.4	70.0
Victim's age**		
Infant/child (1-9)	44.4	0.0
Youth (10-17)	29.6	76.2
Adult (18 or over)	25.9	23.8

*$p<.01$; **$p<.05$.

offense. Similarly, 37.5 percent of the minority youth in this group had been arrested for a prior violent or serious offense as opposed to only 10 percent of the Anglo youth.

The findings of more extensive offense histories among minority youth is not surprising, given recent research on the division processes and probabilities of minority youth being arrested (Smith, 1986). Whether these base rate differences are due to differential offending rates or discriminatory law enforcement practices remains controversial (see Huizinga and Elliott, 1987).

For youth charged with violent crimes, data were also collected on characteristics of the crimes. Table 2 shows information on weapon use, the extent of the injury received by the victim and the age and sex of the victim. Significant differences in the use of weapons by minority and Anglo youth were found, with minority youth more likely to use weapons than Anglo youth (81.1 percent versus 47.1 percent). Some differences also appear in the age and sex of the individuals victimized by minority and Anglo violent offenders. Anglo youth appeared to be more likely to victimize females (53.6 percent versus 30.0 percent) than their minority counterparts. In addition, Anglo youth were significantly more likely than minority youth to victimize infants and children (44.4 percent versus zero percent).

It might be anticipated that these differences in the nature of the violent offenses committed by Anglo and minority youth would affect subsequent processing decisions.

Figure 1
Police Decision Making: Detention

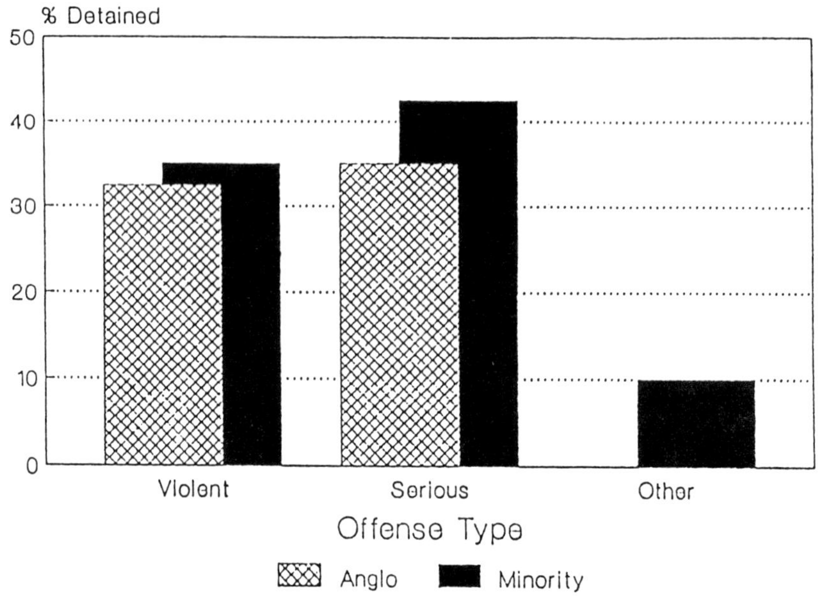

However, the direction such influence might take is hard to predict. For example, if use of weapon and resulting injury is perceived to be more dangerous, then we would expect to find minority youth being treated more severely by the system, based on the characteristics of violent offenses shown in Table 2. On the other hand, victimization of females and young children might be perceived as more dangerous, in which case Anglo youth would be treated more severely. Note that over three-quarters of the victims of minority youth were other youth, aged 10-17; such cases might be perceived by juvenile justice personnel as less threatening to society in general, or these may be seen by system decision makers as evidence of a violent subculture among minority youth, and treated accordingly. How these factors bear on subsequent decisions is a topic of this research.

Police Decision Making

The present discussion begins at the point when a juvenile (defined by law as aged 10 through 17) is taken into custody by a local police officer. Typically, custody involves either taking the youth to the police station for processing or having a parent bring him or her in. In some cases, the contact involves interviewing the youth in his or her home without coming to the station. Our operational definition of custody (apprehension) was the existence of a written police record showing time and location of custody. To examine police processing, data were collected on prehearing detention determinations

Figure 2
Police Decision Making: Referral

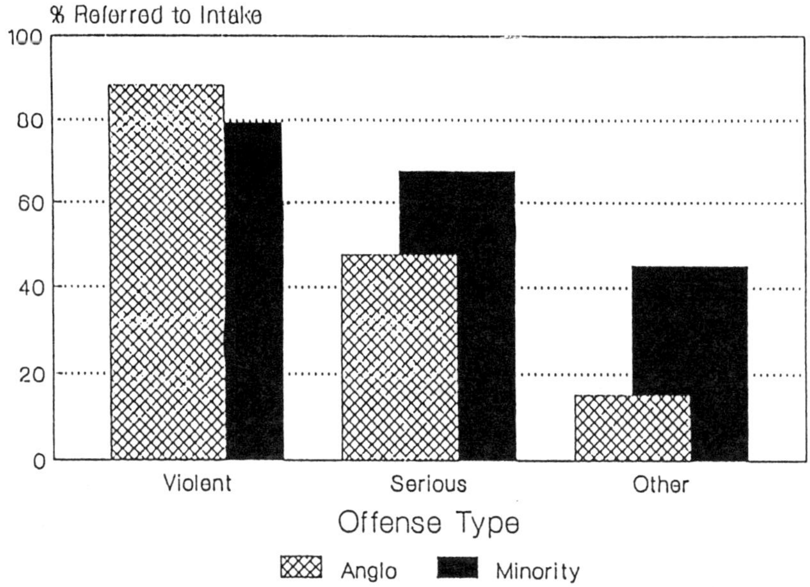

and disposition of the case (referred to juvenile court intake or dismissed). Figure 1 shows the results of police decisions, and Table 3 specifically examines referral decisions controlling for background factors.

Figure 1 suggests that detention decisions are influenced by neither offense severity nor race. Few "other" offenders are detained, but all are minorities. Among serious or violent offenders, differences are not statistically significant.

Figure 2 shows that the police decision to screen cases out of further processing or to refer onward in the system differs significantly by offense severity, and by race in two offense categories. Violent offenders are most likely to be referred (over four out of five cases). Anglo violent offenders are slightly more likely to be referred than are minority violent offenders, which suggests that weapon use and injury are not the most salient factors in making this decision. These mixed results are consistent with prior research on race and preadjudicatory detention, where measurement and design differences have yielded contradictory evidence. Race does influence these decisions, especially less severe offense categories.

Within the "serious" and "other" categories, minority youth are significantly more likely than Anglo youth to be referred for further processing. Table 3 examines these differences in further detail for youth in these two offense categories.

Regardless of the age or family structure of the offender, minority youth are referred at a higher rate. However, police decision making is influenced by offense history characteristics, but not for all offense types. For serious offenders with no offense

Table 3
Police Decision to Refer Serious and Other Youth to Juvenile Court by Ethnicity within Offense Type Controlling for Youth Characteristics (in percentages)

	Serious				Other			
	Anglo		Minority		Anglo		Minority	
	Refer (N=19)	Not Refer (N=21)	Refer (N=27)	Not Refer (N=13)	Refer (N=6)	Not Refer (N=34)	Refer (N=18)	Not Refer (N=22)
Age at Apprehension								
10-12	25.0	75.0	33.3	66.7	0.0	100.0	0.0	100.0
13-15	40.0	60.0	65.2	34.8	16.7	83.3	55.0	45.0
16-17	72.7	27.3	90.0	9.1	18.8	81.3	43.8	56.3
Family status								
Intact	33.3	66.7	53.8	46.2	7.7	92.3	35.7	64.3
Not intact	54.2	45.8	73.1	26.9	19.2	80.8	50.0	50.0
Prior arrest history								
None	29.2	70.8	45.5	54.5	3.7	96.3	9.1	90.9
1-2	70.0	30.0	55.6	44.4	30.0	70.0	63.6	36.4
3 or more	83.3	16.7	85.0	15.0	66.7	33.3	55.6	40.4
Arrest history (severity)								
None	29.2	70.8	45.5	54.6	3.7	96.3	9.1	90.9
Other	71.4	28.6	33.3	66.7	33.3	66.7	42.8	57.1
Serious	77.8	22.2	88.9	11.1	50.0	50.0	75.0	25.0
Violent	0.0	0.0	80.0	20.0	0.0	0.0	66.7	33.0

histories, the disparity in referral rates remains (Anglo 29.2 percent and minority 45.5 percent referred). However, when the serious offender has at least one prior apprehension, the difference disappears. In fact, a slightly higher percentage of serious Anglo offenders with one or two prior offenses are referred to court than similar minority offenders. For "other" offenders, minorities with fewer than two prior offenses are referred to intake more often. However, when minor offenders have three or more prior offenses, the pattern is reversed and Anglo offenders are referred at a slightly higher rate. Thus it appears that police process serious offenders similarly across ethnic categories, but offer informal responses to less severe or one-time Anglo offenders more often than to minority youth. Differentials by race are not evident for violent offenses, regardless of prior record.

Table 4
Prosecutor Decision Making by Ethnicity within Offense Type (Apprehension Charge) (in percentages)

	Violent		Serious		Other	
	Anglo (N=30)	Minority (N=40)	Anglo (N=40)	Minority (N=40)	Anglo (N=39)	Minority (N=40)
Original petition decision						
Petition filed	33.3	52.5	62.5	67.5	25.6	40.0
Dismissed/informal adjudication	66.7	47.5	37.5	32.5	74.4	60.0
Petition charge						
Violent	36.7	45.0	0.0	0.0	0.0	0.0
Serious	0.0	0.0	60.0	67.5	0.0	0.0
Other	0.0	5.0	10.0	2.5	31.6	40.0
No charge	63.3	50.0	30.0	30.0	68.4	60.0
Processing time to prosecutor decision						
Same day	62.1	51.4	26.5	26.3	36.8	28.9
1-3 days	10.3	24.3	23.5	13.2	21.1	34.2
4-7 days	17.2	18.9	35.3	39.5	18.4	10.5
8+ days	10.3	5.4	14.7	21.1	23.7	26.3

Prosecutorial Decision Making

Originally, it was anticipated that prosecutors' decisions would be examined only for those youth from the apprehension sample who were referred by the police to the prosecutor. However, there is an overall racial disparity in police dismissals (75 percent Anglo, 47 percent minority). Accordingly, it was necessary to supplement cases from the apprehension sample with additional youth referred for prosecution.

Information collected on prosecutorial action included the prosecutor's initial decision whether to file a petition or to informally process or dismiss the case;,the petition charge ultimately filed by the prosecutor and the amount of time taken to process the case. These data are presented by ethnicity and offense type in Table 4.

The prosecutor's office files petitions for minority youth at a somewhat higher rate than for Anglo youth across all offense types. Further, for all three offense categories, the prosecutor files charges equivalent to the apprehension charges slightly more often for minority youth than Anglo youth. Though the differences observed were not statistically significant, the consistency in the findings and the large percentage difference in the original petition filing decision for violent offenders (33.3 percent Anglos and 52.5 percent minorities filed) and other offenders (25.6 percent Anglo and 40 percent minorities) suggest that this relationship needs further examination. Controlling for *offender* characteristics fails to identify factors that explain the differences. That is, the relationship between ethnicity and petition filing for violent and other offenders does not change when controlling for the offender's age, family structure, sex or offense history. In virtually all instances, minorities are filed on at higher rates than Anglo youth.

One reason for the differential in cases filed for violent offenses may be that the type of offense differs between Anglo and minority youth. Most of the Anglo violent offenses are sexual assaults on children. Many of these cases are not filed because the victim is too young to testify or the victim's parents do not want to prosecute. Often the parents know the juvenile as a neighbor, friend, relative or baby sitter and drop charges in return for assurances that the juvenile will receive counseling. Minority youth in this sample, on the other hand, are more likely to victimize peers, use weapons and cause injuries. The interpretation of "seriousness" that these decision patterns suggest places young children at the lower level of severity determinations, especially for sexual assault.

Case Outcomes and Judicial Decisions

Data were collected on the outcome of the plea hearing process, as well as the final adjudicatory determination. Plea hearing outcome includes six types of determinations: youth admits guilt to prosecutor's charges; youth pleads guilty to lesser charges; youth pleads guilty to other petition; youth receives continued petition or continued adjudication; youth denies charges; and charges are dismissed. "Continued adjudication" means that the youth has admitted to a charge, but instead of adjudicating him or her a delinquent, the judge continues the hearing for six months (which can later be extended by another six months).[4] During that time the youth is usually placed on informal probation supervision. If he or she does not co-operate or if there are new offenses, the judge may then adjudicate and sentence. Adjudicatory determination is broken down into five categories — violent offense, serious offense, other offense, other petition (charge not specified) and youth not adjudicated. Table 5 presents case outcomes by ethnicity within offense type. Thus any disparities will emerge in plea hearing or adjudicatory outcomes that occur only for particular offense categories.

Minority youth in the violent and serious offense categories are more likely to admit to the prosecutor's charges, whereas Anglo youth more often plead to lesser charges or receive continued adjudication. Although no youth charged with serious offenses had their cases dismissed, Anglo youth charged with serious offenses are twice as likely to be dismissed as minority youth (25 percent Anglo dismissed versus 10 percent of minority youth), and Anglo youth charged with "other" offenses are four times as likely to be dismissed as minority youth (30 percent versus 7.5 percent). Controlling for offense history, Anglo and minority youth charged with serious crimes and possessing no prior offense history receive similar outcomes. However, for those youth with a prior offense, Anglo youth continue to have charges dismissed about one-third of the time, whereas minority youth do not receive dismissals (see Figure 3a).

One possible explanation for these differentials is that Anglo youth are more likely to have private counsel (54.1 percent of those charged with violent offenses and 28.1

Table 5
Case Outcomes by Ethnicity within Offense Type (Petition Charge) (in percentages)

	Violent		Serious		Other	
	Anglo (N=12)	Minority (N=40)	Anglo (N=40)	Minority (N=40)	Anglo (N=40)	Minority (N=40)
Outcomes*						
Guilty, prosecutor's charges	0.0	25.0	12.5	25.0	35.0	27.5
Guilty, lesser charges	58.3	37.5	35.0	25.0	5.0	10.0
Guilty, other petition	8.3	17.5	12.5	27.5	12.5	42.5
Continued petition/ adjudicated	16.7	2.5	10.0	2.5	12.5	7.5
Charges denied	16.7	17.5	5.0	10.0	5.0	5.0
Charges dismissed	0.0	0.0	25.0	10.0	30.0	7.5
Adjudicated charge**						
Violent	16.7	42.5	0.0	0.0	0.0	0.0
Serious	25.0	15.0	27.5	40.0	0.0	0.0
Other	16.7	15.0	27.5	40.0	0.0	0.0
Other petition	0.0	15.0	12.5	25.0	12.5	42.5
None	41.7	15.0	40.0	20.0	47.5	22.5

*p<.05; **p<.01.

percent of those charged with serious offenses), whereas minority youth are more likely to have public defenders or court-appointed attorneys (25.6 percent of those charged with violent offenses and 5.6 percent of those charged with serious offenses). This factor was controlled, with the result that for serious offenders with public attorneys, 78.4 percent of minority youth and 57.1 percent of Anglo youth admitted to charges and 35.7 percent of Anlgo youth had their cases dismissed whereas only 7.1 percent of minority youth had their cases dismissed.

Thus the type of counsel representation in part explains why more of the minority offenders are adjudicated. Certainly, private counsel available more often to Anglo youth appears to help increase the chance of dismissal. Public defenders are more likely to represent minority youth, an artifact of the race/social class interaction. The results suggest poorer representation. However, because offense types vary by race, the results are complex and trends not readily discernible.

Table 6 presents information on judicial disposition by ethnicity within offense type. Youth adjudicated for serious offenses are rarely committed to juvenile corrections. This sentence is dealt much more regularly to youth adjudicated for violent offenses (42 percent of minority violent offenders). However, minority youth adjudicated for serious offenses are about three times as likely as serious Anglo offenders to be committed to

Figure 3a
Case Outcome for Serious Offenders by Number of Prior Arrests

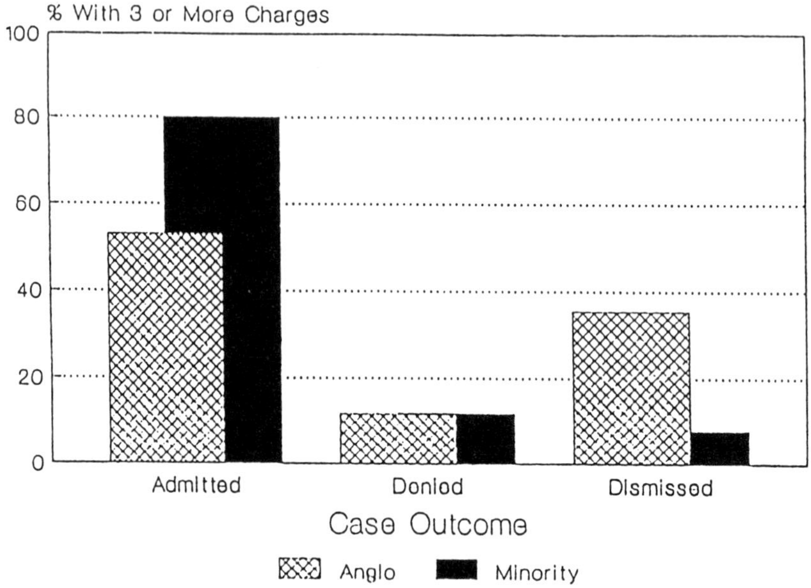

Figure 3b
Case Outcome for Serious Offenders by Severity of Prior Arrests

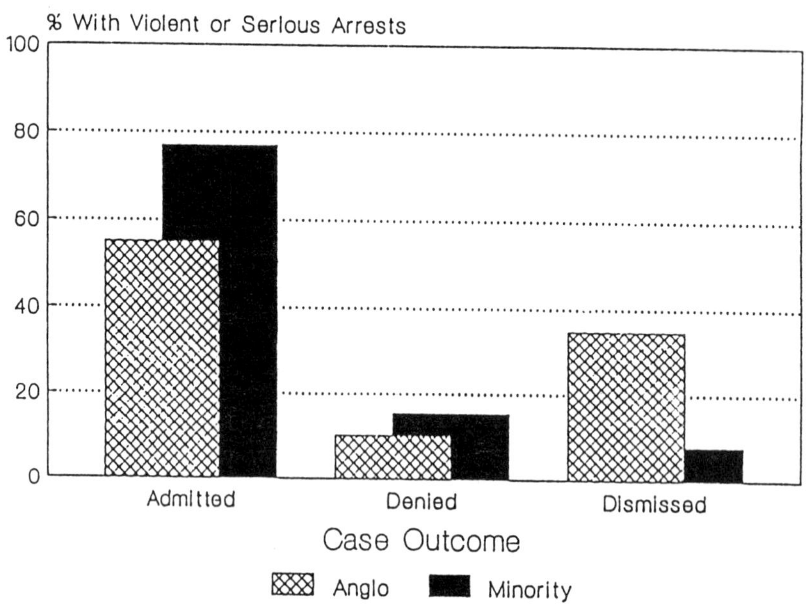

Table 6
Judicial Disposition by Ethnicity Within Offense Type (Adjudicated Charge) (in percentages)

	Violent		Serious		Other*	
	Anglo (N=1)	Minority (N=24)	Anglo (N=36)	Minority (N=39)	Anglo (N=39)	Minority (N=56)
Disposition						
State commitment	0.0	41.7	5.6	15.4	5.1	19.6
Jail/detention	0.0	33.3	33.3	30.8	25.6	33.9
Probation/other**	100.0	25.0	61.1	53.8	69.2	46.4

*"other" offenders significant at .05 level.

**Other dispositions include mental health or social services placements, community services, therapy, and restitution.

juvenile corrections (15.4 percent versus 5.6 percent). Table 6 also displays sentencing patterns for "other" offenders. Minority youth adjudicated for "other" offenses are almost four times as likely as Anglo offenders to be committed to juvenile corrections (19.6 percent versus 5.1 percent). Table 6 also suggests that minority youth, regardless of the instant offense, are committed to juvenile corrections more often than Anglo youth.

Table 7 takes the offense type where the largest disparity appears ("other" offenses) and examines the relationship between ethnicity and sentence controlling for offender characteristics. After controlling for legal representation, age at apprehension, sex of offender, family structure, extent of offense history and severity of offense history, in almost every situation minority youth adjudicated for minor offenses are committed to juvenile corrections more often than Anglo youth. The most dramatic differences are as follows:

- None of the 11 Anglo minor offenders without a prior offense were committed to juvenile corrections; six of the 24 (25 percent) minority offenders adjudicated for such offenses and possessing no priors were committed to juvenile corrections.
- None of the four female Anglo offenders in the sample were committed to juvenile corrections; three of the seven (42.9 percent) minority females were so committed.
- None of the eight Anglo minor offenders coming from intact families were committed to juvenile corrections; three of the 12 (25.0 percent) minority youth from intact families were sent to juvenile corrections.

Probation

Data were collected on system decisions on adjudicated youth placed on probation, including: the sanctions and services required by the judge; the services provided or obtained by the probation department; the frequency of probation officer personal

Table 7
Judicial Dispositions for "Other" Offenders (Adjudicated Charge) by Ethnicity Controlling for Offender Characteristics (in percentages)

	DYS		Jail/Detention		Probation/Other	
	Anglo (N=2)	Minority (N=11)	Anglo (N=10)	Minority (N=19)	Anglo (N=27)	Minority (N=26)
Representation						
Pro se	0.0	0.0	14.3	20.0	85.7	80.0
Public	5.5	26.3	38.9	31.6	55.5	42.1
Private	16.7	12.5	16.7	62.5	66.7	25.0
Age at apprehension						
Under 12	0.0	0.0	0.0	0.0	0.0	100.0
13-15	4.3	21.2	30.4	30.0	65.2	48.5
16-17	8.3	17.4	25.0	39.1	66.7	43.5
Sex						
Female	0.0	42.9	25.0	14.3	75.0	42.9
Male	5.7	16.3	25.7	36.7	68.6	46.9
Family						
Not intact	6.5	18.2	25.8	34.1	67.7	47.7
Intact	0.0	25.0	25.0	33.3	75.0	41.7
Arrest history (extent)*						
No	0.0	0.0	0.0	50.0	100.0	50.0
1-2	0.0	14.3	15.4	42.9	84.6	42.9
3 or more	9.1	20.8	36.4	31.3	54.5	47.9
Arrest history (severity)*						
Violent	20.0	10.0	20.0	60.0	60.0	30.0
Serious	7.1	25.8	35.7	25.8	57.1	48.4
Other	0.0	14.3	25.0	28.6	75.0	57.1
None	0.0	0.0	0.0	50.0	100.0	50.0

*Arrests up to day of adjudication.

contacts with the youth; the number of months the youth actually remained on probation; and the use of and reasons for probation revocation. Very few racial disparities are evident. Minority youth are somewhat more likely to receive educational and vocational services than Anglo youth, in each offense category. Further, minority youth are somewhat more likely to stay on probation for more than 18 months.

Table 8
Judicial Commitment Decisions (in percentages)

	Violent		Serious		Other	
	Anglo (N=3)	Minority (N=15)	Anglo (N=9)	Minority (N=60)	Anglo (N=8)	Minority (N=29)
Minimum sentence						
None	33.3	26.7	44.4	48.3	75.0	72.4
1-12 months	0.0	0.0	0.0	1.7	0.0	0.0
More than 12 months	66.7	73.3	55.6	50.0	25.0	27.6
Use of special status						
None	33.3	21.4	44.4	50.0	75.0	75.9
Repeat/mandatory	0.0	64.3	55.6	50.0	25.0	24.1
Violent	66.7	14.3	0.0	0.0	0.0	0.0
Reasons for commitment*						
Delinquency petition	100.0	73.3	100.0	63.3	50.0	58.6
Revocation for offense	0.0	6.7	0.0	11.7	0.0	3.4
Revocation for technical violation	0.0	20.0	0.0	25.0	50.0	37.9

*"Serious" sample significant at .10 level.

Juvenile Corrections

Data were collected on a variety of decisions made by the juvenile court judge and the juvenile corrections staff regarding youth committed to the state juvenile corrections agency. Since it is the harshest sanction, and also a decision that apparently is biased, we focus on this type of sanction. Table 8 reports information on judicial disposition for committed youth.

Table 8 shows that ethnicity does not affect the specifics of judicial commitments to juvenile corrections. No relationship is found between ethnicity and minimum or maximum sentence to the use of special commitment statutes. The only difference observed is in the reason for committing serious offenders. The instant petition resulting in commitment was a probation revocation for 22 out of 60 (37 percent) serious minority offenders. In contrast, all serious Anglo youth were committed on delinquency petitions rather than probation revocations.

The interpretation of this finding is not clear. One possible explanation is that minority youth are more likely to get a chance on probation, whereas Anglo youth are more likely to be committed to juvenile corrections without a prior period on probation. However, if we assume that both groups are equally likely to be given at least one period of probation prior to commitment (a plausible assumption), the alternative explanation is that the prosecutor is more likely to file a new delinquency petition when an Anglo youth is apprehended for a serious charge, but is more likely to file a probation revocation on a minority youth. Or, since the "threshold" for a court filing may be lowest for minority youth, more minority cases (with less serious charges) are filed, resulting in a broader range of sanctions for a broader array of cases. Because a delinquency petition carries with it the right to a trial by jury, whereas a probation revocation does not (it is heard in trial to the court), a probation revocation is believed to be easier to obtain than an adjudication on a new petition.

Conclusions

Racial discrimination consistently influences juvenile justice processing in this metropolitan area. Specifically, the race of juvenile offenders influences decisions to apprehend, detain, charge, adjudicate and punish juveniles who are accused of a range of offenses. When the Cohen and Kleugel (1978) criteria are applied, differential processing of minority and Anglo youth becomes apparent. Both legal and extralegal factors enter into juvenile justice system decisions. At times, race disparities are confined to less severe offense categories: at other stages they are evident for all offenders. After controlling for a wide range of offense and offender characteristics, and despite the absence of differences between minority and Anglo offenders for factors other than race and social class, the disposition of minority offenders consistently was harsher and more punitive. And, at the "deepest" end of the system where the consequences are most serious, no factor other than race could be identified to explain the harsher response to minority youth.

Though racial disparities are clearly observed at several seemingly separate decision points, no consistent pattern was discernible. Discrimination takes different forms for different decisions and personnel. Direct influences were observed for all levels of severity at certain points, such as detention and charging decisions; at other times race interacts with legal factors (such as offense severity) revealing disparate decisions. Plea hearing outcomes and dispositions, for example, reveal race differences for less serious ("other") offenders but not for violent offenders. The convergence of decision patterns among decision makers of such disparate backgrounds and independent functions is itself surprising. System personnel from police officers to intake staff to prosecutors and judges engaged in similar patterns of case evaluation and disposition. How these patterns can emerge within a system that has been accused often of being "nonsystem" remains a difficult question.

Depending on the decision juncture of the system, race effects were discerned either directly or through controls for offense severity, prior history, or other background factors (such as family). Moreover, the inclusion of factors specific to the offense also did not explain disparities. That is, knowledge of weapon use, victim age and background, or the presence of other mitigating circumstances do not alter the basic finding of racial bias.

The absence of legal factors generally associated with dispositional decisions, particularly prior record, also is surprising. At the earliest stages of the system, it is not unusual to find a combination of legal and historical factors influencing decisions. What was surprising was the relatively low importance of factors other than race as discriminators of youth for purposes of disposition. It is here that legal factors should be weighed most heavily if not exclusively, given the stakes of a dispositional decision. Whether these patterns would emerge from a broader analytic perspective is uncertain. For example, failing to control for offense severity at each decision point would weaken the magnitude of the disparities. The complexity of the patterns of discrimination is reiterated by these findings.

Methodological Implications

The results also illustrate methodological issues in the analysis and detection of racial discrimination in juvenile justice decision making. The analytic strategy demonstrates a convenient way of stratifying offense and offender characteristics to locate disparities by race. By sampling at each decision point, and then controlling for legal and extralegal factors, two distinct trends can be discerned. First, disparities in backgrounds of offenders identically processed to that stage can be analyzed. For example, apprehension and detention decisions can be weighed by equity based on the backgrounds, offense severity and extralegal characteristics of accused youth. Second, differential decision making of youth entering a decision "gate" can also be assessed in a similar fashion. Accordingly, the sequential "in/out" decisions can be analyzed separately to determine points where disparities operate and accumulate in later stages.

The strategy also illustrates the types of sampling strategies and controls necessary to sort out the locations and strength of disparate decisions. This study introduced legal and extralegal factors presumably linked to the perception of offenders by decision makers and their evaluation of offenders' amenability to different sanctions. The sampling strategy overlooks racial prevalence in the justice system, and possibly distorts the magnitude of effects, but overcomes the high attrition rates that characterize previous efforts at discrimination research. The ability to identify racial disparities depends on generating adequate study samples for underrepresented racial or offender groups. Further research should weight these samples and include them in path analytic models to determine the independent and interactive effects of previous stages on subsequent offender profiles and racial disparities. An alternative strategy is to develop independent models for minority and Anglo youth in the justice system to determine how racial differences yield models with disparate parameters and explanatory variables.

Theoretical and Policy Implications

The variation in how racial differentials operate across decision points complicates an understanding of their origins and, in turn, their remedies. It appears that minority youth receive consistently harsher dispositions, but not at all levels of offense severity. Moreover, disparities within offense levels emerge only after introducing controls for other disparate ways to decision outcomes, but the results are identical: minority offenders are at a consistent disadvantage in their efforts to receive equal protection under the law. If the factors of the case do not change as it proceeds through the system, the conclusions of decision makers also remain constant (and discriminatory) and the evidence and factors of the case represent the cumulative efforts of juvenile justice system actors reviewing identical (and presumably refined) information, why should race matter?

This study controlled for potentially mitigating circumstances that offered explanatory factors beyond simple offense and offender characteristics. But there remain potential explanatory factors not examined in this research. For example, the empirical evidence on social class and social status also suggests influences on juvenile court dispositions (McCarthy and Smith, 1986). Both the status position of the neighborhood and the social status of the individual may partially explain differential processing. The present study used weak measures of individual social status, relying primarily on public versus private defense representation and family status as well as the close correlation of race with social class. These are primarily measures of individual position, but overlook the interactive effects of status context and social class with respect to juvenile court dispositions (Johnstone, 1978). Though specific tests of social class were beyond the scope of this inquiry, the inclusion of additional substantive factors in the analyses makes it difficult to imagine factors other than race that explain these findings. Nevertheless, specific measures of social class, status context and neighborhood should be included in future research.

The evidence for racial discrimination in this study is compelling. Its sources may lie in the individual attitudes of decision makers in the system's independent agencies, but it is unlikely that these seemingly isolated decision makers of substantially different backgrounds would produce such consistent, systematic behaviors. Rather than a chance convergence of independent behaviors, they seem to reflect a sociological process, if not a generalized perspective, shared across decision makers of disparate backgrounds. Like other societal institutions, the justice system is not blind to ethnic and racial differences. To understand the differential treatment of minorities in the juvenile justice system, we may turn to the disparate status of minorities in the larger society:

> If discrimination exists in the larger society, it surely creates problems for the disadvantaged and limits their resources to cope with their difficulties. Such persons entering the juvenile justice system may present the kinds of substantive problems that juvenile court officials presumably weigh heavily in dispositional decision making (McCarthy and Smith, 1986: 59).

Racial disparities in juvenile justice make a mockery of the notions of accountability that pervade contemporary juvenile justice policy. In recent years, much ado has been made over the absence of accountability for youthful offenders before the juvenile justice system.[5] The existence of racial bias in juvenile justice undermines accountability for both the system proceedings and its agencies, as well as for youth before the court. When minority youth discern differential and more lenient treatment for their Anglo counterparts, a bitter and ironic form of accountability is taught. The goals of justice are weakened by the practices that lead to racial disparities in the juvenile system.

The disparate treatment of minorities in the justice system is further illustrated by the increasing number of blacks in juvenile and adult correctional facilities (U.S. Department of Justice, 1985). It is important to remember that inequality and disparity are endemic in our society, and that juvenile justice agencies are no less a part of that society than any other institution. The processes that yield economically and socially isolated minority communities also contribute to the systemic responses documented in this study. There is ample evidence that relative deprivation and inequality contribute to higher crime rates (Laub, 1983; Byrne and Sampson, 1986), but the disparities in crime may be as much a societal reaction of justice system decision makers within "high-crime" neighborhoods as the result of socialization processes for youth in those same areas (Smith, 1986). The results suggest a convergence of conflict theory with ecological theories where the hardening of the inner city has been linked to higher rates of official and self-reported crime (Sampson, 1986).[6] The impact of such extralegal factors on sequential decision is an empirical question in need of further research.

The correlates of delinquent conduct differ little in minority and general youth populations (Fagan *et al.*, forthcoming). There is little reason, then, to presume that factors other than neighborhood context, especially socioeconomic isolation, explain differences in official or self-reported crime rates. Removing the economic and social isolation of minority communities may be the most critical step in reducing differential treatment of minority offenders, by neutralizing the nonsubstantive criteria that apparently influence responses to crime. When the economic gaps that isolate neighborhoods and youth within them are narrowed, the gap in perceptions and societal responses may also narrow. Policies that link crime control to neighborhood development may address neighborhood factors that are etiologically relevant to both crime causation and the responses of juvenile justice system officials.

Endnotes

1. See Elliott and Huizinga for a detailed analysis of differential offending rates for minority and Anglo adolescents.
2. Population: 250,000-1,000,000.
3. Violent offenses were major felony crimes against persons, generally UCR Part I Index offenses. Serious offenses were property offenses, generally UCR Part II Felonies, but also lesser felonies against persons. Minor offenses were the equivalent of misdemeanors, but also included some nonviolent felonies (such as selling stolen goods).
4. Although continued adjudication frequently occurs at the dispositional hearing, it is considered to be a plea hearing outcome for purposes of this study so that dispositional data will be limited to those youth actually adjudicated.
5. The American Legislative Exchange Council, supported by a grant from the Department of Justice, recently proposed model juvenile justice codes that would instill "accountability" in the juvenile justice process for youth committing serious offenses. This would take the form of proportionate punishment and a more formalized juvenile justice process.
6. Johnstone (1978) specifically locates conflict theory in this context.

References

Arnold, W.R. 1971. "Race and Ethnicity Relative to Other Factors in Juvenile Court Dispositions." *American Journal of Sociology*. 77: 211-227.

Bailey, W.C. 1981. "Preadjudicatory Detention in a Large Metropolitan Juvenile Court." *Law and Human Behavior*. 5: 19-43.

Bailey, W.C. and R.D. Peterson. 1981. "Legal Versus Extra-legal Determinants of Juvenile Court Dispositions." *Juvenile and Family Court Journal*. XX: 41-59.

Bortner, M.A. *et al.* 1985. "Race and the Impact of Juvenile Deinstitutionalization." *Crime and Delinquency*. 31: 35-46.

Braithwaite, J. 1981. "The Myth of Social Class and Criminality Reconsidered." *American Sociological Review*. 46: 36-57.

Byrne, J. and R. Sampson (eds.). 1986. "Introduction" in *The Social Ecology of Crime: Theory, Research, and Public Policy*. New York: Springer-Verlag.

Carroll, L. and P. Jackson. 1983. "Inequality, Opportunity, and Crime Rates in Central Cities." *Criminology*. 21: 178-194.

Carter, T. and D. Clelland. 1979. "A New-Marxian Critique, Formulation and Test of Juvenile Dispositions As a Function of Social Class." *Social Problems*. 27: 96-108.

Cernkovich, S.A., P.C. Giordano and M.D. Pugh. 1985. "Chronic Offenders: The Missing Cases in Self-Report Delinquency Research." *Journal of Criminal Law and Criminology*. 76: 705-732.

Chused, R.H. 1973. "The Juvenile Court Process: A Study of Three New Jersey Counties." *Rutgers Law Review*. 26: 488-539.

Coates, R., A. Miller and L. Ohlin. 1975. *Diversity in a Youth Correctional System: Handling Delinquents in Massachusetts*. Cambridge: Ballinger.

Cohen, L.E. and J.R. Kluegel. 1978. "Determinants of Juvenile Court Dispositions: Ascriptive and Achieved Factors in Two Metropolitan Courts." *American Sociological Review*. 43: 162: 176.

.... 1979. "Selecting Delinquents for Adjudication: An Analysis of Intake Screening Decisions in Two Metropolitan Juvenile Courts." *Journal of Research in Crime and Delinquency*. 16: 143-163.

Comer, J. 1985. "Black Violence and Public Policy" in L. Curtis (ed.), *American Violence and Public Policy*. New Haven: Yale University Press.

Dannefer, D. and R.K. Schutt. 1982. "Race and Juvenile Justice Processing in Court and Police Agencies." *American Journal of Sociology*. 87: 1113-1132.

Datesman, S.K. and F.R. Scarpitti. 1977. "Unequal Protection for Males and Females in the Juvenile Court" in T. Ferdinand (ed.), *Little Brother Grows Up*. Beverly Hills: Sage.

Dungworth, T. 1977. "Discretion in the Juvenile Justice System: The Impact of Case Characteristics on Prehearing Detention" in T. Ferdinand (ed.), *Little Brother Grows Up*. Beverly Hills: Sage.

Elliott, D.S. and S. Ageton. 1980. "Reconciling Race and Class Differences in Self-Reported and Official Estimates of Delinquency." *American Sociology Review*. 45: 95-110.

Elliott, D.S. and D. Huizinga. 1983. "Social Class and Delinquent Behavior in a National Youth Panel." *Criminology*. 21: 149-177.

Fagan, J.A., E. Piper and M. Moore. 1986. "Violent Delinquents and Urban Youth." *Criminology*. 24: 439-472.

Farrell, R.A. and V.L. Swigert. 1978. "Prior Offense Record as a Self-Fulfilling Prophecy." *Law and Society Review*. 12: 437-453.

Ferdinand, T.N. and E.G. Luchterhand. 1970. "Inner-city Youth, the Police, the Juvenile Court, and Justice." *Social Problems*. 17: 510-527.

Hindelang, M., T. Hirschi and J. Weis. 1981. *Measuring Delinquency*. Beverly Hills: Sage.

Johnstone, J.W.C. 1978. "Social Class, Social Areas, and Delinquency." *Sociology and Social Research*. 63: 49-72.

Kramer, J.H. and D.J. Steffensmeier. 1978. "The Differential Detention Jailing of Juveniles: A Comparison of Detention and Non-detention Courts." *Pepperdine Law Review*. 5: 759-807.

Krohn, M.D. and J.L. Massey. 1980. "Social Control and Delinquent Behavior: An Examination of the Elements of the Social Bond." *Sociological Quarterly*. 21: 529-544.

Langan, P. 1985. "Racism On Trial: New Evidence to Explain the Racial Composition of Prisons in the United States." *Journal of Criminal Law and Criminology*. 76: 666-683.

Laub, J.H. 1983. "Urbanism, Race, and Crime." *Journal of Research in Crime and Delinquency*. 20: 183-198.

Lewis, D.O., S.S. Shanok, R.J. Cohen, M. Grant and E. Ritvo. 1980. "Race Bias in the Diagnosis and Disposition of Violent Adolescents." *American Journal of Psychiatry*. 137: 1211-1216.

Liska, A.E. and M. Tausig. 1979. "Theoretical Interpretations of Social Class and Racial Differentials in Legal Decision-making for Juveniles." *Sociology Quarterly*. 20: 197-207.

Martin, E. 1983. "Minorities in the Juvenile Justice System." Unpublished manuscript, Office of Juvenile Justice and Delinquency Prevention, Washington, D.C.

McCarthy, B.R. and B.L. Smith. 1986. "The Conceptualization of Discrimination in the Juvenile Justice Process: The Impact of Administrative Factors and Screening Decisions on Juvenile Court Dispositions." *Criminology*. 24: 41-64.

McEachern, A.W. and R. Bauzer. 1967. "Factors Related to Disposition in Juvenile Police Contacts" in Klein, M. and B. Meyerhoff (eds.), *Juvenile Gangs in Context: Theory, Research and Action*. Englewood Cliffs: Prentice-Hall.

Meade, A. 1973. "Seriousness of Delinquency, the Adjudicative Decision and Recidivism—A Longitudinal Configuration Analysis." *Journal of Criminal Law and Criminology*. 64: 478-485.

Pawlak, E.J. 1977. "Differential Selection of Juveniles for Detention." *Journal of Research in Crime and Delinquency*. 15: 153-165.

Poole, E.D. and R.M. Regoli. 1980. "An Analysis of the Determinants of Juvenile Court Dispositions." *Juvenile and Family Court Journal*. 16: 23-32.

Reed, W.L. 1984. "Racial Differentials in Juvenile Court Decision-making Final Report." Washington: U.S. Department of Justice, National Institute for Juvenile Justice and Delinquency Prevention.

Sampson, R. 1986. "Crime in Cities: Formal and Informal Social Control" in Reiss, A. Jr. and M. Tonry (eds.), *Crime and Justice: An Annual Review of Research. Vol. 8, Communities and Crime.* Chicago: University of Chicago Press.

Schuster, R.L. 1981. "Black and White Violent Delinquents: A Longitudinal Cohort Study" in McNeely, R.L. and C.E. Pope (eds.), *Race, Crime and Criminal Justice.* Beverly Hills: Sage.

Smith, D.A. 1986. "The Neighborhood Context of Police Behavior" in Reiss, A. Jr. and M. Tonry (eds.), *Crime and Justice: An Annual Review of Research. Vol. 8. Communities and Crime.* Chicago: University of Chicago Press.

Strasburg, P.A. 1984. "Recent National Trends in Serious Juvenile Crime" in Mathias, R. *et al.* (eds.), *Violent Juvenile Offenders: An Anthology.* San Francisco: National Council on Crime and Delinquency.

Sumner, H. 1970. *Locking Them Up.* Davis: Council on Crime and Delinquency, Western Region.

Terry, R.M. 1967a. "Discrimination in the Handling of Juvenile Offenders By Social Control Agencies." *Journal of Research in Crime and Delinquency.* 5: 218-230.

.... 1967b. "The Screening of Juvenile Offenders." *Journal of Criminal Law, Criminology and Police Science.* 58: 173-181.

Thomas, C.W. and R.J. Cage. 1977. "The Effect of Social Characteristics on Juvenile Court Dispositions." *Sociology Quarterly.* 18: 237-252.

Thornberry, T.P. 1973. "Race, Socioeconomic Status and Sentencing in the Juvenile Justice System." *Journal of Criminal Law and Criminology.* 64: 90-98.

Thornberry, T.P. and M. Farnworth. 1982. "Social Correlates of Criminal Involvement: Further Evidence of the Relationship Between Social Status and Criminal Behavior." *American Sociological Review.* 47: 508-518.

Tittle, C.R., W.J. Villemez and D.A. Smith. 1978. "The Myth of Social Class and Criminality." *American Sociological Review.* 43: 643-656.

U.S. Department of Justice. 1985. *Children in Custody.* Washington: Bureau of Justice Statistics.

Wellford, C. 1975. "Labelling Theory and Criminology: An Assessment." *Social Problems.* 22: 332-345.

Wilson, J.Q. 1968. "The Police and the Delinquent in Two Cities," in Wheeler S. (ed.), *Controlling Delinquents.* New York: John Wiley.

Wolfgang, M.E., R.M. Figlio and T. Sellin. 1972. *Delinquency in a Birth Cohort.* Chicago: University of Chicago Press.

CHAPTER 7

RACE, ETHNICITY AND THE SPATIAL DYNAMIC: TOWARD A REALISTIC STUDY OF BLACK CRIME, CRIME VICTIMIZATION AND CRIMINAL JUSTICE PROCESSING OF BLACKS

DANIEL E. GEORGES-ABEYIE
FLORIDA STATE UNIVERSITY

Data on the disproportionality of minority criminality in general, and black criminality in particular, are readily available. Federal, state, and local crime reports document the apparent "tendency" for blacks to be involved in crime and their preponderance in criminal victimization, arrest and conviction statistics. Jurists such as New York State Supreme Court Justice Bruce Wright, former Detroit Records Court Justice (now Congressman) George W. Crockett and former Maryland Justice Joseph C. Howard contend that while Blacks are disproportionately included among the ranks of crime perpetrators and victims, justice is not color-blind (see Georges-Abeyie, 1984a; Ware, 1976; Howard, 1967, 1975). That thesis is also shared by Harvard Law Professor Derrick Bell (1973a, 1973b) and scores of other academicians (*e.g.*, Long, Long, Leon and Weston, 1975; Christianson, 1984; McNeely and Pope, 1981; Baldus, Pulaski and Woodworth, 1983; Georges-Abeyie, 1984b, and the criminal justice "brain trust" of the United States House of Representatives). However, the thesis of a racially conscious criminal justice system has been challenged, in part by the claims of Rand Corporation social scientist Joan Petersilia (1984; 1985; 1988) and in total by Florida International University's William Wilbanks (1987). Petersilia's 1983 study asserts the following:

(1) minority suspects were more likely than whites to be released after arrest; however, after a felony conviction, minority offenders were more likely than whites to be given longer sentences and to be put in prison instead of jail;

(2) in certain states, racial differences in post-sentencing treatment existed in the form of length of sentence served;

---

* Originally published in *Social Justice*, Vol. 16, No. 4: 35-54 (1989).
Reprinted by permission of Global Options.

(3) high post-arrest release rates for minorities do not indicate that police overarrest minorities in proportion to the kind and amount of crime they actually commit;
(4) there are some evident racial differences in criminal motivation, weapons use, and prison behavior, but most are not statistically significant; and
(5) controlling for the other major factors that might influence sentencing and time served, we found that minorities receive harsher sentences and serve longer in prison, all other things being equal. However, racial differences in plea bargaining and jury trials may explain some of the differences in length and type of sentence (Georges-Abeyie, 1984b: 27-29).

In a later study on sentencing and parole reform based on certain guidelines, Petersilia (1988) challenges claims that such guidelines discriminate against blacks. She found that key predictors associated with crime, upon which the guidelines are based, are more prevalent among blacks than among whites. She concludes that racial disparity, not discrimination is the result. Her study of racial equity in sentencing showed that for certain crimes a higher percentage of black and Latino offenders were sentenced to prison than were other offenders. It also showed that certain factors could predict whether a person would be placed on probation or sent to prison, as well as the length of term imposed for those offenders who were imprisoned. In California, however, race did not appear to affect sentencing once other legal "cognizable factors" were controlled for.

Wilbanks argues that the U.S. criminal justice system is essentially "race blind" in its "official" processing of blacks, and that if, or when, race is a factor, the system often operates in a racially biased manner that is less punitive toward the black offender than toward his/her white counterpart. Thus, Wilbanks rejects what he has labeled the "discrimination thesis," that is, the reality of a systematic, systemic racially discriminatory criminal justice system. The Wilbanks thesis, which is a variant of an earlier thesis put forth by Hindelang (1984), correctly notes disproportionate black involvement in Federal Bureau of Investigation Part One offenses. Petersilia rightly notes (as does Wilbanks) that "official" criminal justice agency data on the official, formal processing of blacks might not document discrimination in a "systematic," "systemic" racially conscious manner. The underlying question is: do the Hindelang/Petersilia/Wilbanks findings further society's comprehension of the dynamic of black crime perpetration, criminal victimization and criminal justice agency processing of black suspects and convicted felons and misdemeanants? Further, does the Hindelang/Petersilia/Wilbanks thesis further comprehension of black fear of the police, courts, and corrections — especially among low-income blacks? I think not. In fact, the current array of popular criminological and criminal justice theories fail, for the most part, to offer insight into the dynamic of black criminality, victimization and criminal justice processing because they:

(1) lack a social ecological perspective;
(2) too often focus on the formal decision in the processing of blacks; and
(3) analyze blacks as an ethnic monolith who are often caught up in a criminal justice system which is really a morass of disjointed, interconnected agencies involving both an informal and formal decision making process.

CURRENT CRIMINOLOGICAL/CRIMINAL JUSTICE THEORIES

A cursory review of popular criminology and criminal justice texts[1] and journals[2] reveals the following as the most popular criminology/criminal justice orientations:

(1) psychological and biological explanations that center on personality traits and inner controls developed through the process of socialization during early childhood (Hirschi, 1969), or criminogenic factors associated with temperament, IQ and hormonal abnormalities (Wilson and Herrnstein, 1985); and

(2) sociological explanations that focus on anomie (Merton, 1968), subculture (including the incongruence of being lower class with middle-class values and aspirations [Cohen, 1955]), techniques of neutralization (Sykes and Matza, 1970), differential opportunity (Cloward and Ohlin, 1960), lower-class valuation (Miller, 1970), economic or political power deprivation (Sellin, 1938; Turk, 1971, 1982), differential association (Sutherland and Cressey, 1978) and labeling (Becker, 1963).

What each of these contemporary approaches lacks is:

(1) a social-ecological sensitivity cognizant of diverse black ethnicity, which might result in research that identifies black ethnic specific rates of offending behavior as well as differentials in the processing of ethnic-specific black individuals;

(2) differentials in site and situational realities associated with the rates of crime commission within and outside the spatial domain of the black ghetto and the slum-ghetto; and

(3) possible differentiation in how the criminal justice system processes black suspects who reside within (or outside) the varied spatial domain of the black ghetto and the slum-ghetto.

RACE DOES NOT EQUAL ETHNICITY: REJECTION OF THE BLACK ETHNIC MONOLITH PARADIGM

Wilbanks, Petersilia, Hindelang and others have characterized. black criminality, criminal victimization and criminal justice processing as if Negroid (i.e., black) racial identity equates to ethnic homogeneity. Blacks, however, manifest varied ethnic identities, and these varied black ethnic groups might manifest different rates of criminality and criminal victimization, as well as what Emory Bogardus refers to as "social distance."

In 1926, Bogardus noted the reality and importance of social distance when discussing desired interaction between different ethnic and racial groups. Social distance may be defined as "the degree of closeness or remoteness one desires in interaction with members of a particular group" (Parrillo, 1985: 491). Many factors are involved in the construct of "social distance." They include:

(1) the extent of physiognomic, phrenologic and anatomic difference (skeletal difference), some of which may be viewed as atavisms by the culturally dominant group;

(2) perceived extent of "contributions" to the national development;

(3) perceived extent of cultural and social network differences between minority/out-groups versus majority/in-groups;
(4) perceived threat to the social order;
(5) perceived criminality; and
(6) perceived "intrinsic worth."

Ethnicity and perceived social distance are interconnected; ethnicity affects social distance and social distance may impact perceived "ethnicity." Ethnicity was defined by Gordon (1964) as the intersection of race, nation of origin and religion (a cultural variable). Thus, a traditional application of black ethnic identity would be cognizant of blacks of Caribbean, African, Central and South American origin (e.g., Puerto Rican, Virgin Islands, African-American, Dutch Antilles and so on). The parameters of these cultural-social-spatial identities define more than the contours of national origins; they are the nexus of profound cultural variables such as religion.

Thus, one can, and should, be cognizant of black Puerto Ricans, Cubans, Virgin Islanders, Jamaicans, Africans, African-Americans and others with very different religious traditions (e.g., Protestant, Catholic, Muslim, Baha'i and Jewish). However, black ethnic identities are further subdivided by color and hue realities that affect social networking which ranges from informal social clubs and cliques to formal legal arrangements such as marriage. These color and hue realities engender such social classifications as *moreno, mulatto, blanco sucio, negro* and *pardo*. The ethnic divisions in the Cuban-American community, such as *Marielitos* and Castro-era refugees, mirror social-cultural-spatial realities which include race, color and hue. Linguistic production of the terms Continentals (U.S.-born persons of a West Indian and/or Puerto Rican heritage) and Islanders (native-born persons) within these Caribbean cultures amply demonstrates these social realities along the axes of color and ethnicity. These terms have different meanings in the context of West Indian society, in contrast to their use in Puerto Rico. For a West Indian, these terms refer to intraracial, ethnic identities. For a Puerto Rican, these terms are used to distinguish both inter- and intraracial ethnic identities. The Puerto Rican manifestation of this is reflected in underground Puerto Rican organizations such as the U.S.-spawned Armed Forces for National Liberation (FALN) and the *Macheteros*, which originated in Puerto Rico.

African-American ethnic identifiers often modify as they elaborate upon the classic tripartite ethnic definition bounded by religion, nation of origin and race. These identifiers encompass not only color and hue; they also often distinguish individuals along regional and class lines, as well as on a multitude of indigenous factors. Predominantly geographic "tags" distinguish, for example, between suburban versus urban origin and rearing; East Coast versus West Coast; Southern versus Northern or Midwestern origin, and even ghetto versus slum-ghetto, or non-ghetto origin and rearing. The ghetto versus slum-ghetto, and/or ghetto versus non-ghetto delineators have undergone further development, which can be described as containing an ethclass dimension. This is an economic dimension, characterized by intergenerational poverty, which might be best described in terms of ethcaste parameters.

Thus, should social distance be significant within and between black ethnic groups, then is it not possible that social distance between blacks and whites might impact every phase of the processing of black ethnics? Is it not also conceivable that different black ethnic groups are more involved in extralegal and illegal activity than are others, and that certain black ethnics dominate certain criminal activities (or are believed to) and are thus viewed as more threatening than are other black ethnics (e.g., Jamaican versus Hispanic, African-American versus British West Indian, "dark-skinned" Negroids versus what some blacks have derisively labeled "high yellas" and "brights")? In fact, social distance may influence perceived ethnicity to the extent that black law violators are automatically assumed to be of a specific ethnic origin, that is, labeled Jamaican versus Virgin Islander (when an accent is noted), *Marielito* versus Castro-era Cubano, Afro-American versus West Indian, slum-ghetto versus black suburbanite.

If one can speak of varied white ethnic traditions that include criminal and extralegal behaviors — for example, the criminally violent "Okie" traditions of California's San Joaquin Valley, the "hillbilly" tradition of "moonshining," the "swampbilly" and "swamp rat" traditions of the South Carolina and Georgia lowlands, as well as of the Florida Everglades — then is it not conceivable that certain black ethnics (including the allegedly "crime-prone" Carolina Geechee-Gullah Maroons and Louisiana Creoles) might also be the victims of negative out-group labeling dynamics which lead to invidious processing by the criminal justice system?

The Spatial Factor and Its Significance in Criminal Justice Processing of Black Defendants

Racial segregation has been the spatial reality of American cities from the nation's earliest urbanization (Taeuber and Taeuber, 1965; Weaver, 1967; Wade, 1964; Hawley and Rock, 1973; Johnson, 1972; Spear, 1967; Osofsky, 1968). *De jure* realities established and enforced racial segregation (Bell, 1973b; Long, Long, Leon and Weston, 1975) until the tumultuous 1960s and early 1970s. Contemporary social distance realities (i.e., *de facto* customary practices) maintain a U.S. urbanscape marked by ghettoization and slum-ghettos. However, ghettos (zones of minority-group residential dominance with adequate housing and related characteristics) and slum-ghettos (zones of minority-group residential dominance denoted by inadequate housing, high morbidity and infant mortality rates and related social pathologies) vary in the extent of minority-group residential dominance (Forman, 1971). Black ghetto and slum-ghetto morphologies (Rose, 1971; Grodzins, 1958; Taeuber and Taeuber, 1965; Georges-Abeyie, 1981) are characterized by:

(1) a Zone of Transition, that is, those spatial units in which 30 percent to 49 percent of the resident population is black. This is not a true ghetto or slum-ghetto manifestation. This is the territory rapidly being incorporated into the ghetto or slum-ghetto fringe;

(2) a ghetto/slum-ghetto fringe, that is, those spatial units in which the population is 50 percent to 74 percent black; and

(3) a ghetto/slum-ghetto core, that is, those spatial units in which the population is 75 percent to 100 percent black.

The concept of ghetto/slum-ghetto morphology is important because of the site and situational advantages (or disadvantages) associated with such residential zones. Site is the exact physical location of an event, and situation means the accessibility between two or more sites. Thus, when black crime is discussed, one might note:

(1) the site of the crime's occurrence;
(2) the site of the offender's residence;
(3) the site of the victim's residence;
(4) the site of the initial, or subsequent, encounters between the victim and the assailant;
(5) the degree of difficulty in movement, or extent of distance between the site of victimization and the site of the offender's residence;
(6) the site of the jurors' or jurists' residence; and
(7) the situational factors associated with any of the previously noted sites.

The site of the event, arrest, or of the offender's residence might affect the degree of threat jurors or jurists perceive when reviewing the particulars of a given case. The severity of the threat, anxiety, or danger perceived by the juror or jurist may, in part, be influenced by the zone in which the juror or jurist resides. For example, the juror or jurist may perceive more threat, anxiety, or fear if s/he resides within the same morphological zone of the same ghetto or slum-ghetto, or the same morphological zone of a different ghetto or slum-ghetto as the victim or alleged offender. The more dissimilar the jurors' or jurists' zone of residence is from the site of the criminal event (or site of the alleged criminal's arrest), or the greater the physical distance the juror's or jurist's residence is from the site of the criminal event (or site of the alleged offender's arrest), the less threat the juror or jurist might perceive (i.e., the "distance decay" factor). The more threat, anxiety and fear experienced by the juror (or perhaps the jurist), the less rigorous the evidence need be to convict a defendant regarded as socially distant from the juror or jurist. Also, the less social distance felt by the juror or jurist toward the victim, perhaps the less rigorous need be the evidence for conviction — especially if the juror or jurist perceives great social distance toward the defendant. These site and situational factors compounded by social distance determinants might influence the criminal justice system at all levels of formal and informal decision making — from the initial police response to a call for help, to an issuance of work assignments in the correctional setting, to the decision to parole or not parole a convicted felon.

The varied black ethnic groups may manifest different degrees of social distance toward other black ethnics. In fact, it is conceivable that the ethclass identification of a given member of a black ethnic group may result in that individual feeling considerable social distance toward other members of one's own ethnic group, that is, one might "out-reference" and thus manifest extreme punitive behavior when involved in discretionary situations which involve members of one's own ethnic group. Georges-Abeyie (1981: 101) noted that:

> ...neither the anthropologist, the geographer, nor the social ecologist has examined the relationship of crime to the various zones of black racial ethnic residential dominance....

The urban anthropologist Valentine (1970) noted that black ethnic diversity leads to differing mechanisms of internal community control. The inference is that crime rates may vary with different black ethnic groups, as well as with the extent of black ethnic heterogeneity within the various social-ecological zones of black residential dominance. Thus, the following have been studied with regard to black criminality, criminal justice processing, and criminal victimization:

(1) patterns of white-black (victim-offender) victimization (Davis, 1976; Curtis, 1974, 1975; Georges and Kirksey, 1978);

(2) perceptions of crime in ghetto communities (Knowles and Brewer, 1973);

(3) (rudimentary) acknowledgement of differential nonwhite ethnic group crime rates within nonwhite communities (Kleinman and David, 1973);

(4) the issue of race, status, and criminal arrest (Green, 1970);

(5) racism and discrimination as manifested within the (official decision-making process) of the U.S. criminal justice (system) in such areas as the law, the courts, and sentencing (Crockett, 1969, 1971; Staples, 1975; Somerville, 1968; Lundsgaarde, 1973; Burns, 1973; Bell, 1973a; Thornberry, 1973; Howard, 1975; Carroll and Mondrick, 1976; Jordon, 1974; Long *et al.*, 1975);

(6) minorities as victims of police brutality and other police irregularities (Goldkamp, 1976; Hahn, 1971);

(7) minority attitudes and perceptions of the criminal justice process and the law (Martin and McConnell, 1972; Davis, 1974; Jacob, 1971; Thomas, Cage and Foster, 1976; Hindelang, Gottfredson, Dunn and Parisi, 1973, 1974, 1975, 1976; Furstenberg and Wellford, 1973; Kuykendall, 1970; Hahn, 1971; Knowles and Brewer, 1973; Block, 1974; Smith and Hawkins, 1973); and

(8) studies of black police self-images (Bannon and Witt, 1973; Sax, 1968; Alex, 1982).

However, the research modalities utilized by contemporary social scientists, including Wilbanks (1987) and Petersilia (1984, 1985, 1988), assume ghetto, slum-ghetto and black ethnic uniformity. They ignore the interface of social distance and the complexity of black ethnic diversity and social-ecological morphology. They do not examine the dysfunctional impact of black ethnic heterogeneity within the given morphological zones of a ghetto or slum-ghetto, nor do they examine the site and situational factors within these specific morphological zones. They do not examine the importance of the impact of site and situational factors upon criminal justice practitioners charged with social control activities within the spatial domains of the ghetto and slum-ghetto. They do not examine the interface or site, situation, social morphology and juror/jurist behavior when different black ethnics are involved as defendants.

Significance of Black Ethnic Diversity — The Role of Extralegal Social Controls

If black ethnic diversity is real within the social-ecological zones of a given black ghetto or slum-ghetto, then various extralegal and informal social controls — including ridicule, ostracism, corporal punishment and praise — might be more deficient in some black ghettos and slum-ghettos than others. Extralegal and informal social controls are important mechanisms utilized by the socialization process, which in turn influences the formulation of personality. Black ethnic diversity might also affect the rigor of formal and informal Neighborhood Watch activities, as well as the decision to come (or not to come) to the assistance of a neighbor involved in a criminal incident.

Systematic, Systemic and Capricious Discrimination: The Role of Petit Apartheid Practices and the "Why" of Black Alienation from the U.S. Criminal Justice System

The Hindelang/Petersilia/Wilbanks thesis rejects the existence of systematic or systemic racially discriminatory practices within the U.S. criminal justice system. Petersilia is especially careful to confine her findings and conclusions to specific states — Texas, Michigan and California. Yet, together, they limit their criminal justice analyses to discriminatory practices that are easily defined and observed in the formal decision-making process. The first issue is: what is systematic and/or systemic bias? Current U.S. law and jurisprudence cannot be technically considered "apartheid," since there is only one set of laws and formal legal practices are applicable to whites as well as to blacks and other nonwhites. However, the criminal justice documents Capital *Punishment* (see Schlesinger, 1982) and *Sourcebook of Criminal Justice Statistics* (see Flannagan and Jamieson, 1988) note that certain legal sanctions, such as capital punishment for forcible rape of adult white females, have been almost exclusively reserved for black and other nonwhite offenders. Once sentenced to die, a black is much less likely to have a sentence commuted than is a comparable white person.

Studies that purport to examine racial equity in sentencing note that certain objective non-racial factors appear to be highly correlated with the length of term imposed for those offenders who are imprisoned. These variables include:

(1) having multiple current conviction counts;
(2) having prior prison terms and juvenile incarcerations;
(3) being on adult and/or juvenile probation at the time of arrest;
(4) having been released from prison within 12 months of arrest;
(5) using a weapon;
(6) having a history of drug and/or alcohol addiction;
(7) being over 21 years old;
(8) going to trial and not being released prior to trial; and
(9) having been represented by a public defender.

Perhaps none of these factors could be legitimately used to validate a "discrimination thesis" couched in the rhetoric of systematic and/or systemic bias in the formal decision making practices of the U.S. criminal justice system. The *Webster's New Twentieth Century Dictionary, Unabridged* (1983: 1853) defines "systematic" as:

(1) forming or constituting a system;
(2) based on or involving a system;

(3) made or arranged according to a system, method, or plan; regular or orderly;
(4) characterized by the use of method or orderly planning, methodical;
(5) of or having to do with classification....

"Systemic" is defined by *Webster's* (*ibid.*) as "pertaining to a system."

The essence of the concepts "systematic" and "systemic" is regularity and predictability, that is, if this, then that. Certainly, the U.S. criminal justice system is more a process of interrelated but distinct legal entities than a "true" system. Racist decisions, especially formalized, legally sanctioned decisions involving blacks and other nonwhites, are not predictable. This lack of predictability, however, should not be interpreted as an absence of prejudice or racism. American prejudice (an attitude) is not always made manifest via racism (a behavior). Westie (1965) notes that prejudice can be masked by "general valuations" (i.e., generally verbalized beliefs such as the belief in "equality," "universal brotherhood" and "fair play"); yet, it can be contradicted, in part or in total, via "specific valuations" which express social distance toward certain low-status ethnic groups (e.g. opposition to interracial marriage between blacks and whites or a belief in the greater intrinsic worth or intelligence of whites versus blacks). Westie's acknowledgement of incongruence between general and specific valuations can be taken one step further by noting the *actualization* of the "specific valuation," that is, by noting behavior. The failure of a jury or judge to convict a black person who victimizes another black, or of a non-black who victimizes a black, may not represent an absence of racism but rather the expression of the actualization of a specific valuation, of a social distance which values black life less than white life.

A decision to parole or pardon a black convicted felon, or to sentence such a felon to fewer years than one would a white counterpart with a comparable record, might again be an *actualization* of a negative specific valuation, tempered by social distance, and the juror's (or jurist's) realization that most Part One Index offenses are bound by racial segregation and income realities. Most Index offenses are intraracial and within the same socioeconomic class (robbery and arson may be two exceptions). The absence of predictability in the expression of the "specific valuation" (i.e., in the actualization of the specific valuation) obliges social scientists to question the attribute of "objectivity" associated with "objective" social science methodologies and modalities — such as the "objective" guidelines that eliminate or limit discretion in sentencing. Social scientists must be cognizant of the reality that some acts of law violation are viewed as lesser offending behaviors, as lesser contracultural modalities punished under criminal law statutes, or even treated as tort violations with relatively limited penalties.

Other criminal "modalities" — those disproportionately "perpetrated" by the poor and thus the nonwhite — are considered so dangerous and so injurious that they, in theory, offend the state and are punished as felonies. No objective guideline can be truly racially and ethnically blind if certain racial or ethnic groups, because of their intergenerational socioeconomic status and culture, are compelled or enticed into the very behaviors indexed by objective sentencing or arrest guidelines. Such guidelines are merely indices of race, ethnicity and class, if not color-caste.

Thus, the "real" factors that disproportionately predispose various black ethnic youth to the formal processing of a nondiscriminatory criminal justice system are the labeling of certain behaviors as contracultural (Curtis, 1975), deviant and/or criminal, and the reality of poverty and other slum-ghetto social "pathologies." The poor disproportionately commit criminal violence (which gets reported) and certain property offenses, resulting in their early, youthful immersion into the criminal justice system. *They are processed early and often*. Discretionary decisions by law enforcement officers define their youthful transgressions as "motor vehicle theft" (a felony) rather than "unlawful use of a motor vehicle" (a misdemeanor), "assault" (a felony) rather than "disorderly conduct" (a misdemeanor) and the like. The court funnels these youth under *parens patriae* authority into juvenile services and criminal court rather than into diversion programs. Understaffed public defender agencies too often short-shrift their clients into plea bargains that assure early criminal records. Health care providers (doctors, nurses, psychiatric social workers) note bruised and battered Black flesh at public and private hospitals, and report questionable causations for such wounds to law enforcement authorities — an action that might result in frequent or early arrests of minority adults and youths. Public school teachers and administrators often act in similar ways.

The answer to why many low-income blacks are alienated from the agencies of formal social control (i.e., the police, the courts, etc.) lies in an examination of the racial and ethnic composition of the agents who make up these agencies, as well as in the many petit apartheid realities low-status blacks face on a daily basis. Social control institutions tend to select the most middle-class (or middle-class oriented) Eurocentric blacks available in the minority applicant pool. This selection is assured by a battery of "objective" testing procedures followed by face-to-face interviews. Should progressively oriented departments be cognizant of the need for bilingual or multilingual agents, their selection procedures often remain monocultural and ethnocentric. Are Eurocentric, "objective" test procedures cognizant of the predominantly single-sex orientation of low-status Caribbean recreational institutions, which validate the playing of cards and dominoes, and the consumption of alcohol on the stoop, or the act of just "hanging out" on street corners, rather than bringing males into the home? What is "respectful" in one culture may be considered contracultural in another. Do social control agencies make a concerted effort to select agents who are cognizant of the simple fact that slum-ghetto dwellings lack usable recreation space such as basements and family rooms? Thus, young men are forced outdoors. Are social control agencies cognizant of (much less respectful of) the various informal social controls utilized by different black ethnic groups? Do these agencies realize that virtually every slum-ghetto black youth experiences multidimensional "value-space" (Curtis, 1975) — that is, they embrace the value-space of the dominant WASP middle-aged, male-dominated culture, their own lower-class "subculture" and the contracultural values of toughness, suspicion of the motives of others, pride in physical prowess and fatalism, all of which are instrumental for survival in slum-ghetto environs? Do these agencies realize that blacks of specific ethnic origin often know pals only by their first name or nickname and have no idea of the exact street address of their "homeboy's" residence? That some suspects are not "running a game" when they say they need bail in order to "secure" (i.e., locate) their alibi?

What of the almost omnipresent reality, or threat, of petit apartheid, that is, the informal practices of criminal justice agents and agencies, which include selectively inhumane and demeaning behavior by law enforcement, court and corrections officials directed at nonwhite suspects and arrestees? These acts of intimidation and cruelty are seldom mandated as official agency policy. They may be in the form of insults, rude or indifferent behavior, posturing, or spoken communication. Petit apartheid may also take the form of the decision to stop and question or to stop and frisk. A case in point is the 1988 City of Philadelphia American Civil Liberties Union (ACLU) agreement to halt the Philadelphia Police Department's practice of stopping and questioning black males between the ages of 20 to 40 years of age, ranging in height from five-feet-four-inches to five-feet-ten-inches, and weighing from 120 to 160 pounds, who happened to be in Philadelphia's Center City. The practice became more pervasive when the police were investigating the Center City "stalker incidents." The unofficial search-and-question technique was initiated in an attempt to apprehend a slender black male who was suspected of raping eight females, one Hispanic and seven white.[3] Petit apartheid appears to have also been the reality in suburban Pittsburgh during 1987, when the Homestead Police Department officers made late night, door-to-door requests of all black males in the township to voluntarily submit to fingerprinting and blood tests. The initiative was in response to a series of rapes of elderly white females (and one elderly black female) by a man wearing a ski mask who had a "black-sounding voice."[4] Petit apartheid may have also been the reality of the Lower Providence Township (Montgomery County, Pennsylvania) Police Department's alleged practice of stopping automobiles with "black interiors," that is, with black motorists.[5]

The very wording of the jury's charge may be expressed in terms of considerable social distance toward the defendant, and thus "closeness" toward the defenders of the social order. All of these formal or informal wordings and behaviors may manifest petit apartheid realities. The defendant's opportunity, or lack thereof, to dress appropriately or to not be shackled when first presented to the jury (i.e., the moment a person may "shuffle" or walk into court from the "waiting pen") may be a manifestation of petit apartheid realities that subliminally affect the determinations of both jurors and jurists.

Conclusion

A realistic study of black crime, the criminal victimization of blacks, or the criminal justice system processing of black suspects and defendants must be cognizant of the following:

(1) black ethnic diversity, meaning race does not equate ethnicity;

(2) social distance realities among diverse black ethnic groups, as well as between blacks and whites;

(3) the multidimensional "value-space" which afflicts slum-ghetto black ethnics, a value-space that results in anomie and some contracultural behaviors which may be "criminalizable;"

(4) formal and informal petit apartheid decisions that alienate, anger and often

inflame seemingly minor black-white encounters into more serious conflict situations;

(5) ethnocentric behaviors and beliefs by white agents (or Eurocentric nonwhite agents) of social control who devalue black ethnic cultural expressions and even view some of these subcultural and contracultural traditions as criminally deviant;

(6) the difference between "general valuations," "specific valuations" and the *actualization* of negative "specific valuations," tempered by majority race feelings of considerable social distance toward blacks as well as white expressions of ethnocentrism;

(7) the social-ecological morphology of the ghetto and slum-ghetto, a morphology that results in the establishment of a ghetto transition zone, fringe and core, as well as in differential rates of offending behaviors within each of these zones;

(8) a social-ecological ghetto and slum-ghetto morphology that results in a differential site and situational advantages;

(9) possible differentials in rates of offending behavior by different black ethnic groups;

(10) the false premise of sentencing guidelines and other "objective" criminal justice modalities which are really indices of socioeconomic and racial/ethnic stratification that have taken on color-caste dimensions;

(11) the reality that "objective" guidelines and modalities are not color, race,, ethnic, caste, or class-blind if they directly relate to when and how certain racial, ethnic, or color-caste out-groups become tracked within the criminal justice system;

(12) the importance of the difficult-to-measure, informal criminal justice system decisions which affect black ethnic suspects and offenders from the initial law enforcement response to a call to the decision to grant (or not to grant) parole; and

(13) the need to restructure the concept of ethnicity so that it applies to the African-American experience, and thus does not merely rely upon the traditional tripartite construct of race, nation of origin and religion.

If advertising agencies are cognizant of the conscious as well as the subliminal impact of social distance, race-ethnicity and general physical appearance in the decision-making habits of the American public; if the jury selection process (including preemptory eliminations) is based on skin color, specific religious or political affiliation, or social affinity; if popular mass media magazines, television programming, cinema and audio recordings are cognizant of the power of imagery, which includes the presentation of Eurocentric values, beliefs, and appearances; if "television influences attitudes toward racial or ethnic groups by the status of the parts assigned to their members, the kind of behavior they display within these parts, or even the type of products they promote" (Parrillo, 1985: 65-67); and if phenotype-based ethnic differences have been utilized, such as was employed in the classification of Arizona prisoners then is it not conceivable that black racial and ethnic indicators may consciously or subliminally influence the decision-makers within the U.S. criminal justice system during all or some of its formal and informal processes — even those "objective" processes that focus on formal, easily observed and recorded "empiricisms"? Racially and ethnically impacted empirical procedures that are directly related to when and how often blacks are processed by social control agencies are indices of racial and ethnic discrimination, not just of racial and ethnic disproportionality. Institutional racism is concerned with impact, with result, not intent. Institutions that subordinate individuals because of their race or factors directly related to race (Downs, 1976) are institutionally racist. Thus, "objective" sentencing procedures or petit apartheid law enforcement practices are institutionally racist in impact, if not always in intent.

ENDNOTES

1. For this manuscript, the author conducted a survey of over 40 criminology and criminal justice texts published by leading U.S. publishers.

2. The following journals were reviewed: *Criminology; Journal of Police Studies; Social Justice; Crime and Delinquency; Journal of Research in Crime and Delinquency; Journal of Criminal Law and Criminology; Justice Quarterly News Magazine; Corrections; Police Chief; and Federal Probation.*

3. The so-called Center City "stalker incidents" were covered extensively by *The Philadelphia Inquirer* and *The Philadelphia Tribune* (see, e.g. *The Philadelphia Tribune*, [1988: 1A]). The Center City "stalker incidents," according to Mr. Stefan Presser, who is the Pennsylvania ACLU Legal Director and Chief Attorney on these cases, involved the questioning of 269 black "suspects" not taken into custody, and the taking into custody of 113 additional suspects. The Center City "stalker incidents" involved the wholesale suspension of the Fourth Amendment rights of black males. The City and the ACLU are currently in negotiation for an out-of-court financial settlement for the abuse of numerous black "suspects." Two other petit apartheid incidents involving the City of Philadelphia are noteworthy. "Operation Cold Turkey" (a police label), according to Mr. Presser, involved the round-up of more than 100 Hispanic youths because of the murder of a white police officer in the predominantly Hispanic neighborhood of Spring Garden. The race and ethnicity of the original suspect or suspects were unknown by the Philadelphia Police Department. The case resulted in an out-of-court settlement of over $50,000 by the City of Philadelphia to Hispanic litigants ("suspects"). The City is also involved in a $500,000 settlement for its unlawful stopping of over 1,400 nonwhites (primarily blacks) at 48 intersections within Philadelphia during the police search for the Center City "stalker incidents." All three of the aforementioned incidents involved the abridgement of Fourth Amendment rights of black males and are examples of the petit apartheid realities too often faced by blacks in the U.S.

4. This policy was instituted during the stewardship of Homestead Police Chief Christopher Kelly, currently with the Baldwin Borough Police Department.

5. In November of 1987, the Pennsylvania Human Relations Commission was scheduled to open hearings on the allegations of the aforementioned petit apartheid practices of the

Lower Providence Township Police Department. Two federal lawsuits have been filed in U.S. District Court, in Philadelphia, alleging racial bias in the ticketing of black motorists in Lower Providence Township of Montgomery County. One lawsuit was brought by a group of black motorists; the other by six white former Lower Providence police officers.

REFERENCES

Alex, N. 1982. *Black in Blue.* Englewood Cliffs: Prentice-Hall.

Baldus, D.C., C. Pulaski and G. Woodworth. 1983. "Comparative Review of Death Sentences: An Empirical Study of the Georgia Experience." *Journal of Criminal Law and Criminology.* 74: 661-725.

Bannon, J.D. and G.M. Witt. 1973. "Black Policeman: A Study of Self-Images." *Journal of Police Science and Administration.* 1: 21-29.

Becker, H.D. 1963. *Outsiders: Studies in the Sociology of Deviance.* New York: Free Press.

Bell, D.A. 1973a. *Race, Racism, and American Law.* Boston: Little, Brown and Company.

.... 1973b. "Racism in American Courts: Cause for Black Disruption or Despair?" *California Law Review.* 65: 165-203.

Block, R. 1974. "Why Notify the Police: The Victim's Decision to Notify the Police of an Assault." *Criminology.* 11: 555-569.

Burns, H. 1973. "Black People and the Tyranny of American Law." *Annals of the American Academy of Political and Social Science.* 401: 156-160.

Carroll, L. and M.E. Mondrick. 1976. "Racial Bias in the Decision to Grant Parole." *Law and Society Review.* 11,1: 93-107.

Christianson, S. 1984. "Our Black Prisons" in Georges-Abeyie, D. (ed.), *The Criminal Justice System and Blacks.* New York: Clark Boardman.

Cloward R.A. and L.E. Ohlin. 1960. *Delinquency and Opportunity: A Theory of Delinquent Gangs.* New York: Free Press.

Cohen, A.K. 1955. *Delinquent Boys: The Culture of the Gang.* New York: Free Press.

Crockett, G. 1984. "The Role of the Black Judge" in George-Abeyie, D. (ed.), *The Criminal Justice System and Blacks.* New York: Clark Boardman.

Crokett, G.W. 1969. "Racism in the Law." *Science and Society.* 33: 223-230.

.... 1971. "Racism in the Courts." *Journal of Public Law.* 20, 2: 385.

Curtis, L.A. 1974. *Criminal Violence.* Lexington: Lexington Books.

.... 1975. *Violence, Race, and Culture.* Lexington: Lexington Books.

Davis, J.A. 1974. "Justification for No Obligation: Views of Black Males Toward Crime and the Criminal Law." *Issues in Criminology.* 9: 69-84.

.... 1976. "Black Crime and American Culture." *Annals of the American Academy of Political and Social Science.* 4: 89-98.

Downs, A. 1976. *Urban Problems and Prospects* .2nd edition. Chicago: Rand McNally.

Flannagan, Timothy J. and M. Jamieson. 1988. *Sourcebook of Criminal Justice Statistics.* Washington: U.S. Department of Justice.

Forman, R.E. 1971. *Black Ghettos, White Ghettos, and Slums*. Englewood Cliffs: Prentice-Hall.

Furstenberg, F.F. and C.P. Wellford. 1973. "Calling the Police: The Evaluation of Police Service." *Law and Society Review*. 7, 3: 393-406.

Georges-Abeyie, D. 1981. "Studying Black Crime: A Realistic Approach" in Brantingham, P.J. and P.L. Brantingham (eds.), *Environmental Criminology*. Beverly Hills: Sage.

.... 1984a. "Interview with Judge Bruce McM. Wright" in Georges-Abeyie, D. (ed.), *The Criminal Justice System and Blacks*. New York: Clark Boardman.

.... 1984b. *The Criminal Justice System and Blacks*. New York: Clark Boardman.

Georges, D. and K. Kirksey. 1978. "Violent Crime Perpetrated against the Elderly in the City of Dallas, October 1974-September 1975." *Journal of Environmental Systems*. 7, 2: 149-197.

Goldkamp, J.S. 1976. "Minorities as Victims of Police Shootings: Interpretation of Racial Disproportionality and Police Use of Deadly Force." *Justice System Journal*. 2: 169-183.

Gordon, Milton Myron. 1964. *Assimilation in American Life: The Role of Race, Religion, and National Origins*. New York: Oxford University Press.

Green, E. 1970. "Race, Status, and Criminal Arrest." *American Sociological Review*. 35: 476-490.

Grodzins, M. 1958. *The Metropolitan Areas as a Racial Problem*. Pittsburgh: University of Pittsburgh.

Hahn, H. 1971. "Ghetto Assessments of Police Protection and Authority." *Law and Society Review*. 183: 183-193.

Hawley, A.H. and V.P. Rock. 1973. *Segregation in Residential Areas*. Washington: National Academy of Sciences.

Hindelang, M.J. 1984. "Variations in Sex-Race-Age Specific Incidence Rates of Offending" in Georges-Abeyie, D. *op. cit.*

Hindelang, M., R. Gottfredson, D.S. Dunn and N. Parisi. 1973. *Sourcebook of Criminal Justice Statistics*. Washington: Government Printing Office.

.... 1974. *Sourcebook of Criminal Justice Statistics*. Washington: Government Printing Office.

.... 1975. *Sourcebook of Criminal Justice Statistics*. Washington: Government Printing Office.

.... 1976. *Sourcebook of Criminal Justice Statistics*. Washington: Government Printing Office.

Hirschi, T. 1969. *Causes of Delinquency*. Los Angeles: University of California Press.

Howard, J.C. 1967. *The Administration of Rape Cases in the City of Baltimore and the State of Maryland*. Baltimore: Monumental Bar Association.

.... 1975. "Racial Discrimination in Sentencing." *Judicature*. 59, 3: 120-125.

Jacob, H. 1971. "Black and White Perceptions of Justice in the City." *Law and Society Review*. 6, 1: 69-89.

Johnson, J.W. 1972. *Black Mountain*. New York: Atheneum.

Jordon, V.E. 1974. "The Systems Propagates Crimes." *Crime and Delinquency*. 20, 3: 233-240.

Kleinman, P.H. and D.S. David. 1973. "Victimization and Perception of Crime in a Ghetto Community." *Criminology*. 11: 307-343.

Knowles, L. and J. Brewer. 1973. "The Black Community: Attitudes toward Community Problems, Crime, and the Police." *Police Chief*. 40: 48-51.

Kuykendall, J.L. 1970. "Police and Minority Groups: Toward a Theory of Negative Contacts." *Police* (September-October): 47-55.

Long, E, J. Long, W. Leon and P. Weston. 1975. *American Minorities: The Justice Issue.* Englewood Cliffs: Prentice-Hall.

Lundsgaarde, H.P. 1973. "Racial and Ethnic Classifications: An Appraisal of the Role of Anthropology in the Lawmaking Process." *Houston Law Review* (March).

Martin, J. and J. McConnell. 1972. "Black Militant Ideology and the Law." *Criminology.* 10: 111-116.

McNeely, R.L. and C.E. Pope (eds.). 1981. *Race, Crime and Criminal Justice.* Beverly Hills: Sage.

Merton, R. 1968. *Social Theory and Social Structure.* New York: Free Press.

Miller, W.B. 1970. "Lower-Class Culture as a Generating Milieu of Gang Delinquency" in Wolfgang, M.E. *et al.* (eds.), *The Sociology of Crime and Delinquency.* 2nd edition. New York. John Wiley.

Osofsky, G. 1968. Harlem: *The Making of a Ghetto.* New York: Harper Torchbooks.

Parrillo, V.N. 1985. *Strangers to These Shores* . 2nd edition. New York: John Wiley & Sons.

Petersilia, J. 1984. "Racial Disparities in the Criminal Justice System: Executive Summary of Rand Institute Study, 1983" in Georges-Abeyie, D. *op. cit.*

Petersilia, J., S. Klein, and S. Turner. 1988. *Racial Equity in Sentencing.* Santa Monica: Rand Corporation.

Petersilia, J. and S. Turner. 1985. *Guideline-Based Justice: The Implications for Racial Minorities.* Santa Monica: Rand Corporation.

Rist, R.C. 1970. "Student Social Class and Teacher Expectations: The Self-Fulfilling Prophecy in Ghetto Education." *Harvard Education Review.* 49, 3 (August): 411-451.

Rose, H.M. 1971. *The Black Ghetto.* New York: McGraw-Hill.

Sax, R.M. 1968. "... It Hurts to Be Black in Blue." *Issues in Criminology.* 4: 1-11.

Schlesinger, Steven R. 1982. *Capital Punishment: A National Prison Statistics Report.* Washington: U.S. Department of Justice.

Sellin, Thorsten. 1938. "Culture, Conflict, and Crime." *Social Science Research Council, Bulletin (No. 41).* New York.

Smith, P.W. and R.O. Hawkins. 1973. "Victimization, Types of Citizen-Police Contacts, and Attitudes toward the Police." *Law and Society Review.* 8, 1: 134-152.

Somerville, B. 1968. "Double Standards in Law Enforcement with Regard to Minority Status." *Issues in Criminology.* 4: 35-48.

Spear, A.H. 1967. *Black Chicago.* Chicago: University of Chicago.

Staples, R. 1975. "White Racism, Black Crime, and American Justice: An Application of the Colonial Model to Explain Crime and Race." *Phylon.* 36: 14-22.

Sutherland, E.H. and D. Cressey. 1978. *Criminology.* 10th edition. Philadelphia: Lippincott.

Sykes, O.M. and D. Matza. 1970. "Techniques of Neutralization. A Theory of Delinquency" in Wolfgang, M.E. *et al.* (eds.) *The Sociology of Crime and Delinquency.* 2nd edition. New York: John Wiley.

Taeuber, K.E. and A.F. Taeuber. 1965. *Negroes in Cities.* Chicago: Aldine.

Thomas, C.W., R.J. Cage and S.C. Foster. 1976. "Public Opinion on Criminal Law and Legal Sanctions: An Examination of Two Conceptual Models." *Journal of Criminal Law and Criminology.* 67: 110-116.

The Philadelphia Tribune. 1988. "City Agrees to Stop the Random Arrest of Blacks."

Thornberry, T.P. 1973. "Race Socio-Economic Status and Sentencing in the Juvenile Justice System." *Journal of Criminal Law and Criminology*. 64: 90-98.

Turk, A. 1982. *Political Criminality*. Beverly Hills: Sage Publications.

Turk, A. 1971. *Criminality and the Legal Order*. Chicago: Rand McNally.

Valentine, C. 1970. *Culture and Poverty: Critique and Counter Proposals*. Chicago: University of Chicago.

Wade, R.C. 1964. *Slavery in the Cities*. London: Oxford University.

Ware, G. (ed.). 1976. *From the Black Bar*. New York: G.P. Putnam's Sons.

Weaver, R.C. 1967. *The Negro Ghetto*. New York: Russel & Russel.

Webster's New Unabridged Dictionary. 1983. Second edition. New York: Dorset and Baber.

Westie, F.R. 1965. "The American Dilemma: An Empirical Test." *American Sociological Review*. 30 (August): 531-532.

Wilbanks, William. 1987. *The Myth of a Racist Criminal Justice System*. Monterey: Brooks Cole.

Wilson, James Q. and Richard J. Herrnstein. 1985. *Crime and Human Nature*. New York: Simon and Schuster.

Chapter 8

Spirit-Murdering the Messenger: The Discourse of Fingerpointing as the Law's Response to Racism

Patricia Williams
The City University of New York Law School at Queen's College

Windows and Mirrors

Buzzers are big in New York City. Favored particularly by smaller stores and boutiques, merchants throughout the city have installed them as screening devices to reduce the incidence of robbery. When the buzzer sounds, if the face at the door looks "desirable," the door is unlocked. If the face is that of an "undesirable," the door stays locked. Predictably, the issue of undesirability has revealed itself to be primarily a racial determination. Although the buzzer system was controversial at first, even civil rights organizations have backed down in the face of arguments that the system is a "necessary evil,"[1] that it is a "mere inconvenience" compared to the risks of being murdered,[2] that discrimination is not as bad as assault,[3] and that in any event, it is not *all* blacks who are barred, just "17-year-old black males wearing running shoes and hooded sweatshirts."[4]

Two Saturdays before Christmas, I saw a sweater that I wanted to purchase for my mother. I pressed my brown face to the store window and my finger to the buzzer, seeking admittance. A narrow-eyed white youth who looked barely seventeen, wearing tennis sneakers and feasting on bubble gum, glared at me, evaluating me for signs that would pit me against the limits of his social understanding. After about five seconds, he mouthed, "We're closed," and blew pink rubber at me. It was one o'clock in the afternoon. There were several white people in the store who appeared to be shopping for things for *their* mothers.

I was enraged. At that moment I literally wanted to break all of the windows in the store and *take* lots of sweaters for my mother. In the flicker of his judgmental grey eyes,

* Originally published in *University of Miami Law Review*, Vol. 42, No. 147: 127-157 (September 1987).
Reprinted by permission of University of Miami School of Law.

that saleschild had reduced my brightly sentimental, joy-to-the-world, pre-Christmas spree to a shambles. He had snuffed my sense of humanitarian catholicity, and there was nothing I could do to snuff his, without simply making a spectacle of myself.

I am still struck by the structure of power that drove me into such a blizzard of rage. There was almost nothing I could do, short of physically intruding upon him, that would humiliate him the way he humiliated me. No words, no gestures, no prejudices of my own would make a bit of difference to him. His refusal to let me into the store was an outward manifestation of his never having let someone like me into the realm of his reality. He had no connection, no compassion, no remorse, no reference to me and no desire to acknowledge me even at the estranged level of arm's length transactor. He saw me only as one who would take his money and therefore could not conceive that I was there to give him money.

In this weird ontological imbalance, I realized that buying something in that store was like bestowing a gift: the gift of my commerce. In the wake of my outrage, I wanted to take back the gift of my appreciation, which my peering in the window must have appeared to be. I wanted to take it back in the form of unappreciation, disrespect and defilement. I wanted to work so hard at wishing he could feel what I felt that he would never again mistake my *hatred* for some sort of plaintive wish to be included. I was quite willing to disenfranchise myself in the heat of my need to revoke the flattery of my purchasing power. I was willing to boycott this particular store, random white-owned businesses and anyone who blew bubble gum in my face again.

My rage was admittedly diffuse, even self-destructive, but it was symmetrical. The perhaps loose-ended but utter propriety of that rage is no doubt lost not just to the young man who barred me, but to those who appreciate my being barred only as an abstract precaution, and who approve of those who would bar, even as they deny that *they* would bar *me*.

The violence of my desire to have burst into that store is probably quite apparent to the reader. I wonder if the violence and the exclusionary hatred are equally apparent in the repeated public urging that blacks put themselves in the shoes of white store owners,[5] and that, in effect, blacks look into the mirror of frightened whites faces to the reality of their undesirability; and that then blacks would "just as surely conclude that [they] would not let [themselves] in under similar circumstances."[6]

This article will consider how the rhetoric of increased privatization, in response to racial issues, functions as the rationalizing agent of public unaccountability, and ultimately, irresponsibility. My emphasis will be more on the process of exclusion than on reiterating the substantive literature of silenced voices, a body as great as the history of this nation. I will analyze the language of lawmakers, officials and the public in order to present racial discrimination — so pervasive yet so hard to prosecute, so active yet so unactionable — in a new light. My concern is the need for new tools with which to confront issues such as discriminatory prosecution, prejudice as a silent force in jury reallocation of the burden of proof, the adequacy of an evidentiary system in which relevance and materiality are subjective reflections of self-interested values, private assumptions about race and class, and right and wrong as forces in the allocation and distribution of the resources for survival. To this end, I will examine two cases: the death of Eleanor Bumpurs, an elderly black woman shot by police in the Bronx, and the beating of three black men by white teenagers in the Howard Beach section of Queens.

The second purpose of this article is to examine racism as a crime, an offense so deeply painful and assaultive as to constitute something I call "spirit-murder." Society is only beginning to recognize that racism is as devastating, as costly and as psychically obliterating as robbery or assault; indeed they are often the same. Racism resembles other offenses against humanity whose structures are so deeply embedded in culture as to prove extremely resistant to being recognized as forms of oppression.[7] It can be as difficult to prove as child abuse or rape, where the victim is forced to convince others that he or she was not at fault, or that the perpetrator was not just "playing around." As in rape cases, victims of racism must prove that they did not distort the circumstances, misunderstand the intent, or even enjoy it.

Crimes without Passion

Eleanor Bumpurs and the Language of Lawmakers

On October 29, 1984, Eleanor Bumpurs, a 270-pound, arthritic, 67 year old woman, was shot to death while resisting eviction from her apartment in the Bronx. She was $98.85, or one month, behind in her rent.[8] New York City Mayor Ed Koch and Police Commissioner Benjamin Ward described the struggle preceding her demise as involving two officers with plastic shields, one officer with a restraining hook, another officer with a shotgun and at least one supervising officer. All of the officers also carried service revolvers. According to Commissioner Ward, during the course of the attempted eviction Mrs. Bumpurs escaped from the restraining hook twice and wielded a knife that Commissioner Ward says was "bent" on one of the plastic shields. At some point, Officer Stephen Sullivan, the officer positioned farthest away from her, aimed and fired his shotgun. It is alleged that the blast removed half of her hand, so that, according to the Bronx District Attorney's Office, "[I]t was anatomically impossible for her to hold the knife."[9] The officer pumped his gun and shot again, making his mark completely the second time around.[10]

In the two and one-half year wake of this terrible incident, controversy raged as to whether Mrs. Bumpurs ought to have brandished a knife and whether the officer ought to have fired his gun. In February 1987, a New York Supreme Court justice found Officer Sullivan not guilty of manslaughter.[11] The case centered on a very narrow issue of language pitted against circumstance. District Attorney Mario Merola described the case as follows: "*Obviously,* one shot would have been justified. But if that shot took off part of her hand and rendered her defenseless, whether there was any need for a second shot, which killed her, that's the whole issue of whether you have reasonable force or excessive force."[12] My intention in the following analysis is to underscore the significant task facing judges and lawyers in undoing institutional descriptions of what is "obvious" and what is not, and in resisting the general predigestion of evidence for jury consumption.

Shortly after Mr. Merola's statement, Officer Sullivan's attorney, Bruce Smiry, expressed eagerness to try the case before a jury.[13] Following the heavily publicized attack in

Howard Beach, however, he favored a bench trial. In explaining his decision to request a nonjury trial, he stated:

> I think a judge will be much more likely than a jury to understand the defense that the shooting was justified.... The average lay person might find it difficult to understand why the police were there in the first place, and why a shotgun was employed.... Because of the climate now in the city, I don't want people perceiving this as a racial case."[14]

Since 1984, Mayor Koch, Commissioner Ward, and a host of other city officials repeatedly have described the shooting of Mrs. Bumpurs as completely legal.[15] At the same time, Commissioner Ward has admitted publicly that Mrs. Bumpurs should not have died. Mayor Koch admitted that her death was the result of "a chain of mistakes and circumstances" that came together in the worst possible way, with the worst possible circumstances.[16] Commissioner Ward admitted that the officers could have waited for Mrs. Bumpurs to calm down, and that they could have used teargas or mace instead of gunfire. According to Commissioner Ward, however, these observations are made with hindsight. As to whether this shooting of a black woman by a white police officer had racial overtones, he stated that he had "no evidence of racism."[17] Commissioner Ward pointed out that he is sworn to uphold the law, which is "inconsistent with treating blacks differently,"[18] and that the shooting was legal because it was within the code of police ethics.[19] Finally, city officials have resisted criticism of the police department's handling of the incident by remarking that "outsiders" do not know all of the facts and do not understand the pressure under which officers labor.

The root of the word "legal" is the Latin word *lex*, which means law in a fairly concrete sense — law as we understand it when we refer to written law, codes, and systems of obedience.[20] The word *lex* does not include the more abstract, ethical dimension of law that contemplates the purposes of rules and their effective implementation. This latter meaning is contained in the Latin word *jus*, from which we derive the word "justice."[21] This semantic distinction is not insignificant. The word of law, whether statutory or judicial, is a subcategory of the underlying social motives and beliefs from which it is born. It is the technical embodiment of attempts to order society according to a consensus of ideals. When society loses sight of those ideals and grants obeisance to words alone, law becomes sterile and formalistic; *lex* is applied without *jus* and is therefore unjust. The result is compliance with the letter of the law, but not the spirit. A sort of punitive literalism ensues that leads to a high degree of thoughtless conformity. This literalism has, as one of its primary underlying values, order — whose ultimate goal may be justice, but whose immediate end is the ordering of behavior. Living solely by the letter of the law means living without spirit; one can do anything as long as it comports with the law in a technical sense. The cynicism or rebelliousness that infects one's spirit, and the enthusiasm or dissatisfaction with which one conforms is unimportant. Furthermore, this compliance is arbitrary; it is inconsistent with the will of the conformer. The law becomes a battleground of wills. The extent to which technical legalism obfuscates and undermines the human motivations that generate our justice system is the real extent to which we as human beings are disenfranchised.

Cultural needs and ideals change with the momentum of time; redefining our laws in keeping with the spirit of cultural flux keeps society alive and humane. In the Bumpurs case, the words of the law called for nonlethal alternatives first, but allowed some officer discretion in determining which situations are so immediately life-endangering as to require the use of deadly force.[22] This discretionary area was presumably the basis for the claim that Officer Sullivan acted legally. The law as written permitted shooting in general, and therefore, by extension of the city's interpretation of this law, it would be impossible for a police officer ever to shoot someone in a specifically objectionable way.

If our laws are thus piano-wired on the exclusive validity of literalism, if they are picked clean of their spirit, then society risks heightened irresponsibility or the consequences of abominable actions. Accordingly, Jonathan Swift's description of lawyers weirdly and ironically comes to life: "[T]here was a Society of Men among us, bred up from their Youth in the Art of proving by words multiplied for the Purpose, that White is Black and Black is White, according as they are paid. To this Society all the rest of the People are Slaves."[23] We also risk subjecting ourselves to such absurdly empty rhetoric as Commissioner Ward's comments to the effect that both Mrs. Bumpurs' death and racism were unfortunate, while stating "but the law says...."[24] Commissioner Ward's sentiments might as well read: "The law says...and therefore the death was unfortunate but irremediable; the law says...and therefore there is little that can be done about racism." The law thus becomes a shield behind which to avoid responsibility for the human repercussions of both governmental and publicly harmful private activity.[25]

A related issue is the degree to which much of the criticism of the police department's handling of this case was devalued as "noisy" or excessively emotional. It is as though passionate protest were a separate crime, a rudeness of such dimension as to defeat altogether any legitimacy of content. We as lawyers are taught from the moment we enter law school to temper our emotionalism and quash our idealism. We are taught that heartfelt instincts subvert the law and defeat the security of a well-ordered civilization, whereas faithful adherence to the word of law, to *stare decisis* and clearly stated authority, would as a matter of course lead to a bright, clear world like the Land of Oz, in which those heartfelt instincts would be preserved. Form is exalted over substance, and cool rationales over heated feelings. But we should not be ruled exclusively by the cool formality of language or by emotions. We must be ruled by our complete selves, by the intellectual and emotional content of our words. Governmental representatives must hear the full range of legitimate concerns, no matter how indelicately expressed or painful they may be to hear.

But undue literalism is only one type of sleight of tongue in the attainment of meaningless dialogue. Mayor Koch, Commissioner Ward and Officer Sullivan's defense attorneys have used overgeneralization as an effective rhetorical complement to their avoidance of the issues. For example, allegations that the killing was illegal and unnecessary and should therefore be prosecuted, were met with responses such as "The laws permit police officers to shoot people,"[26] "As long as police officers have guns, there will be unfortunate deaths"[27] and "The conviction rate in cases like this is very low."[28] The observation that teargas would have been an effective alternative to shooting

Mrs. Bumpurs drew the dismissive reply that "there were lots of things they *could* have done."[29]

Privatization of response as a justification for public irresponsibility is a version of the same game. Honed to perfection by President Reagan, this version holds up the private self as indistinguishable from the public "duty and power laden" self. Public officials respond to commentary by the public and the media as though it were meant to hurt private, vulnerable feelings. Trying to hold a public official accountable while not hurting his feelings is a skill the acquisition of which would consume time better spent on almost any conceivable task. Thus, when Commissioner Ward was asked if the internal review board planned to discipline Officer Sullivan, many seemed disposed to accept his response that while he was personally very sorry she had died, he could not understand why the media was focusing on him so much. "How many other police commissioners," he asked repeatedly, "have gotten as much attention as I have?"[30]

Finally, a most cruel form of semantic slipperiness infused Mrs. Bumpurs' death from the beginning. It is called victim responsibility.[31] It is the least responsive form of dialogue, yet apparently the easiest to accept as legitimate.

All these words, from Commissioner Ward, from the Mayor's office, from the media and from the public generally, have rumbled and resounded with the *sounds* of discourse. We want to believe that their symmetrical, pleasing structure is the equivalent of discourse. If we are not careful, we will hypnotize ourselves into believing that it *is* discourse.

Howard Beach and the "Private Property" of Neighborhood

In the early morning hours of December 20, 1986, three young black men left their stalled car on Cross Bay Parkway, in the New York City borough of Queens, and went to look for help. They walked into the neighborhood of Howard Beach, entered a pizzeria, ordered pizzas and sat down to eat. An anonymous caller to the police reported their presence as "black troublemakers." A patrol car came, found no trouble and left. After the young men had eaten, they left the pizzeria and were immediately surrounded by a group of eight to ten white teenagers who taunted them with racial epithets. The white youths chased the black men for about three miles, catching them at several points and beating them severely. One of the black men died as a result of being struck by a car as he tried to flee across a highway. Another suffered permanent blindness in one eye.[32]

In the extremely heated public controversy that ensued, as much attention centered on the community of Howard Beach as on the assailants themselves. A veritable Greek chorus formed, comprised of the defendants' lawyers and resident after resident after resident of Howard Beach, all repeating and repeating and repeating that the mere presence of three black men in that part of town at that time of night was reason enough to drive them out. "They had to be starting trouble."[33] "We're a strictly white neighborhood."[34] "What were they doing here in the first place?"[35]

Although the immensely segregationist instincts behind such statements may be fairly evident, it is worth making explicit some of the presuppositions behind such ululations.

Everyone who lives here is white.
No black could live here.
No one here has a black friend.
No white would employ a black here.
No black is permitted to shop here.
No black is ever up to any good.

These presuppositions themselves are premised on lethal philosophies of life.

1. "It's Better to be Safe than Sorry"

"Are we supposed to stand around and do nothing while these blacks come into our area and rob us?"[36] one woman asked a reporter in the wake of the Howard Beach attack. A twenty-year-old, who had lived in Howard Beach all of his life, said, "We ain't racial.... We just don't want to get robbed."[37] The hidden implication of these statements is that to be safe is not to be sorry, and that to be safe is to be white and to be sorry is to be associated with blacks. Safety and sorrow, which are inherently alterable and random, are linked to inalterable essences. The expectation that uncertain conditions are really immutable is a formula for frustration; it is a belief that feeds a sense of powerlessness. The rigid determinism of placing in the disjunctive things that are not in fact disjunctive is a setup for betrayal by the very nature of reality. The national repetition that white neighborhoods are safe and blacks bring sorrow is an incantation of powerlessness. And, as with the upside-down logic of all irrational incantations, it imports a concept of white safety that almost necessarily endangers the lives as well as the rights of blacks.

It is also an incantation of innocence and guilt, much related to incantations that affirmative action programs allow presumably "guilty" blacks to displace "innocent" whites.[38] (Even assuming that "innocent whites" were being displaced by blacks, does that make blacks less innocent in the pursuit of education and jobs? If anything, are not blacks *more* innocent in the scheme of discrimination?) In fact, in the wake of the Howard Beach incident, the police and the press rushed to serve the public's interest in the victims' unsavory "guilty" dispositions. They overlook the fact that racial slurs and attacks "objectif[y] people — the incident could have happened to any black person who was there at that time and place. This is the crucial aspect of the Howard Beach affair that is now being muddied in the media. Bringing up [defendants' past arrest records] is another way of saying, 'He was a criminal who deserved it.'"[39] Thus, the game of victim responsibility described above is itself a slave to society's stereotypes of good and evil.

It does no good, however, to turn race issues into contests for some Holy Grail of innocence. In my youth, segregation and antimiscegenation laws were still on the books in many states. During the lifetimes of my parents and grandparents, and for several hundred years before them, laws prohibited blacks from owning property, voting and learning to read or write. Blacks were, by constitutional mandate, outlawed from the hopeful, loving expectations that being treated as a whole, rather than three-fifths of a human being can bring. When every resource of a wealthy nation is put to such destructive ends, it will take more than a few generations to mop up the mess.[40]

We have all inherited that legacy, whether new to this world or new to this country. It survives as powerfully and invisibly reinforcing structures of thought, language and law. Thus, generalized notions of innocence and guilt have little place in the struggle for transcendence; there is no blame among the living for the dimension of this historic crime, this national tragedy.[41] There is, however, responsibility for never forgetting one another's histories, and for making real the psychic obliteration which lives on as a factor in shaping relations, not just between blacks and whites,[42] or blacks and blacks,[43] but also between whites and whites. Whites must consider how much this history has projected onto blacks the blame for all criminality, and for all of society's ills. It has become the means for keeping white criminality invisible.[44]

2. "Discrimination Doesn't Hurt as much as Being Assaulted" or "A Prejudiced Society is Better than a Violent Society"

The attempt to split bias from violence has been this society's most enduring and fatal rationalization. Prejudice does hurt, however, just as the absence of prejudice can nourish and shelter. Discrimination can repel and vilify, ostracize and alienate. White people who do not believe this should try telling everyone they meet that one of their ancestors was black. I had a friend in college who, having lived her life as a blonde, grey-eyed white person, discovered that she was one-sixteenth black. She began to externalize all the unconscious baggage that "black" bore for her: the self-hatred that is racism. She did not think of herself as a racist (nor had I) but she literally wanted to jump out of her skin, shed her flesh and start life over again. She confided in me that she felt "fouled" and "betrayed." She also asked me if I had ever felt this way. Her question dredged from some deep corner of my suppressed memory the recollection of feeling precisely that, when at the age of three or so, some white playmates explained to me that God had mixed mud with the pure clay of life in order to make me.

In the Vietnamese language, "the word 'I' (toi) ... means 'your servant'; there is no 'I' as such. When you talk to someone, you establish a relationship."[45] Such a concept of "self" is a way of experiencing the other, ritualistically sharing the other's essence, and cherishing it. In our culture, seeing and feeling the dimension of harm that results from separating self from "other" requires more work.[46] Very little in our language or our culture encourages or reinforces any attempt to look at others as part of ourselves. With the imperviously divided symmetry of the marketplace, social costs to blacks are simply not seen as costs to whites,[47] just as blacks do not share in the advances whites may enjoy.

This structure of thought is complicated by the fact that the distancing does not stop with the separation of the white self from the black other. In addition, the cultural domination of blacks by whites means that the black self is placed at a distance even from itself, as in the example of blacks being asked to put themselves in the position of the white shopkeepers who view them.[48] So blacks are conditioned from infancy to see in themselves only what others who despise them see.[49]

It is true that conforming to what others see in us is every child's way of becoming socialized.[50] It is what makes children in our society seem so gullible, so impressionable, so "impolitely" honest, so blindly loyal and so charming to the ones they imitate.[51] Yet this conformity also describes a way of being that relinquishes the power of independent ethical choice. Although such a relinquishment can have quite desirable social consequences, it also presumes a fairly homogeneous social context in which values are shared and enforced collectively. Thus, it is no wonder that western anthropologists and ethnographers, for whom adulthood is manifested by the exercise of independent ethical judgment, so frequently denounce tribal cultures or other collectivist ethics as "childlike."

By contrast, our culture constructs some, but not all, selves to be the servants of others. Thus, some "I's" are defined as "your servant," some as "your master." The struggle for the self becomes not a true mirroring of self-in-other, but rather a hierarchically-inspired series of distortions, where some serve without ever being served, some master without ever being mastered, and almost everyone hides from this vernacular domination by clinging to the legally official definition of "I" as meaning "your equal."

In such an environment, relinquishing the power of individual ethical judgment to a collective ideal risks psychic violence, an obliteration of the self through domination by an all-powerful other. In such an environment, it is essential at some stage that the self be permitted to retreat into itself and make its own decisions with self-love and self-confidence. What links child abuse, the mistreatment of women and racism is the massive external intrusion into psyche that dominating powers impose to keep the self from ever fully seeing itself.[52] Because the self's power resides in another, little faith is placed in the true self, that is, in one's own experiential knowledge. Consequently, the power of children, women and blacks is actually reduced to the "intuitive," rather than the real; social life is necessarily based primarily on the imaginary.[53] Furthermore, because it is difficult to affirm constantly with the other the congruence of the self's imagining what the other is *really* thinking of the self, and because even that correlative effort is usually kept within very limited family, neighborhood, religious, or racial boundaries, encounters cease to be social and become presumptuous, random and disconnected.

This peculiarly distancing standpoint allows dramas, particularly racial ones like Howard Beach, to unfold in scenarios weirdly unrelated to the incidents that generated them. At one end of the spectrum is a *laissez faire* response that privatizes the self in order to remain unassailably justified. At the other end is a pattern that generalizes individual or particular others into terrifyingly uncontrollable "domains" of public wilderness, against which proscriptive barriers must be built to protect the eternally innocent self.

a. Privatizing Innocence

The prototypical scenario of the privatized response is as follows:

> Cain: Abel's part of town is tough turf.[54]
> Abel: It upsets me when you say that; you have never been to my part of town.
> As a matter of fact, my part of town is a leading supplier of milk and honey.[55]

> Cain: The news that I'm upsetting you is too upsetting for me to handle. You were wrong to tell me of your upset because now I'm terribly upset.[56]
> Abel: I felt threatened first. Listen to me. Take your distress as a measure of my own and empathize with it. Don't ask me to recant and apologize in order to carry this conversation further.[57]

This type of discourse is problematic because Cain's challenge in calling Abel's turf "tough" is transformed into a discussion of the care with which *Abel* challenges that statement. While there is certainly an obligation to be careful in addressing others the obligation to protect the feelings of those others gets put above the need to protect one's own. The self becomes subservient to the other, with no reciprocity, and the other becomes a whimsical master. Abel's feelings are deflected in deference to Cain's, and Abel bears the double burden of raising his issue properly *and* of being responsible for its impact on Cain. Cain is rendered unaccountable for as long as this deflection continues because all the fault is assigned to Abel. Morality and responsiveness thus become dichotomized as Abel drowns in responsibility for valuative quality control, while Cain rests on the higher ground of a value-neutral zone.

Caught in conversations like this, blacks as well as whites will feel keenly and pressingly circumscribed. Perhaps most people never intend to be racist, oppressive, or insulting. Nevertheless, by describing zones of vulnerability and by setting up fences of rigidified politeness, the unintentional exile of individuals as well as races may be quietly accomplished.

b. Publicizing Guilt

Another scenario of distancing self from the responsibility for racism is the invention of some great public wilderness of others. In the context of Howard Beach, the specter against which the self must barricade itself is violent: seventeen-year-old black males wearing running shoes and hooded sweatshirts. It is this fear of the uncontrollable, overwhelming other that animates many of the more vengefully racist comments from Howard Beach, such as, "We're a strictly white neighborhood.... They had to be starting trouble."[58]

These statements set up angry, excluding boundaries. They also imply that the *failure* to protect and avenge is bad policy, bad statesmanship and an embarrassment. They raise the stakes beyond the unexpressed rage arising from the incident itself. Like the Cain and Abel example, the need to avenge becomes a separate issue of protocol and etiquette — not a loss of a piece of the self, which is the real cost of *real* tragedies, but a loss of self-regard. By self-regard, I do not mean self-concept as in self-esteem; I mean that view of the self that is attained by the self stepping outside the self to regard and evaluate the self. It is a process in which the self is watched by an imaginary other, a self-projection of the opinions of real others, where "I" means "your master" and where the designated other's refusal to be dominated is felt as personally assaultive. Thus, the failure to avenge is felt as a loss of self-regard. It is a psychological metaphor for whatever trauma or original assault that constitutes the real loss to the self.[59] It is therefore more abstract, more illusory, more constructed, and more invented. Potentially, therefore, it is less powerful than "real" assault, in that with effort it can be unlearned as a source of vulnerability. This is the real message of the attempt to distinguish between prejudice and violence: names, as in the old "sticks and stones" ditty, although undeniably and powerfully influential, can be learned or undone as motivation for future destructive action.[60] As long as they are *not* unlearned, however, the exclusionary power of such free-floating emotions makes its way into the gestalt of prosecutorial and jury decisions and into what the law sees as crime, or as justified, provoked or excusable.[61] Law becomes described and enforced in the spirit of our prejudices.[62]

The Evidentiary Rules of Legitimizing Turf Wars

The following passage is a description of the arraignment of three of the white teenagers who were involved in the Howard Beach beatings:

> The three defense lawyers also tried to cast doubt on [the prosecutor's] account of the attack. The lawyers questioned why the victims walked all the way to the pizza parlor if, as they said, their mission was to summon help for their car, which broke down three miles away.... At the arraignment, the lawyers said the victims passed two all-night gas stations and several other pizza shops before they reached the one they entered.
>
> A check yesterday of area restaurants, motels and gas stations listed in the Queens street directory found two eating establishments, a gas station and a motel that all said they were open and had working pay phones on Friday night.
>
> A spokesman for the New York Telephone Company, Jim Crosson, said there are six outdoor pay telephones...on the way to the pizzeria.[63]

In the first place, lawyers must wonder what relevance this has. Does the answer to any of the issues the defense raised serve to prove that these black men assaulted, robbed, threatened or molested these white men? Does it even prove that the white men *reasonably* feared such a fate? The investigation into the number of phone booths per mile does not reveal why the white men would fear the black men's presence. Instead, it is relevant to prove that there is *no* reason a black man should walk or just wander around the community of Howard Beach. This is not semantic detail; it is central to understanding burdensomeness of proof in such cases. It is this unconscious restructuring of burdens of proof into burdens of white over black that permits people who say and who believe that they are not racist to commit and condone crimes of genocidal magnitude. It is easy to rationalize this as linguistically technical, or as society's sorrow. As one of my students said, "I'm so tired of hearing the blacks say that society's done them wrong." Yet these gyrations kill with their razor-toothed presumption. Lawyers are the modern wizards and medicine people who must define this innocent murderousness as crime.

Additionally, investigations into "closer" alternatives eclipse the possibility of other explanation. They assume that the young men were not headed for the subway (which was in fact in the same direction as the pizzeria), and further, that black people must have documented reasons for excursioning into white neighborhoods and out of the neighborhoods to which they are supposedly consigned.

It is interesting to contrast the implicit requirement of documentation imposed on blacks walking down public streets in Howard Beach with the implicit license of the white officers who burst into the private space of Mrs. Bumpurs' apartment. In the Bumpurs case, lawmakers consistently dismissed the availability of less intrusive options as presumption and idle hindsight.[64] This dismissal ignored the fact that police officers have an actual burden of employing the least harmful alternatives. In the context of Howard Beach, however, such an analysis invents and imposes a burden on nonresidents to stay out of strange neighborhoods. It implies harm in the presence of those who do not specifically "own" something there. Both analyses skirt the propriety and necessity of public sector responsibility. Both redefine public accountability in privatized terms. Whether those privatized terms act to restrict or expand accountability is dichotomized according to the race of the actors.

Finally, this factualized hypothesizing was part of a news story, not an editorial. "News," in other words, was reduced to hypothesis based on silent premises: they should have used the first phone they encountered; they should have eaten at the first "eating establishment;" they should have gone into a gas station and asked for help; surely they should have had the cash and credit cards to do any of the above or else not travel in strange neighborhoods. In elevating these to relevant issues, however, *The New York Times* did no more than mirror what was happening in the courtroom.

The Appropriation of Psychic Property

In an ill-fated trip to the neighborhood of Jamaica, in the borough of Queens, Mayor Koch attempted to soothe tensions by asking a congregation of black churchgoers to understand the disgruntlement of Howard Beach residents about the interracial march by 1400 protesters through "their" streets. He asked them how they would feel if 1400 white people took to the streets of the predominantly black neighborhood of Jamaica.[65] This remark, from the chief executive of New York City, accepts and even advocates a remarkable degree of possessiveness about public streets. This possessiveness, moreover, is racially rather than geographically bounded. In effect, Koch was pleading for the acceptance of the privatization of public space. This is the *de facto* equivalent of segregation. It is exclusion in the guise of deep-moated private property "interests" and "values." In such a characterization, the public nature of the object of discussion, the street, is lost.[66]

Mayor Koch's question suggests that 1400 black people took to the streets of Howard Beach. In fact, the crowd was integrated — blacks, browns and whites, residents and nonresidents of Howard Beach. Apparently, crowds in New York are subject to the unwritten equivalent of Louisiana's race statutes (which provide that 1/72 black ancestry renders a person black) and to the Ku Klux Klan's "contamination by association" standard ("blacks and white-blacks" was how one resident of Forsythe County, Georgia described an interracial crowd of protesters there).

On the other hand, if Mayor Koch intended to direct attention to the inconvenience, noise and pollution of such a crowd in those small streets, then I am sympathetic. My sympathy is insignificant, however, compared to my recognition of the necessity and propriety of the protestors' spontaneous, demonstrative, peaceful outpouring of rage, sorrow and pain.

If, however, Mayor Koch intended to ask blacks to imagine 1400 angry white people descending on a black community, then I agree, I would be frightened. This image would also conjure up visions of 1400 hooded white people burning crosses, 1400 Nazis marching through Skokie and 1400 cavalry men riding into American Indian lands. These visions would inspire great fear in me, because of the possibility of grave harm to the residents. But there is a difference, and that is why the purpose of the march is so important. That is why it is so important to distinguish mass protests of violence from organized hate groups that openly threaten violence. By failing to make this distinction, Mayor Koch created the manipulative specter of unspecified mobs sweeping through homes in pursuit of vague and diffusely dangerous ends. From this perspective, he appealed to thoughtlessness, to the pseudoconsolation of hunkering down and bunkering up against the approaching hordes, to a glacially overgeneralized view of the unneighborhooded "public" world.

Moreover, the Mayor's comments reveal that he is ignorant of the degree to which the black people have welcomed, endured and suffered white marchers through their streets. White people have always felt free to cruise through black communities and to treat them possessively. Most black neighborhoods have existed only as long as whites have permitted them to exist. Blacks have been this society's perpetual tenants, sharecroppers and lessees. Blacks went from being owned by others to having everything around them owned by others. In a civilization that values private property above all else, this effectuates a devaluation of humanity, a removal of blacks not just from the market, but from the pseudospiritual circle of psychic and civic communion. As illustrated in the microcosm of my experience at the store,[67] this limbo of disownedness keeps blacks beyond the pale of those who are entitled to receive the survival gifts of commerce, the property of life, liberty and happiness, whose fruits our culture places in the marketplace. In this way, blacks are positioned analogically to the rest of society, exactly as they were during slavery or Jim Crow.[68]

There is a subtler level to the enactment of this dispossession. The following story may illustrate more fully what I mean: not long ago, when I first moved back to New York after some 20 years, I decided to go on a walking tour of Harlem. The tour, which took place on Easter Sunday, was sponsored by the New York Arts Society, and except for myself, was attended exclusively by young, white, urban, professional real estate speculators. They were pleasant looking, with babies strapped to their backs and balloons in their hands. They all seemed like very nice people.

Halfway through the tour, the guide asked the group if they wanted to "go inside some churches." The guide added, "It'll make the tour a little longer, but we'll probably get to see some services going on. ... Easter Sunday in Harlem is quite a show." A casual discussion ensued about the time that this excursion might take.

What astonished me was that no one had asked the people in the churches if they minded being stared at like living museums. I wondered what would happen if a group of blue-jeaned blacks were to walk uninvited into a synagogue on Passover or St. Anthony's of Padua in the middle of High Mass. Just to peer, not pray. My overwhelming instinct is that such activity would be seen as disrespectful.

Apparently, the disrespect was invisible to this well-educated, affable group of people. They deflected my observations with comments such as, "We just want to look;" "No one will mind;" "There's no harm intended." As well-intentioned as they were, I was left with the impression that no one existed for them whom their intentions could not govern.[69] Despite the lack of apparent malice in their demeanor,[70] it seemed to me that to live so noninteractively is a liability as much as a luxury. To live imperviously to one's impact on others is a fragile privilege, which depends ultimately on the inability of others to make their displeasure known.

The Gift of Intelligent Rage

Owning the Self in a Disowned World

Reflecting on Howard Beach brought to mind a news story from my fragmentary grammar school recollections of the 1960s: a white man acting out of racial motives killed a black man who was working for some civil rights organization or cause. The man was stabbed 39 times, a number which prompted a radio commentator to observe that the point was not just murder, but something beyond.

What indeed was the point, if not murder? I wondered what it was that would not die, which could not be killed by the fourth, fifth, or even tenth knife blow; what sort of thing that would not die with the body but lived on in the mind of the murderer. Perhaps, as psychologists have argued, what the murderer was trying to kill was a part of his own mind's image, a part of himself and not a real other. After all, statistically and corporeally, blacks as a group are poor, powerless and a minority. It is in the minds of whites that blacks become large, threatening, powerful, uncontrollable, ubiquitous and supernatural.

There are certain societies that define the limits of life and death very differently than our own. For example, death may occur long before the body ceases to function, and under the proper circumstances, life may continue for some time after the body is carried to its grave.[71] These non-body-bound, uncompartmentalized ideas recognize the power of spirit, or what we in our secularized society might describe as the dynamism of self as reinterpreted by the perceptions of other.[72] These ideas comprehend the fact that a part of ourselves is beyond the control of pure physical will and resides in the sanctuary of those around us. A fundamental part of ourselves and of our dignity is dependent upon the uncontrollable, powerful, external observers who constitute society.[73] Surely a part of socialization ought to include a sense of caring responsibility for the images of others that are reposited within *us*.[74]

Taking the example of the man who was stabbed 39 times out of the context of our compartmentalized legal system, and considering it in the hypothetical framework of a legal system that encompasses and recognizes morality, religion and psychology, I am moved to see this act as not merely body murder but spirit-murder as well. I see it as spirit-murder, only one of whose manifestations is racism — cultural obliteration, prostitution, abandonment of the elderly and the homeless and genocide are some of its other guises. I see spirit-murder as no less than the equivalent of body murder.

One of the reasons that I fear what I call spirit-murder, or disregard for others whose lives qualitatively depend on our regard, is that its product is a system of formalized distortions of thought. It produces social structures centered around fear and hate; it provides a tumorous outlet for feelings elsewhere unexpressed.[75] For example, when Bernhard Goetz shot four black teenagers in a New York City subway, an acquaintance of mine said that she could understand his fear because it is a "fact" that blacks commit most crimes. What impressed me, beyond the factual *in*accuracy of this statement,[76] was the reduction of Goetz' crime to "his fear," which I translate to mean *her* fear. The four teenage victims became all blacks everywhere, and "most crimes" clearly meant that most *blacks* commit crimes.

In the process of devaluing its image of black people, the general white population seems to have been socialized to blind itself to the horrors inflicted by white people. One of the clearest examples of the mechanics of this socialized blindness is the degree to which the public and the media in New York repeatedly and relentlessly bestialized Goetz' victims. Images of the urban jungle, of young black men filling the role of "wild animals," were favorite journalistic constructions. Young white urban professionals were mythologized, usually wrapped in the rhetorical apparel of lambs or sheep, as the tender, toothsome prey.[77] The corollary to such imagery is that the fate of those domesticated white innocents is to be slaughtered in confrontation, the dimensions of which thus become meaninglessly and tragically sacrificial.[78] Locked into such a reification, no act of the sheep against the wolves can ever be seen as violent in its own right, because active sheep are so *inherently* uncharacteristic, so brave, so irresistibly and triumphantly parabolic. Thus, when prosecutor Gregory Waples cast Goetz as a "hunter" in his final summation, juror Michael Axelrod said that Waples "was insulting my intelligence. There was nothing to justify that sort of [characterization]. Goetz wasn't a hunter."[79]

Furthermore, most white people do not seem to feel as criminal the dehumanizing cultural images of sterile, mindless white womanhood and expressionless, bored but righteous, assembly-line white manhood.[80] For example, although it is difficult to document in any scientific way, I think many whites do not expect other whites to rape, rob, or kill them.[81] They are surprised when it happens. Perhaps they blind themselves to the warning signals of approaching assault. Some do not even recognize it when it does happen; they apologize for the assailant, think it must have been their fault; *they* misperceived the other's intent.[82]

The following vignette may better illustrate what I mean:

> A lone black man was riding in an elevator in a busy downtown department store. The elevator stopped on the third floor and a crowd of noisy white high school students got on. The black man took out a gun and shot as many of

> them as he could before the doors opened on the first floor. ... the rest fled for their lives. The black man later explained to the police that he could tell from the students' "body language," from their "shiny eyes and big smiles," that they wanted to "play with him, like a cat plays with a mouse." Furthermore, the black man explained, one of the youths had tried to panhandle money from him and another asked him, "How are you?" "That's a meaningless thing," he said in his confession, "but in certain circumstances, that can be a real threat." He added that a similar greeting had preceded the vicious beating of his father, a black civil rights lawyer in Mississippi, some time before. He confessed that he intended to murder the high school students.

My guess is that most white Americans would view the severe contextual misapprehensions of the black gunman as a form of serious insanity. Although degrees of sympathy might vary, I suspect that the social consensus would be nearly unanimous that he presents a danger to himself and to others and should therefore be institutionalized or imprisoned. The above story is, however, with minor character alteration, consistent with a videotaped confession by Bernhard Goetz.[83] Nevertheless, the public overwhelmingly presumed Goetz innocent. Most accounts did *not* propose that he be institutionalized, but pointed instead to the failure of public institutions to engage in *more* such punitive activities. Bernhard Goetz' defense blatantly reflected this consensus in its claim, not that Goetz was temporarily insane, but rather that he acted *reasonably* under the circumstances.[84] It is reflected as well in the degree to which the public devoured, *ex post facto*, stories about the deviant behavior of the victims in this case.[85] Goetz became a cited authority and favorite interviewee on the subject of crime in New York. "Criminals," he declared, must realize that being shot is a "risk they are going to have to take."[86] I can think of no better example of the degree to which criminality has become lodged in a concept of the black "other."

If Americans are subject to such utter emotional devastation, it is no wonder that the urge to act as a victimizer is so irresistible; it appears to be the only right thing, the only defensible thing to do. It is no wonder that society has created in blacks a class of ready-made, prepackaged victims. To discount as much violence as we do in this society must mean that we have a very angry population suppressing explosive rage. Most white Americans, at least those in urban areas, have seen the angry, muttering "lunatic" black person who beats the air with his fists and curses aloud. Most people cross the street to avoid him; they don't choose him to satisfy their need to know the time of day. Yet for generations, and particularly in the wake of the foaming public response to incidents like Howard Beach, the Goetz shooting,[87] and Forsythe County, that is precisely how white America has looked to many black Americans.

For these reasons, I think we need to elevate what I call spirit-murder to the conceptual, if not punitive level of a capital moral offense.[88] We need to see it as a cultural cancer; we need to open our eyes to the spiritual genocide it is wreaking on blacks, whites and the abandoned and abused of all races and ages. We need to eradicate its numbing pathology before it wipes out what precious little humanity we have left.

Mirrors and Windows

The night after the Bumpurs story became public, I dreamed about a black woman who was denied entry to a restaurant because of her color. In response, she climbed over the building. The next time she found a building in her way, she climbed over it, and the next time and the next and the next. In time, she became famous, as she roamed the world, traveling in determined straight lines, wordlessly scaling whatever lay in her path, including skyscrapers. Well-meaning white people came to marvel at her and gathered in crowds to watch and applaud. She never acknowledged their presence, but went about her business in unsmiling silence. The white people grew angry and condemned her for failing to appreciate their praise and rejecting their gift of her fame. I stood somewhere on the periphery of this dream and wondered what unspoken rule, what deadened curiosity kept anyone from ever asking why.

Upon waking, I asked myself a progression of "why's" about the Bumpurs death. My life experiences had prepared me better to comprehend and sympathize with the animating force behind the outraged, dispossessed knifewielding of Mrs. Bumpurs.[89] What I found more difficult to focus on was the "why," the animus that inspired such fear, and such impatient contempt in a police officer that the presence of six other heavily armed men could not allay his need to kill a sick old lady fighting off hallucinations with a knife. It seemed to me a fear embellished by something beyond Mrs. Bumpurs herself; something about her enlarged to fill the void between her physical, limited presence and the "immediate threat and endangerment to life" that filled the beholding eyes of the officer. Why was the sight of a knife-wielding woman so fearfully offensive to a shotgun-wielding policeman that he felt that blowing her to pieces was the only recourse, the only way to preserve his physical integrity? What offensive spirit of his past experience raised her presence to the level of a physical menace beyond real dimensions? What spirit of prejudgment and of prejudice provided him with such a powerful hallucinogen?

However slippery these questions may be on a legal or conscious level, unresponsiveness to them does not make these issues go away. Failure to resolve the dilemma of racial violence merely displaces its power. The legacy of killing finds its way into cultural expectations, archetypes and "isms." The echoes of both dead and deadly others acquire a hallucinatory quality; their voices speak of an unwanted past, but also reflect for us images of the future. Today's world condemns those voices as superstitious and paranoid. Neglected, they speak from the shadows of such inattention, in garbles and growls, in the tongues of the damned and the insane. The superstitious listen, and perhaps in the silence of their attention, they hear and understand. So-called enlightened others who fail to listen to the voices of demonic selves, made invisibly uncivilized, simply make them larger, more barbarously enraged, until the nearsightedness of looking-glass existence is smashed in upon by the terrible dispossession of dreams too long deferred.

ENDNOTES

1. Gross, "When 'By Appointment' Means Keep Out," *NY Times*, 17 Dec. 1986 p. B1, col. 3.

2. *Ibid.*

3. Letter to the Editor from Michael Levin and Marguerita Levin, *NY Times*, 11 Jan. 1987 p. E32, col. 3 [hereinafter Letter to the Editor].

4. *Ibid.*

5. Gross, *supra* note 1.

6. Letter to the Editor, *supra* note 3. The fact that some blacks might agree with the store owners shows that some of us have learned too well the lessons of privatized self-hatred and rationalized away the fullness of our public, participatory selves.

7. That the framework of society dictates the nature of an offense is not a recent phenomenon:

> Radical criminologists have traditionally argued that the definition of offenses is historically contingent, a function of the needs of the dominant class at any point in history. Many activities that seem totally unexceptionable on their face (for instance, hunting in England on medieval common grounds) turns into the capital offense of poaching as the ascending bourgeoisie wants to consolidate its control over land as a commercial factor of production and to proletarianize the peasantry by denying it sources of sustenance other than wages for hired work.... At the same time, as activities harmless to all but the rulers are outlawed, obviously harm-causing activities that are routinely performed by the dominant classes (*e.g.*, spewing carcinogens into the air and water) tend to be noncriminal or, even when criminalized (*e.g.*, white-collar crimes like embezzlement and price-fixing), punished trivially and rarely.

Kelman, "The Origins of Crime and Criminal Violence" inD. Kairys (ed.) *The Politics of Law*. (1982), p. 218.

8. The tragedy of Eleanor Bumpurs was put in an ironic perspective by one citizen who asserted:

> What has not been made clear in discussion relating to this case is that Mrs. Bumpurs was evicted on a default judgment of possession and warrant of eviction issued without any hearing of any kind. She was never personally served because, allegedly, she was not at home on the two occasions the process server says he called. Since Mrs. Bumpurs did not appear in court to answer the petition for her eviction, the default judgment for possession and warrant for her eviction were signed by the Civil Court judge solely on the papers submitted. From what we know now...there is serious doubt about the validity of those papers.
>
> Only last year, in announcing the indictments of five process servers, the Attorney General and the New York City Departments of Consumer Affairs and Investigation issued a report on service of process in Civil Court, finding that at least one-third of all default judgments were based on perjurious affidavits....

NY Times, 19 Mar. 1987 p. A26, col. 4.

9. *NY Times*, 12 Jan. 1987 p. B2, col. 5.

10. *NY Times*, 27 Feb. 1987 p. B1, col. 2.

11. *Ibid.* The case was not brought to trial until January, 1987. Initially, a grand jury indicted Officer Sullivan for reckless manslaughter. Two lower courts rejected the indictment, but in 1986, the Court of Appeals of New York reversed and ordered a trial regarding the second shot.

12. *NY Times*, 26 Nov. 1986 p. B6, col. 3 (emphasis added).

13. *Ibid.*

14. *NY Times*, 12 Jan. 1987 p. B2, col. 3.

15. Remarks of Benjamin Ward, Police Commissioner of New York City, at City University of New York (CUNY) Law School (Nov. 1985) (audiotape on file at CUNY) [hereinafter Ward].

16. *NY Times*, 21 Nov. 1984 p. B3, col. 1.

17. *Ibid.* Against this, it is interesting to note that in New York City, where blacks and latinos account for close to half the population, "86.8 percent of police officers are white; 8.6 percent are black; 4.5 percent Latino; and 0.1 percent Asian or American Indian." "Fact Sheets on Institutional Racism," Council on Interracial Books for Children (January 1982).

18. Ward, *supra* note 15.

19. Raab, "Ward Defends Police Actions in Bronx Death," *NY Times*, 3. Nov. 1984, § 1, p. 27, col. 1.

20. *Webster's Ninth New Collegiate Dictionary* (1983), p. 682.

21. *Ibid.* p. 655.

22. Laws requiring police officers to use nonlethal alternatives are prevalent in this country.

> [N]ationwide, a majority of the states have specific provisions governing the use of deadly force. Approximately twenty-four states have codified the common-law 'fleeing felon' rule under which a law enforcement officer is justified in using deadly force in order to arrest any person suspected of committing any felony. Primarily because of the considerable discretion inherent in the choice to use deadly force, provisions of the Model Penal Code have called for state statutes requiring the decision to use deadly force be based on the concern for immediate public safety rather than the fact that a felony, in name only, has been committed.
>
> As a general proposition, efforts to control the use of deadly force have not fared too well over time. For example, the Missouri legislature rejected the suggestion of its advisory committee to limit the use of deadly force when he or she 'reasonably believes' such force is necessary. Of the states evaluated, over half dealt with the issue of the use of force, but few adhered to the standard of the Model Penal Code concerning the police decision to use force. The approach of the legislatures evaluated has to be described as one of maintaining extensive discretion in the use of force — not of limiting it.

Williams, "The Politics of Police Discretion," in C. Pinkele and W. Loutham (eds.), *Discretion, Justice, and Democracy*, (1985), p. 23.

23. J. Swift, *Gulliver's Travels* (1726).

24. Ward, *supra* note 15.

25. "Th[e] process of allowing the structures we ourselves have built to mediate relations among us so as to make us see ourselves as performing abstract roles in a play that is produced by no human agency is what is usually called...reification. It is a way people have of manufacturing necessity: they build structures, then act as if (and genuinely come to believe that) the structures they have built are determined by history, human nature, economic law." Gordon, "New Developments in Legal Theory" in *The Politics of Law*, supra note 7, p. 289; see also United States Commission on Civil Rights, *Who is Guarding the Guardians? A Report on Police Practices* (1981).

26. Raab, *supra* note 19.

27. *Ibid.*; Ward, *supra* note 15.

28. This was part of the basis on which two lower courts had vacated the 1985 grand jury indictment of Officer Sullivan, before it finally was reinstated in November, 1986, and the basis on which the Police Benevolent Association protested Officer Sullivan's being tried at all. See *NY Times*, 26 Nov. 1986, p. B1, col. 5.

29. Ward, *supra* note 15; see also *NY Times*, 21 Nov. 1984, p. B3, col. 1 (Mayor Koch's description of the Bumpurs incident).

30. Ward was the first black commissioner in the history of the New York City Police Department. Compared to other responsible officials, he was subjected to a glaringly excessive degree of scrutiny.

31. *NY Times*, 13 Jan. 1987, p. B1, col. 4. The hypothesized failure of Mrs. Bumpurs' children to look after her actually became a major point in Officer Sullivan's defense attorney's opening statement and closing argument. Ironically, "a former employee of the Housing Authority said that, three weeks before Mrs. Bumpurs' death...her relatives tried to make a payment of about...half of the rent she owed...but the former Authority employee, Joan Alfredson,...who was a bookkeeper, said she turned down the payment because she was forbidden to accept partial payment without the written consent of a supervisor." *Ibid.*

32. *NY Times*, 6 Jan. 1987, p. B1, col. 4.

33. *NY Times*, Dec. 23, 1986, at B4, col. 6.

34. *Ibid.*

35. *NY Times*, 29 Dec. 1986, p. B3, col. 3. The pinnacle of legitimacy to which this particular question arose is, to me, the most frightening aspect of this case. For example, when Mayor Koch was asked why he thought the young men were walking around Howard Beach, he dignified the question with the following answer: "I don't know...and neither did the 12 or so people who beat them. Because they didn't ask them. They didn't talk to them" (*ibid*). One is left to speculate that if the attackers, these self-annointed gatekeepers, *had* asked and gotten an answer like "none of your business" they then would have been entitled to beat and attack in the fullness of public spirited zeal. One wonders further, what explanation really would have been a sufficient "open sesame" to allow young black males to continue unmolested passage into the sanctified byways of Howard Beach?

36. *Village Voice*, 6 Jan. 1987, p. 16, col. 1.

37. *Ibid.*

38. Professor Richard Delgado has written extensively on how such analyses are used to undercut affirmative action:

> A 'we they' analysis...justifies a disadvantage that we (the majority) want to impose on ourselves to favor *them* (the minority). This type of thinking, however, leaves the choice of remedy and the time frame for that remedy in the hands of the majority; it converts affirmative action into a benefit, not a right. It neglects the possibility that a disadvantaged minority may have a moral claim to a particular remedy.
>
> The inner-circle commentators rarely deal with issues of guilt and reparation. When they do, it is often to attach responsibility to a scapegoat, someone of another time or place, and almost certainly of another social class than that of the writer. These writers tend to focus on intentional and determinable *acts* of discrimination inflicted on the victim by some perpetrator and ignore the more pervasive and invidious forms of discriminatory *conditions* inherent in our society. This 'perpetrator' perspective deflects attention from the victim-class, the Blacks, Native Americans, Chicanos, and Puerto Ricans who lead blighted lives for reasons directly traceable to social and institutional injustice.

Delgado, "The Imperial Scholar," *U. PA. L. REV.* 132 (1984): 561, 570-71.

39. Reid, "Visible Man," *Village Voice*, 6 Jan. 1987 p. 15, col. 3.

40. In an interview with Alton Maddox and Vernon Mason, attorneys for the victims of the Howard Beach attack, a reporter asked if "too much" was being made of this case:

> Maddox: We've had too many murders, so you can never make too much out of a case when you've seen too many other similar murders. What happens is that the rage expands and it continues to expand as the establishment continues to whitewash these cases....
>
> Mason: I think it is a tribute in a commemorative way, almost a memorial way, that we have our dead who spiritually are rising up from their graves now — Willie Turks, Michael Stewart, Eleanor Bumpurs, Darryl Dodson [all New Yorkers killed in recent white-on-black violence] and so many other people over the ages who have been the victims of injustice. We have had to live with all of that. We have had to absorb all of that. There is something to be said about the adage that if a Black person is not psychologically ill or paranoid, then something's wrong with him. We've had to absorb all of that pain with no justice.
>
> We as a people have had to deal with a distorted, bizarre way of dealing with our pain over a period of years. That rage that Alton was talking about, it didn't disappear; people still remember. It expands.

City Sun, 1-13 Jan. 1987, p. 7-8.

41. Delgado has stated:

> Emphasizing utility or distributive justice as the justification for affirmative action has a number of significant consequences. It enables the writer to concentrate on the present and the future and overlook the

> past.... The past becomes irrelevant; one just asks where things are now and where we ought to go from here, a straightforward social-engineering inquiry.... But...it robs affirmative action programs of their moral force in favor of a sterile theory of fairness or utility. No doubt there is a great social utility to affirmative action, but to base it solely on that ground ignores the *right* of minority communities to be made whole, and the *obligation* of the majority to render them whole.

Delgado, *supra* note 36, p. 570.

42. During a trip to Howard Beach that was to be his effort to promote racial harmony, Mayor Koch asserted that "most robberies were committed by blacks...." *NY Times*, 29 Dec. 1986, p. B3, col. 5.

43. Mayor Koch went on, moreover, to reassure his all-white audience that "most of the victims were black, too." *Ibid.*

44. *Ibid.*; see *supra* note 43.

45. D. Berrigan and T. Nhat Hanh, *The Raft is Not the Shore*, (1975) p. 38.

46. Lacan wrote:

> Who, if not us, will question once more the objective status of this 'I', which a historical evolution peculiar to our culture tends to confuse with the subject? This anomaly should be manifested in its particular effects on every level of language, and first and foremost in the grammatical subject of the first person in our languages, in the 'I love' that hypostatizes the tendency of a subject who denies it. An impossible mirage in linguistic forms among which the most ancient are to be found, and in which the subject appears fundamentally in the position of being determinant or instrumental of action.
>
> Let us leave aside the critique of all the abuses of the *cogito ergo sum*, and recall that, in my experience, the ego represents the center of all the *resistances* to the treatment of symptoms. It was inevitable that analysis, after stressing the reintegration of the tendencies excluded by the ego, in so far as they are subjacent to the symptoms that it tackled in the first instance, and which were bound up for the most part with the *failures* of Oedipal identification, should eventually discover the 'moral' dimension of the problem.

J. Lacan, "Aggressivity in Psychoanalysis" in *Ecrits: A Selection*, (1977) pp. 23-24.

47. The starkest recent example of this has been the disastrous delay in responding to the AIDS epidemic; as long as AIDS was seen as an affliction affecting Haitians, Hispanics, Africans and other marginalized groups such as intravenous drug users and homosexuals, its long-term implications were ignored. "Health Experts Fault U.S. on Response to AIDS," *NY Times*, 12 Aug. 1987, p. A20, col. 1.

48. See Letter to the Editor, *supra* note 3.

49. See generally K. Clark, *Dark Ghetto* (1965); K. Clark, *Prejudice and Your Child*, (1955); J. Comer and A. Poussaint, *Black Child Care* (1975); W. Grier and P. Cobbs, *Black Rage* (1968).

50. See generally Selznick, "Law, Society and Moral Evolution" in P. Schucman (ed.), *Readings in Jurisprudence and Legal Philosophy*, 931 (1979); 947-49.

51. "[T]he Oedipal identification is that by which the subject transcends the aggressivity that is constitutive of the primary subjective individuation. I have stressed elsewhere how it constitutes a step in the establishment of that distance by which, with feelings like respect, is realized a whole affective assumption of one's neighbur [sic]." Lacan, *supra* note 46, p. 23.

52. See generally A. Miller, *The Drama of Gifted Child,* (1984).

53.

> An example relevant to the development of 'legal reification' can be found in any first grade classroom. It is 8:29 and children are playing, throwing food, and generally engaging in relatively undistorted communication. At 8:30 the teacher ... calls the class to attention: it is time for the 'pledge of allegiance.' All face front, all suffer the same social rupture and privation, all fix their eyes on a striped piece of cloth. As they drone on, having not the slightest comprehension of the content of what they are saying, they are nonetheless learning the sort of distorted or reified communication that is expressed in the legal form. They are learning, in other words, that they are all abstract 'citizens' of an abstract 'United States of America,' that there exists 'liberty and justice for all,' and so forth — not from the content of the words, but from the ritual which forbids any rebellion. Gradually, they will come to accept these abstractions as descriptive of a concrete truth because of the repressive and conspiratorial way that these ideas have been communicated (each senses that all the others 'believe in' the words and therefore that they must be true), and once this acceptance occurs, any access to the paradoxically forgotten memory that these are mere abstractions will be sealed off. And once the abstractions are reified, they can no longer be criticized because they signify a false concrete.

Gabel, "Reification in Legal Reasoning," in *3 Research in Law and Sociology*, 25, 26-27.

54. The following newspaper account describes an encounter between Mayor Koch and a black congregation in Jamaica, Queens: "In discussing the Howard Beach incident, Mr. Koch asked the people in Morning Star [Baptist Missionary Church] whether, if three white men were walking in Harlem after midnight, 'do you believe they would be absolutely safe?'"

"'Yes,' the congregation chorused. The Mayor did not think so, but said he was glad they did." *NY Times*, 29 Dec. 1986, p. B3, col. 6.

In reading this, I had trouble discerning the Mayor's motivation in asking such a question. Was the Mayor implying that blacks *would* support racial violence if it occurred in reverse? If, as the story implies, Koch thought the congregation would say 'no,' what he then would have "shown" is that racism is just human nature after all; that public absolution is simply a matter of pointing a finger and wailing "well you did it too;" and that death in "turf wars" — or over eviction notices — isn't really racism, but just part of life.

55. Rev. Dr. Timothy Mitchell, pastor of Ebenezer Missionary Baptist Church stated, "What happened to Michael Griffith [who was killed in the Howard Beach incident] can

happen to any of us.... The issue is whether we are free to walk around in our city and be seen and accepted and protected as God's children." *NY Times*, 29 Dec. 1986, p. B3, col. 1.

56. Dr. Gerald Schulze, a physician at Coney Island Hospital stated, "I don't want to continue to hear Howard Beach is a hotbed of racial violence because it isn't." *NY Times*, 23 Dec, 1986, p. B4, col. 4.

57. When Alan Hendrickse, the leader of the mixed race chamber of the South African Parliament, decided to go swimming at a "whites only" beach, President Botha demanded that he either apologize or resign, or he would "have no choice but to dissolve the Parliament.... When he started marching in on the beach, he embarrassed me and broke the rules of Parliament.... It is a question of procedure." *NY Times*, 22 Jan. 1987, p. A3, col. 6.

58. *NY Times*, 23 Dec. 1986, p. B4, col. 6.

59. Inner rage tends to burn out our connections to the real world. It tends to overwhelm reason and to destroy the faces and beings of others. In our anger we can only see ourselves. The inability to imagine the experience of the stranger, of the other, was exactly what made the Holocaust possible. The Nazi success in dehumanizing their victims has left us with such rage that we too can dehumanize, erase the individual faces of others. We must find a way to let our anger burn freely, openly without consuming or perverting ... otherwise we remain victims forever.

Roiphe, "The Politics of Anger," 1 *Tikkun*, 18 (1986), 22.

60. Professor Robert Cover discussed the relation of "name-calling" to the power of the judiciary as follows:

> The judge in imposing a sentence normally takes for granted the role structure which might be analogized to the 'transmission' of the engine of justice. The judge's interpretive authorization of the 'proper' sentence can be carried out as a deed only because of these others; a bond between word and deed obtains only because a system of social cooperation exists. That system guarantees the judge massive amounts of force — the conditions of effective domination — if necessary. It guarantees — or is supposed to — a relatively faithful adherence to the word of the judge in the deeds carried out against the prisoner.... If the institutional structure — the system of roles — gives the judge's understanding its effect, thereby transforming understanding into 'law,' so it confers meaning on the deeds which effect this transformation, thereby legitimating them as 'lawful.' A central task of the legal interpreter is to attend to the problematic aspects of the integration of role, deed, and word, not only where the violence (*i.e.*, enforcement) is lacking for meaning, but also where meaning is lacking for violence.

Cover, "Violence and the Word," *Yale Law Journal* 95 (1986): *Yale L.J.*, 1601, 1619 (1986).

61. *Ibid.* at 1629.

62. In describing the degree to which subway gunman Bernhard Goetz was made a folk hero after he shot four young black men, Kenneth Clark stated:

> There is no question that society must be protected from those who assault, rob or otherwise violate others. These forms of lawless behavior must be punished. But they cannot be punished constructively by the

> lawlessness of another individual. Frustration, fear and outrage afflict both the rejected and the 'respectables.' This common predicament blurs the boundaries between the lawful and the lawless. As a society adjusts to, or rewards, its accepted cruelties and continues to deny their consequences, it makes heroes of lawless 'respectables' and in so doing develops a selective form of moral indignation and outrage as a basis for the anomaly of a civilization without a conscience.

Clark, "In Cities, Who Is the Real Mugger?" *NY Times*, 14 Jan. 1987, p. A19, col. 1.

63. *NY Times*, 24 Dec. 1986, p. B4, col. 6.

64. See *supra* note 16 and accompanying text.

65. See *supra* note 35 and accompanying text.

66. Walt Whitman recognized a world in which nature knows no boundaries:

> I guess [the grass] is a uniform hieroglyphic, And it means, Sprouting alike in broad zones and narrow zones, Growing among black folks as among white.... I give them the same, I receive them the same.

W. Whitman, "Song of Myself," in *Leaves of Grass,* (1977) p. 39.

67. The microcosm to which I am referring is the experience of being excluded, not that of not being able to get into that store *per se.*

68. It is in understanding the degree to which black buying power is nevertheless a sustaining component in even the strongest white economies that reveals the logic behind the controversial boycott of white-owned businesses, called for by some black leaders in the wake of Howard Beach. Rev. Calvin O. Butts III of the Abyssinian Baptist Church said, "We're talking about getting the kind of respect that comes from the power of our vote and our buying power." *NY Times*, 22 Jan. 1987, p. B3, col. 4.

69. For an analysis that elevates precisely this thinking to normative principles of "good intentions" in the law, see Simon, "Racially Prejudiced Governmental Actions: A Motivation Theory of the Constitutional Ban Against Racial Discrimination," *San Diego Law Review*, 156 (1978): 1041.

70. Professor Charles Lawrence aptly described this lack of malice in the following:

> It is common for racial minorities, especially those who find themselves relatively isolated in predominantly white institutions, to have white colleagues express stereotyped or derogatory views either by way of direct statements or by unstated but implicit assumptions.... It is obvious to the minority person that the speaker has not intended a racial slight — his tone is friendly and candid — and that he is unaware of the attitudinal source of the inadvertent derogation. And when other whites are present, they are unlikely to hear or be sensitive to the connotations of the demeaning remark.

Charles Lawrence, "The Id, the Ego, and Equal Protection: Reckoning with Unconscious Racism," *Stanford Law Review*, 39: 317, 341, n.100.

71. Death under these circumstances is, in the mythology of most cultures, associated with some sort of initiatory transformation. Shamanism, fraternities and Christianity thus all share elements of suffering, death, and resurrection.

> [T]he same symbolism occurs again in the Buddhist tradition: the monk gives up his family name and becomes a 'son of Buddha'... because he is 'born among the saints.' ... But this initiatory birth implied death to profane existence.... [I]n Hinduism as well as in Buddhism ... the yogi 'dies to this life' to be reborn into another mode of being, that which is represented by 'liberation.'

M. Eliade, *Myths, Dreams and Mysteries*, trans. P. Mairet (1975), p. 227.

72. Such ideas are found in many cultures other than our own:

> In the West, the loss of the sense of self...is often regarded as a sign of madness, but in India the loss of the sense of Self...as distinct from God ...is the key to enlightenment.... Because they move as far away as possible from the terrifying brink of solipsism, Indians tend to rush to the other extreme of attributing an external reality to the internal mental constructions of other people.... In this way, it is possible to get gobbled up by dragons that *other* people believe in.

W. O'Flaherty, *Dreams, Illusion, and Other Realities*, (1984) p. 121.

73. Creating a self-identity through the eyes of others is not a new phenomenon:

> [A]ll the sociologists of the 'primitive mind' busy themselves around this profession of identity, which, on reflexion [sic], is no more surprising than declaring, 'I'm a doctor' or 'I'm a citizen of the French Republic' and which certainly presents fewer logical difficulties than the statement, 'I'm a man', which at most can mean no more than, 'I'm like he whom I recognize to be a man, and so I recognize myself as being such.' In the last resort, these various formulas are to be understood only in reference to the truth of 'I is an other', an observation that is less astonishing to the intuition of the poet than obvious to the gaze of the psychoanalyst.

J. Lacan, "Aggressivity in Psychoanalysis," in *Ecrits: A Selection, supra* note 46, p. 23.

74. Lacan permits us to explore the relations between the unconscious and human society.

> One way of describing his work is to say that he makes us recognize that the unconscious is not some kind of seething, tumultuous, private region 'inside' us, but an effect of our relations with one another. The unconscious is, so to speak, 'outside' rather than 'within' us — or rather it exists 'between' us, as our relationships do.

T. Eagleton, *Literary Criticism* (1983), p. 173..

75. Undoubtedly, something that is not expressed does not exist. But the repressed is always there — it insists, and it demands to come into being. The fundamental relation of man with this symbolic order is precisely the same one which founds this symbolic order itself — the relation of non-being to being.

Lacan, "Sign, Symbol, Imaginary" in M. Blonsky (ed.), *On Signs* (1985), p. 209.

76. In 1986, whites were arrested for 71.7 percent of all crimes; blacks and all other races accounted for the remaining 28 percent (T. Flanagan and K Jamieson (eds.) *Sourcebook of Criminal Justice Statistics* (1986) p. 300. Furthermore, there is evidence that "whites commit more crimes, and that white offenders have consistently lower probabilities of arrest than do either blacks or Mexican-Americans. This is particularly striking for

armed robbery and burglary" (J. Petersilia, *Racial Disparities in the Criminal Justice System* (1983), p. 44). "Controlling for the factors most likely to influence sentencing and parole decisions, the analysis still found that blacks and Hispanics are less likely to be given probation, more likely to receive *prison* sentences, more likely to receive longer sentences, and more likely to serve longer time." *Ibid.*, p. xxiv.

77. A typical example of this was the front page story of the *New York Post* of 15 June 1987, two days before the jury returned a verdict which cleared Goetz of all but illegal gun possession. The article, excoriating the prosecutor's office for even *bringing* the case, ran under an enormous heading referring to the victims as "predators."

78. Black attempts to invert this imagery have been logical but largely lost efforts. See, e.g. Flake, "Blacks Are Fair Game," *NY Times*, 19 June 1987, p. A35, col. 3.

79. *NY Newsday*, 17 June 1987, p. 5, col. 2.

80. The short stories of Joyce Carol Oates and Raymond Carver often present characters who provide the prototype of what I mean. They describe people of warmth, compassion and variety trapped in lives whose permitted limits flatten them like the roles of a situation comedy. These people adjust their exteriors to required expectations, but every now and then the repressed passion flares in sometimes wonderful, but more often destructive or self-destructive ways. See R. Carver, *Will You Please Be Quiet, Please?* (1978); J. Oates, *Marriages and Infidelities*, (1972).

81. According to the Bureau of Justice Statistics, fifty-four percent of violent crimes are committed by friends, acquaintances or relatives of the victims. "In the last four years, fewer than half, or 46 percent, of reported violent crimes were committed by complete strangers...." *NY Times*, 22 Jan. 1987, p. A24, col. 1. A most tragic example of this is the strangulation death in Central Park of college student Jennifer Levin. If public response is a measure of anything at all, what fueled the fascination with that case was the fact that David Chambers, the socialite who allegedly killed her, wasn't supposed to be the *type* of person who robbed, raped or murdered. Such typology interferes with a lot of people seeing a lot of reality. See Riley, "An Aggressive Defense — or 'Obscene' Quest?" *National Law Journal*, 13 April 1987, p. 1.

82. In a now famous videotape, Bernhard Goetz described to police in New Hampshire his intention to inflict as much harm as he could. He detailed his wish to see his victims dead; said that if he had to do it over again, he'd do the same or worse, and expressed a retrospective desire to gouge their eyes out. Yet in finding him "not guilty" of each of twelve counts of attempted murder, assault and reckless endangerment, the jury entirely discounted this confession. "We felt he said a lot of things he was unsure about. He had nine days of thinking about what happened and reading newspapers, and combined with the guilt, we felt that he may have gotten confused. His own confusion coupled with his feelings of guilt might have forced him to make statements that were not accurate." *NY Times*, 30 April 1987, p. B6, col. 2.

83. *Ibid.*

84. See Fletcher, "Goetz: Crazed Gunman or Good-Guy Defender?," *L.A. Times*, 17 May 1987, § V, p. 1, col. 4; Restak, "The Fiction of the Reasonable Man," *Washington Post*, 17 May 1987, p. C3, col. 1.

85. The criminal propensities of Goetz' victims — ranging from allegations of rape to robbery — were used not just in the context of whether deadly force should have been used

defensively, but were used to show why the four young men de*served* to be the objects of his intent to kill. *NY Times*, 28 April 1987, p. B1, col. 5. (Imagine in the case of the black gunman in the elevator, a public inquiry that focused attention on any prior racist statements of the white high schoolers, on their history of drinking and driving, on how they treated their girlfriends, on whether any of them had ever shoplifted and whether they were only in the department store to do so again. Imagine what might have happened if the black men in the Howard Beach case, even after the first few beatings, had decided to "defend" themselves by pulling guns and shooting repeatedly, to kill.)

86. *L.A. Times*, 24 Mar. 1987, Part 1, p. 4, col. 3.

87. There is a doorway on East 13th Street in New York City that for months had a huge piece of brown paper taped to it, and the legend "Goetz" written across it. It reminded me of the banners hung in windows for the parades of astronauts and other heroes. In fact, a parade was all that the Goetz hoopla lacked to make it into a proper festive event. After delivering their verdict, "defense attorney Nark Baker said the jurors asked for and received Bernhard Goetz' autograph on their jury certificates." *NY Newsday*, 17 June 1987, p. 40, col. 2.

88. See, e.g. Delgado, "Words That Wound: A Tort Action for Racial Insults, Epithets and Name-Calling," *Harv. C. R.-C.L. Law Review*, 17 (1982): 133.

89. I know few blacks who have not had some encounter with police intimidation. My earliest remembrance of such an instance was when I was about nine and my sister was about seven. My family was driving to Georgia to see my father's relatives. Two highway patrolmen stopped our car on a deserted stretch of highway in South Carolina. They were attracted to the Massachusetts license plate, and they wanted to know what "y'all" were doing in those parts. They inquired about the weather in Boston, they fondled my father's driver's license with great curiosity and they admired the lines of the car. They were extremely polite, their conversation a model of southern hospitality and propriety. Throughout the entire 15 or 20 minutes of our detention, one officer questioned my mother and father in soothing, honeyed tones; the other held a double-barreled shotgun through the rear window, pointed at my sister and me. If he had "accidently" shot us both, our deaths would have been, like that of Eleanor Bumpurs, entirely legal in the state of South Carolina.

Chapter 9

Discrimination Revisited: An Exploration of Frontstage and Backstage Criminal Justice Decision Making

Timothy S. Bynum
Michigan State University
Raymond Paternoster
University of Maryland

Abstract: While both the labeling and conflict perspectives suggest that more severe criminal sanctions are imposed on lower-class and minority defendants, prior research has not consistently revealed such disparity. Most studies, however, have focused primarily on highly visible decisions. The authors argue that discrimination is more likely to be found in the backstage regions of criminal justice decision making. Focusing on decisions about sentencing to and release from prison, the present analysis suggests that although Native Americans have not been more severely treated at sentencing (a frontstage decision), they are less likely to be paroled (a backstage decision) than similar non-Indian offenders.

Introduction

The relationship between "extra-legal" attributes and criminal justice system processing has occupied the attention of legal scholars and sociologists for over twenty years. One such attribute which perhaps has received the most attention is the race of the defendant. This interest in race is rooted in two major theoretical traditions; the conflict perspective and labeling theory.

Conflict theorists have generally emphasized the role of economic, political and cultural power in the creation and maintenance of social order (Coser, 1956; Dahrendorf, 1957; Collins, 1975). In terms of legal system processing this has meant that criminal sanctions are used by the powerful as a mechanism through which those who threaten the interests of the *status quo* may be controlled (Gordon, 1973; Spitzer, 1975; Quinney,

* Originally published in *Sociology and Social Research*, Vol. 69, No. 1: 90-108 (October 1984).
Reprinted by permission of University of Southern California.

1977). As power is distributed along class and racial lines in American society, threats to the existing power structure are seen by conflict theorists as identified by class and racial group membership. Members of racial minorities, inasmuch as they are disproportionately members of the lower economic class, can be expected to be subject to more frequent and more severe treatment at all levels in the criminal justice system. In an early statement of the conflict position, Chambliss (1969: 86) noted this tendency of class bias in American criminal justice:

> A consequence of the unequal ability of members of different social classes to reward the legal system is that at every step of the legal process the lower class person is more likely to feel the sting of the law enforcement process.

Although most conflict theorists speak in terms of *class* conflict and *class* bias in the operation of the legal system, conflict theory can also be used to derive propositions about racial disparity. Although there is a strong relationship between race and social class position, this is not to say that race and class effects are coterminous. Racial disparity and class bias, though interrelated, are independent features of differential legal processing.

Within the conflict perspective, there are several reasons to expect racial disparity within official criminal justice activities. One of these emphasizes the powerlessness of racial minorities in American society. Conflict theorists, such as Turk (1969: 163) suggest that racial minorities are more likely to receive harsh treatment in the legal system because they lack sufficient resources and power relative to norm enforcers:

> ...there is no doubt that nonwhites in the United States are more powerless than are whites to affect legal decisions or to resist their implementation.... every indicator continues to point to the relatively disadvantaged position of the nonwhite in this country.

According to Turk, the relative powerlessness of nonwhites will ensure a one-way flow of criminalization because their behavior is both more subject to criminal definition and because (*ibid.*: 169) "nonwhites are less able than whites to resist enforcement." The relative inability to resist enforcement occurs not only at the police "street level" of justice but at bail, access to counsel, sentencing and beyond.

Labeling theorists entertain a similar expectation concerning the discriminatory application of the criminal sanction to racial minorities. One reason for this expectation is identical to that offered by conflict theorists — the relative lack of power of racial minorities and the threat to social order posed by the powerless in the eyes of the powerful. Similar to Turk's (1969: 70) contention that "the greater the power difference in favor of norm enforcers over resisters, the greater the probability of criminalization" is the claim of one labeling theorist (Lofland, 1969: 14) that:

> ...deviance is the name of the conflict game in which individuals or loosely organized small groups *with little power* are feared by a well-organized, visible, minority or majority who have a large amount of power [emphasis added].

Furthermore, just as Turk expressed that the greater probability of criminalization for blacks in America is, in part, a product of their powerlessness, Becker (1963: 1213) noted that:

> The degree to which an act will be treated as deviant depends also on who feels he has been harmed by it. Rules tend to be applied more to some persons than others.... the law is differentially applied to Negroes than whites.

In his discussion of labeling processes, Schur (1971) noted that outcomes of deviant events are not determined solely by the behavior of deviance-processing organizations. Between those labeling and those being labeled there is considerable bargaining and negotiation that significantly influences whether a deviant label is applied and if so, of which type. In terms of negotiation and bargaining over the application of criminal labels, racial minorities, because of a lack of resources (competent legal counsel, bail money, etc.) are more likely to find themselves in a disadvantageous position, and so receive more severe treatment.

In addition to the relative power position of nonwhites, conflict and labeling theorists posit other reasons for expecting racial disparity in the outcomes of legal processing. Turk (1969: 169-170), for instance, claims that nonwhites are more likely to be criminalized than whites because they are more likely to disagree over legal norms and because they are less likely to make "realistic" or "sophisticated" (i.e., conflict-reducing) moves *vis-à-vis* norm enforcers. In a similar vein, labeling theorists would predict a greater severity of treatment for minorities because of the existence and use of racial stereotypes at the organizational-processing level (Lofland, 1969, Simmons, 1969; Schur, 1971; Hawkins and Tiedeman, 1975). The stereotyping of particular racial minorities as "crime prone" and the considerable discretion within which such typifications could operate would be expected to result in minority group members being more severely sanctioned by deviance control organizations.

As can be seen, there are important theoretical convergences between the conflict and labeling perspectives which would lead theorists from both traditions to predict racial disparity in the application of legal sanctions. Theorists from both perspectives would agree that in American society racial minorities have been economically and politically suppressed, putting them in a subordinate position both in organizationally-based negotiation processes and in large-scale power conflicts. In addition, there is a rich tradition of stereotypes around their criminality, stereotypes shared not only by the general public but by "norm enforcers."

Although the expectation that racial minorities will receive harsh treatment by the legal system is derived from at least two well-established theoretical perspectives, the empirical evidence in support of it has been less than conclusive. Research on the relationship between suspect's race and the decision to make an arrest have provided inconsistent support for the racial disparity hypothesis. While most studies have shown that blacks are more likely to be arrested, some researchers have concluded that this is due to legal considerations, such as the seriousness of the offense (Terry, 1967; Black and Reiss, 1970; Black, 1971), the antagonistic demeanor of black suspects (Black,

1971), or the dispositional preference of complainants (Black and Reiss, 1970; Lundman *et al.*, 1978). Other studies, however, have suggested that the race/arrest relationship is not artifactual (Black, 1968; Lundman, 1974; Visher, 1983; Smith, 1984).

Research on the relationship between race and the sentencing decision has been no more conclusive. While some studies have found that the race of the defendant does affect either the type or length of sentence (Chiricos, *et al.*, 1972; Thomas and Cage, 1977; Lizotte, 1977; Liska and Tausig, 1979; Thornberry, 1979; Farnworth and Horan, 1980; Unnever, 1982), others have found either very weak or no such effect (Burke and Turk, 1975; Chiricos and Waldo, 1975; Berstein *et al.*, 1977; Cohen and Kluegel, 1978; Hagan *et al.*, 1979).

It might appear from the literature on racial correlates of arrest and sentencing that the conflict and labeling proposition about racial disparity in legal decision making has been discredited. Consideration of the *context* of the arrest and sentencing decisions within the overall system of social control, however, may bring to light both a possible interpretation of the lack of evidence of racial disparity at these levels and suggestions for alternatives research strategies. In examining why so little support for the racial bias hypothesis has been found, it is helpful to remember that some legal decisions are highly visible ceremonies, taking place in the "front region" (Goffman, 1959) of the legal system. Inasmuch as sentencing is a public ceremony, conducted in places easily accessible to public view, as is the decision to arrest in the presence of a complainant, it behooves the personnel in the system to follow the officially espoused ideology of egalitarianism. Operating under an official ideology of equal treatment before the law, and hemmed in by the public and quasi-public nature of its proceedings, police and court workers are at times relatively restricted in the opportunity to use extra-legal information in decision making. This is not to say, of course, that there is no disparity along racial lines in the legal system; rather it is to say with Green (1964: 357) that if there is, it is "more apt to occur in the less public phases of the administration of justice."

If there is racial bias in the criminal justice system, then it is more likely to appear in less visible ceremonies. Goffman (*ibid.*: 113) has referred to these regions of social interaction as "backstages." As "backstage" areas, the events occurring within them are often totally withheld from public view: "the back region will be the place where the performer can reliably expect that no member of the audience will intrude." Shielded from public scrutiny, the performance of actors "backstage" may often violate official or public expectations. Indeed, as Goffman (1959: 112) makes clear, because they are not open to public view, backstage events may deliberately contradict the impression created in the more visible front region:

> ...when one's activity occurs in the presence of other persons, some aspects of the activity are expressively accentuated and other aspects, which might discredit the fostered impression, are suppressed. It is clear that accentuated facts make their appearance in what I have called a front region; it should be just as clear that there may be another region — a "back region" — where the suppressed facts make an appearance.

> A back region or backstage may be defined as a place, relative of a given performance, where the impression fostered by the performance is knowingly contradicted as a matter of course.

In the front region, ceremonies such as police-suspect-complainant interactions and criminal trials, are deliberately imbued with a spirit of legal equality, while discrimination may yet appear in backstage events, with "suppressed facts making an appearance." A limitation of previous studies on the role of race in legal decision making, then, is that they have often been conducted in frontstage regions.

There are, however, regions in the legal process which are more nearly protected from public inspection and scrutiny, regions where only criminal justice system actors have access. In these areas research showing racial disparity in treatment has been more consistent. Studies on the prosecutor's issuing of arrest warrants (Hepburn, 1978); access to private counsel (Swigert and Farrell, 1977; Unnever, 1982), and release on bail (Lizotte, 1977; Unnever, 1982; Bynum, 1982) show either a direct or indirect effect for the defendant's race. One other backstage, low-visibility decision point in the criminal justice process which has received relatively little research attention is the granting of parole.

Except in those states with rigorous determinate sentencing laws, the decision to release an offender from incarceration has been in the hands of paroling authorities. With but few exceptions parole decisions have been made at hearings conducted within prison walls beyond the purview of all but parole board members and inmates. In addition, paroling authorities have virtually unguided and untrammeled discretion (Stanley, 1976; Coffee, 1978; von Hirsch and Hanrahan, 1979). The few studies that have focused on the impact of race on paroling decisions suggest that at this stage racial minorities may receive more severe treatment than whites. In their study of parole decision making, Carroll and Mondrick (1976) found that black inmates served a significantly longer proportion of their sentence than whites before being released on parole. In a study of early exit from prison on "shock probation," Peterson and Friday (1975) found that race was the strongest factor in predicting this form of release.

In summary, the inconsistent evidence found in previous research for the unequal treatment of racial minorities in legal processing may reflect the *context* within which that treatment takes place. Frontstage regions are exposed to public intervention and intrusion, making it difficult for norm enforcers to depart from the espoused ideology of equal legal treatment. Such departures from the official ideology of the legal system can more readily be conducted in hidden or backstage regions, such as parole hearings. Past research has ignored this contextual element, which may explain the inconsistencies in the literature.

A second limitation of this racial disparity literature is that for the most part studies on the effect of race in legal system decision making have restricted their attention to the difference in how whites and blacks are treated. Little research has been done on how the legal system treats other minorities, even though in some states Chicanos and Native Americans comprise a significant proportion of the nonwhite population. Of the published literature, only the studies of Lundman (1974), Hall and Simkus (1975), Lizotte (1977), Hagan (1975), Hagan *et al.*, (1979) and Unnever (1982) have included nonblack samples.

An examination of the legal treatment experienced by Native Americans would provide a clear test of the conflict/labeling hypothesis since they are perhaps the most oppressed minority group in American society (Talbot, 1981).

In summary, although the proposition that racial minorities will be more severely treated by the legal system is predicted by two major theoretical perspectives, research efforts to date have been inconclusive. This may reflect the fact that researchers have ignored an important contextual variable, the location of the event in the front or backstage of legal processing. In addition, the scope of their inquiry has been unnecessarily restricted to an examination of black-white differentials, with little attention directed toward the treatment of other racial minorities.

This paper reports on an attempt to explore criminal justice decision making in a backstage region. It focuses on how one American minority group, the Native American, fares in the decision to grant parole. In keeping with previous research findings and the theoretical expectations they have given rise to, we hypothesize that although Native Americans may not be treated more severely in the frontstage sentencing decision, they are more likely to receive more harsh treatment in the backstage decision to release on parole. In an earlier study, Swift and Bickel (1974) found that Native Americans in the federal prison system served 15 percent more time in prison than whites before being released on parole. It is not dear from the Swift and Bickel study, however, whether this was due to racial discrimination since they also reported that Indians received longer sentences than whites, and they did not consider other relevant parole criteria such as prison infractions and prior criminal history. The present study will incorporate controls for relevant legal factors and social characteristics in an attempt to more precisely address the issue of parole release and Native Americans.

Data and Method

The data employed in this analysis came from an Upper Plains state with a relatively large Native American population. At the time of the study an indeterminate sentencing system was in effect, with inmates being eligible for parole after serving one-fourth of their maximum sentence. Furthermore, there were no parole guidelines in operation which would restrict parole board decisions. Thus, in the absence of such formal criteria, parole board members possessed wide discretion in the granting of release from prison.

In order to allow sufficient time for most offenders to either be paroled or released, data were gathered from institutional records for a cohort of offenders admitted to the state prison system during 1970. Excluded from the sample were those offenders who were not eligible for release during this period (i.e., those serving life or extremely long sentences). Thus, all individuals in the sample had completed their sentence either through release on parole or serving their maximum sentence.[1] Excluded, too, were categories of offenses so singular (e.g. child molesting, extortion [total excluded = seven]) that their inclusion might have distorted the analysis. This procedure resulted in a sample of 137 offenders, of which 54, or 39 percent, were Native Americans.

In the following analysis, several approaches are used to determine the severity of sanction imposed as well as the importance of various factors in the parole decisions. Initially, the relationship between the independent variables and two indicators of sanction severity, mean length of sentence imposed and proportion of time served prior to parole, are explored. Rather than simply looking at time served before parole this latter measure relates time served to sentence imposed to obtain a single measure of severity of sanction.[2] An offender who serves two years of a four-year sentence has served longer than one who has served 18 months of a two-year sentence, but the second offender has clearly been punished proportionately more severely. Following such a procedure overcomes a traditional weakness in parole studies and one that is particularly problematic for Swift and Bickel's (1974) earlier study of parole decisions involving Native Americans.

In the multivariate analysis that follows, release on parole was analyzed to determine the unique contribution of each of the independent variables to the parole decision. While this is a straightforward question in multivariate analysis, traditional solutions (e.g. multiple regression) are inappropriate in such situations with a dichotomous dependent variable (i.e., released or not released on parole) (Palmer and Carlson, 1976; Hanushek and Jackson, 1977; Swafford, 1980; Bynum, 1982). A logistic regression (logit) model was adopted to determine the contribution of each of the independent variables to the probability of release on parole. This nonlinear solution involves fitting a logistic function to the data in which the dependent variable is the natural logarithm of the odds of success (being paroled) rather than failure (not being paroled). The coefficients derived through this method indicate the addition each independent variable makes to the odds of success.

Two independent variables representing the "legal" factors influencing the parole decision were used: the number of prior felony convictions of the offender and the number of major infractions committed while incarcerated. (Major infractions were defined according to Department of Corrections policy and included such actions as assaults, refusing to obey orders and possession of weapons.) Sixty-five percent of the sample had at least one prior felony conviction and 50 percent had at least one major prison infraction. Additional information concerning behavior in prison that may influence parole decisions, such as participation in correctional programs, was not available. While having finalized a parole plan including adequate job and living arrangements is an important aspect of the actual date of release, in this study the release date was calculated using the date of parole approval which may have been in advance of the submission of a complete parole plan.

Three independent variables — Indian status, age at admission to prison and educational level — were urged to represent the impact of social factors upon parole decisions. Further measurements of social status, such as income or occupation, were not consistently available. A dummy variable was used to represent Indian and non-Indian.[3] The mean age at admission was 29.3 years, while the mean educational level was 9.5 years.

Table 1
Mean Length of Sentence Imposed by Race for Burglary Offenses and for all Offenses Combined

	Overall	Age		Education		Prior Convictions	
		25 and Under	Over 25	Through 9th	10th and Above	None	One or More
All Cases							
Indian (N = 51)	18.6‡	20.0	17.4‡	19.5	18.1†	17.3	19.7†
Non-Indian (N = 82)	26.5	23.9	29.6	22.5	29.9	24.7	28.6
Burglary Cases							
Indian (N = 19)	16.2†	18.6	13.6*	17.0	14.9	16.8	16.0‡
Non-Indian (N = 24)	24.8	21.5	30.4	24.3	25.3	20.0	28.9

* $p < .05$
† $p < .01$
‡ $p < .001$

Findings

To examine the differences between front and backstage ceremonies, Tables 1 and 2 present the relevant independent variables, the mean length of sentence imposed and the proportion of time served. The length of sentence imposed is a decision made in a front region (courtroom) where the theme of equality is paramount. The proportion of time served is the outcome of a variety of events played out backstage and it is here that we would expect nonlegal criteria (e.g. race) to become important.

Although most individuals in the sample were serving sentences for property crimes, the variation in type of offense may be responsible for a portion of the variation in the dependent variables. While analysis based upon a single offense does not negate the potential importance of the type of offense, it does control for the influence of this factor in decisions regarding those individuals sentenced for this offense. Thus, a secondary analysis was conducted on a reduced sample of offenders sentenced for burglary offenses only (n = 43). Table 1 presents the mean length of sentence imposed for both the full (all offenses) and reduced (burglary offenses) samples. In both cases the difference between sentences imposed upon Indians and non-Indians was statistically significant. But it is important to note that sentences imposed upon Indians were shorter than sentences imposed upon non-Indians. In the full sample, non-Indians received an average sentence of 26.5 months while the sentences given Indians averaged 18.6 ($p < .001$).[4] More importantly, in the more homogeneous sample of burglary cases, non-Indians received significantly ($p < .01$) longer sentences than Indians (24.8 and 16.2 months respectively). Table 1 also presents a comparison of the mean length of sentence imposed for Indians and non-Indians under first-order controls for age, education and prior convictions. For both samples, in each of the categories of the control variables non-Indians received longer sentences than Indians. Particularly interesting is the length of sentence imposed among different categories of age at admission. While the difference between sentences imposed on Indians and non-Indians age 25 and under was slight, there was a sizable and significant difference between older inmates. This is particularly the case in the burglary sample: the average sentence imposed on whites (30.4 months) was over twice as long as the sentence imposed on older Indian defendants (13.6 months). A similar situation was observed when controls were introduced for prior felony convictions. In the burglary sample, those non-Indians who had one or more prior convictions received sentences that averaged over a year longer than the sentences imposed on Indians with similar records.

Thus, in the frontstage region of sanctioning, Native Americans are apparently not only not subjected to more severe sanctions, they are seemingly sentenced more leniently. Several comments are in order about this apparent anomaly. First, and most important, since these data come from only an incarcerated population, we are limited in our ability to make conclusions about the sentencing process. Furthermore, it is altogether possible that Indians may be less likely than whites to be sentenced to nonincarcerative sanctions. Such a situation would result in Indians being sentenced to prison for less serious offenses; a fact that may explain the consistently shorter sentences Indians received.

The second dependent variable of interest in this analysis was the proportion of sentence served before release from prison. Table 2 presents the mean proportion of sentence served for Indians and non-Indians and the first-order controls for age, education, major prison infractions and prior convictions. In the all-cases combined sample, non-Indians served an average of 75 percent of their sentence before release from prison, while Indians served an average of 86 percent of the sentence imposed. This difference is even more striking in the burglary sample, where non-Indians served an average of 64 percent and Indians served an average of 84 percent of their sentence. (This difference is significant at the .01 level in both samples.) Furthermore, in each category of the control variables, Indians served a larger proportion of their sentence than non-Indians. These relationships are particularly strong in the burglary sample. Indians with at least one prior conviction served an average of 94 percent of their sentence while non-Indians with similar criminal records served on the average only 66 percent of the sentence imposed. The findings were similar for Indians who were older, had more education and had committed more prison infractions.

Table 2
Mean Proportion of Sentence Served by Race for Burglary Cases and for all Offenses Combined

	Overall	Age		Education		Major Infractions		Prior Convictions	
		25 and Under	Over 25	Through 9th	10th and Above	None	One or More	None	One or More
All Cases									
Indian (N = 51)	8.6‡	.77	.92*	.86	1.84	.84	.91*	.71	.89*
Non-Indian (N = 82)	.75	.71	.82	.82	.67	.76	.75	.65	.80
Burglary Cases									
Indian (N = 19)	.84†	.77	.93*	.83	.88	.86†	.84	.59	.94‡
Non-Indian (N = 24)	.64	.60	.70	.67	.61	.58	.69	.47	.66

* p < .05
† p < .01
‡ p < .001

Table 3 presents the zero-order correlations between the full range of the variables used in this analysis for both the all-cases and burglary sample. In both samples, Indians were found to be slightly older, to have more prior convictions, to have fewer major prison infractions, to receive shorter sentences and to serve a higher proportion of the sentence imposed. In addition, there was little evidence of multicollinearity (at the zero-order level), with the highest correlation between — not unexpectedly — age and prior convictions.

These results tend to support the hypothesis that members of racial minorities may receive disparate treatment in the backstage regions of criminal justice decision making. One explanation of the finding that Indians serve a higher proportion of their sentence is that they get shorter sentences, that is, those offenders receiving short sentences are more likely to complete a larger proportion of their time before being released. With a 12-month sentence, the parole authority may simply not bother to grant parole for such a short period of supervision. The data in Table 3 lend evidence to such a tendency: in both samples there was a negative association between sentence length and the proportion of sentence served. Since Indians more often received shorter sentences (all cases,

Table 3
Zero-Order Correlation Coefficients
Burglary Offenses Only

	Sentence Length	Proportion of Sentence Served	Indian	Prior Convictions	Major Infractions	Age	Education
Sentence Length		-.274	-.429	.057	.374	-.078	-.029
Proportion of Sentence Served	-.209		.479	.448	.177	.367	.137
Indian	-.276	.238		.132	-.213	.145	-.092
Prior Convictions	.152	.340	.142		.193	.626	.011
Major Infractions	.381	.154	-.068	-.017		-.183	-.082
Age	-.009	.165	.079	.520	-.229		-.052
Education	-.071	.118	.064	-.065	.036	-.133	

r=-276; burglary cases, r=-429), the apparent discrimination in release from prison may be due to this paroling practice. However, when a control is introduced for the length of sentence imposed, the correlation between being an Indian and the proportion of sentence served is reduced from .24 to .14 (the partial correlation was significant at .05), while in the sample of burglary offenders this correlation was reduced from .48 to .32 ($p < .05$). Thus, while these partial correlations are smaller than the corresponding zero-order relationships, it is clear that the difference in the proportion of sentence served by Indians and by non-Indians cannot be accounted for solely by the fact that Indians received shorter sentences than non-Indians.

Table 4 presents the results of the logit analysis. Since the dependent variable was based upon only the parole decision, the length of sentence was introduced as an independent variable in these equations. The independent variables in this analysis were effect coded in the following manner: Indian (1), non-Indian (-1); Sentence one year or less (-1), Sentence over one year (1); No major infractions (-1), One or more major infractions (1); No prior convictions (-1); One or more prior convictions (1); Less than tenth grade education (-1); Completed tenth grade or higher (1); Twenty-five years

Table 4
Logit Results

	All Cases (N = 132)	Burglary Cases (N = 43)
Indian	-.311*	-1.634†
Sentence Length	.703‡	.196
Major Infractions	-.231	-1.137
Prior Convictions	-.408*	-1.645†
Education	.229	-.736
Age	.230	.344
Constant	.443	1.491
x^2	45.432	16.284

* $p < .10$
† $p < .05$
‡ $p < .01$

old or younger (-1); Over 25 years old (1). The pattern of findings obtained from this procedure is consistent with the previous relationships. Within the all-cases sample we observe that the equation is dominated by the length of sentence. That is, among all inmates, those individuals who have over a year sentence are more likely to be paroled than those serving shorter sentences. However, given that there is a wide variation among types of crimes in this group and that sentence length varies according to type of offense, sentence length may be acting as a proxy for type and/or seriousness of offense in this heterogeneous offense group. In addition, being an Indian and having prior felony convictions were also marginally significant (p.< .10) in this equation.

The above interpretation is supported in the more homogeneous group of burglary offenders as the importance of the length of sentence was dramatically reduced. In this equation, being an Indian and having prior offenses were significantly related ($p < .05$). Although within this group of offenders Indians were significantly less likely to receive parole, those individuals serving burglary sentences who had prior felony convictions were also less likely to receive parole regardless of race. The Chi-square values reported represent a goodness of fit test and indicate an adequate fit of the models to the observed data (see Hanushek and Jackson, 1977).

An interesting property of the logit procedure is that it allows for a computation of the probabilities of success (parole) given certain characteristics. By substituting the effect codings for offender characteristics in the equation and multiplying the coefficients, the log of the odds of success may be obtained. By taking the antilog of this number, one may calculate the probabilities of parole for different categories of offenders. (See Swafford, 1980, for a particularly helpful discussion of the interpretation of findings from logit analysis.) Through such a procedure the different probabilities of parole for Indians and non-Indians controlling for other relevant factors may be observed. For example, an Indian offender who was in prison for a burglary offense, was serving a sentence of less than one year, had at least one prior convictions, had no major prison infractions, had less than a tenth grade education and was over 25 years old would have a probability of parole of .56. However, a similar non-Indian offender would have a probability of parole of .98. Similarly, an Indian burglary offender who was serving a sentence over one year, had no major infractions, had at least one prior conviction, had over a tenth grade education and was over 25 years old would have a probability of parole only .22; yet a similar non-Indian offender had a probability of parole of .90. Thus, there appears to be a dramatic and significant difference in the likelihood of parole for similar Indian and non-Indian offenders.

Discussion

The conflict and labeling perspectives hypothesize that legal sanctions will be more severely imposed on members of racial minorities. While little support for these expectations can be found in the literature, it could be that discriminatory treatment in the legal system is most likely to occur in backstage decisions that are highly discretionary and not very visible. Further, there has been little study of discriminatory treatment of non-black minority groups. The data presented in this study reveals the existence of differential treatment of Native Americans in a low-visibility criminal justice decision — the decision to grant parole. The logit analysis reported here showed that of several explanatory variables, race was a major determinant of parole release, with American Indians significantly less likely to be released than whites.

The major questions about these findings may now be raised: what is it about being a Native American that may induce the parole board to impose a more severe sanction? Do Indians have a higher recidivism rate and are parole boards simply following a policy of predictive restraint? Are Native Americans more likely to be seen by parole board members as more in need of "prison treatment and education" than whites? Hawkins' (1971) study of parole in New York demonstrated the importance of the inmate's appearance and demeanor at the parole hearing in determining parole release. In a similar vein, Piliavin and Briar (1964) found that demeanor was of major importance in the police decision to arrest and that demeanor was strongly correlated with race. Thus, blacks were more likely to be seen as having a "bad attitude" than whites and consequently were handled more severely. It is possible that a similar process may be occurring in the decision to grant parole, with Indians being perceived as having a poor presence at their parole hearing and consequently treated more harshly. They may also be viewed as having inadequate community support, such as a poor prospect for employment or an unstable living arrangement. This is compatible with Talbot's (1981) description of high rates of unemployment, poverty, idleness and family disruption in Indian society. Although suggestive, at present there are no data to address these questions — clearly, they warrant further study. An important direction for future research would be direct observational data of parole board members' attitudes and perceptions of Native Americans, as well as the behavior of Indian inmates in the parole hearing.

While the present study has found support for the hypothesis that Native Americans are likely to receive more harsh treatment in backstage legal decisions, a major anomaly of these findings remains unexplained. If Native Americans were the object of discriminatory treatment, why did they receive significantly shorter sentences? There are several possible interpretations for this phenomenon. First, Indians might be given prison sentences for offenses or in circumstances for which whites would receive probation. If whites are generally given probation for less serious crimes and only incarcerated for serious offenses, or when less serious crimes have serious factual elements associated with them, then their sentence length in the aggregate may actually be as long as or longer than those received by Native Americans. Rather than reflecting judicial leniency for Indians, however, this reflects the fact that for similar offenses Indians are less likely to receive nonincarceral dispositions. In this case, it would appear consistent to argue that Indians who receive a relatively short term of incarceration were actually being treated more harshly than similarly situated whites who avoided incarceration. Thus, what is needed to supplement the present length-of-incarceration argument is an analysis of the *type* of sentence given to similar Indian and white offenders. Hall and Simkus (1975) performed such an analysis and reported that for similar offenses, Native Americans were more likely to be incarcerated than whites.

Secondly, the shorter sentences given to Native Americans might reflect the fact that their crimes are most likely to be directed against other Indians rather than whites, and these offenses may be perceived as either less severe or less threatening than those that cross racial boundaries. This suggests the idea of a *race-specific* definition of offense severity and may account for the shorter sentences of some Indians.

While the findings from this study differ from a number of other studies dealing with the treatment of other racial minorities in the legal system, they are consistent with other studies about the discriminatory legal treatment of Native Americans. This consistently reported disparity at several decision points may suggest the existence of cumulative discrimination (Liska and Tausig, 1979) that should be addressed through a more comprehensive analysis of the treatment of Native Americans at each stage of the criminal justice process.

Endnotes

1. Those offenders who were paroled and returned to prison as a result of parole violation were included in the parole group even though they may have served their complete sentence, since they at one point did receive a favorable parole decision.
2. In this state "good time" was awarded at a rate of two months for every ten months of good behavior. Thus, for a one-year sentence an inmate would have to serve 10 months unless he committed prison infractions that would result in the loss of this good time.

Proportion of time served was computed by calculating the actual sentence (sentence imposed minus good time) and viewing the time served as a percentage of this amount. Thus, those inmates who were released at the expiration of sentence would have a proportion of time served equal to 1.0. However if an inmate lost good time and was released at his sentence expiration, the proportion of time served might be greater than 1.0 All variables were measured continuously except race which was coded "1" for Indians and "0" for non-Indians .

3. Although 83, or 60 percent, of the sample were not Indians, only three were non-white.

4. T-tests were used in determining the significance of the difference of means in Tables 1 and 2.

REFERENCES

Becker, H. 1963. *Outsiders: Studies in the Sociology of Deviance.* New York: Free Press.

Berstein, I. W. Kelly and P. Doyle. 1977. "Societal reaction to deviants: The case of criminal defendants." *American Sociological Review.* 42: 743-755.

Black, D. 1968. "Police encounters and social organization: An observational study." Department of Sociology, University of Michigan, Ann Arbor (unpublished).

.... 1971. "The social organization of arrest." *Stanford Law Review.* 23: 63-77.

Black, D. and A. Reiss. 1970. "Police control of Juveniles." *American Sociological Review.* 35: 63-77.

Burke, P. and A. Turk. 1975. "Factors affecting post-arrest dispositions: A model for analysis." *Social Problems.* 22: 313-332.

Bynum, T. 1982. "Release on recognizance: Substantive or superficial reform?" *Criminology.* 20: 67-82.

Carroll, L. and M. Mondrick. 1976. "Racial bias in the decision to grant parole." *Law and Society Review.* 11: 93-107.

Chambliss. W. 1969. *Crime and the Legal Process.* New York: McGraw-Hill.

Chiricos, T. P. Jackson and G. Waldo. 1972. "Inequality in the imposition of a criminal label." *Social Problems.* 19: 533-572.

Chiricos, T. and G. Waldo. 1975. "Socioeconomic status and criminal sentencing: An empirical assessment of a conflict proposition." *American Sociological Review.* 40: 753-772

Coffee, J. 1978. "The repressed issues of sentencing: Accountability, predictability, and equality in the era of the sentencing commission." *Georgetown Law Review.* 66: 976-1 107

Cohen, L. and J. Kluegel. 1978. "Determinants of juvenile court dispositions: Ascriptive and achieved factors in two metropolitan courts." *American Sociological Review.* 43: 162-179.

Collins, R. 1975. *Conflict Sociology: Toward An Explanatory Science.* New York: Academic Press.

Coser, L. 1956. *The Foundations of Social Conflict.* London: Free Press

Dahrendorf, R. 1957. *Class and Class Conflict in Industrial Society.* Stanford: Stanford University Press.

Farnworth, M. and P. Horan. 1980. "Separate justice: An analysis of race differences in court processes." *Social Science Research.* 9: 381-399.

Goffman, E. 1959. *The Presentation of Self in Everyday Life.* Garden City: Doubleday.

Gordon. D. 1973, "Capitalism, class and crime in America." *Crime and Delinquency.* 19: 163-186.

Green, E. 1964. "Inter- and intra-racial crime relative to sentencing." *Journal of Criminal Law, Criminology, and Police Science.* 55: 348-358.

Hagan, J. 1975. "Parameters of criminal prosecution: An application of path analysis to a problem of criminal justice." *Journal of Criminal Law and Criminology.* 65: 536-544.

Hagan, J., J. Hewitt and D. Alwin. 1979. "Ceremonial justice: Crime and punishment in a loosely coupled system." *Social Forces.* 58: 506-527.

Hall, E. and A. Simkus. 1975. "Inequality in the types of sentences received by Native Americans and Whites." *Criminology.* 13: 199-222.

Hanushek, E. and J. Jackson. 1977. *Statistical Methods for Social Scientists.* New York: Academic Press.

Hawkins, K. 1971. "Parole selection: The American experience," Ph.D. Dissertation, The University of Cambridge.

Hawkins, R. and G. Tiedeman. 1975. *The Creation of Deviance.* Columbus: Merrill Publishing.

Hepburn, J. 1978. "Race and the decision to arrest: An analysis of warrants issued." *Journal of Research in Crime and Delinquency.* 15: 54-73.

Liska, A. and M. Tausig. 1979. "Theoretical interpretations of social class and racial differentials in legal decision-making for juveniles." *Sociological Quarterly.* 20: 197-207.

Lizotte, A. 1977. "Extra-legal factors in Chicago's criminal courts: Testing the conflict model of criminal justice." *Social Problems.* 25: 564-580.

Lofland, J. 1969. *Deviance and Identity.* Englewood Cliffs: Prentice-Hall.

Lundman, R. 1974. "Routine police arrest practices: A Commonwealth Perspective." *Social Problems.* 22: 127-141.

Lundman, R., R. Sykes and J. Clark. 1978. "Police control of juveniles: A replication." *Journal of Research in Crime and Delinquency.* 15: 74-91.

Palmer, J. and P. Carlson. 1976. "Problems in the use of regression analysis in prediction studies." *Journal of Research in Crime and Delinquency.* 13: 64-81.

Peterson, D. and P. Friday. 1975. "Early release from incarceration: Race as a factor in the use of shock probation." *Journal of Criminal Law and Criminology.* March: 79-87.

Piliavin, I. and S. Briar. 1964. "Police encounters with juveniles." *American Journal of Sociology.* 70: 206-214.

Quinney, B. 1977. *Class, State and Crime.* New York: McKay.

Schur, E. 1971. *Labeling Deviant Behavior: Its Sociological Implications.* New York: Random House.

Simmons, J. 1969. *Deviants.* Berkeley: Glendessary Press.

Smith, D. 1984. "The organizational context of legal control." *Criminology.* 22: 19-38.

Spitzer, S. 1975. "Toward Marxian theory of deviance." *Social Problems.* 22: 638-651.

Stanley, D. 1976. *Prisoners Among Us: The Problem of Parole.* Washington: Brookings.

Swafford, M. 1980. "Three parametric techniques for contingency table analysis: A non-technical commentary." *American Sociological Review.* 45: 664-690.

Swigert, V. and R. Farrell. 1977. "Normal homicides and the law." *American Sociological Review.* 42: 16-32.

Swift, B. and G. Bickel. 1974. *Comparative Parole Treatment of American Indians and Non-Indians at United States Federal Prisons.* Washington: Bureau of Social Science Research.

Talbot, S. 1981. *Roots of Oppression: The American Indian Question.* New York: International Publishers.

Terry, R. 1967. "The screening of juvenile offenders." *Journal of Criminal Law, Criminology and Police Science.* 58(2): 173-181.

Thomas, C. and R. Cage. 1977. "The effects of social characteristics on juvenile court dispositions." *Sociological Quarterly.* 18: 237-252.

Thornberry, T. 1979. "Sentencing disparities in the juvenile justice system." *Journal of Criminal Law and Criminology.* 70: 164-171.

Turk, A. 1969. *Criminality and Legal Order.* Chicago: Rand McNally.

Unnever, J. 1982. "Direct and organizational discrimination in the sentencing of drug offenders." *Social Problems.* 30: 212-225.

Visher, C. 1983. "Gender, police arrest decisions and notions of chivalry." *Criminology.* 21: 5-28.

von Hirsch, A. and K. Hanrahan. 1979. *The Question of Parole: Retention, Reform or Abolition?* Cambridge: Ballinger.

Chapter 10

Black People[1] and Criminal Justice in the U.K.

Iain Crow
Senior Research Officer, NACRO

Abstract: Until recently, relatively little research had been carried out on criminal justice and black people in the U.K., but this is now changing. The indications of work to date are that black people's experience of criminal justice in the U.K. is very different from that of white people. One consequence of this is that the number of black people in Prison Department establishments is disproportionately greater than their representation in the population as a whole. However, the process by which this comes about is a complex one, reflecting not only the way that black people are dealt with by different criminal justice agencies, but also their position in society at large. The available evidence shows that, while some differential sentencing cannot be ruled out as an explanation for the disproportional representation of black people in the prison population, what seems to be more important is what happens prior to sentence, in that black people are differentially apprehended, charged and brought to court in the first instance. In view of this it is not surprising that relations between black people and the police are often troubled. This article highlights the interdependence of the criminal justice process and the way that decisions taken at one stage of the process can affect subsequent decisions, and thus be responsible for black people perceiving the whole system as discriminatory.

For some time evidence has been available which shows that in various aspects of social life in the U.K. black people are at a disadvantage compared with white people, and are discriminated against, both directly and indirectly. Unemployment, even before the rise in mass unemployment of recent years, has been higher among black people,

* Originally published in *The Howard Journal*, Vol. 26, No. 4: 303-314 (November 1987).
Reprinted by permission of Blackwell Publishers.

and black people have generally found employment in lower status, low income sectors of the labour market (Barber, 1985; Department of Employment, 1984; Smith, 1981). In housing there has been evidence in the past of discrimination, particularly with regard to local authority allocation procedures. Recent studies indicate that, although direct discrimination is now much reduced, there are still distinct differences in the housing conditions of different ethnic groups (Smith and McIntosh, 1974; Smith and Whalley, 1975; Brown, 1984). There has also been concern about underachievement by black pupils in an educational system largely geared to the white majority (Little, 1975). Because the evidence of disadvantage and discrimination is so well documented and so widespread it is not surprising that many black people believe that what is needed is not more research but more action.

When it comes to the criminal justice system, however, much less empirical material is available regarding the position of ethnic minorities in this country. At the end of the 1970s it would have been hard to come up with more than a handful of references on the topic, except for writings on relations between black people and the police. In the 1980s we are seeing a change in this situation. Not only has there been continuing, indeed heightened, interest in policing but there has also been an increase in research on such matters as sentencing and prisons. Some probation services have become more aware of the fact that they operate in a multiracial society and have carried out reviews of their working practices. This increasing attention to ethnic minorities and various aspects of the criminal justice system is in part a reflection of a growing awareness of past neglect. But it also reflects changes in U.K. society as a whole, which means that no part of that society can ignore the demands of multiracialism, the need for equal opportunities and for anti-racist policies.

Black People as Victims

A study carried out in 1980 of samples of West Indian and white people, in an area of Manchester with a high ethnic minority population, found that there was little difference between the two ethnic groups as far as their experiences of being the victims of crime were concerned (Tuck and Southgate, 1981). Such differences as there were (white people were more likely to experience attempted break-ins and theft from outside the house) could be attributed to environmental factors such as the kind of locality and type of house people lived in. Since that study was conducted, however, there has been growing concern about the increasing incidence of racial attacks in several parts of the country. A Home Office (1981a) report found that black people suffered disproportionately from racially motivated attacks, Asians faring worst of all, and that the incidence of such attacks appeared to be on the increase. It was also found that the victims of such attacks did not always report offenses. Lack of confidence in the police and other authorities were cited as the main reasons for this. The report stated that:

> There was a widespread feeling in both Asian and black communities that the police should do far more to respond to the problems experienced by the ethnic minorities and to prevent racial offences (p. 17).

The fears expressed in the 1981 Home Office report that such attacks were on the increase appear to have been borne out by more recent studies indicating that such incidents are becoming not only more numerous, but also more violent and likely to result in fatalities (Gordon, 1986; Walmsley, 1986).

Recorded Crime and Policing

There is no evidence that black people are more likely than white people to commit crimes or that the size of the ethnic minority population is related to the level of recorded crime in an area (Stevens and Willis, 1979); an inner-city area with a lot of social problems is likely to have a higher than average level of crime, regardless of the ethnic composition of the area. In the past some figures have been produced, most notably by the Metropolitan Police in a press release issued on 10 March 1982, of certain recorded crimes by perceived ethnic group of the suspect. Such measures are highly unreliable, however, and their publication has been criticized because they are not only misleading but damaging to community relations (Smith, 1982). Another, more detailed, examination of the available statistics found that

> [i]nsofar as the victims' assessments of their assailants are valid, a disproportionately large number of non-white persons appear to have committed those offences of street robbery and snatches which were recorded (Home Office, 1983: para. 30 (ii)).

Again, such conclusions need to he viewed with caution, not only because of the unreliability of the sources, but because of the need to take account of socio-economic and demographic factors. It has long been established that known offending correlates with social problems, such as bad housing and other aspects of inner-city deprivation. Offending is also more common among the young. Since ethnic minority groups are particularly susceptible to such deprivation and have a high youthful population, then a high level of representation among known offenders may be expected. In 1979 Stevens suggested that since the young and unemployed are disproportionately involved in crime, and since the proportion of young and unemployed who are black will increase, so that proportion of blacks involved in crime will increase:

> The main point of this article has been to suggest that black representation among the young and unemployed will almost certainly increase, and therefore that black representation among those arrested and convicted is also likely to increase, and that the absolute numbers of blacks arrested and convicted will increase rapidly in the 1980s and perhaps beyond (Stevens, 1979: 17).

Both the study by Stevens and Willis (1979) and the Home Office Statistical Bulletin referred to above found that black people were disproportionately more likely to be arrested than would be expected from their numbers in the population, but also further pointed out that differences in arrest rates between different ethnic groups can be largely accounted for by demographic and socio-economic factors.

Of course the likelihood of anyone appearing in official crime figures is affected by the extent to which crimes are reported, by variations in recording practices and by policing itself in such matters as stopping, searching, arresting and the bringing of charges. The likelihood of apprehension for crime is also related to socio-economic status and social disadvantage (Stinchcombe, 1963). Pease (1984), analyzing data from the British Crime Survey, concluded that the likelihood of victims reporting crimes to the police is affected by the perceived ethnic origin of the perpetrator. As a consequence "the first stage in making offenders available to the penal system is discriminatory" (p. 8).

As mentioned earlier, policing is one area of the criminal justice system that has attracted particular attention over a number of years. In 1972 Humphrey wrote: "To many Blacks in our inner cities, police harassment has become a way of life" (p. 11). Since then there has been an accumulation of evidence testifying to the troubled nature of relationships between police and black people culminating, but sadly not ending, with the report on the Brixton riots of 1981 by Lord Scarman (Scarman Report, 1981). Studies have found that young blacks are disproportionately more likely to be the subject of police stop and search powers (Willis, 1983) and were more likely to be arrested for suspicious behavior, "sus," before its repeal (Demuth, 1978). When apprehended, black juveniles are less likely than their white peers to be referred to the police juvenile bureau and are less likely to be cautioned, prosecution being more likely (Landau, 1981; Landau and Nathan, 1983). An extensive investigation by the Policy Studies Institute, commissioned by the Metropolitan Police, found that among men aged 15 to 24 the proportion of West Indians stopped by the police was considerably higher than that for whites or Asians. Those classified as being of West Indian or African origin accounted for 17 percent of people arrested but for only five to six percent of the population of London (Smith and Gray, 1983). Sixty-three percent of contacts between young West Indians were adversarial in nature, compared to only 25 percent for young whites. Racial prejudice was found to be present in many instances. The study stated:

> Although it has less effect on policing behaviour than might be expected, the level of racial prejudice in the (Metropolitan) Force is a cause of serious concern (p. 351).

Gaskell (1986), in a study comparing the attitudes of black and white young males towards the police, found evidence to suggest that, although young blacks have more negative attitudes to the police than young whites, they are not anti-police merely because the police are seen as symbols of an oppressive white society. Nor are they more hostile solely as a result of higher unemployment levels among young blacks. It is concluded that past policing strategies themselves have contributed to blacks' hostile attitudes to the police. Given the findings of the studies referred to, it is not surprising that the level of complaints against the police has been found to be higher among ethnic minorities, although complaints made by black people have been less frequently substantiated than those made by whites (Stevens and Willis, 1981). It was also found that the circumstances in which black, white and Asian complaints arose were not very different from each other.

It is relevant to note that many of the studies of crime and policing have focused on London and the Metropolitan Police. London may reflect what is to be found in other conurbations or it may be that the picture is different elsewhere. The survey in Manchester referred to earlier (Tuck and Southgate, 1981) found that there was little difference in whether those of West Indian origin and whites reported being the victims of crime and little difference in their experience of contact with the police (in contrast to the P.S.I. study), including being stopped and searched. The social characteristics of the area that people lived in were more important in all these respects:

> The data do not suggest a community strongly alienated from the local police. Differences of experience by age or by ward within the area were more substantial than ethnic differences. (Tuck and Southgate, 1981: 33)

Despite the lack of differences, black people were twice as likely as whites to feel they had wanted to complain about the police and a greater frequency of anti-police feeling was found among blacks, indicating that perhaps the data do not tell the whole story. Thus it is possible that experiences and practices do vary from place to place and there is a need to know more about what happens in different places. Hopefully the development of local crime surveys will contribute to this to some extent, but there is also a need for studies similar to that carried out by the Policy Studies Institute in the Metropolitan Police Force area to be conducted in other force areas.

The limited geographical coverage of studies to date means that care needs to be exercised in deriving any general conclusions. One thing that is important about the material on black people, crime and policing, however, is that where discrimination does occur, it will feed through to the rest of the criminal justice system. Decisions made at an early stage of the criminal justice process may affect later decisions, such as sentencing. Likewise, differences between ethnic groups found at a later stage of the process, such as the proportion of people from different ethnic groups in prison, may well have their origins in what happens at these early stages. Such disparities may appear to give credibility to the notion that black people are more likely to commit crime whereas, in fact, they are more likely to be a consequence of the criminal justice process itself. If black people are more likely to be reported, stopped, searched, arrested and charged and if, as some of the evidence suggests, this process of discrimination starts among the youngest age group, then black people are going to appear in court earlier and more often than are comparable whites. So, although more has been written about ethnic minorities and policing than about other aspects of the criminal justice system, it is important to place this material in relation to the criminal justice process as a whole.

THE COURTS

Relatively little is known about black people and the courts. The Home Office Statistical Bulletins (Home Office, 1983, 1984) reported that, in the Metropolitan Police area, the ethnic distribution of those found guilty or cautioned was similar to that for those arrested. Using data from a study of Crown Courts in London and Birmingham covering 1,476 cases in all, of which 339 involved non-whites, McConville and Baldwin (1982) came to the conclusion that

> there appears to be no evidence of direct systematic bias on racial lines in sentencing in the Crown Court. The implication is that defendants are treated equally once they attain the status of convicted persons: not necessarily fairly or appropriately, but equally (658).

However, the researchers point out that their finding does not mean that discrimination does not occur at other stages of the criminal process, for example "in connection with policing, arrest patterns, bail status or jury selection" (658).

Another study covered nine courts: four juvenile, three magistrates' and two Crown Courts in different parts of the country. The survey covered 668 cases of which 124 involved non-white defendants. Information was obtained about the characteristics of the defendants and various aspects of how each case was handled, such as whether people were remanded on bail, whether they were legally represented and whether social enquiry reports were available, as well as on defendants' previous criminal history and the nature of the present offense. This study also found no evidence that people from different ethnic groups were sentenced differently:

> The conclusion indicated by the data is that, in criminal justice terms, the different ethnic groups present similar patterns of crime, their cases are handled in similar ways and the sentences they are given are similar (Crow and Cove, 1984: 416).

Again, however, this negative finding is accompanied by the caveat that it only provides information on what happened in certain courts at a certain time and does not mean that discrimination never occurs. Attention is also drawn to one significant finding: black offenders in the sample were more likely to have been brought to court on charges which involved no loss or damage. This is consistent with an earlier Home Office study (Stevens and Willis, 1979) showing that, in crimes of violence, "there is a higher possibility that a coloured attacker will cause no injury than a white attacker" (37). This suggests that some element of differential processing takes place at an earlier stage than the court appearance. If this is so, it will add to the disparity accounted for by factors mentioned earlier, like youth and unemployment, to produce a proportion of black people appearing as defendants which is relatively high compared to their representation in the population as a whole. In the study by McConville and Baldwin, over 15 percent of those in the London Crown Court sample and over a quarter of those in the Birmingham Crown Court sample were nonwhite. Sixteen percent of the sample in Crow and Cove's study were nonwhite.

A more recent study in two magistrates' courts in West Yorkshire, involving 1,173 cases, differed from the earlier studies in finding both a smaller proportion of black defendants (5.5 percent) and some differences in sentencing. In particular, black offenders were less likely to receive a probation order but more likely to receive a community service order than whites. Black offenders were also less likely to be given a sentence of imprisonment. In common with the previous research, however, this study also points to the earlier stages of the criminal process as a source of discrimination:

> As the sample of black defendants was younger than that of whites this may suggest that black people are being apprehended by the police and prosecuted more often than whites, and that this process may start at an earlier stage for blacks (Mair, 1986: 153).

Some individuals and agencies have begun conducting local surveys of sentencing patterns in courts in their areas and these will add to the limited picture so far available. The real need, however, is for a comprehensive research project to be carried out, rather than having to rely on piecemeal data from different sources.

The Prisons

Concern has been expressed about the number of black people in penal establishments. In 1981 the *Report on the Work of the Prison Department* (Home Office, 1981b) stated that the proportion of the prison population from the ethnic minorities was growing. In some young offender establishments in the south east black people constituted more than a third of the inmate population. Fludger (1981), looking at borstals prior to their abolition found that, while the number of people of West Indian, Indian or Pakistani descent within the 15 to 19 age range in the general U.K. population was 4.3 percent, those born in the West Indies made up about four percent of the borstal population and those of West Indian origin but born in the U.K. made up a further 2.5 percent. It was also found that trainees of West Indian or Asian parentage had fewer previous convictions than trainees of U.K. ethnic origin, suggesting that West Indians and Asians have reached borstal on the strength of a shorter criminal record. This is what one would expect to find on the basis of' material presented above concerning the likelihood of black people being more likely to be protected against earlier and more readily than white people in similar situations.

The borstal system has subsequently given way to youth custody centers, but another study of establishments in London and the southeast found the same process at work:

> The most striking feature to arise from this research is the disproportionately large population of black Afro-Caribbean youths in the youth custody system.... Given the evidence that many young offenders ultimately serve adult prison sentences, it is possible that the social composition of young offender centres will become a feature of future adult prison populations (Guest, 1984).

Until recently no data was available about the ethnic composition of the prison population as a whole. In 1982 the Home Office established an ethnic monitoring system and the first results of this were published in 1986 (Home Office, 1986). This showed that the proportion of people in the prison population from ethnic minority groups is higher than their representation in the population as a whole. Among prisoners under sentence, the proportion known to be from ethnic minorities was 12 percent for male young offenders and about 11.5 percent for adult males, compared with six percent and five percent respectively in the comparable age groups in the general population. For females the corresponding proportions were 12 percent and 16 percent, compared with six percent and five percent respectively in the comparable age groups in the general population. Ethnic minority prisoners were also found to be serving longer sentences, but this was largely explicable in terms of the type of offenses involved (drug offenses were more prevalent among black prisoners), previous convictions, age, geographical area and type of court. Not explicable by such means were the findings that black prisoners had fewer previous convictions than white prisoners sentenced for the same type offense, and were more likely to have been remanded in custody. Thus the bulletin again raises the question of whether black people have been dealt with differently from white defendants by the courts. But it does not make it possible to know whether this might be a result of the way they are dealt with at an even earlier stage; for example, whether black people are charged differently to white people.

The prison system lies, in one sense, at the end of the criminal justice process. A disproportionately high number of black people in penal establishments is therefore likely to be a net reflection of the disproportionality occurring at earlier stages of the process (and not, as mentioned earlier, proof that black people are more likely to commit crime). In another sense, as the quotation from Guest (1984) above reminds us, the prison system may also be only one point on a circuit which leads to deviancy amplification. The information about the number of black people in penal establishments also underlines the need for a clearly defined race relations policy in the establishments to avoid racial discrimination occurring inside prisons. The Prison Department has taken steps in this direction by requiring the appointment of race relations liaison officers in each establishment and by setting up training courses in race relations for the liaison officers and governors.

Probation

Non-custodial options which offer the possibility of avoiding imprisonment are provided by the probation service. Unfortunately, just as the indications are that ethnic minorities are over-represented in penal establishments, so they appear to be under-represented in the preparation of social enquiry reports and on probation orders (Whitehouse, 1978). Where black people do appear to be over-represented on probation caseloads is on post-custody licenses and after-care (Taylor, 1981). Evidence that black people are less likely to receive a probation order comes from the study by Mair (1986) reported above. The study by Crow and Cove (1984) also tends in the same direction. Although in this latter study no overall differences in sentencing were found, when cases remanded for reports are excluded from the analysis, 11 percent of white defendants were given probation orders compared to only seven percent of black defendants. Unlike the prisons, there is no general ethnic monitoring system for the probation service. As a result, information is piecemeal, depending on individual services' preparedness to come to grips with operating in a multi-racial society. One of the reasons for ethnic minority clients figuring less prominently on non-custodial caseloads may be that the predominantly white service is unable to meet the demands of black offenders. In an effort to overcome such disparities the West Midlands Probation Service, together with NACRO, set up a project in 1979 to enable the Service to develop closer links with young black offenders in the Handsworth area of Birmingham in the hope that this would have an impact on sentencing. The results of the pilot study showed that, while the probation offices involved did work more with young black offenders, and there was an increase in the use of probation orders for them, the level of custodial sentences for black offenders did not decrease and the increase in probation orders was largely at the expense of other non-custodial disposals (Crow *et al*., 1982).

COMMENT

Although the information that is available about black people and criminal justice in this country is limited in several respects, one of the things the material does illustrate is the inter-relatedness of the criminal justice process. The interdependence of the criminal justice system is becoming increasingly recognized (Moxon, 1985). It needs to be realized that this interdependence also extends to and affects the way black people experience the system. Thus, discrimination at one part of the process, direct or indirect, is likely to feed through to other parts and reinforce black people's perception of the whole system as racist. This can only have disastrous consequences. The research to date shows that undoubtedly policing is a major problem area. But there is no basis for complacency elsewhere in the system. Anti-racist policies need to be pursued by the courts, the probation services and the prison service as much as by the police. Surveys which have inquired into black peoples' views of criminal justice show that there is a lack of confidence in the U.K. criminal justice system (Tuck and Southgate, 1981; Brown, 1984; King and May, 1985). The quality of justice is not solely a matter of concern for black people, however: the importance of justice being seen to be manifestly fair and equal is something that concerns us all.

Nor can the criminal justice system be seen in isolation from the discrimination which ethnic minorities experience in other areas of social life, such as employment, housing and education. Notwithstanding the research by Gaskell (1986) referred to earlier, they will all tend to be seen as part and parcel of a racist society. The process was summarized in another of the studies referred to earlier:

> Disproportionate unemployment among young people of a particular ethnic group arising out of racial discrimination, would increase the vulnerability of that group to the temptations of crime and vandalism.... The age structure, socioeconomic levels and unemployment rates of (a minority group) may increase the likelihood of its members being found in borstal (Fludger, 1981: 1).

One of the main problems, as far as the criminal justice system is concerned, is that it is almost wholly a white dominated structure and this is reflected in the way it is staffed. Whether one looks at the police, judiciary, magistracy, probation service or Boards of Visitors, ethnic minority representation is minimal and, where it does occur, is rarely found at the more senior levels. Clearly there are many problems to be overcome, not least the fact that suspicion of the criminal justice system makes it difficult for those from ethnic minority backgrounds to become part of it. Realistically, adequate ethnic minority involvement in the criminal justice system may take some time to achieve. But a more immediately achievable aim should be to give those who already operate the system an increased amount of training in working in a multi-racial society. Although some training along these lines already occurs, a recent report suggests that there is still much room for development (NACRO, 1986).

White cultural dominance extends to the research itself. Much of what has been reported here is the result of data collected by white researchers and officials. What it fails to do, so far at least, is adequately to comprehend black people's experience of the criminal justice process. For example, whether or not there is any objective proof of bias in sentencing, the reality for the young black person in a courtroom is that of being surrounded by white authority. The black community's knowledge of the criminal justice system is less likely to be found in academic journals. This article has highlighted the fact that, although research on ethnic minorities and criminal justice in the U.K. is increasing, there are still many respects in which it is inadequate. The lack of a black perspective is one of these inadequacies. What is needed is more research by black researchers and the incorporation of different strands of research, reflecting more adequately ethnic minority perspectives. It is also important to recall what was said at the beginning of this article: that black people have become impatient with research in other areas, often feeling that what is needed is not research but action. Future research on criminal justice matters should therefore be capable of being demonstrably related to developments in policy and practice. This need not dilute the quality of research. But, if research becomes seen as merely a substitute for action, this will engender cynicism among black people about it, decrease their inclination to co-operate in it and this, in turn, will affect the quality of the research and thus diminish its value.

One way in which both research and policy could be advanced significantly and soon is by the extension of ethnic monitoring. This should cover the staffing of criminal justice agencies, the way different ethnic groups are dealt with by those agencies and the availability of services for black offenders. There is no reason in principle why existing statistical series should not incorporate ethnic data in the same way they currently do age and sex. Individual courts and probation services could also benefit from maintaining ethnic records on a local basis.

ENDNOTE

1. The term 'black' in this paper is used to refer to people of African, West Indian and Asian origin.

References

Barber, A. 1985. "Ethnic origin and economic status." *Employment Gazette.* 93: 467-77.

Brown C. 1984. *Black and White Britain: The Third PSI Surveys.* London: Policy Studies Institute.

Crow, I. *et al.* 1982. *The Handsworth Alternative Scheme: Report on the Pilot Period.* London: NACRO.

Crow, I. and J. Cove. 1984. "Ethnic minorities and the courts." *Criminal Law Review.* 413-17.

Demuth, L. 1978. *SUS: A Report on the Vagrancy Act, 1824.* London: Runnymede Trust.

Department of Employment. 1984. "Unemployment and Ethnic Origin." *Employment Gazette.* 92: 260-4.

Fludger, N. 1981. *Ethnic Minorities in Borstal.* London: Directorate of Psychological Services, Home Office Prison Department.

Gaskell, G. 1986. "Black Youth and the Police." *Policing.* 2 (1): 26-34.

Gordon, P. 1986. *Racial Violence and Harrassment.* London: Runnymede Trust.

Guest, C. 1984. *A Comparative Analysis of the Career Patterns of Black People and White Young Offenders.* MSc Thesis, Cranfield Institute of Technology.

Home Office. 1981a. *Racial Attacks.* London: Home Office.

.... 1981b. *Report of the Work of the Prison Department.* London: H.M.S.O.

.... 1983. "Crime statistics for the metropolitan police district analysed by ethnic group." *Statistical Bulletin.* 22/83. London: Home Office Statistical Department.

.... 1984. "Crime statistics for the metropolitan police district by ethnic group, 1977-1983." *Statistical Bulletin.* 22/84. London: Home Office Statistical Department.

.... 1986. "The Ethnic Origin of Prisoners: The Prison Population On 30 June 1985 and persons received, July 1984-March 1985." *Statistical Bulletin 17/86.* London: Home Office Statistical Department.

Humphrey, D. 1972. *Police Power and Black People.* London: Panther.

King, M. and C. May. 1985. *Black Magistrates.* London: Cobden Trust.

Landau, S.F. 1981. "Juveniles and the Police." *British Journal of Criminology.* 21: 27-46.

Landau, S.F. and G. Nathan. 1983. "Selecting delinquents for cautioning in the London Metropolitan Area." *British Journal of Criminology.* 23: 128-49.

Little, A. 1975. "The Educational Achievement of Ethnic Minority Children in London Schools" in Verma, G. and C. Bagley (eds.), *Race and Education Across Cultures.* London: Heinemann.

McConville, M. and J. Baldwin. 1982. "The Influence of Race on Sentencing in England." *Criminal Law Review.* 652-8.

Mair, G. 1986. "Ethnic Minorities, Probation and the Magistrates Courts: A Pilot Study." *British Journal of Criminology.* 26: 147-55.

Moxon, D. (ed.). 1985. *Managing Criminal Justice.* London: Home Office Research and Planning Unit.

NACRO. 1986. *Black People and the Criminal Justice System.* London: NACRO.

Pease, K. 1984. "Crime, Race and Reporting to the Police." Unpublished paper. University of Manchester.

Scarman Report. 1981. *The Brixton Disorders: Report of an Inquiry by the Rt. Hon. Lord Scarman OBE.* London: H.M.S.O.

Smith, D. 1981. *Unemployment and Racial Minorities.* Policy Studies Institute Report No. 598. London: Policy Studies institute.

Smith, D.J. and J. Gray. 1983. *Police and People in London. Vol. IV: The Police in Action.* London: Policy Studies Institute.

Smith, D.J. and A. Whalley. 1975. *Racial Minorities and Public Housing.* London: Political and Economic Planning.

Smith, L.J. and N. Mcintosh. 1974. *The Extent of Racial Discrimination.* London: Political and Economic Planning.

Smith, S. 1982. *Race and Crime Statistics.* London: Board for Social Responsibility, Church of England.

Stevens, P. 1979. "Predicting Black Crime." *Home Office Research Unit Bulletin.* 8: 14-17.

Stevens, P. and C.F. Willis. 1979. *Race, Crime and Arrests.* Home Office Research Study No. 58. London: H.M.S.O.

Stevens, P. and C.F. Willis. 1981. *Ethnic Minorities and Complaints Against the Police.* Research and Planning Unit Paper 5. London: Home Office.

Stinchcombe, A.L. 1963. "Institutions of Privacy in the Determination of Police Administrative Practice." *American Journal of Sociology.* 69: 150-60.

Taylor, W. 1981. *Probation and After-Care in a Multi Racial Society.* London and Birmingham: Commission for Racial Equality and West Midlands Probation Service.

Tuck, M. and P. Southgate. 1981. *Ethnic Minorities, Crime and Policing: A Survey of the Experience of West Indians and Whites.* Home Office Research Study No. 70. London: H.M.S.O.

Walmsley, R. 1986. *Personal Violence.* Home Office Research Study No. 89. London: H.M.S.O.

Whitehouse, P.D. 1978. "Ethnic Minorities." *West Midlands Probation Service Bulletin.* Birmingham: West Midlands Probation Service.

Willis, C. 1983. *The Use, Effectiveness and Impact of Police Stop and Search Powers.* Research and Planning Unit Paper No. 15. London: Home Office.

Chapter 11

Racism and the Innocence of Law

Peter Fitzpatrick
Darwin College, The University

> ...with us there is nothing more consistent than a racist humanism since the European has only been able to become a man through creating slaves and monsters.[1]

Introduction

In liberal views of the world, law is manifestly incompatible with racism. Where racist practice infects law that can only be something aberrant and remediable. Exploring the British situation as a case, I will argue that on the contrary racism is compatible with and even integral to law. I try to show that the very foundational principles of law as liberal legality import racism into law, those principles of equality and universality which stand in their terms opposed to racism. The aim is not to dismiss law, nor to expose liberal legality as a sham. But neither is it to retrieve law and add to the list of obviously desirable variants on how to combat racism through law, such as recent "left strategies."[2] The point is, rather, to make such "acts, gestures, discourses which...had seemed to go without saying become problematic, difficult, dangerous."[3] A note on the term racism: I will use it in an extended way to cover both belief and practice.

Liberal Capitalism and the Specificity of Racism

Initially, I will set the argument in contrary Marxist views of racism. One, usually attributed to Marx, sees a fundamental incompatibility between racism and capitalism of

* Originally published in *Journal of Law and Society*, Vol. 14, No. 1: 119-132 (Spring, 1987).
Reprinted by permission of Blackwell Publishers.

a developed, liberal variety. With its integral assertions of equality and universalist morality, such a capitalism stands opposed to racist divisions and this for good economic reasons.[4] Far from seeing such capitalism and racism as opposed, the alternative Marxist tradition finds them compatible, even symbiotic. In economic terms racism operates to provide cheap labour and to constitute a sector of 'the reserve army of labour.' Politically, racism divides the working class and counters the transformative potential of that class. There are numerous dimensions to this. In the annals of war and imperialism, race has often served to unite a 'white' working class and bourgeoisie. Racial division has been a powerful strategic tool of employers both in undermining white workers and in gaining their support.

These abrupt accounts may seem overly functionalist. But they do have large historical warrants. So much is that so that in the dispute between them one cannot be accepted as right and the other dismissed as wrong. What they support, rather, is a picture of conflicting forces within capitalism. And what this disagreement indicates is the inability of Marxism to provide a surpassing theoretical elaboration that encompasses racism. This need not provoke a rejection of Marxism, nor should it occasion surprise if we see Marxism as confronting a specific history of liberal capitalism. That confrontation does have things to say about racism. But it could also be the case that engaging with a specific history of racism can say things about liberal capitalism. In those rare moments when critical social theory has considered racism, it has tended to be taken on as an extra, as a discrete actor in a scenario devised without it in mind. Or that has been so until recently. There are now emergent academic visions not just of the historical specificity of race but also of its current centrality and significance.[5] It is, however, difficult to establish the significance of racism in a society whose self-presentation denies that significance. Monuments to liberalism can hardly acknowledge foundations of racism. It follows that racism in its legitimate forms will not be explicit. It will be found in forms of, for example, crime and social degeneration, community and culture, nation and society. That is, the form both substitutes for explicit racism and provides a means of asserting that what is involved is not racism but something different.

The liberal denial of racism prompts certain strategies in establishing its significance. One could be seen as a root-and-branch strategy, a strategy that seeks constitutive compatibilities between liberalism and racism. This large challenge has begun to be taken up in philosophical and historical work.[6] As I interpret it, this work points to the origins of racism in the liberal Enlightenment project which, with its claims to universality, comprehensiveness and consistency, sets a fateful dimension. It can only relate to those excluded from the project through slavery or semi-slavery by saying that they are qualitatively different. This imperative, this terrifying consistency puts the enslaved and the colonised beyond the liberal equation of universal freedom and equality by rendering them in racist terms as qualitatively different. This identity in essential difference, particularly in the figure of the feckless African, becomes a counter in the making of the disciplined, 'liberal' individual in the West. Racism was, in short, basic to the creation of liberalism and the identity of the European.

Another strategy for extracting racism's significance entails a short-cut through liberalism. This could be called a strategy of telling instances. By this I mean instances, often seemingly insignificant or evanescent, which convincingly anticipate or provoke demotic responses. Jokes and politicians provide an abundance of these. Take the statement on 30 January 1978 of Thatcher as leader of the parliamentary opposition, a statement which immensely boosted both the popularity of the Conservative party and the salience of 'immigration' as an electoral issue. She said:

> ...that people are really rather afraid that this country might be swamped by people with a different culture. And, you know, the British character has done so much for democracy, for law, and done so much throughout the world, that if there is a fear that it might be swamped, people are going to react and be rather hostile to those coming in.[7]

As Martin Barker has so skillfully shown, all the elements of racism are contained in this and numerous other recent political evocations of culture, community and the miasma of unexpired imperial dreams.[8] To take one other instance, Crossman's diaries as a cabinet minister provide a candid account of anticipating a demotic response. The Labour government in the 1960s changed its policy and practice on immigration to an "illiberal" one so as to "out-trump the Tories," otherwise "we would have been faced with certain electoral defeat in the West Midlands and the South East."[9]

So far, there are two broad lines to the argument. One focuses on liberal capitalism and traces a basic conflict within it in that liberal capitalism opposes yet is maintained by racism. The other line of argument focuses on racism. It asserts the specificity and the significance of racism. That dimension intersects with the history of liberal capitalism indicating integral connections between racism and liberalism. I will now add law to the mixture.

Law as Racism

Liberal cosmology provides a particular protection of law's innocence. Law is radically separate from 'material life' and can also act on and order that life: with liberal society "[p]articular self-interest must be constrained by universalistic legal and motivational structures; in this sense, the formal rationality of civil society must dominate the substantive rationality of material life."[10] In line with assertions of the centrality and significance of racism, we may ask what point is to be given to the experience of those for whom law is not separate from, much less able to order or correct that part of material life called racism. Lord Scarman could provide a celebrated confirmation that... '[i]nstitutional racism' does not exist in Britain" in a report that was an instance of it.[11] In this he was implicitly confronting and dismissing a phrase that black people used to encapsulate their experience of law and of state action.[12] That experience is not simply a contained 'different voice' which stands along with, if opposed to, liberal self-presentation. It can also be given point in founding a critical engagement with that self-presentation. An immediate problem is the powerful closure erected around liberal legality. Being radically separate from and ordering material life, law cannot be brought into definitively complicitous comparisons with that life. Sympathetic connections between law and racism can be presented as exceptional and remediable, with the exceptional serving to contrast and confirm the great virtue of the norm.[13] Indeed, the very terms of that separation — terms of universalistic ordering, terms operatively realised in liberal legality — are ostentatiously opposed to racism. Against accusations of racism, then, law's innocence is unassailable.

If we 'respect' the terms of separation, that is, if we are not simply to reduce them to something else such as economic relations or treat them merely as a mask for something else, then the only way of integrally linking law with racism is to attack the foundation and show that those very terms of separation are racist. Law could then be seen as contradictory, as integrally opposed to and supportive of racism. I will argue that, metaphorically speaking, law positively acquires identity by taking elements of racism into itself and shaping them in its own terms. Yet law also takes identity from its opposition to and separation from racism. But this very opposition is not innocent for it operates by containing and constraining law. Law, as a result, and contrary to the principle of universality, is unable assuredly to counter racism. This is not just to say, along with assertions of critical legal scholars about the family and workplace, that by not entering areas where racism or sexism is prevalent law implicitly confers powers on those who are dominant within them.[14] Such a line of argument leaves law competent to intervene and counter that power and, of course, liberal legality is only a claim about competence, about being able to cover things, not about actual coverage. The point here is that racism marks constitutive boundaries of law, persistent limits on its competence and scope. Being so limited, law proves to be compatible with racism. I will argue, further, that it is the combination of this compatibility with law's claims to universalist competence that creates and heightens racism.

I will try to support that ambitious agenda in a way that may seem disappointingly and inaptly modest. That is, I will explore particular aspects of the operation of the *Race Relations Act 1976*. Although there may be a provocative persuasiveness in establishing racism in legislation aimed at countering it, there does remain the small problem of how the general assertions about law and racism that I have just indicated can be established in such a particular way. But to borrow from Foucault's "rule of double conditioning," a localized exercise of power with its "precise and tenuous relations" is effective only as a distinct but related part of a "general strategy" of power. The general strategy is, in turn, distinct but dependent for its effectiveness on the localized exercise of power.[15] The study of the localized is, in this light, necessary. It will also implicate the general. Specifically, an exploration of certain "precise and tenuous relations" involved in the *Race Relations Act* reveals persistent limits beyond which law will not proceed, limits erected in an overlapping of confining categories and discretions, and in the constitution of a domain of the normal. When we seek to move beyond these limits, we find on their borders "general strategies" drawing on racism, strategies which involve the power of capital and nation. This general dimension makes intelligible what would otherwise be mysterious in the limiting of localized instances. The approach from a localized instance cannot, of course, present some comprehensive, much less structured picture of the general. But I am arguing that effective general elements are invoked by it.

THE BOUNDS OF LAW IN THE *RACE RELATIONS ACT*

The British *Race Relations Act 1976* enabled people to take civil action in respect of discrimination in certain areas of life on "racial grounds."[16] Persons discriminate if on racial grounds they treat someone less favorably than they treat or would treat others. There is also indirect discrimination which is the imposition of requirements or conditions having a discriminatory effect in that they disproportionately disadvantage racial groups, are to the detriment of the person alleging discrimination and cannot be otherwise justified. For example, educational requirements for a job that are in excess of what can be justified for the work to be done could indirectly discriminate against racial groups who are educationally 'disadvantaged.'

Almost all cases brought under the legislation concern employment. Employment cases are taken to an administrative court called an industrial tribunal. Awards which may be made in employment cases comprise damages for material loss and for injury to feelings, a declaration of the rights of the complainant and a recommendation that the employer take remedial action. Damages cannot be awarded in cases of indirect discrimination whilst there is no intent to discriminate. The Act also constitutes and empowers a governmental Commission for Racial Equality which is "to work towards the elimination of discrimination." Greatest emphasis is given to its broad power to investigate discriminatory practices, to issue non-discrimination notices and take court proceedings to have these enforced.

I will explore employment cases under the legislation, focusing on aspects of universalistic legal ordering. These are the form of universal individual right and the mode of adjudication, adjudication being the subjection of competing claims to universally applicable, impartially applied standards. I do not make the common, but infinitely contestable assertion found in critical legal studies that with legislation like this the form of right constitutes racial (or gender) oppression in terms of the action of individuals and thereby denies its wider 'social' or 'structural' determinants.[17] But this branch of critical legal studies is a source of assertions suggesting boundaries imported by the form of right, boundaries we can seek in the legislation and in the legal processes it generates. This will involve the mundane and the obvious — quotidian rules of evidence and questions about the burden of proof, for example. But, as I try to show, a multitude of oppressions are effected by the mundane and the obvious.

Right is attached to the individual legal actor who has to assert this right against the person allegedly in breach of a correlative duty. That breach is a matter of individual wrongdoing. It is something aberrant, a particular episode which disturbs the normal course. It calls for the occasional and discontinuous intervention of legal remedies. These remedies, in turn, need only reassert the normal course, need only focus on the act of the wrongdoer and correct or compensate for it. The form of right deals with deviation, and racism in liberal societies has to be a deviation. This correspondence provides a temptation to which the *Race Relations Act* succumbs in the basic remedy against 'discrimination.' In legal and liberal terms discrimination is a matter of intentional wrongdoing inflicted by one individual on another. The only significant remedy provided in the legislation is damages seen as redress, as affirming the norm. The complainant, the person wronged, has the onus of establishing that the norm has been disturbed. This 'burden of proof' is in practice a heavy one. As I will show later, industrial tribunals reflect the ethos of law and liberalism and take racial discrimination to be exceptional indeed.[18] There is also the banal paradox that making discrimination legally culpable has rendered it more elusive and intractable to remedial action. Unless the person supposedly discriminating is unaware or intemperate enough to provide it, it is difficult to get direct evidence of discrimination. The evidence, that is, will usually be circumstantial. Such evidence is never conclusive. It is clear from the cases that circumstantial evidence is accepted as proving discrimination, as discharging the burden of proof, only very exceptionally. Such constant rejections of complainants are facilitated by narrowing the type of knowledge that can be used in support of a claim. This narrowing is in terms of the individualistic nature of the relation and dispute between the parties. There is a concretising here of the form of right in the adversarial process. The adversaries, for example, are to be left on their own. The tribunal will only rarely help a litigant and it often explicitly refuses to do so. Evidence going beyond these individualistic dimensions will be rejected or given little weight. Instances of such evidence include social survey evidence of racial disadvantage in employment generally or statistical information about the 'racial' composition of the employer's workforce. In the same vein, the remedy of recommending that the employer take remedial action cannot extend beyond what is necessary to redress the adverse effect on the complainant. But the most potent dimension of individuality in the legal process here is that of intention. The unsurpassed aptness of a rejected applicant is not evidence of racial discrimination because she or he may have been rejected on other grounds. And such grounds, as tribunals repeatedly recognize, can include the most vague and the most irrational. Constantly, tribunals uphold employers' purported rejection of applicants in such terms as demeanor, personality, ability to fit in and even in terms of favoritism on the part of the employer. Obviously, racially-based decisions can be thus justified or obscured with ease. Tribunals also engage here in a revealing slippage, one that purports to follow on from intentionality but goes beyond legal justification in such terms. For what they assert is that such decisions are the prerogative of the employer, that they have to accept the employer's assessment and even the terms in which it is made. As a matter of course the impermeability of the employer's power is affirmed.

It is convenient now to be fair and credit the legislation with attempts to transcend the limits imported by the form of right and the related idea of discrimination. But these attempts, I now argue, end up confirming and reinforcing the original limits. The Commission for Racial Equality is given ostensibly broad powers to investigate discrimination and to issue a non-discrimination notice. Any threat that this power may be effective is avoided by its reduction in the lineaments of the form of right. Thus, a non-discrimination notice can only relate to particular acts. The Commission's power to issue a *subpoena* for information is restricted to investigations where the Commission suspects a named person of discriminatory acts, and there has already to be material supporting "a reasonable suspicion."[19] That position is reached with the aid of judicial interpretation, an interpretation which reflects a splenetic attitude to conferring judicial-type power on an administrative body thereby denying, in the view of the judges, adequate protection for the individual: "[y]ou might think that we are back in the days of the Inquisition.... You might think that we were back in the days of the General Warrants," thought Lord Denning. He appropriated control of this power for the judges, where it has remained. The court was "free to balance the public interests involved," those between the "immense powers" given to the Commission "to compel the disclosure of confidential information" and "the importance to the public services and industrial concerns" of preserving that confidentiality.[20] Less spectacularly, the Act in s.38(3)(a) confers a similar discretion by obliquely applying rules of evidence relating to discovery. A similar story can be told about discovery in its more general application in cases before tribunals. Discovery does have a particular significance in such cases for it is "designed to offset the probative disadvantage which the complainant would otherwise suffer" because evidence of discrimination will usually be in the hands of the employer.[21] Discovery tends to be successful when the information is narrowly focused on the applicant or the alleged act of discrimination. But 'confidentiality' almost invariably excludes discovery of more extensive information held by the employer such as details of the competitors for a job or for promotion. Inevitably, it is for the tribunal to exercise a discretion here in terms of what is "necessary for dispensing fairly of the proceedings."[22] In short, where the Act provides modes compensating for the limits entailed in the form of right, the limits are extended to confine these modes. Should this not suffice to protect the portals of capital, then adjudicators are to exercise their discretion, in both senses of the word.

The most revealing instance of this strategy is provided by indirect discrimination. Such discrimination is, in part, constituted in categories of the form of right. Action is brought by the individual who must have sustained harm. But there is no purposive wrongdoing involved. The causal element springs from the disproportionate effect the employer's "requirement or condition" has on a racial group. Tenaciously, the form of right shapes the outcome because damages cannot be awarded whilst the employer did not intend to discriminate. But the core of indirect discrimination, the salience of the effect on a racial group, goes beyond the realm of individual right. Here, legal enquiry and legal ordering cannot be confined to some episodic wrongdoing. They must now penetrate the realm of the employer, examining and assessing potentially any "requirement or condition" relating to employment. But the potency of indirect discrimination was soon countered in judicial applications of the exemption from indirect discrimination of a requirement or condition shown to be justifiable. This was rendered in terms of, variously, what was reasonable or commonsensical, or what was acceptable to right-thinking people and such, or it was simply a question of fact unique to each case. Judicial creativity enters again with an expedient balancing, the desirability of eliminating discrimination being balanced against the demands of the employer's enterprise. In this, judges and tribunals again explicitly recognize that employers are to be left with their autonomy; they ought to be able to decide what is best for business.

In looking at the two types of universalistic ordering, I have so far concentrated on the form of right and have considered the mode of adjudication only from that perspective. Adjudication sustained the form of right as a confining category and restrained extensions beyond it by the apt use of discretion and the recognition of the employer's autonomy. I will now focus more exclusively on the process of adjudication. We can start with the banality that law cannot be mechanically applied. Adjudication requires a productive impetus, a positive going-out to recognize and shape claims. We can continue with another banality: that, as it is usually put, the values of adjudicators influence their decisions. I will try to establish this not in the sense of values intruding on otherwise pristine standards and processes of adjudication, but in the sense of values constituting these standards and processes. Such standards and processes, in turn, form a particular but comprehensive perspective which quite simply includes the interests of some and excludes the interests of others. This is not a matter of remediable bias or some such. It is a matter of a whole sensibility. Adjudicators cannot be responsive to interests they cannot comprehend. Nor can they respond through standards and processes that obscure and deny these interests rather than reveal them. The productive impetus needed to recognize claims in adjudication does not operate to recognize claims founded in such interests. Where the claims are insistent and potentially disruptive, they are explained away as something else, something understood within the particular perspective, understood in the domain of the normal. I will now expand and illustrate that argument.

Adjudicative standards and processes are not pure creations. They are responsive to and draw on wider rationalities operating beyond adjudication and law. With industrial tribunals, there is an explicit mode of incorporating such wider rationalities, since, in addition to a legally qualified chairperson, tribunals are composed of two 'wing' members drawn respectively from employers' and trade union organizations. Such people are likely to be more responsive to 'good industrial relations' than to adopt a radical view towards the notorious racism of employers and trade unions.[23] They are not likely to transcend the traditional hostility of employers and unions to anti-discrimination legislation.[24] The failure, for example, of "industry machinery" to discern discrimination under the previous *Race Relations Act* was almost complete.[25] The point can be made dramatically by looking at cases where a wing member has some specialist background in 'race relations.' Commenting on "the experience of adjudication in the first eighteen months of the Act," Lustgarten notes that "in *every* case in which there was a split tribunal decision against the complainant, the non-specialist wingmen joined the chairman to make the majority."[26] That experience, with but few exceptions, has continued since. We are, it would seem, dealing here with two worlds. The inability of industrial tribunals to respond to one of them was starkly evident even before the *Race Relations Act* of 1976 in cases of unfair dismissal brought under employment protection legislation. Despite numerous such cases involving a racial element, "[i]n not one case … [had] there been an express finding that dismissal was for racial reasons."[27] Nor does the legally qualified chairperson inhibit the abject responsiveness of wing members to prevailing rationalities. The chairperson is more likely than these members to find against the complainant. But disagreement among tribunal members is quite exceptional. Uniformity is promoted in the chairperson's tending to be a dominating influence. This dominance is fostered in the technical nature of the process. Despite original aspirations to informality and accessibility, industrial tribunals have become increasingly legalistic. Hence, although they are never great, the chances of success are very slim without expert assistance.[28] Often tribunals assert that they are not bound by technical rules of evidence, such as the rule against admitting hearsay evidence, but almost as often this is merely a prelude to applying such rules. More generally, the crudities of such rules, of the adversarial process, of the standard tricks of advocacy designed to block the truth, all serve to exclude evidence of an often subtle and intractable racial oppression.[29] This, in sum, is a circumscribed ritual of reassertion of a world in which such oppression is non-existent or rare.

What if evidence of racial discrimination survives these exclusions? Exceptionally, a complainant will succeed as a result. Much more usually, the evidence is made to conform to the domain of the normal in two ways. In one, apparent evidence of the employer's discrimination is understood by the tribunal as something else. So, a particular hostility to the applicant is understood as a communications problem, as bad management practice, or as the result of pressure or health problems. Alternatively, the domain of the normal reduces evidence of the employer's discrimination to a less challenging dimension. So, the complainant is, in terms of the common *canard*, paranoid or over-sensitive or the acts complained of are "trivial."[30] But this is the "triviality of the sand," to borrow Auden's phrase. What is happening is that the massive reality of oppression is being rejected or reduced to the insignificant, whereas the employer's reality is being accepted and elevated to the determinant. It is not so much a matter that the employer's account is believed whereas the complainant's is not. The grinding normality is that the employer's account serves to call forth and to confirm what is already there, what is already known.

Of course, industrial tribunals are not the sole occupants of the field of adjudication. But they do have something close to sole occupancy of a crucial part of it. Factual questions and questions of the weight of evidence will, as a matter of law, rarely be disturbed on appeal. Appellate courts will have a decisive influence on tribunals in determining questions of law and thereby providing precedents which tribunals have to follow. There is also the vaguer question of appellate 'values' influencing tribunals. On both these counts the constant refrain has been one of restriction, reinforcing the perspective generated within tribunals. In its interpretation, race relations legislation has not been construed expansively under, say, the 'mischief rule' as befits the remedying of an acknowledged social evil. Rather, appeal courts see the Race Relations Acts as having to be interpreted strictly, especially as they restrict "the liberty which the citizen has previously enjoyed at common law" to discriminate.[31] Such judicial invocation of positive legal liberties also characterizes, as we have seen, the balancing of confidentiality and the employer's autonomy against the desirability of eliminating discrimination. This line of argument may accord well with the demonstration by critical legal scholars (and others) that "the legal process at large and its discrete doctrinal components...are fundamentally indeterminant and manipulable," and that adjudication draws on no ultimate and principled resolution but is, rather, a "political" process.[32] The argument here is different, however. We have seen that in the process of adjudication some elements when weighed in the balance have more or less persistently been found wanting. What happens is that these seeming choices are not simply made, but themselves make the community of law. With this community, apparently disjoint or indeterminant elements do configure in hierarchies which, if not invariant, are at least usual. Judges relate to the overall ordering ethos of community in such ultimate and revealing terms as what is "sensible" and "reasonable," what conforms to "the fitness of things," and to "common sense."[33] These are not masks for an unbounded, 'political' discretion. They are, rather, borders beyond which the recognition of constraint cannot proceed in terms of the community's particular traditions and particular rationalities.

LAW, RACE AND THE LIBERAL WORLD

This community of law, like any community, is not generated purely internally. Through industrial tribunals, as we have seen, the community of law incorporates and integrally relies on a particular yet operatively comprehensive perspective. This perspective joins with the confining categories and obscuring discretions of the form of right and of the legal process to set law's bounds. These bounds restrict law but in so doing they maintain its integrity in its relation to the power of employers.[34] Law is, however, constituted not just in opposition to other types of power but also in the positive assimilation of wider, sustaining identities. There are identities predisposed toward racism with which law is intimately involved. One is the modern figure of society as a contained unit with a 'typical' membership.[35] The other is the distinct but not greatly dissimilar figure of the nation: liberal "legality...celebrates and elevates the law to an exalted status as the expression of unity in the nation."[36] Neither these identities nor law take on a racist dimension without its specific historical addition. Such an addition is, of course, frequent and Britain is conspicuously not an exception. In line with my earlier argument, the addition of racism effects the unity of society and nation and serves to constitute the identity of its members.

I will now explore law's connections with the particularity of society and nation and relate these connections to law's universalistic pretensions. The argument will develop through instances. One is the very genius of the common law with its combination of universalistic "reason" with a "strange and...incoherent" (English) particularism.[37] In Dicey's seminal account of constitutional law, the combination becomes a prerogative of the 'English.' The resulting "rule of law" is not English in the sense that it should be confined to England. It is just that in less happy climes, such as Belgium, its existence is much more attenuated.[38] Adjusting Dicey's paean to our concern with a more mundane reality of legal procedure, Lord Denning recently could find a betrayal of 'England' and Empire in a small challenge posed by the European Communities (Amendment) Bill to the "English adversary system."[39] To put the argument before instances descend any further, such ethnocentric elevations of law are an inevitable reconciliation of law's palpable national connections with its transcendent universalist claims.[40] In the result, law is captured as an expression of national superiority. When that superiority incorporates racism, law is likewise captured as an expression of it.

It is hardly surprising, then, that the resort to law as a symbol of race and nation should be so facile, so common and so effective.[41] Thus, to return to the stratagem of the telling instance and to Thatcher's contribution, she precisely echoes the imperialist claim to law as a gift we gave them, gave those "people with a different culture," people who did not have law, who did not give it to the world and who in remaining essentially alien have failed to assimilate the gift adequately. Almost in passing, the not-so-distinctive contributions of the higher judiciary to this 'new racism' have also at times assumed telling dimensions.[42] But for law the most telling has probably been the immense popular response to Powell's speech in 1968, in which racial division in Britain prompted some characteristic visions: "[l]ike the Roman, I seem to see 'the River Tiber foaming with much blood'." His prop and target were provided by the then Race Relations Bill, an anti-discrimination measure even more limited and more anaemic than the current legislation. Yet Powell presented it with great effect as "a one-way privilege," as "legal weapons" which "the stranger" can now use "to overawe and dominate the rest."[43] Gilroy has acutely located a potency of Powell's appeal here in the "debasement" and "perversion" of what was pure law and English law. This "ultimate symbol of national culture" is traduced through "blacks being afforded limited legal protection."[44]

Indeed, both the critics and the supporters of race relations legislation agree that its purpose is to bring black people 'discriminated' against into society.[45] But, as the aptly named Whitelaw as Home Secretary put it: for equal rights, responsibilities and opportunities to be extended to such people, they should "demonstrate their commitment to our society" and abandon cultural and linguistic isolation.[46] The Race Relations Acts are seen not just as a powerful means for black people to achieve this, but also as a privilege given to them and as an advantage over white people. This is not just Powell's perception but a popular one.[47] It is also, incidentally, one that is wrong in that the legislation protects people of any race and cases brought by white people are not infrequent. But the error is much more extensive than that. The race relations legislation has had little reforming effect.[48] The failure of the oppressed successfully to use such powerful, privileging legal means thus confirms their essential inadequacy. Reform, in the guise of a succession of Race Relations Acts, like so much reform becomes part of the problematic, creating and sustaining that which it purports to counter.

Law, in short, is tied to a particular community which excludes those whom law would include through race relations legislation. In the liberal world-view, as we saw, law erects a universal inclusiveness, transcending and ordering material life. It is true that law as legal rules only directs what should happen and so cannot be held specifically accountable. But the liberal world-view does entail a general and a strong claim for law's competence. If the powerful and persistent ministrations of law do not bring certain racial identities into society that must be because the identities are essentially different and naturally incapable. This is but a continuation of that legacy of the Enlightenment in which those constantly beyond the liberal equation have to be qualitatively different from those within it.

Conclusion

I started questioning the manifest opposition between liberal legality and racism by drawing on a conflict in Marxist accounts of racism. This conflict indicated that racism was incompatible yet symbiotic with liberal capitalism in Britain. This same conflict pointed towards the specificity and the enormous significance of racism. But no matter what the significance of racism, law seemed to escape any complicitous connections with it. This was because, in the liberal world-view, law was a form of universalistic ordering which transcended material life. Yet if the universalistic terms of that transcendence could, paradoxically, be held racist, then law could still be rendered accountable. To begin establishing that, I took a seemingly perverse course of looking at instances of universalistic legal ordering which were not only minutely localized but also explicitly opposed to 'racial discrimination.' These instances were the operation of the form of right and of the mode of adjudication in employment cases under the *Race Relations Act* of 1976.

A detailed study of such instances showed that there were certain persistent limits, certain bounds beyond which law did not proceed in countering racism. What, in an immediate sense, stood on the other side of those bounds and checked law's advance was the power and autonomy of employers. Law thus marked out areas in which the racism of employers could operate. But the relation of law to racism was seen to be more intimate. Between law and the employer, mediating and constituting the necessary distance separating them, was a comprehensive yet particular perspective generated in adjudication which 'naturally' and racially set law's limits and, in the same moment, denied effect to the contrary experience of black people. This perspective inhabited the community of law which, in turn, evoked and integrally relied on a wider, racially-conceived society and nation. For these entities, law was an operative figure of great social impact. In this, law was seen to be readily involved in extensive racist strategies. Its contributions to racism were also more distinctive, however. Law's claims to universalistic ordering contrasted with its confinement in terms of specific national community. The disjunction, as we saw, is resolved by making that community and its law the incarnation of a rational universal ordering. Those of a 'different culture' are not, however, merely excluded from superior reason. When, as in the *Race Relations Act*, its beneficent and potent modes are extended to them in terms of universalistic ordering but then withdrawn in implicit terms of community, a gap opens which is filled by the attribution to them of an insuperable inadequacy.

Endnotes

1. J.-P. Sartre, "Preface" to F. Fanon, *The Wretched of the Earth* (1967), p. 22.
2. See G. Ben-Tovim *et al.*, "Race, Left Strategies and the State," *Politics and Power* 3 (1981), p. 153.
3. M. Foucault, "Questions of Method: An Interview with Michel Foucault," *I. & C.*, 8 (1981), p. 3, 12.
4. See A. Szymanski, "Race, Sex and the U.S. Working Class," *Social Problems* 21 (1973-74), p. 706 for an account and strange application of these Marxist views on race.
5. See, for example, *The Empire Strikes Back: Race and Racism in 70s Britain* (Centre for Contemporary Cultural Studies, 1982).
6. See, for example, P. Fryer, *Staying Power: The History of Black People in Britain* (1984) chap. 7.
7. As quoted in M. Barker, "Racism — The New Inheritors," *Radical Philosophy* 21 (1984), p. 2, 4.
8. *Ibid.*
9. As quoted in J. Rex and S. Tomlinson, *Colonial Immigrants in a British City: A Class Analysis* (1979), p. 61.
10. Poole, "Reason, Self-Interest and 'Commercial Society:' The Social Content of Kantian Morality," *Critical Philosophy* (1984), p. 24, 42.

11. *The Brixton Disorders 10-12 April 1981: Report of an Inquiry by the Right Honourable the Lord Scarman, O.B.E.* (Penguin, 1982) p. 209; Barker and Beezer, "The Language of Racism," *International Socialism* (1983), p. 108.

12. A. Sivanandan, "Race, Class and the State: The Black Experience in Britain," *Race and Class* XVII (1976), p. 347.

13. For example, Scarman *op. cit.*, p. 119.

14. *Cf.* some targets of Rose's analysis in this collection.

15. M. Foucault, *The History of Sexuality Volume I: An Introduction* (1981), pp. 99-100.

16. The summaries in the text are supported in ss. 1, 2, 6, 17, 20, 43, 48-51 and 54-58 of the Act.

17. For example, Freeman, "Legitimizing Racial Discrimination Through Antidiscrimination Law: A Critical Review of Supreme Court Doctrine," *Minnesota Law Review* 62 (1978), p. 1049.

18. Statements about legal process draw on a survey of judgments in cases before industrial tribunals and employment appeals tribunals. The records of most are kept in the Central Office of the Industrial Tribunals. I will happily supply people interested with record numbers of cases supporting or instancing the various statements. I will refer here to cases from which quotations are taken. The name of a case followed only by a number refers to its record in the Central Office.

19. *R.* v. *Commission for Racial Equality, Ex parte Hillingdon Borough Council,* [1982] 1 Q. B. 276.

20. *Science Research Council* v. *Nassé,* [1979] 1 Q.B. 144 at pp. 172-73.

21. *British Library* v. *Palyza and Another,* [1984] I.C.R. 504 at p. 508.

22. *Ibid.*, p. 507.

23. *Francis* v. *Newey and Eyre Limited,* 20743/80.

24. See, for example, A. Lester and G. Bindman, *Race and Law* (1972), pp. 126-130.

25. Select Committee on Race Relations and Immigration, *Minutes of Evidence (Race Relations Board), Session 1973-74,* (24 January 1974) p. 28.

26. L. Lustgarten, *Legal Control of Racial Discrimination* (1980), p. 196 (his emphasis).

27. I. A. Macdonald, *Race Relations: The New Law* (1977), p. 122.

28. V. Kumar, *Industrial Tribunal Applicants Under the Race Relations Act 1976: A Research Report* (1986).

29. On tricks of advocacy see Paynter, "Presenting Your Case: A Guide to Effective Advocacy Before the Industrial Tribunal: Part Two," *The Lawyer* (1984), p. 14. Other points were dealt with earlier.

30. *Shah* v. *Richards Longstaff Ltd,* 26623/84. On the *canard* see D. J. Smith, *Unemployment and Racial Minorities* (1981), p. 158.

31. *Per* Lord Diplock in *Dockers' Labour Club and Institute, Ltd.* v. *Race Relations Board,* [1974] 3 All E.R. 592 at p. 598.

32. Hutchinson and Monahan, "Law, Politics and the Critical Legal Scholars: The Unfolding Drama of American Legal Thought," *Stanford Law Review* 36 (1984), p. 199 at pp. 211-12.

33. P. Goodrich, *Reading Law: A Critical Introduction to Legal Method and Techniques* (1986), p. 152.

34. The point is developed more generally in Fitzpatrick, "Law and Societies," *Osgoode Hall Law Journal* 22 (1984), p. 115.

35. P. Hirst and P. Woolley, *Social Relations and Human Attributes* (1982), chaps. 2 and 3.

36. C. Sumner, *Reading Ideologies: An Investigation into the Marxist Theory of Ideology and Law* (1979), p. 293.

37. D. Little, *Religion, Order and Law: A Study in Pre-Revolutionary England* (1969), p. 172.

38. A. V. Dicey, *Introduction to the Study of the Law of the Constitution* (1885), chap. 4.

39. 480 *H.L. Debs.*, cols. 249-51, 265 (8 October 1986).

40. Law's inter- and sub-national existences do not detract from its powerful national configuration.

41. For an enthralling account and analysis of instances see P. Gilroy, *'There Ain't No Black in the Union Jack': The Cultural Politics of 'Race' and Nation* (forthcoming), chap. 3.

42. Barker and Beezer *op. cit.*, and Lester and Bindman *op. cit.*, pp. 90-91.

43. E. Powell, *Freedom and Reality* (1969), pp. 286, 289.

44. *Ibid.*, chap. 3.

45. For example, Sivanandan *op. cit.*, and Home Office, *Racial Discrimination* (1975; Cmnd. 6234), p. 6.

46. "Whitelaw Seeks to Reassure Immigrants on Equal Rights," *The Guardian*, 12 July 1980.

47. See, for example, A. Phizacklea and R. Miles, "Working-class Racist Beliefs in the Inner City," in R. Miles and A. Phizacklea (eds.), *Racism and Political Action in Britain* (1979), p. 113.

48. C. Brown and P. Gay, *Racial Discrimination: 17 Years After the Act* (1985).

Chapter 12

Policing and Urban Unrest: Problem Constitution and Policy Response

John Solomos
Tim Rackett

Abstract: The 1980s were an important period in the racialization of debates about law and order, crime and policing in British society. This was so in at least two ways. First, the politicization of the black youth unemployment issue helped to focus attention on the inter-relationship between 'race,' unemployment, urban unrest and crime. Second, the riots during 1980-1 and 1985 forced the issues of 'black crime' and violence on the streets onto the mainstream political agenda. The widespread coverage given to the issue of 'race' in connection with the riots helped to open up a wider debate about issues such as 'mugging' and 'black crime.'

Civil disorder and unrest were recurring phenomena in many inner-city areas during the 1980s. In 1980, 1981 and 1985 major riots in Bristol, London, Liverpool and Birmingham commanded the headlines and became a key theme in policy debates about the future of the inner cities. It is also the case that in each *year since 1980 there have been examples of serious street disorder. These outbreaks of disorder have presented a major challenge to the Conservative Government's image as the guardian of public order. More importantly, however, they have given added urgency to the long-running debate about the future of Britain's inner cities. The sight of violent confrontations on the streets of major cities helped to stimulate yet further the acrimonious political debate about how to regenerate depressed inner-city localities (Robson, 1988).*

This chapter explores the political and policy debates surrounding the major outbreaks of urban unrest during 1980-1 and 1985, and the ever-present threat of more violent disorder. After providing a brief overview of the chronology of urban unrest during the 1980s, the chapter concentrates on two main themes. First, the political

* Originally published in *Out of Order: Policing Black People*, edited by Ellis Cashmore and Eugene McLaughlin: 42-63 (1991). Reprinted by permission of Routledge, Inc.

debates about the origins and causes of the unrest are assessed, and second, the impact of the unrest on the policy agenda is examined. This entails a review of the impact of the Scarman Report, and other important policy documents, on the agenda of both the government and other political institutions. Finally, the chapter concludes by providing some reflections about the prospects during the decade ahead.

THE POLITICS OF RACE AND POLICING

The 1970s witnessed a complex process by which sections of the black communities in Britain's inner-city areas, particularly young blacks, came to be seen as intimately involved in (a) particular forms of streetcrime and (b) confrontations with the police which represented a challenge to the maintenance of law and order (Solomos, 1988). This process of racialization involved the construction of complex images of 'race' as a causal factor in the development of violence and disorder in British society. It also provided a clear example of the ways in which 'race' can easily become a symbol to which are attributed a variety of meanings.

A good example of this process occurred during the aftermath of the 1980-1 riots in Bristol, Brixton, Toxteth and elsewhere. In March 1982, the Metropolitan Police decided to release a racial breakdown of those responsible for street robberies, a statistical breakdown which it had not published previously, although it had been collating such statistics for some time (Scotland Yard, Press Release, 10 March 1982; *Guardian*, 11 March 1982). The police statistics showed a marked rise in street robberies, but the crucial statistic which the press and the media picked on was concerned with the 'disproportionate involvement' of young blacks in street crimes such as 'mugging,' purse snatching and robbery from stores. The press reaction to the press release varied from sober commentaries on the nature and limitations of the statistics, sensational headlines about 'black crime,' to the *Sun's* "The Yard blames black muggers." But a common theme was the argument that the statistics, along with the riots during 1980-1, were further evidence of the consequences of letting in alien communities to settle in the very heart of Britain. The *Daily Telegraph* articulated this argument succinctly:

> Over the 200 years up to 1945, Britain became so settled in internal peace that many came to believe that respect for the person and property of fellow citizens was something which existed naturally in all but a few. A glance at less fortunate countries might have reminded us that such respect scarcely exists unless law is above the power of tribe, or money, or the gun. But we did not look; we let in people from the countries we did not look at, and only now do we begin to see the result. Many young West Indians in Britain, and, by a connected process, growing numbers of young whites, have no sense that the nation in which they live is part of them. So its citizens become to them mere objects of violent exploitation.
>
> (11 March 1982)

Such an argument amounted to a direct link between 'race' and 'crime.' A similar tone was adopted by papers such as the *Daily Mail* and the *Sun*, which went even further in their use of images of 'mugging' — harking back to Enoch Powell's 1976 definition of mugging as essentially a 'black crime.'

A year later the intervention of Harvey Proctor, the right-wing Tory MP, helped to secure the release of similar figures by the Home Office and led to a similar wave of articles in the press about the 'rising wave' of crime in areas of black settlement. Since then the Metropolitan Police have been much more reticent about publishing such statistics, because of their potentially volatile political impact.

Not surprisingly, however, the issue of the involvement of young blacks in criminal or quasi-criminal activities remains a key area of concern for the police and other institutions, both locally and nationally. Because of this climate of official concern the issues of 'crime' and 'violence' remain central to the full understanding of how contemporary ideologies about young blacks as a social category were formed and how they are being transformed.

What is clear is that the successive shifts in political language about the black youth question throughout the period since the early 1970s have involved the issues of policing and 'black crime' as a central theme. Whether in terms of specific concerns about 'mugging,' 'street crime' or with more general concerns about the development of specific subcultures, such as Rastafarianism, among young blacks, the interplay between images of 'race' and 'crime' has remained an important symbol in political language. Since the late 1970s, and particularly after the 1980-1 riots, political debates about the 'black crime' issue have also been overdetermined by the phenomenon of urban unrest and civil disorder. But even within this context the issues of 'race, crime and the ghetto' remain the bedrock for the shifts in official ideologies and public debate about 'black youth.'

This also helps to explain the increasingly politicized nature of the response to black youth unemployment and violent urban unrest (Solomos, 1988). The ideological construction of the involvement of young blacks in mugging and other forms of street crime provided the basis for the development of strategies of control aimed at keeping young blacks off the streets and keeping the police in control of particular localities which had become identified both in popular and official discourses as 'crime-prone' or potential 'trouble spots.' It also helped to bring to the forefront a preoccupation with the social and economic roots of alienation and criminal activity among young blacks. This was reflected in the debate about the impact of unemployment on young blacks, but it was also reflected in the increasing preoccupation of the police and other social control agencies with particular localities where relations between the police and sections of the black community were becoming tense and politicized. This concern became apparent in the context of the responses of the police to the waves of urban unrest during the 1980s. The unrest raised important questions about the nature of policing and law and order in inner-city multi-racial areas, and it is to this issue that we now turn.

Policing, Legitimacy and Urban Unrest

The first notable instance of urban unrest during the 1980s took place in the St. Paul's district of Bristol on 2 April 1980. The immediate reaction to this event was one of shock and surprise, with public and media attention focusing particularly on the interplay between racial and social deprivation in the area (Joshua and Wallace, 1983). A year later further serious violence occurred during the weekend of 10-12 April 1981 in the Brixton area of south London, which resulted in many injuries and widespread damage, and attracted enormous media attention.

Further disturbances took place in many parts of the country in July 1981. On Friday 3 July a pitched battle occurred in Southall between hundreds of skinheads and local Asian people, and the police quickly became embroiled. On the same night in the Liverpool 8 district of Merseyside, an apparently minor incident sparked off rioting which lasted until Monday 6 July. The disorder in Liverpool 8 was particularly violent. For the first time ever in Britain, CS gas was fired at rioters by the police. Looting and arson was widespread, and the damage was estimated at some £10 million. On the night of 7-8 July 1981, disorder occurred in Moss Side, Manchester. During the following week disturbances were reported in places such as Handsworth in Birmingham, Sheffield, Nottingham, Hull, Slough, Leeds, Bradford, Leicester, Derby, High Wycombe and Cirencester.

Disorder again erupted in Brixton on 15 July 1981. At 2.00 a.m. 11 houses in Railton Road were raided by 176 police officers, with a further 391 held in reserve. The police had warrants to look for evidence of unlawful drinking and to search five houses for petrol bombs, although no evidence of either was found. During the operation the houses sustained very considerable damage — windows, sinks, toilets, floorboards, furniture, televisions and personal possessions were smashed. The resultant outcry led to an internal inquiry which exonerated those involved and stated that the police officers had been issued with sledgehammers and crowbars "to effect speedy entry." Compensation of £8,500 for structural damage, and further sums for damage to personal property, were paid by the Metropolitan Police. This raid, and the resultant violence on the streets of Brixton, convinced many people that the way policing is carried out is a vital factor in the context of urban unrest. An inquiry into the Railton Road raid by the Police Complaints-Board discovered "serious lapses from professional standards" and an "institutional disregard for the niceties of the law" (Benyon and Solomos, 1987).

Disorder was again evident in 1982 and in subsequent years, although on a reduced scale (Benyon and Solomos, 1987). The attention of the news media was firmly focused on the Falklands, and so few accounts of disturbances in British cities were reported. It is clear, though, that urban unrest continued to occur in parts of London and Liverpool, and similar disorder seems to have taken place in 1983. The following year, the Metropolitan Police Commissioner, Sir Kenneth Newman, reported that during 1984 there were many mini-riots which had the potential to escalate to Brixton 1981 proportions and he added: "London is nowadays a very volatile city."

A MORI opinion poll in February 1985 reported that 64 percent of those surveyed expected further riots to occur in British cities, and seven months later their fears were justified. In September and October 1985 serious urban unrest again became the focus of popular attention. The first eruption occurred on Monday 9 September 1985 in the Lozells Road area of Handsworth, Birmingham. The riot resulted in the deaths of two Asian men, Kassamali and Amirali Moledina, who suffered asphyxiation in their burning post office. One hundred and twenty-two other people, mainly police, were reported injured and the value of damaged property was put at £7.5 million. Further rioting occurred the next day when Douglas Hurd, the Home Secretary, visited the area. Other disturbances, widely regarded as 'copycat,' were reported elsewhere in the West Midlands, for example in Moseley, Wolverhampton and Coventry, and in the St. Paul's district of Bristol.

The Handsworth/Soho/Lozells area, with a population of 56,300, is regarded by Birmingham City Council as the most deprived district in the city. Unemployment is a major affliction, and at the time of the riots 36 percent of the workforce in Handsworth was out of work, while the figure for people under 24 was 50 percent. It is an area in which it was claimed that reasonably good relations existed between young blacks and police, as a result of the practice of community policing introduced in the late 1970s. However, at the end of 1981 a new superintendent instituted changes which included moving a number of the area's community police-officers to other duties and clamping down on the activities by local youths which had previously been tolerated.

These changes resulted in an increase in tension between youths and the police. In July 1985 two serious disturbances occurred in Handsworth, but both were played down and went unreported in the media. The context within which the eruption on 9 September occurred was thus one of deteriorating relations between young people, especially blacks, and the police, as well as one of widespread unemployment and social disadvantage. The tinder merely required a spark, which was provided when a black youth became involved in an altercation with an officer over a parking ticket. It was alleged that during the incident, at which more police arrived, a black woman was assaulted. Three hours later some 45 buildings in Lozells Road were ablaze.

Brixton was the scene of the next outbreak of violent disorder, during the weekend of 28-9 September 1985. Seven hundred and twenty-four major crimes were reported, 43 members of the public and ten police officers were injured, and 230 arrests were made. As in Handsworth, the event which led to the rioting involved police-officers and a black person. At 7.00 a.m. on 28 September armed police entered Mrs. Cherry Groce's house in Normandy Road, Brixton, looking for her son. Two shots were fired by an officer, and a bullet damaged Mrs. Groce's spine causing permanent paralysis. At 6.00 p.m. the local police-station was attacked with petrol bombs, and during the next eight hours large numbers of black and white people took part in burning and looting which caused damage estimated at £3 million. During the riot a freelance photographer sustained injuries from which he died three weeks later.

Two days after Mrs. Groce was shot, rioting occurred in Liverpool 8. In this instance, the disturbances were precipitated when four black men were refused bail at Liverpool Magistrates' Court. During the summer there had been reports of rising tension in the area, and on 30 August a crowd demonstrated outside Toxteth police station and then attacked police-cars and the station itself. A number of assaults on police officers were also reported. As in Brixton and Handsworth, police relations with youths, and especially young black people, were a significant factor in the explosive mixture, and in Toxteth, too, the disorder was precipitated by an incident involving police-officers and black people.

The most serious of the disorders occurred at Broadwater Farm Estate, in Tottenham, London. The rioting began at about 7.00 p.m. on Sunday 6 October 1985, and during a night of extraordinary violence Police Constable Keith Blakelock was stabbed to death, 20 members of the public and 223 police-officers were injured and 47 cars and some buildings were burned. Guns were fired at the police, causing injuries to several officers and reporters, and the police deployed CS gas and plastic bullets, although these were not used.

As in Handsworth, Brixton and Toxteth, the context within which the disturbances occurred in Tottenham was one of deteriorating relations between the police and young people, especially black, and the trigger event involved police officers and black people (Gifford, 1986). The chief superintendent for the area was a firm believer in community policing, and he put as his first priority the prevention of public disorder. However, it is clear that many of his police constables and sergeants did not agree with this approach. During the summer of 1985 there was evidence of increasing tension, and a prominent member of the Hornsey Police Federation was quoted as saying that rank-and-file officers "desperately wanted to go in hard and sort out the criminals." Some serious incidents occurred during this period on the Broadwater Farm Estate, such as an attack on police by youths which resulted in one officer sustaining a bad head wound, and there was also a series of attacks on an Asian-owned supermarket. Senior police officers appeared to play these incidents down, but black youths of the estate complained they were increasingly harassed by the police.

The incident which precipitated the riot began when police officers stopped a car driven by Floyd Jarrett, a 23-year-old black man well-known in the area. One of the officers decided to arrest Jarrett for suspected theft of the car, but after an altercation Jarrett was in fact charged with assaulting a police officer. On 13 December 1985 Jarrett was acquitted of this charge, and was awarded £350 costs against the police. While he was detained at the police-station a number of police officers used a key taken from the arrested man to enter his mother's home. During the police search of the house Mrs. Cynthia Jarrett collapsed. The family alleged that her death was caused by a police officer who pushed her over; the police denied that this had occurred. On 4 December 1985 the inquest returned a verdict of accidental death. Mrs. Jarrett was certified dead at 6.35 p.m. on Saturday 5 October, and news of the tragedy spread quickly around the estate during the evening. The next day, after sporadic incidents, violent disorder erupted at about 7.00 p.m.

Disorder occurred again in 1986. During the spring there were renewed reports of increasing tension in some areas. In Notting Hill, for example, there were allegations of assaults by the police and the planting of drugs, while in Nottingham a number of forced entries into black people's homes and a series of street searches caused widespread anger. On the Broadwater Farm Estate virtually every black male under 30 was interrogated — over 350 people were arrested, although most were released without charge. In July 1986 the Metropolitan Police mounted a huge raid in Brixton, involving nearly 2,000 officers, aimed at selected premises in which cannabis offenses were allegedly being committed.

In early September 1986 serious disorder occurred on the streets of the North Prospect Estate in the Devonport constituency of Plymouth. A large crowd of white youths set up burning barricades, and smashed windows, doors and fences on the estate. A few days later the Avon and Somerset Police organized a large raid in the St. Paul's district of Bristol. Almost exactly one year after the Handsworth riots, 600 police moved into the area to search several premises in connection with drugs and drinking offenses. The reaction was serious rioting and attacks on the police involving petrol bombs, bricks and stones.

The Policy Impact of Urban Unrest

Reactions to the riots have concentrated on a number of key variables that are said to characterize the localities in which the riots have occurred. Lord Scarman's report on the 1981 disorders highlighted the importance of unemployment, urban deprivation, racial disadvantage, relations between young blacks and the police, the decline of civic consent and political exclusion as the key issues. Other reactions have concentrated on the issue of the interplay between inner-city decay and racial disadvantage in contemporary Britain. Yet others have argued that the unrest can be seen as a symptom of the breakdown of law and order in British society (Gaffney, 1987; Hall, 1987; Keith, 1987).

The main issues that were prominent in debates during 1980-1 were 'race' and 'law and order.' This was by no means an accident, since throughout the 1970s a powerful body of media, political and academic opinion had been constructed around the theme of how Britain was drifting into a 'violent society,' and how the basis of consent was being shifted by the pressures of immigration and the growth of multi-racial inner-city areas.

A glimpse of the impact of the 1980-1 riots at this level can be achieved through two important debates in Parliament. The first took place in the midst of the July 1981 riots, and had as its theme "Civil Disturbances." The tone of the debate was set by Home Secretary William Whitelaw's introductory statement in which he spoke of (a) the need to "remove the scourge of criminal violence from our streets," and (b) the urgency of developing "policies designed to promote the mutual tolerance and understanding upon which the whole future of a free democratic society depends" (*Hansard,* 8, 16 July 1981: col. 1405). The "scourge of criminal violence" was, Whitelaw argued, a danger to the whole framework of consent and legality on which the political institutions of British society were based. In reply Roy Hattersley, the Shadow Home Secretary, supported the call for the immediate suppression of street violence, but warned that the roots of such riots could not be dealt with until all people felt they had a stake in British society (*ibid.*: cols. 1407-9).

The second debate took place on 26 November 1981, on the publication of the Scarman Report, and had as its theme "Law and Order." The importance of the riots in pushing the law and order issue, and specifically policing, onto the main political agenda was emphasized by the Liberal leader, David Steel, who argued that "urgent action" to prevent a drift into lawlessness was necessary from both a moral and political perspective (*Hansard*, 13, 26 November 1981: cols. 1009-1). A subsequent debate on the same issue in March 1982 was also full of references to the experience of 1981, the impact of street violence, crime, decaying urban conditions, the breakdown of consent between the police and many local communities and the spectre of "more violence to come" if changes in both policing tactics and social policy were not swiftly introduced (*Hansard*, 20, 25 March 1982: cols. 1107-81).

The need to support the police was accepted by both the Labour and Conservative speakers in the parliamentary debate on the riots, and was established as a benchmark for the official response to the riots long before the Scarman Report was published in November 1981. Any substantive disagreement centered around the issue of what role social deprivation and unemployment had in bringing young people to protest violently on the streets.

Intermingled with the discourses about race and law and order were constant references to unemployment, particularly among the young, and various forms of social disadvantage and poverty (Solomos, 1988: 186-90). Throughout 1980 and 1981 debates about the riots in the media, Parliament and in various official reports hinged around the interrelationship between racial law and order and social factors. The importance of this debate can be explained, partly, by the political capital which the Opposition could make from linking the social and economic malaise of the country at large with violent street disturbances. Conversely, throughout this period government ministers strenuously denied that unemployment and social deprivation were significant causes of urban unrest.

Although the Scarman Report is often taken to be the central text which argues for a link between 'social conditions' and 'disorder,' the terms of the debate were by no means set by Scarman. During both April and July 1981 vigorous exchanges took place in the press and in Parliament about the role that deteriorating social conditions and unemployment may have played in bringing about the riots. During the 16 July parliamentary debate on "Civil Disturbances," Roy Hattersley's formulation of this linkage provided a useful summary of the 'social conditions' argument. After some preliminary remarks about the Labour Party's support for the police, he went on to outline his opposition to the view of the riots as essentially anti-police outbursts:

> I repeat that I do not believe that the principal cause of last week's riots was the conduct of the police. It was the conditions of deprivation and despair in the decaying areas of our old cities — areas in which the Brixton and Toxteth riots took place, and areas from which the skinhead invaders of Southall come.
>
> (*Hansard*, 8, 16 July 1981: col. 1408)

Much of the subsequent controversy about this analysis centred on the question of youth unemployment. Hattersley had suggested that the riots were a 'direct product' of high levels of youth unemployment, and a furious debate ensued in both Parliament and the media about this assertion.

The final symbolic cue used to make sense of the 1980-1 protests is more difficult to categorize, but its basic meaning can be captured by the term 'political marginality.'

While a number of discussions of the roots of urban unrest in the USA have noted the salience of political marginality in determining participation in violent protests (Skolnick, 1969; Fogelson, 1971; Edelman, 1971; Knopf, 1975), this issue has received relatively little attention in Britain. Nevertheless, during the 1980-1 events and their aftermath the political context was discussed from a number of perspectives.

The Scarman Report, for example, located part of the explanation for the riots in the feelings of alienation and powerlessness which were experienced by young blacks living in depressed inner-city areas. A successful policy for tackling the roots of urban disorder was seen as one which sought to involve all the community in dealing with the problems of each area so that they could come to feel that they have a stake in its future (Scarman, 1981: para. 6.42).

Where such arguments did not fit in with the overarching themes of race, violence and disorder and social deprivation they were either sidelined or pushed into the sub-clauses of official reports. The Scarman Report, for example, contained the following policy proposal: "I recommend that local communities must be fully and effectively involved in planning, in the provision of local services and in the management and financing of specific projects" (Scarman, 1981: para. 8.44). Such a move towards greater political integration was seen by Lord Scarman as essential if the gap between inner-city residents and the forces of law and order was to be bridged. But the concern with overcoming political marginality remained on the sidelines of the main public debate because it questioned the perception of the rioters as driven by irrational, uncivilized and criminal instincts. This did not, however, stop the question of political marginality and the need to reform existing policies from being raised at all, as can be seen subsequently by the attempts after 1981 to introduce measures both locally and nationally which were meant to address some of the grievances of the rioters and to ensure that further disturbances did not occur. Aspects of these measures are considered further on in the chapter.

Police Responses

In the aftermath of the Scarman Report's publication police opinion was divided on the question of whether its proposals for reforming the police and the adoption of new methods of policing could be implemented, or whether such changes could insure against further violence and unrest. Sim (1982) has argued that the police were particularly worried by Scarman's recommendations that they should (a) tackle racial prejudice and harassment, (b) improve their methods of policing inner-city multi-racial areas and (c) develop new methods of managing urban disorder. He sees the police and sections of the media and right-wing parliamentarians as launching a counter-offensive to counteract criticisms of the police handling of the riots or their handling of the black community in general.

Certainly even before the publication of the Scarman Report the police and sections of the media were engaged in constructing a rather different explanation of the riots and of the participants in such events. From the very first confrontation in Bristol on 2 April 1980 the issue of race was a prime concern of the popular media. Under the headline

"Riot Mob Stone Police" the *Daily Mail* talked of "mobs of black youths" roaming the streets (3 April 1980). This was a theme repeated in the coverage of the *Sun, Daily Star* and *Daily Express* during this period.

During both the Brixton riot of April 1981 and the nationwide riots of July 1981 the press was full of images, both pictorial and written, that emphasized that 'race' was somehow a central variable or even the main one. The strength of these images is particularly clear during July 1981 when headlines proclaimed the hatred that blacks had for the police, their alienation or detachment from the mainstream values of British society and the growth of racial tension in certain important localities. Among the early reports on the riots the *Daily Mail's* headline proclaimed simply: "Black War on the Police" (6 July 1981). This was perhaps the most extreme, but the *Sun* was only marginally less direct when it talked of "The Cities that Live in Fear," while the *Daily Mirror* proclaimed the words of Merseyside's Chief Constable, Kenneth Oxford, when it argued: "This was not a race war. It was blacks versus the police."

During July 1981 a number of accounts of the events focused on the issue of the family background of riot participants and the decline of 'firm parental control' over children. Kenneth Oxford made a number of statements which argued that the main responsibility for the riots lay with parents who either could not control their children or who did not care. The *Daily Telegraph* reported Mr Oxford as saying:

> What in the name of goodness are these young people doing on the streets indulging in this behaviour and at that time of night? Is there no discipline that can be brought to bear on these young people? Are the parents not interested in the futures of these young people?
>
> (8 July 1981)

According to this model the cause of the riots lay not in the conflict between young people and the police but in the failure of families to control the actions of their children. Such arguments were articulated with regularity throughout the period of the riots. Both the Prime Minister, Margaret Thatcher, and the Home Secretary, William Whitelaw, supported such arguments. *The Times* reported the Prime Minister as saying that if the parents could not control the actions of their children, what could the government do to stop them from engaging in "hooliganism" and a "spree of naked greed" (10 July 1981). At the same time the Home Secretary was reported as saying that the government was looking at plans to involve parents in "the consequences of offenses committed by their children" (*The Times,* 10 July 1981).

Such arguments were not necessarily linked to race, but, as we saw earlier, Lord Scarman himself partly explained the drift of black youngsters into crime and violence by reference to the weak family units of the West Indian communities. And during 1981 much media coverage was given to the supposed weakness of the West Indian family and the isolation of young blacks from both their families and society as a whole. Moreover, the history of political responses to black immigration is deeply infused with the notion that blacks were intrinsically a 'problem,' either in social or cultural terms. Thus even when such arguments were not about 'race' *per se*, popular common sense helped to link the notion of 'weak family structure' to the West Indian communities; and it was a short step from this to explaining the riots as an outcome of pathological family structures.

Arguments around the question of the family were linked to other issues: e.g. the crisis of youth, the growth of violence in society generally, the phenomenon of 'youth hooliganism,' the drift of young people into crime. Whether such images were based on factual evidence or not they succeeded in becoming part of the public debate about the 1980-1 riots and became even more important during 1985. By becoming part of public debate they helped to construct a model of the riots which saw them as the outcome of causes which were outside of the control of either the government or the police. They thus helped to deflect attention away from the "broader social context" of Lord Scarman's report and towards specific social problems which undermined law and order.

What Kind of Reform?

Despite widespread predictions of further unrest in the aftermath of 1981, the scale and the location of the 1985 riots seem to have surprised even some of the most astute commentators. Handsworth, for example, was presented even shortly before September 1985 as a 'success story' in terms of police-community relations. The outbreak of violence in this area was therefore widely presented as an aberration. Similarly the spread of violence in London to areas such as the Broadwater Farm Estate in Tottenham was seen as a break from previous experience, which had centered on areas such as Brixton.

There are many continuities between 1980-1 and 1985 in relation to the 'common-sense' images used in the press and television to cover the events. But responses in 1985 were different, at least in terms of degree, and probably in relation, to the extent to which the riots were seen as a 'race' phenomenon by a wider body of opinion. The ambiguities and sub-clauses to be found in much of the press coverage during 1980-1 had at least acted as a countervailing tendency against the more extreme forms of discourse which blamed the riots completely on black people.

During the 1985 riots and their immediate aftermath, the imagery of 'race' was used by sections of the press without the sense of ambiguity which could still be found in 1980-1. The 'silence over race' was breached in 1980-1, but in 1985 debate about racial issues was taken a step further. Peregrine Worsthorne, for example, used the ferocity of the confrontations in Handsworth, Brixton and Tottenham to argue that there was a major question mark over the possibility of assimilating the "coloured population" into mainstream "British values" (*Sunday Telegraph*, 29 September 1985). To be sure, there was still a strong response opposing Enoch Powell's call for repatriation, from all shades of political opinion, but the racialization of public debate about the 1985 riots went much further than 1980-1.

In this context it was the externality of British Afro-Caribbeans and Asians which was highlighted rather than the racist institutions and processes which worked against blacks at all levels of society. The usage of 'race' during the September-October 1985 period took on new meanings, which had little if anything to do with the impact of racism as such, since the emphasis was on the cultural characteristics of the minority communities themselves. After Handsworth part of the press response was to blame the riot on rivalry between West Indians and Asians, and even after the arguments were criticized by local residents and community leaders they were used to 'explain' what happened. In addition, the questions of whether the cultures and values of the black communities, their family structures and their political attitudes 'bred violence' were constantly raised (van Dijk, 1988).

The actual 'facts' of who was arrested during the riots, whether black or white, were hardly debated, since it was assumed that they were mostly black and mostly unemployed and involved with crime (Keith, 1987). The imagery of the 'black bomber' used in Handsworth was extended to the notion that there were groups of alienated and criminalized young blacks who saw the riots as a chance to engage in an 'orgy of looting.' The Dear Report on Handsworth captures this image and links it to the social condition of young blacks:

> The majority of rioters who took part in these unhappy events were young, black and of Afro-Caribbean origin. Let there be no doubt, these young criminals are not in any way representative of the vast majority of the Afro-Caribbean community whose life has contributed to the life and culture of the West Midlands over many years and whose hopes and aspirations are at one with those of every other law-abiding citizen. We share a common sorrow. It is the duty of us all to ensure that an entire cultural group is not tainted by the actions of a criminal minority.
>
> (Dear, 1985: 69)

This 'black' criminal minority was constructed not only into the leading force behind the riots, but sometimes as the only force. Indeed, throughout September and October 1985, and during the following months, the imagery of race continued to dominate debate both about the causes and the policy outcomes of the riots. As pointed out earlier, the 'social causes' argument was another major plank of public debate about the 1980-1 riots, particularly in relation to the highly politicized issue of unemployment. During 1985 this issue was raised once again, though by then the extent of mass unemployment and urban de-industrialization and decay was more stark than it had been in 1981. Images of 'urban decay,' 'tinderbox cities' and 'ghetto streets' linked up with the images of 'race inequality' and 'black ghettos' to produce an analysis more complex but contradictory.

An interesting mixture of the various images was provided by a story in the *Daily Telegraph* under the headline "Broadwater Farm: Like the Divis Flats with Reggae" (8 October 1985). The *Daily Mirror* described the estate as "Living Hell," and quoted one resident as saying that "You've no idea how awful daily life is" (8 October 1985). Such images were reworkings of arguments already used about Toxteth in 1981 and Brixton in 1981, but they were used more widely than in 1980-1. Even the *Daily Mail*, which deployed the clearest use of 'race' and 'outside agitator' type arguments, ran a major story on Broadwater Farm under the headline "Burnt-out hulks litter this concrete jungle. Despair hangs heavy" (8 October 1985). A number of stories using such imagery were run by both the quality and popular press during this period, but similar arguments are to be found in parliamentary debates (*Hansard*, 84, 21 October 1985: cols. 30-46 and col. 388) and even in official reports produced by the police on the riots in Birmingham and London.

The 'cities of inner despair' were conceived as the breeding ground for disorderly protest, and however hard the government tried to break the causal link between the two it was forced to take on board the need to restore order not only through the police but through promises of help for the inner cities. Much as in 1980-1, the 'social causes' argument cannot be seen separately from the broader debate about the future of the British economy and society. The government's record on unemployment was a heavily politicized issue, and, just as in 1981, it vehemently denied any responsibility for the riots through its pursuit of free-market policies. But the government did find a way of accepting a link between the riots and social problems without bringing its main policies into the debate: namely by linking the growth of violent disorder to crime and drugs.

The emphasis on 'crime' and the 'criminal acts' of the rioters in the official responses to the 1985 riots took a general and a specific form. The general form relied on the argument that the riots were not a form of protest against the insufferable social conditions of inner-city areas or the actions of the police, but a 'criminal act' or a 'cry for loot.' This was an argument put most succinctly by Geoffrey Dear, Chief Constable for the West Midlands (Dear, 1985) and by Douglas Hurd, the Home Secretary, in relation to Handsworth. But it recurred as a theme in official and press responses to the other riots. The specific form was built upon the notion that the outbreak of violence in Handsworth and Brixton, in particular, was brought about by 'drug barons' who saw the police attempting to curb their activities and control 'their territory.' Numerous examples of this line of argument can be found in Dear's report on Handsworth, and in press coverage during the riots.

Taking the specific argument about the role of drugs and 'drug barons' in stimulating the riots, this seems to have served two purposes. First, it distanced the riots from the social, economic, political and other grievances which had been linked to them, by locating the cause outside of the 'social problems' of inner-city dwellers and in the 'simple greed' of the drug barons to accumulate 'loot.' Second, just as Dear's image of a few hundred 'young black criminals' was used to explain what happened in Handsworth, the problem of drugs was used to explain what happened at a national level. The issue of drugs provided an everyday image, already a national issue through saturation media coverage and public debate, around which the police, the Home Office and other institutions could de-politicize the riots.

Responding to the Handsworth events, Douglas Hurd was moved to argue forcibly that such events were senseless and reflected more on those who participated in them than on the society in which they took place: "The sound which law abiding people in Handsworth heard on Monday night, the echoes of which I picked up on Tuesday, was not a cry for help but a cry for loot" (*Financial Times*, 13 September 1985). The Chief Constable for the West Midlands, Geoffrey Dear, took this argument further by pointing out that the day before the riots a successful carnival had taken place, with the support of local community leaders. He drew the conclusion from this that the riot "came like a bolt out of the blue" (*Guardian*, 21 November 1985). Such language focused attention on the individuals or groups who were 'breaking the law,' 'committing criminal acts' and threatening the interests of the law-abiding 'majority.'

In terms of economic and social policies the impact of the 1980-1 riots was equally ambiguous and contradictory. Part of this ambiguity, as outlined above, resulted from the government's strenuous efforts to deny any link between its policies and the outbreak of violence and disorder. This denial was particularly important, since at the time the Thatcher administration was going through a bad period in terms of popular opinion on issues such as unemployment, social services and housing. While Lord Scarman was careful not to enter the political dispute between the government and the Labour Party on issues such as unemployment and housing, his call for more direct action to deal with these problems, along with racial disadvantage, posed a challenge to the political legitimacy of the policies which the government had followed from 1979 onwards. It also posed a delicate problem for the Home Secretary himself, since Lord Scarman had been appointed by him to carry out his inquiry. Having spent the whole summer denying any link between its policies and the riots, the government had to tread wearily in responding to the economic and social policy proposals of the Scarman Report when it was published in November 1981.

The parliamentary debate on the report showed the Home Secretary adopting a two-pronged strategy in his response. First, he accepted many of the recommendations of the report, particularly in relation to the role of the police. Additionally, he accepted the need to tackle racial disadvantage and other social issues. Second, he emphasized the government's view that, whatever broader measures were taken to deal with racial and social inequalities, the immediate priority was to restore and maintain order on the streets. When the Home Secretary talked of the need for the Government to give a lead in tackling racial disadvantage he therefore saw this as an issue for the longer term. On the other hand, he was much more specific about the reform of the police and the development of new tactics and equipment for the management of urban disorder (*Hansard*, 14, 10 December 1981: cols. 1001-8).

In 1985, however, the government specifically rejected calls for another Scarman type inquiry, arguing that since the riots were a 'criminal enterprise' it was useless to search for social explanations or to have yet another report advising it about what to do. Implicitly the government was saying that it knew what the problems were, and how they could be tackled.

Some senior policemen, like Metropolitan Police Commissioner Sir Kenneth Newman, wanted to stress the link between the response of the police and other areas of 'social policy' (Metropolitan Police, 1986). Within the context of this perspective it was necessary to develop complex forms of 'social policing' in which the actions of the police were linked to those of other agencies, such as social workers and youth workers.

The official government response, however, attempted to decontextualize the riots and see them as the actions of a small minority who were either criminalized or influenced by extreme political ideas. The dominant approach of the government attempted to emphasize two main arguments:

(1) that the riots were 'a lust for blood,' an 'orgy of thieving,' 'a cry for loot and not a cry for help;'

(2) that the riots reflected not a failure to carry out the "urgent programme of action" recommended by Lord Scarman in 1981, but were the outcome of a spiralling wave of crime and disorder in inner-city areas.

The logic of this approach, articulated by Home Secretary Douglas Hurd most clearly, was that the riots were both 'unjustifiable' and a 'criminal activity.' In a widely reported speech to police chiefs at the time of the disorders Hurd made this point clear:

> Handsworth needs more jobs and better housing. But riots only destroy. They create nothing except a climate in which necessary development is even more difficult. Poor housing and other social ills provide no kind of reason for riot, arson and killing. One interviewer asked me whether the riot was not a cry for help by the rioters. The sound which law-abiding people heard at Handsworth was not a cry for help but a cry for loot. That is why the first priority, once public order is secure, must be a thorough and relentless investigation into the crimes which were committed.
>
> (*Daily Telegraph*, 14 September 1985)

Such arguments resonated throughout the media and in the various parliamentary debates during September and October 1985. They become part of the symbolic political language through which the riots were understood by policy-makers and by popular opinion.

Since the 1985 unrest, and particularly after the 1987 general election, the government has announced a number of initiatives on the inner cities, and it has presented these as part of an effort to rejuvenate depressed areas on a sound basis. The evidence that has emerged since then, however, points to a major discrepancy between the government's promises of action and the allocation of resources to implement them (Robson, 1988). It is perhaps too early to reach a conclusion on this point, but a repeat of the period of inaction between 1982 and 1985 seems to be evident, within the current political context. A number of local authorities have attempted to take more positive action to deal with the issues raised by the 1985 riots, but their experience has shown that such local initiatives are often severely limited by the actions of national government, the police and broader economic and political pressures.

In the years since 1981 the one consistent response to urban unrest has been the provision of more resources, more training and more equipment to the police. Instead of tackling the causes of urban unrest, the government has built up forces to deal with the manifestation of those root conditions.

Increasingly the most strident political voices are raised in the name of free enterprise and law and order, not for equity and social justice. For the New Right and other influential sectors of political opinion the attempt to achieve racial equality through legal and political means is at best naive political folly, and at worst a restriction on the workings of the market. The present political climate gives little cause for optimism that a radical change in governmental priorities in this field is likely (Solomos, 1989).

The government's plan of *Action for Cities* (DoE, 1988), issued after Mrs. Thatcher's post-1987 election promise, says very little directly about racial inequality. It remains to be seen whether it will suffer the fate of numerous other initiatives on the inner cities and fade into obscurity. But one thing seems clear: during the past decade the government has been more intent on reducing the powers of local authorities than on providing for fundamental changes in the social conditions of the inner cities.

Conclusion

Finally, what of the prospects for the future? Certainly the experience of the past decade makes it difficult to be optimistic about the chances of a radical change in public policy in this field. As the predominant political ideas have shifted to the right, so the probability of the political action required at the national level to tackle the roots of racism and social disadvantage has diminished. The situation, however, is by no means static. The frequency of outbreaks of urban unrest during the 1980s indicates that the continued exclusion of black communities and other inner-city residents may result in the repudiation of political authority, manifest as civic indifference, as a refusal to comply with laws and directives or as open conflict and violence. While the excluded black and white citizens of urban areas seem set to continue to suffer deprivations and injustice, it cannot be assumed that they will do so in silence.

In recent years the Conservative administrations have proclaimed their intention of regenerating the inner cities, largely through free-market oriented programs of action. Again there is little room for optimism that such strategies will substantially improve the position of the most deprived citizens of the inner cities. Unless radical action is taken, British cities seem poised to become yet more turbulent, brutalized and trouble-torn. The remedy of using tough policing is merely tackling the symptoms of the disorder, and is liable to exacerbate the underlying malaise.

What the outbreaks of urban unrest during the 1980s showed clearly is that political institutions have yet to address seriously the question of how to overcome the exclusion of large sections of the black population from equal citizenship and full political rights. Recent political developments do not show any indication that the present administration is prepared to make major initiatives in this area. Short of radical and imaginative reforms it is likely that during the 1990s there will be further outbreaks of violent urban unrest, and this will have major implications for the role of the police in British society.

Chapter 13

The Mohawk-Canada Crisis: Native Peoples, Criminalization and the Justice System

Thomas O'Reilly-Fleming

The University of Windsor

Introduction: The State as Criminal

The social control of aboriginal peoples in Canada, Australia and the United States has resulted in their marginalization, and engendered vulnerability in terms of the criminalization of their struggles for autonomy and independence. The attack upon native Canadians, a diverse collection of 650 bands comprising 350,000 Status Indians and 25,000 Inuit (Ratner, 1990: 59; York, 1990) who reside in ten provinces has been constant and devastating. First Canadians who are last in line for justice have been treated as outcasts with well documented results, most centrally in the cultural isolation of confinement to postage stamp parcels of 'reserve' land through consistent government rejection of treaties and exploitation of resources to the benefit of multi-national corporations (Adele and Stasiulis, 1989; Asch, 1984; Badcock, 1976; York, 1990; Miller, 1991). Natives have a reduced life expectancy (Ratner, 1990), have suicide rates that are far greater than that recorded in the general population (York, 1990), suffer from wide-scale unemployment and have lost generations of children to white child welfare workers who removed native children from reserve settings, often to be fostered and adopted into white homes (O'Reilly-Fleming, 1991; Ratner, 1990; York, 1990). Central to the argument presented in this paper is the fact that natives are grossly overrepresented in the criminal justice system where men, women and children fill jail cells (Shorten, 1991). In Manitoba and Saskatchewan, natives comprise ten percent of the province's population but make up 60 percent or more of persons serving sentences of incarceration (Havemann, 1985; Hylton, 1983; Jackson, 1988; York, 1990: 146). A joint federal-provincial

---

* Reprinted by permission of the author.

task force not surprisingly concluded that "racism exists in our criminal justice system.... ignorance of aboriginal people...appears to be a large part of the problem of racism." (*Globe and Mail*, November 12, 1991: 1).

While racism is explicit in the excessive incarceration of native peoples in the prison system one must look to the hegemonic control of native land claims by the Canadian government and its native policies to provide a framework for understanding of the recent militancy of native groups. Since it is not within the scope of this article to provide a complete dissection of either land claims disputes or governmental policies, an overview of key issues since 1969 will be provided. In 1969, a federal government white paper called for the repeal of the *Indian Act*, the extinguishment of treaty rights, the closing of reserves and assimilation of natives into the dominant culture (Little Bear, Boldt and Long, 1981; Little Bear and Boldt, 1988). This proposal ignored five years of negotiations with native peoples setting the tone for government negotiations which has persisted until today (Weaver, 1981).

By 1982, native leaders were forced to lobby in Great Britain to ensure their treaty rights when the Canadian Constitution was repatriated as the Canadian government would not listen to them (Ponting, 1986; Purich, 1986). In 1983, the First Ministers' Conference which included the Prime Minister as well as the premiers of all Canadian provinces rejected native self-government, declaring it to be 'too vague' a concept, and cut the meetings short (Cohen, 1991: 258-260). Within a month, Mulroney was to extend a similar conference in order to ensure the rights of French Canadians were enshrined in the Meech Lake Accord granting them 'distinct society' status. As George Erasmus, Chief of The Assembly of First Nations (1989: 1) wrote, "There are obviously two standards that the prime minister and the premiers follow: one for themselves, and another for the aboriginal peoples."

In 1990, Elijah Harper, Manitoba's only native member of the Manitoba legislature, stopped the passage of the Meech Lake Accord singlehandedly by filibustering until the adoption deadline passed. Native leaders rejected Prime Minister Mulroney's promise of a special commission to address their needs (Cohen, 1991; York, 1990), aware of endless Royal Commissions which together comprise only so much yellowing paper. The stage was now set for a further deterioration of relations between Native Canadians and authorities as Mulroney's dream of being the father of a new, united Canada lay in ruins defeated by a native parliamentarian brandishing an eagle feather and the anger of generations of native peoples.

The actions of the Canadian government at all levels can be interpreted as criminal and intended until recently to see the disappearance of native peoples into the melting pot of Canadian society. When this strategy failed following 1969, their approach can best be summarized as following a three-pronged attack: (1) to systematically deny significant land claims to native peoples through the administration of law; (2) to give native peoples a voice at conferences which will represent little more than token representation; and (3) to impose policies which impact with dire consequences on native peoples making many of them into 'criminals' through their interaction with 'white' law.

In the remaining portion of the article I wish to explore the context of the Canada-Mohawk crisis which illustrates several of the levels of criminalization of activities experienced by native peoples in Canada. First, the crisis is seen to underscore the inability of native groups to gain sovereignty over lands. Their efforts to protect their lands, and hence their people since the two are often inextricable, are further monopolized by the dominant culture in Canada to characterize their protest as criminal action. Second, government views on natives which protect compliant native leaders and their followers while discrediting the actions of protestors are seen as not only divisive to immediate and long-term native interests but as a further attempt at criminalization. Finally, in the aftermath of Oka it is argued that not only are policies of stripping natives of their lands continuing, but that verdicts now being handed down in the Oka cases further propagate the concept of native versus native in terms of criminal versus law-abiding 'Indians.' In the wider context of government native relations law is viewed as a weapon of social control (Turk, 1985) wielded by Indian Affairs officials and other officers of the law as a means of dividing native peoples. As one of the leading researchers on native policies commented on returning from discussions with officials of the Indian Affairs Department, "The bureaucrats said, 'They'll do as we say or they won't do anything'" (Weaver, 1991).

Oka: A Failure of Law and Spirit

In the spring of 1990, Mohawks of the Kanesatake Reserve near Oka, Quebec set up a roadblock to protest the expansion of a golf course on 22 hectares of land which was originally seized from the Mohawk peoples by an illegal action on the part of religious authorities some two centuries ago. On July 11, 1990 hundreds of armed Quebec Provincial Police (Sûreté) stormed the roadblock, and in the resultant battle, as Mohawks returned police fire, officer Marcel Lemay was killed. This set off a summer of siege that was to become widely known as the Oka Crisis. More properly, these events were the Canada-Mohawk crisis (Doxtater, 1991), a dispute between two independent nations, the latter contained by the oppression of the former. The disputed land at Oka assumed the status of a symbol of the frustration native peoples had begun to rebel against as their land claims were turned aside, and their peoples were being systematically criminalized by the 'justice' system (MacLaine and Baxendale, 1990).

The role of the federal and provincial governments in the Canada-Mohawk crisis reflected a long-standing attitude which adopted a stance of ignoring Native demands as a method of governance. Friederes (1983) noted the unscrupulous policies which have left the vast majority of the hundreds of native land claims unresolved until the present. The catalogue of government stall tactics have included the forbiddance of non-natives as advocates (until 1951), laws which did not permit band funds or personal contributions by natives to be used for making claims and other policies which simply dismissed claims without legal access to the reasons they were denied. Friederes (1983) noted that "The realization that Natives can act independently in a manner contrary to government policy has occurred only recently." Government policies have viewed natives largely as what Foucault (1977) terms "docile bodies" much like children who do not know what is good for them. In this schema there are 'good' natives who follow the directives of the Indian Affairs Department, and 'bad' natives who wish to assert their independence and resurrect their nations.

The Mohawk people spent the next two months under siege from the Quebec provincial police and later the Canadian army. The federal government refused for several weeks to become involved in the dispute, claiming that the land issue was outside of their jurisdiction. The events of the summer revealed the racist sentiments of the Quebec police, and perhaps of the wider society as daily actions against the Mohawks provoked not only national but international outrage and interventions. The police began by refusing food and medical supplies to pass beyond the barriers despite court orders to this effect. When women and children attempted to leave the reserve police stood idly by while Oka residents hurled rocks at a caravan of cars, resulting in the death of a Mohawk elder. By the end of July (*Globe and Mail*, July 28, 1990: A6) Canadians had begun to support the native point of view as live coverage of the events at Oka were recorded by the Canadian Broadcasting Company and broadcast directly into millions of viewers' homes. Police refused to permit visits by The Quebec Human Rights Commission, Elijah Harper or Jesse Jackson who came to investigate allegations by the people trapped on the reserve of violations of human rights. By August 15, the Canadian army had deployed troops near Oka joining thousands of Quebec police (*Globe and Mail*, August 15, 1990: Al, A2). On September 17, (*Globe and Mail*, September 17, 1990: A3) the army tightened its grip on the Mohawk reserve. All supplies entering the reserve were cut off, reporters were ordered out, and telephone communications cut. From this point forward all 'news' on Oka was provided by the Canadian army, who began a systematic portrayal of the Mohawk warriors as experienced criminals. The army first produced a video documenting the various weapons possessed by the warriors manning the barricade, and attempted to demonstrate that the trenches and defensive structures built within the reserve were constructed by veteran soldiers.

On September 21, the army alleged, through its exclusive control of the media, that the warriors negotiating at Oka were 'criminals' (*Globe and Mail*, September 21, 1990: A8). Kim Campbell, Minister of Justice claimed that, "The Warriors do not represent *legitimate* [my emphasis] native grievances." While several have been involved in the sale of cut-rate gas and cigarettes on Canadian reserves, and in disputes at Akwesasne over legalized gambling, their characterization as 'criminals' in this context represented a feeble attempt to justify the use of the army in a civilian context (York and Pindera, 1991). The presence of the army at Oka lent credence to Mohawk assertions that the Quebec police were guilty of innumerable brutalities against their people and simply could not be trusted.

The portrayal of oppressed peoples as criminals, and their treatment as such by the criminal justice system is a tactic long employed by dominant cultures. The warriors at Oka came to be portrayed by the Deputy Minister of Native Affairs, Harry Swain as a "criminal organization," a form of mafia (*Toronto Star*, July 24, 1990: Al, A20; *Globe and Mail*, July 24, 1990: Al, A2) at a time when the United Nations was considering a probe of the situation. Swain in the same interview described the actions of the warriors as one of "hijacking" the dispute while at the same time "traditional leaders" had been "terrorized" by the warriors. Further it was argued that the warriors 'leading' the revolt were not really 'Canadians' but Americans who had entered the country illegally, conveniently ignoring the Mohawk stand of sovereignty. While it is not arguable that there are factions and differing opinions within the Mohawk community (*Akwesasne Mohawk Nation*, 1990) the depiction of Mohawk warriors as constituting an arm of an organized crime syndicate demonstrated a complete lack of understanding of the power structure of native organizations, and did not reflect the support being given to the actions of the warriors and the other residents of the reserve by native peoples across the country who joined in symbolic barricades as a display of unity. The overcriminalization of the activities of marginal groups who are, in fact, not criminals at all, is a tactic that has been used before by social control agencies within Canada (Fleming, 1983) against a variety of groups. Ovide Mercredi, now chief of The Assembly of First Nations, said "They're insensitive and they have no respect for Indian people. Their strategy is to make us seem unreasonable." (*Globe and Mail*, July 24, 1990: Al). Moreover, Mercredi reaffirmed the position of Chiefs across the country when he commented that "There is community support for the barricades and for self-defense."

In the end more than 50 natives were taken into custody after a stand-off of 78 days by the army and the provincial police with little resistance. The first two to be prosecuted became recognizable across Canada for their tactics of overt resistance and taunting of army troops. Ronald Cross, more widely known by his alias "Lasagna," was sentenced to 52 months in federal prison. Gordon Lazore, known as "Noriega," was given a 23-month prison term. In his decision Justice Benjamin Greenberg commented upon the "contempt, discrimination and racism" that native Canadians have suffered. Greenberg, adopting the divisive approach which has long characterized government and judicial relations with native peoples, linked the majority of Cross's sentence to his assault against another Mohawk, Francis Jacobs (*Windsor Star*, February 15, 1992: A12). Jacobs had proposed a conciliatory approach with negotiators during the crisis and was viewed as a pawn of the government. Thus, the wider political implications of the Canada-Mohawk crisis were submerged as the judiciary chose to portray the events in terms of the government's depiction of the siege, as being propelled by 'criminal' natives who 'hijacked' law-abiding natives. The trials of the remaining Mohawks will take place in the next year, while much of the "deep anger and rage" (*Windsor Star*, February 15, 1992: A12) that precipitated the Canada-Mohawk crisis remains unabated.

NATIVE LAND AND NATIVE RIGHTS: "AT THE PLEASURE OF THE CROWN"

The criminalization of native peoples within Canada is likely to continue and escalate as further erosions of native power and resources occur. Courts in Canada continue to strip Native bands of title to their ancestral lands (Brody, 1991; Miller, 1991; Richardson, 1991). In the case of *Delgamuukw v. British Columbia,* Chief Justice Allan McEachern has ruled that the claim of the Gitskan and Wet'suwet'en Indians of aboriginal right and ownership of 57,000 square kilometers of territory has no validity. McEachern argued that native rights exist at "the pleasure of the Crown." Therefore, the government of British Columbia could dispose of these lands as they saw fit regardless of whether they constituted part of the ancestral lands of these aboriginal people. While one member of parliament pronounced that this was a simple declaration of "cultural genocide," business leaders celebrated the decision as it clears the way for forestry, mining and resource extraction industries to exploit the lands. The Minister of Indian Affairs, Tom Siddon, welcomed the decision, echoing the government stance that native land claims are, in large part, frivolous; "it is a very important decision which will give us important insight into the existence and meaning of aboriginal rights in Canada" (*The Financial Post*, March 9: 1). The decision virtually reversed some slight recognition of aboriginal title that had resulted from earlier decisions in the Supreme Court of Canada (Cassidy, 1991).

The decision of McEachern in *Delgamuukw* reflects the role of the state as oppressor and as legal authority over natives. He wrote:

> they must understand...that our Courts are Courts of law which labour under disciplines which do not always permit judges to do what they subjectively think (or feel) might be the right or just thing to do in a particular case.

Mandel's (1986: 90) observations concerning the role of the judiciary are informative in this context when he wrote that, "It is probably most helpful in this context to think of judges as lawyers whose clients are the status quo." Offe (1984) was to make a similar observation in arguing that judges find themselves unable to make decisions which may be just, but which run contrary to the wishes of the ruling class, since in the Canadian context their appointment is through political channels.

Following the Canada-Mohawk crisis, native attempts to negotiate special status for aboriginal peoples in the new Canadian constitution have largely followed the schema suggested earlier in this article. Aboriginal peoples were allowed to address hearings on the future of Canada held across the country, but when Ovid Mercredi asked for 'distinct society status' for aboriginal peoples the same as that accorded to Quebec's francophone population he was met with outrage on the part of the Quebec delegation and Joe Clark, the minister responsible for these hearings. Clark informed Ovide Mercredi that there was "no time and no money" to consider native demands in a special conference, nor could they expect either distinct society status or full self-government in the new constitution. Natives were to be seen and heard but simply not listened to!

Canada's aboriginal peoples exist as distant figures in the national landscape, part of a 'third world' that few citizens bother to explore (Krotz, 1992). Pope John Paul has declared the conditions that many Canadian natives live under to be worse than that suffered by blacks in the 'homelands' of South Africa. Few know that the reserves were used as a model for these race camps (York, 1990).

Canada continues to criminalize native peoples across a wide variety of life activities. They fill our prisons. Native children have filled our residential schools and now fill our juvenile facilities. Native lands are removed by 'white' laws, which natives are required to respect while cases like *Delgamuukw* are decided by "white man's law...although the aboriginal laws which they recognize could be relevant." White judges do not respect native law, but there is no crime in this. When natives show disrespect for white law, they become criminals. Aboriginal peoples who have lived in Canada for thousands of years are not entitled to self government, and are treated as child-like wards of The

Indian Affairs Department. The claims of French Canadians to "distinct society" status are honored despite their small numbers and relatively short history in Canada. But the francophones do not have claim to millions of kilometers of land, land which has unlimited potential for exploitation by multi-national resource development corporations or government projects like James Bay 1 and 2 (Clement, 1977; O'Connor, 1973; Wright, 1979).

If aboriginal peoples in Canada are going to change their status as fodder for criminalization, they must do so through the assertion of their autonomy and independence as the first people of the nation. As Chief David Perly of the Tobique Indian reserve commented, "We are not children who have to be controlled, guided and directed by the federal officials. Let us take control of our own life" (York, 1990: 266). Until this occurs, native Canadians are likely to remain the victims of Canadian criminal injustice.

References

Abele, F. and D. Stasiulis. 1989. "Canada as a White Settler Colony: What About Natives and Immigrants?" in Clement, W. and G. Williams (eds.), *The New Canadian Political Economy*. Kingston: McGill-Queen's University Press, pp. 240-276.

Akwesasne Mohawk Nation. 1990/91. Publication of the Tribal Council of The Akwesasne Tribal Council.

Asch, M. 1984. *Home and Native Land: Aboriginal Rights and the Canadian Constitution*. Toronto: Methuen.

Badcock, W.T. 1976. *Who Owns Canada?: Aboriginal Title and Canadian Courts*. Ottawa:CASNP.

Brody, H. 1991. *The Peoples Land*. Toronto: Douglas and McIntyre.

Cassidy, F. (ed.). 1991. *Reaching Just Settlements: Land Claims in British Columbia*. Lantzville: Oolichan.

Clement, W. 1977. "The corporate elite, the capitalist class and the Canadian state" in Panitch, L. (ed.), *The Canadian State: Politial Economy and Political Power*, Toronto: University of Toronto Press, pp. 225-250.

Cohen, A. 1991. *A Deal Undone: The Making and Breaking of the Meech Lake Accord*. Toronto: Douglas and McIntyre.

Doxtater, T. 1991. *Reflections on the Mohawk-Canada Crisis*. Paper presented to The Windsor Society of Criminology, March 1991.

Erasmus, G. 1989. "Twenty Years of Disappointed Hopes" in Erasmus, G., *Drumbeat: Anger and Renewal in Indian Country*. Toronto: Summerhill, pp. 1-42.

Financial Post. 1991. "Native Ruling frees resource projects." 9 March, p. 1.

Fleming, T. 1983. "Criminalizing a Marginal Community" in Fleming, T. and L.Visano (eds.), *Deviant Designations: Crime, Law and Deviance in Canada*. Toronto: Butterworths, pp. 37-61.

Foucault, M. 1997. *Discipline and Punish*. New York: Pantheon.

Friederes, J.S. 1983. *Native People in Canada: Contemporary Conflicts.* Scarborough: Prentice-Hall.

Giddens, A. 1982. *Profiles and Critiques in Social Theory.* London: Macmillan.

Globe and Mail, Oka coverage, 13 July 1990 to 29 September 1990, 76 newspaper articles.

Havemann, P. *et al.* 1985. *Law and Order for Canada's Indigenous People.* Regina: Prairie Justice Research, University of Regina.

Harris, M. 1986. *Justice Denied: The Law versus Donald Marshall.* Toronto: MacMillan.

Hylton, J. 1983. "Locking Up Indians in Saskatchewan" in Fleming, T. and L. Visano (eds.), *Deviant Designations: Crime, Law and Deviance in Canada.* Toronto: Butterworths, pp. 61-71.

Jackson, M. 1988. *Locking Up Natives in Canada: A Report of the Canadian Bar Association on Imprisonment and Release.* Ottawa: CBA.

Krotz, L. 1992. *Indian Country: Inside Another Canada.* Toronto: McClelland and Stewart.

Little Bear, L., M. Boldt and J. Long (eds.). 1984. *Pathways to Self-Determination: Canadian Indians and the Canadian State.* Toronto: University of Toronto Press.

Little Bear, L. and M. Boldt (eds.). 1988. *Governments in Conflict?: Provinces and Indian Nations in Canada.* Toronto: University of Toronto Press.

MacLaine, C. and M. Baxendale. 1990. *This Land is Our Land: The Mohawk Revolt at Oka.* Toronto: Optimum.

Mandel, M. 1986. "The Legalization of Prison Discipline in Canada." *Crime and Social Justice.* 26: 79-94.

Miliband, R. 1969. *The State in Capitalist Society.* London: Weidenfeld and Nicholson.

Miller, J.R. 1991. *Sweet Promises: A Reader in Indian-White Relations.* Toronto: University of Toronto Press.

O'Connor, J. 1973. *The Fiscal Crisis of the State.* New York: St. Martin's.

Offe, C. 1984. *Contradictions of the Welfare State.* Cambridge: MIT Press.

O'Reilly-Fleming, T. and P. O'Reilly-Fleming. 1990. "To the Medicine Wheel: Legal Issues in the Repatriation of Native Children to the Reserve." Paper presented to The Canadian Sociology and Anthropology Association, Victoria, British Columbia, June.

Ornstein, T. 1973. *The First Peoples in Quebec.* Montreal: Thunderbird Press.

Ponting, J. (ed.). 1986. *Arduous Journey: Canadian Indians and Decolonization.* Toronto: McClelland and Stewart.

Purich, D. 1986. *Our Land: Native Rights in Canada.* Toronto: James Lorimer.

Ratner, R.S., J. McMullan and B. Burtch. 1987. "The Problem of Relative Autonomy and Criminal Justice in the Canadian State" in Ratner, R.S. and J.McMullan (eds.), *State Control: Criminal Justice Politics in Canada.* Vancouver: University of British Columbia Press.

Ratner, R.S. 1990. "Child Welfare Services for Urban Native Indians." Report to The United Native Nations, May.

Richardson, B. 1991. *Strangers Devour the Land.* Douglas and McIntyre.

Shorten, J. 1991. *Without Reserve.* Edmonton: Newest.

Toronto Star, Oka Coverage, 12 July 1990 to 25 September 1990, 23 newspaper articles.

Weaver, S. 1981. *Making Canadian Indian Policy: The Hidden Agenda, 1968-1970.* Toronto: University of Toronto Press.

.... 1991. "Native Politics After Oka." Talk presented to The Department of Sociology and Anthroplogy, University of Windsor, March 1991.

Windsor Star 1992. "Mohawks get jail for standoff role." 15 February, p. A12.

Wright, E.O. 1979. *Class, Crisis and the State.* London: Verso.

York, G. 1990. *The Dispossessed: Life and Death in Native Canada.* London: Vintage.

York, G. and L. Pindera. 1991. *People of the Pines: The Warriors and the Legacy of Oka.* Toronto: Little Brown.

LEGISLATION

The Indian Act, Revised Statutes of Canada, 1970, Vol. IV, Chapters 1-6.

CASES CITED

Delgamuukw v. *British Columbia.* 1991. B.C.J. No.525. Smithers Registry No. 0843.

Chapter 14

Discrimination, Disadvantage and Police-Work

Tony Jefferson

> Within ten years Britain will have solved its 'black problem' — that is the message of the White Paper — but 'solved' in the sense of having diverted revolutionary aspiration, into nationalist achievement, reduced militancy to rhetoric, put protest to profit and, above all, kept a black under-class from bringing to the struggles of the white workers political dimensions peculiar to its own historic against capital. All these have been achieved in some considerable measure in the past decade and a half — through immigration control and social control — and the process has already thrown up the class of collaborators so essential to a solution of the next stage of the problem: the political control of a rebellious 'second generation.' And it is to this exercise that the White Paper addresses itself.
>
> (Sivanandan, 1976: 347)

> The best contribution criminology can make to socialist politics is to concern itself with specific analyses of crime and crime policies.
>
> (Hogg, 1988: 97)

Abstract: Rereading Sivanandan's uncompromising mid-1970s account of "the black experience in Britain" is salutary, since it reminds us, forcibly and with considerable rhetorical skill, of the absolute importance of the political economy of immigration for a proper understanding of the story. But, from the vantage-point of the late 1980s, a decade of radical Conservative administrations and the new 'left realism' this has evoked, it is now equally revealing for its neglect of another level of analysis, namely,

* Originally published in *Out of Order: Policing Black People*, edited by Ellis Cashmore and Eugene McLaughlin: 109-133 (1991). Reprinted by permission of Routledge, Inc.

anything to do with 'crime and crime policies.' Moreover, since analytical accounts at either level do not necessarily ring true at the level of experience, we need also to understand how the relevant social processes are understood and experienced by those subject to them. In other words, if we wish to produce an understanding of 'race and police-work' which is faithful to all the complexities of the reality covered by that phrase — my object in what follows — we shall need to explore what we know at all these levels. Hopefully, this will prove to be a critical but cumulative journey.

In order to do this I intend, first, to take a historical look at the political economy of police-work in order to identify the organic (or structural) features of the relationship between police and ethnic minorities. Second, I propose to take a closer look at the present in order to identify the particular, contemporary processes which, in conjunction with the organic features, are determining police-black relations. Then I shall look at the debate about race and crime. And, finally, I will examine what we know of the attitudes, perceptions and experiences of ethnic minorities. Though I do not expect to be able to resolve all the problems posed en route, I do hope this stock-taking will leave us better placed to do so.

Two caveats, finally: because space is at a premium, race and ethnicity are used interchangeably throughout, Cohen's valuable strictures to the contrary notwithstanding (Cohen, 1988: 24); secondly, and also for reasons of space, I shall confine myself to a discussion of British data and materials, which means, broadly speaking, to the experiences of Afro-Caribbeans (Blacks) and Asians (from the Indian subcontinent).

Policing the 'Roughs'/Policing Race: A Political Economy of Police-Work

Up until relatively recently a conservative, evolutionary picture of the emergence and development of modern police-work dominated accounts, with the idea of the restrained use of force as a central feature. From this perspective, the widespread cross-class hostility to the very idea of a permanent, paid police-force in the late eighteenth and early nineteenth centuries ensured that the resulting force was unarmed, without special powers and charged to use the minimum force necessary. This restrained approach quickly won over the middle classes, and eventually the working classes, once the benefits of a more orderly and less crime-prone society became evident, and the fears (of intrusion, surveillance, loss of liberty, etc.) proved relatively groundless. With increased acceptance went a reduction in the sort of hostility and violence (from both sides) characteristic of early police-public contacts. This new 'maturity' in police-public relations inaugurated a 'golden age of policing,' which in turn provides further vindication of the restrained approach. A key problem for this conservative perspective is how to explain interruptions to this evolutionary progress — the continuation of conflict or any remaining police-public hostility (both of which characterize police-black relations currently) — without invoking exceptional or pathological explanations.

Such accounts have been challenged by radical alternative accounts which start with the function of the new police. Whether the object of policing was crime, disorder, culture or morals, the function remained broadly the same, namely, the coercive imposition of a 'new civility' on the swelling labouring classes of the growing towns and cities of Victorian England. This coercive, class-based 'civilizing' function at the heart of the police role — captured neatly in Storch's notion of the early police as 'domestic missionaries' (1976) — not only accounts for the initial hostility and violence of police-public contacts, but also its continuation in working-class communities. 'Restraint' may characterize the police handling of the middle classes, but not the disorderly and criminal activities of the working classes. The 'golden age of policing' is thus a convenient myth. If the touchstone for evaluating policing is the experience of working-class communities and not an undifferentiated 'public,' conflict and hostility, not acceptance, is the enduring legacy. A key problem for this approach is the inverse of the former, namely, how to explain the general legitimacy police have acquired for much of the time with significant majorities of the population, including working-class communities (for fuller treatment of both sorts of account, see Brogden, *et al.* 1988: 49-100; Reiner, 1985a: 9-82).

The resolution to this dilemma of whether police-work is best conceived primarily in terms of 'acceptance' or conflict can be found in a third approach, which is based on a recognition that both — acceptance and conflict — are *contingent*, not inevitable, features of police-public relations. The idea that consent is always conditional derives from Gramsci, for whom the question of consent was crucial. If traditional Marxism had emphasized the centrality of understanding the role of conflict between the classes for political or social analysis, Gramsci was one of the first to recognize the importance of consent for understanding how advanced capitalist democracies worked. He recognized that the strength of 'civil society' in such societies rendered an 'old-style' revolutionary seizure of state power redundant. He also recognized that a well-developed civil society made coercion a strategy of last resort; what happened when the ideological struggle to produce consent failed. Both the 'ruling bloc' (the ruling class and its allies from other classes) and its opponents were constantly struggling to widen their sphere of influence by winning over allies to their vision of the world. To the extent that a ruling bloc was successful in such a struggle, its dominance could be said to be 'hegemonic.' To the extent that it failed to do so, it was appropriate to talk of a 'crisis of authority.' Such moments of instability might have many outcomes, including, if the alliance of radical forces failed to produce a successful counter-hegemony (and as Gramsci knew to his personal cost), the horrors of fascism and other 'exceptional' modes of capitalist rule. The idea of politics as the outcome of the balance of forces at particular moments, and of this balance being constantly in flux as each side enjoins the ideological struggle in order to 'win friends and influence people' (and disturb their opponents' similar attempts), renders a very different historical framework to those of the two previously looked at. Rather than the conservative idea of history as progress, or the radical one of history as constant conflict, what we have here is the idea of history as a series of moments or 'conjunctures,' each more or less stable, each more or less hegemonic (or consensual). Whilst long-term 'organic' trends determined by the mode of production set certain limits, within these limits political outcomes are the product of (or *contingent* upon) the successful (or unsuccessful) management of the political field. And crucial to such management is the 'battle of ideas.' (For an elaboration of Gramsci's key ideas, see

Gramsci, 1971.)

Phil Cohen's article (1979) on the changing nature of the policing of Islington before and after the First World War is an excellent example of this 'contingent' approach applied to the history of police-work. The basic argument runs something like this. Like the radical approach outlined above, the starting-point is the idea of the new police having a 'civilizing' mission ultimately motivated by economic considerations which was fiercely resisted by the city slum-dwellers who bore its brunt. However, and here the importance of ideology and consent becomes crucial, this mission embodies a *contradictory* function. On the one hand, the relentless pursuit of the mission — the enforcement of 'statutory norms of public order' (*ibid.*: 120) in working-class neighborhoods where strong countervailing norms operated — could not help but overstretch limited resources and feel oppressive to the community on the receiving end. Hence the fierce community resistance. On the other hand, anything less than full enforcement threatened the very idea which gave the new police-force its general legitimacy, namely, impartial law enforcement. The result was to confront "the force...with the impossible choice of enforcing law or order" (*ibid.*: 130).

In terms of 'consent,' the problem was one of competing ideologies: the old ideology of what was acceptable public behavior in working-class neighbourhoods — the *popular* notion of public order espoused by the new urban proletariat; and the new "juridical ideology of crime" (*ibid.*: 128) — the unpopular bourgeois legal order "in which the bourgeoisie has enshrined its version of the rights of capital and the obligations of labour" (*ibid.*). In other words, 'proletarian order' versus 'bourgeois law.' The solution to the "impossible choice" was, eventually, compromise: a change from the "outright physical confrontation" characteristic of policing in Islington before the First World War to "an unwritten system of tacit negotiation" (*ibid.*: 123) in the post-war period. In practice this meant "turning half a blind eye to the rule book" and "turning the other half of the blind eye to a good deal of minor infringement" (*ibid.*: 130).

This change — from confrontation to negotiation — was not just attributable to the new ideological function of the police. A whole host of changes, especially structural changes in the labor market, assisted. Critical to the latter was the growing divide between the declining 'informal' casual labour market and the developing formal economy, with its 'labour aristocracy' at the apex and gradations of other skilled, semi- and unskilled workers beneath. Whilst those in the casual, informal economy — led by the costermongers (barrow traders) — remained committed to the traditional street culture with its associated popular institutions and mores, those in the regular economy, led by the 'labour aristocrats,' like the "skilled print and railway workers" (*ibid.*: 124), were establishing and participating in a whole range of new institutions — political, cultural and social — and developing a new morality to match. This new morality Cohen has termed "public propriety" (*ibid.*). In short, a structurally-based divide was beginning to open up between those workers with a stake in the new urban order (the "respectables") and those without (the "roughs"). This division, and the associated development of the notion of "public propriety," provided the material basis for the change from confrontation to negotiation, namely, "an alliance between the spokesmen of proletarian patriarchy [the "respectables"] and the enforcers of bourgeois law and order [the police]" (*ibid.*: 132).

However the willingness to allow certain notions of community 'order' to prevail over juridical notions of bourgeois 'law' does not eliminate the ideological importance of the latter. In other words, the contradictory choice of law or order remains. The organizational solution has been to institutionalize this contradiction in the form of an internal division of labor. Within this, some officers, like local beat coppers, have the task of "maintaining negotiated order;" others, "like the Special Patrol Group and Regional Crime Squads" are charged with restoring "statutory order without regard for any of the factors constraining the operations of the local force" (*ibid.*: 134). The consequence is the constant undermining of each other's work:

> The more resources allocated to increasing the efficiency of repressive policing, the more manpower has to be poured into 'community relations' to restabilize the public image of the force. The more technologically sophisticated, and hence impersonal, the systems of surveillance, the more home-beat coppers are needed on the ground.
>
> (*ibid.*: 133)

Finally, the fragility of negotiated settlements is emphasized, and the connection between class and race is made. Because of the way in which the labor force under capitalism is constantly being recomposed and relocated, any negotiations made with existing communities will need to be constantly renegotiated with any new group of workers (or 'non-workers') generated by these changes in the division of labor. To illustrate, Cohen particularly mentions changes in the juvenile labor market and the arrival after the Second World War of "immigrant workers." The temptation for the police with such 'new social forces' is to take the easy way by "falling back on the more or less brutal reimposition of statutory public order when policing these groups" (*ibid.*: 132). Thus it is that the idea of 'negotiated' consent is necessarily contingent; new contingencies constantly threaten the unstable equilibria of existing accommodations.

The advantages of this kind of approach over the others are, hopefully, obvious: it requires neither exceptional nor pathological explanations for the re-emergence of hostility and violence, yet it can also explain why much public-order policing is relatively peaceful, and why there is strong support for the police amongst the working class. In short, neither consensus nor coercion are seen as inevitable features of police-public relations; rather each is regarded as contingent. And Cohen offers an account of the relevant contingencies operating at a crucial transitional moment in the "policing of the working class city," and points — with his references to the arrival of "immigrant groups" and the simultaneous developments of community relations and Special Patrol Group type policing — to their contemporary relevance.

Within this approach, then, "immigrant workers" become heirs to the coster tradition — the new "roughs" who understand only the "brutal reimposition of statutory public order" — and the explanation of why race has become such a significant modality of police-public conflict is given a firm, structural basis.

The strengths of such an account lie in the way processes of marginalization and criminalization are connected to broad shifts in the political economy, and in emphasizing the importance of law and the legal mandate (the contradictions between law and order), as well as ideology ("public propriety"), in mediating such shifts. But there are limitations too: an overemphasis on proactive crimes (crimes which come to light through police-initiated activity and which are sometimes regarded as 'victimless,' e.g. offenses related to prostitution, drunkenness, drugs, gambling, etc.) and a comparative lack of attention to reactive ones (crimes to which police react indirectly, upon citizen request, and which collectively constitute the broad range of conventionally perceived 'normal' crimes, e.g. burglary, thefts, frauds, assaults, etc.). This has the effect of playing down intra-group crime. Moreover, lumping different ethnic groups together as "immigrant workers," as Cohen does, obscures the possibility of differences between racial groups.

Crisis, the New Right and Paramilitarism: Race, Riots and Policing in the Present Conjuncture

For our purposes, the inner-city riots of the 1980s offer, in condensed form, the most pertinent comment on police-black relations in the present conjuncture. But to fully understand these, the nature of the conjuncture needs briefly to be established.

In broad terms, the present moment is framed, first, by a general crisis of hegemony and, second, by the particular response of the radical right. Loosely speaking the 1960s witnessed a breakdown in the consensual hegemony that had characterized the 1950s and ushered in the more coercive, less hegemonic 1970s and 1980s. Of course, 1968 was pivotal here, as was Mr. Heath, who made the first attempt in the early 1970s at a radical right solution to Britain's economic ills, only to be brought down by working-class solidarity and union resistance across a broad front. Jim Callaghan's subsequent attempts to revive social democracy's flagging fortunes via a new 'social contract' with the unions proved, in the event, to be both ill-fated and temporary. Consequently Thatcherism, hatching in the opposition wings since the mid-1970s, was able to take up the reins of office and, in the new highly divided climate, complete the attempted Heathian revolution.

This has involved a triple-pronged attack: economic, ideological and political. In the economic field it has entailed putting the fight against inflation and uncompetitiveness above the evils of recession, a strategy which resulted in huge losses to Britain's industrial manufacturing base, a massive rise in unemployment, cuts in the social wage and a growing divide between the 'haves' and the 'have-nots.' In short, the economics of Thatcherism have meant a relative worsening of the position of the most disadvantaged groups in society — amongst which the young, and especially black youth, have been particularly prominent.

Ideologically, it has entailed a combination of transforming diffuse social anxieties into a series of moral panics through the process of scapegoating deviant and dissenting groups, reducing all dissensual voices to manifestations of a single, undifferentiated 'threat' — 'the enemy within' (e.g. striking miners), and then denying dissent any political meaning by labelling it 'criminal,' or, where the label 'violent' could be attached, any meaning whatsoever (e.g. striking miners, inner-city 'rioters,' Irish republicans). The overall achievement of this set of changes has been the installation of an ideological repertoire capable of reading all dissent as part of a violent conspiracy against 'our' way of life requiring legal constraint and firmer control. Once again black youth — first through the early 1970s mugging scare, then through the more general mid-1970s equation of blacks and crime, finally as 1980s 'rioters' — have figured prominently in all this.

If dissent is part of a conspiracy, then 'legal constraint and firmer control' is justified. And there is no doubt that greater coercion has been at the heart of the political attack. This increase in coercion has entailed an extraordinary "mobilisation of legal instruments against labour, political dissent and alternative lifestyles" (Hall *et al.*, 1978: 284), starting in the early 1970s, and the gradual institutionalization of a paramilitarized policing response to strikes, protest and inner-city crime. The sorry history of police-black youth relations through the 1970s and 1980s bears witness to the role black youth have played in this moving up of coercive gear. (For a fuller account of this crisis of hegemony, see Hall, *et al.*, 1978: 218-323).

Casting our minds back to Phil Cohen's historical account of policing in Islington can now assist our understanding of this conjunctural coincidence, namely, a breakdown of hegemony and the simultaneous emergence of a more coercive, paramilitarized policing response. The essential features of the current breakdown of hegemony have been, to simplify, an economic crisis in which the accompanying recomposition and relocation of the labor force has entailed a massive (and, for some, seemingly permanent) shake-out of labor, and the creation of what might crudely be called 'the new lumpen' or, as some see it, a new 'under-class' (cf. Auletta, 1982); a political crisis characterized by a tough 'law and order' response to increasing numbers of belligerent dissidents of all persuasions; and an ideological crisis in which a repertoire of negative evaluations is constantly applied to all forms of dissent, and which in turn is constantly being challenged. The essential feature of the paramilitary response has been a rough and uncompromising 'no nonsense' approach to the swift re-imposition of (an essentially police-defined sense of) 'order.'

Applying Cohen's terminology, the paramilitary response represents the option of last resort — the "falling back on the more or less brutal reimposition of statutory public order" (1979: 132) on those groups (in this case 'the new lumpen,' in which sections of male, especially black, youth figure prominently, and militant dissidents of all kinds — pickets, demonstrators, etc.) with whom the (preferred) negotiated approach — the 'unwritten system of tacit negotiation' (*ibid.*: 123) — has never been properly established or has broken down. This breakdown may be fairly temporary, in the case of say a particular industrial dispute, or, in the case of some highly alienated groups, Afro-Caribbean youth for example, apparently irrevocable.

The irony of this, as Cohen points out, is that the straightforward repressive legal approach constantly threatens to undermine the order it is designed to uphold (witness the way the repressive Swamp'81 contributed to the first Brixton riots), a dilemma Cohen refers to as the police's "impossible choice of enforcing law or order" (*ibid.*: 130). The result is that "the more resources allocated to increasing the efficiency of repressive policing, the more manpower has to be poured into 'community relations' to restabilize the public image of the force" (*ibid.*: 133). And that is precisely what has happened. The growth of paramilitarism has been accompanied by a parallel growth in community-relations policing (i.e. all forms of policing variously concerned with the question of 'negotiated' rather than strictly 'legal' order). Moreover, and in line with this logic, such initiatives are largely aimed at those groups furthest removed from the existing "tacit negotiations," such as youngsters in Northern Ireland (in the form of police-run blue-lamp discos), and the black communities (to whom community-relations departments owe their very existence: cf. Judge, 1974: 201).

If paramilitarism belongs broadly to the moment of hegemonic breakdown, certain features of the Thatcherite years have exacerbated the situation. In the first place, the multiple crises — economic, political and ideological — signalling the breakdown of hegemony have continued to worsen, and hence to stimulate further paramilitary developments. Secondly, these developments are increasingly technologically sophisticated, which not only makes them more dangerous, most obviously in the case of the new weaponry, but which also makes them prey to "technological drift:" the internal technological dynamic whereby the technologically feasible constantly threatens to pre-empt the politically desirable. Thirdly, the present Conservative government is *committed* to the tough political response, unlike say the social democratic government of the Callaghan years which also presided over paramilitary developments, but less willingly. Within this political climate paramilitarism is not only a 'necessary evil,' but is seen as a positive weapon to enforce key changes (witness the absolutely central role of the police in breaking the miners' strike of 1984/5: McCabe and Wallington, 1988: 130). Finally, and most depressingly, there is the crisis of alternatives, evidenced by the surprising degree of support the government managed to maintain even while implementing a highly divisive strategy. Though there is a debate about the relative strength of the New Right's ideological hold which is beyond the scope of this chapter (which from the vantage-point of 1930 is clearly weakening), I subscribe to Hall's idea that, generally speaking, these have been years characterized by 'authoritarian populism' (but see Hall 1988a and 1988b; Jessop *et al.*, 1984). Jointly these features — the intensity of the conflicts to be policed, the technological capacity of police, the willingness of the government to sanction 'tough' methods, the relative support for these and the absence of ideas about alternatives — provide the essential conjunctural backcloth to an adequate understanding of the riots. But, before we turn to consider them briefly, one final point about paramilitary policing (given policing's importance to the 'riots' story) seems worth making, namely, its inherent tendency to amplify the very problems of disorder it is designed to quell. As I have argued at greater length elsewhere (Jefferson, 1987b: 17-53; and 1990), this tendency stems from the very nature of the paramilitary approach: the use of specially trained, usually male, officers in large numbers and their deployment in groups offering each other unconditional support; the anticipation of trouble; the provision of equipment and lethal weaponry to deal with it, violently if necessary; and the employment of pre-emptive and offensive tactics, simply to exert control or as a means of dispersal.

Benyon's review of "interpretations of civil disorder" (Benyon, 1987: 23-41) makes it evident that understanding this backcloth — the downside of Thatcherism — is a prerequisite for understanding the riots. Having looked at the range of interpretations, he lists five "characteristics...common to the areas where rioting...occurred in the 1980s" (*ibid.*: 33), namely:

> (1) *Racial disadvantage and discrimination are major afflictions.* A significant proportion of the population in each area in which rioting occurred is Afro-Caribbean or Asian...
> (2) *Unemployment is high,* and particularly affects youth, and especially young black (i.e. Afro-Caribbean people)...
> (3) *Deprivation is widespread:* environmental decay, poor educational and social service provision, inadequate recreational facilities and crime are problems...
> (4) *Political exclusion and powerlessness are evident,* in that there are few institutions, opportunities and resources for articulating grievances and bringing pressure to bear on those with political power...
> (5) *Mistrust of, and hostility to, the police is widespread* among certain sections, particularly the young. There is disquiet about police tactics, such as stop-and-search, and allegations are frequently made about harassment, abuse and assault...
>
> (*ibid.*: 33-5; emphases in original)

Though "opinions varied as to which of the...five factors were the most significant" (*ibid.*: 35), "the immediate precipitants or trigger events in each case involved police officers and black people" (*ibid.*: 33).

This brief conjunctural analysis confirms, then, the historical evidence of the previous section, namely, that the basic problem stems from the 'ongoing' police mission of policing the poor and powerless — a process which affects blacks particularly adversely, not only because of their concentration amongst the disadvantaged and unemployed, but also because of the evils of racial disadvantage and discrimination. Its strengths lie in pointing towards the relationship between economic crisis and ideological signification in the criminalization process (the scapegoating of black youths), and in showing how a repressive response (legal coercion and paramilitary policing) can itself become part of the problem (i.e., result in outbreaks of disorder). However, once again the approach tends to downplay the relationship between disadvantage and 'normal' crime and, perhaps in consequence, the relationship between policing developments and normal crime. Possible differences *between* races, for example, Asians and Afro-Caribbeans, also tend to be obscured.

Race and Crime Statistics

If, so far, the question of 'ordinary crime' has been relatively sidelined in considering the relation between police and ethnic minorities, it seems fairly obvious that any consideration of police-work that neglects their 'bread and butter' work is insufficient. And ordinary crime is, of course, a genuine concern of victims, as the recent upsurge of victimization studies has revealed — though whether 'fear of crime' outstrips the level of crime remains contentious (cf. Walklate, 1989: 25-51). However, the difficulties of drawing conclusions from any published criminal statistics, because of the series of decisions about whether to report and to record that lie behind their construction, are now well documented. So caution is necessary. Where race is also an issue, this is even more the case —as the fairly contentious debate about race and crime statistics has shown (cf. Bridges, 1983a, 1983b; Gilroy, 1982, 1983; Gutazmore, 1983; Lea and Young, 1984). With these strictures in mind, let us briefly review what is presently known.

The broad picture looks something like this. So far as stops are concerned, the evidence we have — gleaned either from police records or from surveys of the general public and mostly relating to London — suggest that black males, particularly young black males, have a higher chance of being stopped by the police than white males (cf. Willis 1983: 14). However, a survey in Manchester conducted by Tuck and Southgate (1981), the one study that compared "black and white groups *living in the same areas*, found no difference between the rates at which they were stopped by the police" (Walker, 1987: 49; my emphasis). What this suggests, as Walker points out, is that the decisive factor in determining who gets stopped may be less race than (broadly speaking) 'class' — a possibility supported by the Policy Studies Institute (PSI) findings that the stop rate was higher for the unemployed than those in work, and, for vehicle stops, for unskilled manual workers than professional and managerial workers (Smith, 1983).

This interpretation finds further support in our own recent Leeds-based study (Walker *et al.*, 1989). Our findings based on police records which were *not* 'within area' comparisons support the general conclusion mentioned above of disproportionate stopping of black males. However, when we made 'within area' comparisons (our attempt to hold social class constant) a more complex picture emerged, for disproportionate stopping of black males was confirmed to areas with less than ten percent non-whites. In the areas with more than ten percent non-whites — the relatively disadvantaged areas — it was only the *white* arrests rate which was disproportionate (*ibid.*, 1989: 7). Asians, by contrast, both in London and Leeds, had a comparatively low stoprate, regardless of area (Smith, 1983: 96, 98; Walker *et al.*, 1989: 9).

When it comes to arrests, similar points can be made, though it should be noted that we have data only for London and Leeds. The London data (see, for example, Home Office, 1989) revealed black over-representation in all offence groups, though when age was controlled for in the earlier analysis (Stevens and Willis, 1979) — necessary because "known offenders tend to be young, and...the black population tends to be younger than the white" (Walker, 1987: 40) — this was particularly accounted for by four offence categories, namely, assault, robbery, "other violent theft" and "other indictable offenses." However, social class, also critical to arrest rates, given the established relationship between low social class and known offenders, was not controlled for.

In Leeds we also found that black males — in two age-groups (11-21) and (22-35) — were disproportionately arrested, when arrest rates were considered simply in relation to the city of Leeds as a whole (Walker *et al.*, 1989: 7). But, once again, when 'within area' comparisons were made, a pattern identical to the one we found for stops emerged. So the 'area effect' — area being some sort of rough control for class —seemed to be consistent. Whilst we would need to know more about any differences in policing between these areas, as well as whether race affected public reporting and police recording practices (something our study was not designed to uncover), before we are in a position to explain this pattern, it does at least suggest that area of residence/social class is an influential factor that should not be ignored in analyzing race and crime statistics. (For a fuller discussion, see Jefferson *et al.*, 1990.)

Asians, underrepresented in the overall arrest rate in London and Leeds (Stevens and Willis 1979; Walker *et al.*, 1989), present, once again, a markedly different picture.

Though there have been some studies of police cautioning of juveniles (e.g. Batta *et al.*, 1978; Landau, 1981; Farrington and Bennett, 1981; Landau and Nathan, 1983), and one looking at police decisions to prosecute (Cain and Sadigh, 1982), these have proved difficult to interpret for various reasons and hence, for brevity's sake, will not be dealt with here.

Given the above findings, the question of interpretation remains. Is the black over-representation in the police statistics a consequence of their involvement rate in crime, or has it more to do with police discrimination? It may be worth reminding ourselves, first, of the proactive/reactive distinction — the former referring to police-initiated, the latter to citizen-initiated, acts. Stops clearly come under the heading proactive — as do certain offenses, most notoriously the now abolished "sus" offenses (for which the black arrest rate in London far exceeded the white rate in its 1970s heyday (Demuth, 1978: 40-1), a factor which was certainly influential in its eventual abolition). Moreover, certain offenses — such as "robbery" and "other violent theft" (two of the four categories, it should be remembered, for which Stevens and Willis (1979) found a disproportionate black arrest rate in London once age was controlled for) — are highly subjective categories for recording purposes (cf. Stevens and Willis, 1979: 41; Blom-Cooper and Drabble, 1982). And then there is the question of the importance of 'demeanor' in determining who gets stopped and arrested, with 'disrespect' more often being rewarded with arrest for 'contempt of cop' (cf. Piliavin and Briar, 1964) — a fate to which the more hostile black youths are perhaps particularly prone (cf. Jefferson, 1988: 528).

But, when all is said and done, most commentators conclude that at least part of the explanation for higher black arrests has to be the result of higher offending behavior (cf. Stevens and Willis, 1979; Smith, 1983; Reiner, 1985b; Benyon, 1986; Lea and Young, 1984). Monica Walker's graphic calculations that "black people must have four and a half times the chance of being arrested for burglary (compared to white people)...[and] 14 times...more often...for a robbery if the offender rates were the same" (1987: 40) would seem to make 'implausible' the idea that all of the black over-representation can be accounted for simply by discrimination — though Walker does point out that her calculations are based on "arrests and not convictions" (*ibid.*).

If black over-offending constitutes at least part of the explanation for their high arrest rates, then it puts back squarely on the agenda the question of disadvantage and crime. For, if blacks are disproportionately involved in known offending behavior, they also have much higher rates of social disadvantage, being more likely to live in poorer housing in deprived areas, attend worse-off schools and, in the job market, to find manual (rather than non-manual) jobs or be unemployed (cf. Brown, 1984). Since known offenders are disproportionately drawn from the ranks of manual workers, the unemployed and the socially deprived, the higher black arrest and offender rates should not particularly surprise.

But, finally, we must confront the question of Asians, who are also subject to disproportionate levels of disadvantage (cf. Brown, 1984: 315-18), including, we might add, an even greater likelihood (than blacks) of being victims of racist attacks (Home Office, 1981). However, their arrest rates, as we have seen, do not match their levels of disadvantage. Though I have no space to explore this properly — and, in truth, little research exists to help here — it seems clear that we will need to look towards certain cultural factors (probably those to do with family and community structure and religion) for an explanation (cf. Bains, 1988). Whatever the answer, it certainly suggests that the link between deprivation and offending is not unmediated — a point I shall return to briefly in the following section.

What the race and crime debate has done — its strength — has been to put the issue of ordinary (i.e., largely 'reactive') crime back on the agenda and, in so doing, to have refocused on the offender. It has, at least indirectly, reaffirmed the traditional link between disadvantage and crime (to complement that between disadvantage and crime control which we saw in the first section above). But it has also revealed that race needs to be conceptualized in the plural, given the differences in stop and arrest rates found between blacks and Asians.

The limitations of the approach, if taken on its own, are that the comparative statistical approach — the typical methodological tool — serves to obscure the more general point about the police focus on deprived areas. This, in turn, effectively severs any link with political economy and effectively removes from the agenda any sense of the broader ideological role of discussions about crime.

Attitudes, Perceptions and Experiences: Ethnic Views 'From Below'

> At the end of the summer term, 1984, a crowd of between 30 and 40 schoolchildren aged 14 to 16 from Stockwell Park School, South London, were celebrating the end of term, shouting and throwing bags of flour at each other (an end-of-term tradition) outside the school gate. Three police transit vans pulled up and the children were confronted by 15 police officers who, the children say, bashed their heads against the pavement and the side of the van. Five children were arrested and charged with assaulting the police. The charges against them were later dropped.
>
> (Institute of Race Relations, 1987: 34)

Whatever comparative statistical reality and its meaning, there is no doubt that the experiential meaning of policing for black people, especially for black youth, over the past 20 years or so, has been one of a hostile and alien force — one which has subjected their communities to aggressive, harassing and intimidatory 'overpolicing,' yet has been only indifferent or halfhearted in the face of black and Asian victims of racist attacks. The evidence for this conclusion comes from the many deplorable case-studies assiduously collected in many forms by the communities themselves, and the various surveys of attitudes, perceptions and experiences.

One of the most persistent collators of cases has been the Institute of Race Relations. Its evidence submitted to the Royal Commission on Criminal Procedure and published in 1979 under the title *Police Against Black People* is a horrifying catalog of general harassment, neglect and misconduct — none of which is regarded as exceptional.

In 1987 this 68-page pamphlet was reprinted as an Appendix to a new Institute publication, *Policing Against Black People*. The only changes between the two publication dates have been for the worse: hence the catalogue of abuses, at 93 pages, was longer, and the title had been changed — to signify, in Sivanandan's introductory words, the 'more systematic police surveillance and special policing of whole communities' now 'required' by the growth of unemployment, social deprivation and racism (Institute of Race Relations, 1987: viii). If all this is unfamiliar, *Policing Against Black People* should be compulsory reading; or you could try the recent Independent Committee of Inquiry Report (1989) into the death of Colin Roach published as *Policing in Hackney 1945-1984*; or the recent report of racism in Liverpool, *Loosen the Shackles*, by Tony Gifford and colleagues (1989). It does not matter where you turn, the experiences are depressingly similar.

The survey evidence broadly mirrors this black antipathy to police, though the Policy Studies Institute (PSI) survey of Londoners reminds us that the hostile views of West Indians in London "by no means amount to a complete rejection of the present policing system" (Smith and Gray, 1983: 332). Age is especially critical: "there is a dangerous lack of confidence in the police among substantial numbers of young white people and a disastrous lack of confidence among young people of West Indian Origin" (*ibid.*). In conformity with the cases cited by the Institute of Race Relations, black youth were much more likely to believe that the police abuse their power, use excessive force and fabricate evidence.

Our own survey in Leeds supports such findings. When it came to attitudes to the police, blacks had the highest (of all racial groups) overall 'disapproval' score, and they were less likely (when asked what they would do on witnessing various crimes) to co-operate with the police. About one half of blacks thought that the police were guilty of various malpractices — that they used threats, employed unnecessary violence, took inaccurate records and fabricated evidence — and thought police discriminated against non-whites. The figures for whites (who lived in the same areas, it should be added) were similar, unlike in London, where all areas were included (Walker *et al.*, 1989: 96-8).

Asian attitudes and perceptions, echoing the situation we found with stops and arrests, were different. In London the PSI found Asians to be less critical than West Indians (except with regard to racial attacks), though more so than whites (Reiner, 1985b: 173). In Leeds we found that Asians held significantly less critical attitudes than both blacks and whites (Walker *et al.*, 1989: 16).

One obvious way of explaining any differences between blacks, whites and Asians would be in terms of differences in experiences. Does the fact that Asians have fewer arrests and stops account for their more positive attitudes? The short answer is 'no.' What Smith found from his PSI data was that although there was "a strong relationship between people's hostility towards the police and their perceptions of their personal experience of contact with police officers" (1987: 70), this was not a total explanation because he also found that "people of West Indian origin who report *no* personal adversarial contact with the police are still more hostile to the police than white people, who have not had contact with the police of this kind" (*ibid.*: 71; emphasis in original).

Our own Leeds study endorses this: "Although all the measures of attitude to the police were related to stops etc, and Asians were slopped less and whites more than blacks, differences between races on attitude were consistent regardless of the number of stops" (Walker *et al.*, 1989: 18).

Smith's explanation of this — what he calls "the extra element in the formation of the views of West Indian people" (1978: 72) which accounts for this greater hostility — is in terms of "a sense of solidarity with all other people belonging to the same ethnic group," a "collective consciousness" which in its developed form becomes "some kind of political ideology" (*ibid.*). By this Smith means "a coherent view within the collective consciousness about what is to be done in response to what is perceived as being police oppression and also oppression by wider forces in society" (*ibid.*). In other words, the *collective* experience of racial discrimination appears to have produced both a collective consciousness and a political ideology to match which is over and above the particular experiences of prejudice and discrimination suffered by *individuals* within the group. The political implications of this distinction are important and I shall return to them in the conclusion.

If a "collective consciousness" beyond that of the experiences of individuals explains some of the black hostility to police, it may be that a different "collective consciousness" is informing the markedly more conforming behavior and attitudes of Asians. It can only be speculative to proceed further at this stage, but one point seems worth making. If, as I have argued elsewhere, the consequence of the mutual hostility between blacks and police is a "self-fulfilling prophecy" which can produce a "deadly dynamic of mutual distrust, tension, hostility, and, eventually, hatred" (Jefferson, 1988: 537), it may well be that more positive and conforming Asian attitudes are 'rewarded' with more positive police attitudes, one consequence of which is the more favorable Asian stop and arrest figures that we have seen. In other words, what we are witnessing in police-Asian relations is a self-fulfilling prophecy of a more positive kind. One small piece of evidence from our Leeds study lends this notion some support; we found Asian juveniles significantly more likely to be cautioned and adults to have "no further action" taken after arrest. On the other hand, there is also evidence of conflictual relations between police and some sections of Asian youth in places like Southall (e.g. April 1979 — see NCCL, 1980) and Bradford (most recently in connection with Salman Rushdie). But, as Bains' (1988) thoughtful insider view of youth politics in Southall reveals, the picture is fraught with complications such that generalizations in this area are very hazardous.

The strengths of these accounts of experiences and attitudes are that they act as a reminder of what policing feels like for those groups routinely on the receiving end, i.e., from below. In that sense it provided the human stories to complement Cohen's political economy of police-work outlined in our first section above. It also reminds us of the limits of the quantitative approach: comparative statistics deal in outcomes, not the quality of interactions preceding these. So far as black people are concerned, these interactions have clearly been found wanting. The surveys also show that the relationship between attitudes and experiences is complex, not simple. Though black and Asian experiences of discrimination and disadvantage — when measured by certain objective indices (such as earnings or level of unemployment) — are similar, their subjective perceptions and attitudes are not identical.

What is missing most from these accounts is any strong sense of ordinary crime and of justified policing of it. Moreover, though these accounts are compatible with the political economy outlined in our first section above, they do not themselves deliver one.

Summary and Conclusions

What our broad historical overview established is the importance of situating crime and its control within a broad structural framework constituted by the economic, political and ideological changes to which societies are constantly subject. From this perspective, law, ideology and the process of criminalization are as problematic as the 'crime' they seek to control. Proceeding from this starting-point, we found that 'policing race' is but a contemporary manifestation of the traditional police role of 'policing the powerless.'

One conclusion from this establishment of a historical link between policing and social disadvantage is that of the need to address questions of social disadvantage as well as of policing. Lord Scarman made the point after the 1981 Brixton riots: "urgent action is required if the social conditions which underlay the disorders in Brixton and elsewhere are to be corrected" (Scarman, 1981: 6.42).

But, if anything, the situation is getting worse, as Benyon and Solomos (1987: 192) gloomily conclude in their review of "the roots of urban unrest:" "Unemployment is higher, housing is worse, incomes have fallen, crime is higher, and black people continue to suffer from racism and exclusion." Downes and Ward (1986: 61) make a similar point in the conclusion to their review of the debate about police accountability: social justice, not policing, is the key to social order.

> Rather than place policing at the centre of a socialist response to crime, we would emphasise
> the cardinal importance of social Justice as the only legitimate basis of order, and the need for a range of social and environmental measures to improve the quality of life, as well as preventing some kinds of crime, in those neighbourhoods most afflicted by crime and insecurity.

Questions of police accountability bring us to our conjunctural analysis. Here a closer look at these same structural processes in operation currently showed how a worsening (for the already disadvantaged) economic situation coupled with a tougher political response and ideological attacks on all forms of dissent has made a repressive, paramilitary policing response a central feature — and how the 'riots' are symptomatic of the resulting complete breakdown of relations between police and sections of the powerless.

One conclusion from this is that so long as paramilitarism is seen as part of the solution and not part of the problem (cf. Waddington, 1987; Jefferson, 1990), and as long as questions of police discretion and accountability are not tackled (cf. Jefferson and Grimshaw, 1984), policing has itself now become part of the social disadvantage experienced by the powerless, perhaps even its cutting edge.

The debate about race and crime statistics also reminded us of the importance of 'social disadvantage,' but from the 'other' side. Here, the narrow focus on ordinary crime (not the processes of criminalization) and (primarily) the offender re-emphasized the link between disadvantage and crime — even if the issue of disadvantage (ironically) has been obscured by the focus on the race of offenders. At the same time, in identifying the differences between blacks and Asians it *also* rendered the link between crime and disadvantage problematic.

Three conclusions follow from this. First, failing to take crime seriously in its own terms means not seeing that a common response to disadvantage is a diffuse, apolitical and sometimes amoral frustration that is highly negative in its consequences (cf. Rook, 1979). Second, such failure also entails ignoring the fact that victims of crime are invariably similarly disadvantaged. Thirdly, the apparently different response of Asians to similar levels of disadvantage places the need to take cultural as well as structural factors seriously firmly on the agenda.

When we turn, finally, to what all this feels like 'from below,' we find that those having most negative contacts with police — young blacks —have the most hostile attitudes, and that these are often very critical indeed. But we also saw that there is no simple one-to-one equation between experiences and attitudes; and that, in the case of Asians, high levels of disadvantage and discrimination can be associated with positive attitudes to the police.

Two general conclusions flow from this, if we intend to 'take racism seriously.' The first is the need to see racism in the plural; the second is that 'success' in this area, ultimately, is a subjective category. The perceptions and attitudes of the system's most disadvantaged groups, not so-called objective dimensions of discrimination and disadvantage, will, and do, determine the level of social tranquillity (though, of course, the former are profoundly influenced by the latter). What all this points towards, generally, is the deep-rooted complexity of the issues involved — a point only underlined by the ethnic conflicts that accompanied the democratic explosions of 1989 around Eastern Europe. For better or for worse we had better get used to that fact, and attempt to respond — both intellectually and politically — in ways which do it justice.

CHAPTER 15

POLICE ACCOUNTABILITY AND BLACK PEOPLE: INTO THE 1990S

EUGENE McLAUGHLIN

> The idea of the democratic control of the police has rarely excited interest in Britain.
>
> (B. Cox, 1975)

> We hear a lot nowadays about the much heralded concept of 'democratic community policing' and the need for more involvement by local representatives in the management of police officers.
>
> (J Anderton, 1981)

> Whatever happened to police accountability?
>
> (R. Reiner, 1989b)

Political theorists are agreed that in liberal democracies officials and institutions of governance should be accountable, having a 'continuing obligation to explain and justify their conduct in public' (Day and Klein, 1989: 7). Upon such accountability, it is argued, rests the unique legitimacy of the liberal democratic state. However, the institution of the police rests uncomfortably within this particular state form: "The police more than any institution exhibit an antagonism, both in concept and practice, to some of the basic precepts of a democratic society. In many respects, the phrase 'democratic police force' is a contradiction in terms" (Berkeley, 1969: 1-2).

The police are empowered to infringe upon the liberties of citizens and are legally entitled to use force and violence to uphold law and order. The police deal in and with conllict and are empowered by the state to do so. In a democracy the key problem is to

* Originally published in *Out of Order: Policing Black People*, edited by Ellis Cashmore and Eugene McLaughlin: 109-133 (1991). Reprinted by permission of Routledge, Inc.

make sure that there are structures of accountability to ensure that citizens' liberties are not infringed upon in an unjust manner or unnecessarily by the police and that the police do not use force and violence in the carrying out of their duties (for a full discussion of definitional issues of policing see Reiner, 1989a: 3-4).

During the 1970s and 1980s the issue of whether the police were accountable became an important political issue in Britain. Although the traditional structures of legal, organizational and political accountability looked formally extensive, the substantive reality was very different. The post-war period saw the decline of the political dimension of accountability with the rise to prominence of legal accountability:

> Unlike other institutions, the police apparatus can legitimately justify the absence of a formal political relation — portrayed as partisan — by reference to the legal relation. Within policing ideology the gradual disappearance of the practice of political control is viewed as a progressive reform in the direction of the political dimension — the obligation to act according to legal not political direction (Brogden 1982: 122).

Such a development would not necessarily have been problematic if the mechanism of legal accountability had proved to be effective. However, concern began to be expressed that the judiciary was not only unwilling and incapable of calling the police to account but in fact *was* uncritically sanctioning the constant attempts by the police to extend their powers. In addition it was becoming apparent that the mechanism for pursuing complaints against the police was fundamentally flawed because it was the police who were in charge of investigating themselves.

For civil libertarians the worrying conclusion was reached that the structures of democratic accountability supposedly governing the police had atrophied. The consequences of this breakdown of accountability were most acute in Britain's inner cities, where the phrases "out of control" and "out of order" became commonplace to describe the type of policing that black people were being subjected to. This led to renewed demands and policies being formulated which were geared towards strengthening the democratic accountability of the police. Central to those demands and policies was the belief that the political dimension of accountability had to be re-prioritized to bring policing of black people under control. This chapter documents how such demands and policies were neutralized in the course of the 1980s and the implications for policing in the 1990s.

Renewed Concerns About Policing

As the 1960s and 1970s progressed, policing in Britain was placed back on the political agenda as it became more and more controversial. This was virtually inevitable given the changes that had been effected by the 1964 *Police Act*, the 1972 *Local Government Act* and the internal organizational changes that took place in the post-war period. It was specifically because the 1964 Act failed to resolve the problems arising from the lack of police accountability that the issue was destined to resurface. In fact this was virtually inevitable because first, the powers of the police had been expanded, second, the structures of democratic accountability had been legislatively weakened as a consequence of the *Police Act* and finally the political and economic climate had changed and the public-order role of the police was once more prioritized. Certain sections of the community, most notably black people, were particularly vulnerable to such developments. The empowerment of the police always has drastic implications for the powerless.

The growing concern about the nature of policing in this period covered a diversity of matters (Jefferson and Grimshaw, 1984: 1-8; Reiner, 1985a: 61-80; Morris, 1989: 144-51). First, apprehension was voiced about the increasing gap between the police and the community. Larger impersonal and professionalized forces and changes in operational philosophy were the corollary of the structural changes that had taken place in the postwar period. These technocratic forces did not feel the need to negotiate their presence in neighbourhoods, to cultivate the consent of the community or to take into account the needs of the community. Policing strategies were decided upon, implemented and changed without consultation. Thus, a "unit beat" (with panda cars and two-way radios) system was introduced and then replaced by "fire-brigade" (aggressive response) policing at the professional discretion of the chief constables and under the sponsorship of the Home Office. Such changes had a considerable impact upon the subculture of the lower ranks and the abrasive manner in which they dealt with the public, particularly in the inner cities (Stephens, 1988: 9).

Second, there was concern about the growing catalogue of police malpractice in relation to the planting of evidence, instances of extensive police corruption, the policing of public order, the use of specialist troubleshooting units such as the Special Patrol Groups, saturation policing methods, fire-brigade policing methods, anti-subversion and intelligence gathering activities and the application of new control technologies such as computers and surveillance equipment (Jefferson and Grimshaw, 1984: 4-8). Allied to this was the seeming incapability of the complaints system to provide an effective means of redress for those on the receiving end of police deviance and malpractice. Third, the words and actions of senior police officers in the 1970s became more pronounced and controversial (Reiner, 1980; 1983). The professional corporate managers of the police-service, both as individuals and through the Association of Chief Police Officers (ACPO), began to assert their professional autonomy. This expressed itself in two key ways. First, they vociferously challenged any possible encroachment upon their powers. And second, through their perfection of the art of political lobbying and utilization of moral panics about rising crime rates and social deviance, they exacted more powers and resources (Hall *et al.*, 1978; Hough and Heal, 1979; Campbell, 1987). When challenged to account for the behavior of the forces under their command, chief police officers responded in a manner which attempted to define any questioning of the police as an attempt to subvert the democratic process (Levenson, 1981: 43).

However, it was not only chief officers who were intervening in the political process. The Police Federation, as the powerful representative of the junior ranks, became more and more strident in interventions. In 1975, supported by the Superintendents' Association, the Federation launched a law and order campaign. Between 1977 and 1978 it engaged in a wage dispute with the Labour government which resulted in the recommendation of a 40 percent pay rise. In 1979 the Federation attempted to intervene in the national electoral process through a national press campaign by asking voters to consider where the candidates stood on law and order. It was in this year also that the Police Federation broke with tradition and appointed as its Parliamentary adviser a government rather than an opposition MP (Reiner, 1980; 1983).

The fourth level of concern centered upon the manner in which the main political parties began to focus upon the issue of law and order as a basis upon which to mobilize electoral support. When in opposition in 1977 the Conservatives made an unprecedented intervention by giving full support to the pay claims of the Police Federation. In 1978 the Labour conference saw the party try to wrest the issue of law and order from the Conservatives. As a consequence, in the run-up to the 1979 election both parties tried to outdo each other in their commitment to law and order expenditure and the fight against crime.

As Jefferson and Grimshaw have made clear: "Crystallizing practically all these controversial causes for concern and providing throughout the most acute and persisting examples for campaigners, has been the issue of police-black relations" (1984: 7). The evidence submitted by the Institute of Race Relations (IRR) to the Royal Commission on Criminal Procedure in 1979 documented two decades of black people's experience of unaccountable racist policing. There were two main groupings of complaint emanating from such policing practices. The first group of complaints related to the overpolicing of black political, social and cultural events. This involved raids on black meeting places and the deployment of specialist troubleshooting police units in black neighbourhoods. The second group related to the failure of the police to protect black neighbourhoods from acts of racial terrorism. In addition to complaining about over- and underpolicing, the IRR also provided evidence concerning the use of police powers on the streets and in the police stations to harass and unjustly prosecute black people. Such allegations were confirmed by other research carried out into the state of police-black relations on the 'front lines' of Britain's inner cities (Hunte, 1966; Humphry, 1972; Humphry and John, 1972; Pulle, 1973; Bethnal Green and Stepney Trades Council, 1978; AFFOR, 1978; NCCL, 1980). It is worth remembering that in the early 1970s Derek Humphry and Gus John argued that the relationship between the police and black men in Handsworth was "one of war," whilst Margaret Simey was warning that the policing black people were subject to in Liverpool "could lead to civil war in the city" (Humphry and John, 1972: 13-17).

However, when those concerned about the practices and policies of the police demanded accountability from that institution they were faced with chief officers who had been legally, organizationally and politically empowered during the previous 20 years. They also had to face the consequences of the constant redefining of the role and the position of the police authorities in that period, formally, substantively and ideologically. The 1964 *Police Act* and 1972 *Local Government Act* reshaped them in terms of their composition, powers and the size of the forces for which they were supposed to be responsible. As a consequence they had "passive and quiescent" committees who were both unwilling to call and incapable of calling the chief constables to account (McCabe and Wallington, 1988: 135).

Renewed Demands for Democratic Accountability

In the late 1970s the party consensus was broken when the Conservative Party made both law and order and the Labour Party's stance on the matter key electoral issues. Both the Conservatives and the right-wing media, in the run-up to the 1979 election, sought to establish in the eyes of the electorate that the Labour Party was weak on law and order (Phipps, 1988). One of the traditional weaknesses of the Labour Party was exaggerated by the support the Conservative Party gave to strong law and order measures during this campaign. The response of the Labour Party was essentially contradictory. As indicated above, in the run-up to the election the party tried to compete with the Conservative Party on the issue of law and order. However, the Left of the Labour Party also attempted to place the interests of those subject to discriminatory policing practices on the political agenda. The resultant campaign for democratic accountability of the police was most intense in London since there was no semblance of substantive accountability.

In November 1979 and March 1980 Labour MP Jack Straw introduced (unsuccessfully) Bills into Parliament proposing amendments to the 1964 *Police Act* to strengthen the powers of police authorities and to set up a police authority for London (Jefferson and Grimshaw, 1984: 150-6; Oliver, 1987: 68-70). Between March 1980 and the local government elections of 1981 the issue of police accountability and demands for a police authority for London achieved recognition within the electoral manifesto of the London Labour Party (Bundred, 1982). After Labour's victory the Greater London Council set up a non-statutory police committee and support unit as part of its election manifesto promise to campaign for a democratically accountable police force. Within this initiative administrative and financial support was made available to police monitoring groups to enable them first, to act as the 'eyes and ears' of the police committee, second, to articulate the concerns of the community and third, to link the committee to the community (Walker, 1986). Such monitoring groups had their origins in the campaigns around policing issues that had been waged by black communities since the 1960s. These campaigns concerned racist practices, corruption, deaths in police custody and general policing strategies on the streets. The outcome of some of the campaigns was the development of community-based police monitoring groups. Such groups involved themselves in what Walker (1986: 45) has defined as "community defense" and "para-legal defense," i.e., the monitoring of policing practices, providing support and advice for those in difficulties with the police, campaigning for changes in the structure of police accountability and disseminating counter information. Elsewhere in England, after the county council elections of 1981, radicalized Labour administrations were returned to power who were determined, like the Labour Party in London, to have an input into the manner in which policing was carried out in their areas. Most of the Labour parties in the metropolitan areas had manifestos which called for changes in the 1964 *Police Act* to give police authorities the right to take decisions on matters of policy and in relation to the deployment of police officers and senior promotions.

The civil disturbances of 1981 added impetus to the demands that the police should be accountable to the elected representatives of local communities. All the simmering issues and concerns of the 1970s took on a new urgency as the inner cities burned:

> The riots of the spring and summer of that year, and the Scarman Report on the Brixton disorders, were a turning point in the increasingly politicized debate about police organization and strategy, and the accountability and constitutional position of the police (Reiner, 1985a: 170).

The response of the British state to the disturbance of 1981 and the intense debate about police accountability was formally extensive but geared towards a substantive defense of the *status quo*. Support was given to the enhancement of the paramilitary response capabilities of the police whilst the 1984 *Police and Criminal Evidence Act* and 1986 *Public Order Act* were eventually passed, legislatively empowering the police (Zander, 1985; Hillyard and Percy-Smith, 1988; Douzinas *et al.*, 1988). In addition, the Scarman inquiry addressed the issue of the democratic accountability of the police, particularly the constitutional position of the Metropolitan Police. Although Lord Scarman saw accountability as being important, he rejected demands for a police authority for London and more powers for the existing authorities. Instead he recommended statutory community consultation with the police which did not address the interests, needs and the demands of those sections of the community who had suffered from racist policing practices. The consultation structures were given a specific remit in relation to facilitating community involvement in crime control and prevention. Thus, the interests of those for whom *the police were the problem* were once more defined out by Scarman's recommendations. As Darcus How commented, Scarman had failed to "grasp the nettle" (1988: 57-70).

The Mid-1980s: The Resolution of the Struggles for Democratic Accountability

In the bitter struggles for democratic accountability that took place during the first half of the 1980s, chief police officers, most notably in Greater Manchester and Merseyside, asserted their autonomy from the radicalized police authorities. Chief constables refused to account for the manner in which the 1981 civil disturbances were policed. They also refused to allow any discussion of what they defined as operational matters, e.g. the manner in which black communities were policed. In addition, national developments in policy matters were decided upon by the Home Office and senior officers without reference to the police authorities, most notably on issues such as the National Reporting Centre, mutual aid arrangements and the acquisition of riot equipment, including plastic bullets (McCabe and Wallington, 1988). Such was the determination of chief police officers to make sure that they retained their autonomy from political accountability that James Anderton, the Chief Constable of Greater Manchester, demanded the abolition of the police authorities: "You cannot police a community by Police Authorities. Unless I am very much mistaken the majority of the public would prefer policing at the discretion of their Chief Constable rather than policing with the consent of the Police Authorities" (Anderton, 1985).

In July 1985 the local government bill became law, abolishing the Labour-controlled metropolitan county councils and the Greater London Council as from 1 April 1986. As a result joint boards were established to discharge the duties of the troublesome police authorities. Strict central government guidelines were laid down concerning the composition and powers of the new boards. The act changed the form of political representation that had previously existed on the police authorities. The joint boards were to consist of councilors nominated directly by the constituent councils reflecting, as far as possible, the party balance of power on the respective councils. The boards were subject to the financial control laid down in the 1984 *Rates Act* for three years. The Home Secretary was given potential control over the day-to-day running of the Joint Boards through being given a say in decisions concerning staffing and the allocation of resources. In addition, the Home Secretary was allotted the power to restructure Joint Boards through first allowing district councils to become separate police authorities and second, amalgamating different police areas. Thus, this act gave central government unprecedented formal control over the previously troublesome police authorities. There can be little doubt that the Conservative government, through the passing of the *Local Government Act*, found a convenient means of putting to an end the unceasing demands for democratic accountability of the police. As Loveday has noted:

> The view of the Home Office is that members and Chief Constables are now working together satisfactorily and that this positive relationship presents a strong contrast with the conflict which characterized the operation of the earlier Metropolitan County Police Committees. It is quite clear that this perception is one that is shared by both Chief Constables and most members serving the Joint Boards for police in the Metropolitan areas (Loveday, 1988: 25).

In addition to the neutralization of the police authorities, there were a series of other developments, in relation to the politics of crime and policing, that were to have a significant impact upon the campaign for strengthening the democratic accountability of the police. First, there was the emergence within the Conservative government's law and order project of a concern with crime prevention. Second, there were organizational and policy changes that took place within the police. Finally, there was the impact of left new realist criminology within the overall campaign by the Labour Party to prove itself acceptable to the British electorate. The overall consequence of such developments was the reemergence of a bipartisan discourse on crime and the community which covered crime prevention, fear of crime and victims of crime (Reiner, 1989b).

The Government, Crime Prevention and Active Citizenship

As in the first years of the 1980s, the government continued to prioritize law and order. There was the substantial allocation of resources to the police, the augmentation of the court system, a substantial prison building program, and legislation covering all aspects of the criminal justice system (Savage, 1989; Pilger, 1990). This continuing emphasis on law and order meant that there was no public inquiry into the controversial policing of the 1984-5 coal dispute. In addition, when Handsworth and Broadwater Farm erupted there was no repeat of the Scarman inquiry. Instead, at the Conservative

Party conference the Home Secretary announced the strengthening of public-order legislation and the upgrading of the riot capabilities of the police.

However, the government did have to face the consequences of its political utilization of the issue of crime. Although spending on law and order had increased in real terms by 31 percent, it had little effect on the increasing crime rate. As Savage (1989) has noted, the spending had neither prevented crime, deterred criminals, protected people, eradicated fears, helped victims nor reformed offenders. In this context the limitations of the role of the police in fighting crime were becoming apparent. Criticisms of the government's law and order policies were fueled by the publication of the first national crime survey, which, for the first time, attempted to provide an accurate picture of the extent and the nature of crime in Britain. This survey demonstrated that although crime was much more prevalent than indicated by official statistics, it was of a petty nature. The survey also emphasized that the fear of crime was out of proportion to the risk of being a victim of crime. The survey concluded that more police officers was not the answer to such fears (Hough and Mayhew, 1983: 34). Such conclusions stimulated further debate and studies about the extent, nature and fear of crime, the victims of crime and the effectiveness of the police in controlling crime.

The response of the government was two-fold. First, there was the emergence of the concept of the "active citizen:"

> At the very centre of our ideas on how to control crime should be the energy and initiative of the active citizen. His or her contribution must be mobilized and should be the core of the radical rethinking we need on prevention and control of crime (John Patten, Minister of State, Home Office 1988).

Through the propagation of the notion of active citizenship, the role of the community of active citizens in taking responsibility for the curbing of crime was stressed. The proper role of the community in policing matters was participating actively in consultative arrangements, neighborhood watch schemes, victim support schemes and the special constabulary to help in the fight against crime (Hope and Shaw, 1988; Maguire and Pointing 1988; Mawby, 1988; Leon, 1989; Walklate, 1989). Second, to complement the efforts of the community, a powerful multi-agency approach emerged not only to harness all the criminal justice and related agencies, but also voluntary efforts, central government departments and the media. In April 1986 a ministerial group on crime prevention was set up to co-ordinate the crime prevention strategies of twelve different government departments (*Police Review*, 18 April 1986). All the resultant proposals emphasized the role that statutory authorities should play in co-operating with the police in the fight against crime. Thus, a total community policing strategy was being implemented by the government in relation to crime control. Morgan has also pointed out that this strategy was useful within the government's overall campaign to curb public expenditure (1989: 7-8). Despite public pronouncements to the contrary, community crime control was considerably cheaper than allocating unlimited resources to the police.

THE POLICE AND THE COMMUNITY: TOWARDS A COMMON PURPOSE

The potentially damaging critique of policing that could have developed about increasing crime rates and the manifest failure of the police to control crime failed to materialize. Kenneth Newman, the Commissioner of the Metropolitan Police, the force which was most vulnerable to such a critique, incorporated the criticisms and public debate to neutralize demands for the democratic accountability of his force. The result was the unveiling, from 1983, of a corporatist (multi-agency) community policing strategy aimed at re-establishing the authority and legitimacy of the force. Hence, Newman's strategy and philosophy neatly dovetailed with the government's approach to the problem of crime.

Central to this strategy was mobilizing active community consent in the fight against crime and educating the community about the realistic role of the police in that fight. Newman supported the Scarman consultative arrangements as forums where the consent of community representatives could be mobilized and where the education of the community could take place. Neighborhood watch, crime prevention schemes, victim support schemes and the special constabulary were designated as the means through which the community could participate with the police in the fight against crime. Community beat officers were given a key role in forging a new relationship between the force and the community. Newman also pressed for corporatist policing strategies to be implemented, under the aegis of the police, to deal with the problems of difficult inner-city areas. In addition Newman embarked upon the attempted internal reorganization of the force. In order to put more bobbies back on the beat, civilianization of those tasks not requiring the skills and powers of police-officers took place. Through the implementation of "policing by objective" programs there was the prioritization of particular crimes that were of community concern. Furthermore, the public-order capabilities of the force were enhanced through the acquisition of new equipment, the upgrading of paramilitary training and the re-organization of mobilization procedures to deal with the front lines (symbolic locations) of London's black neighborhoods. Such a strategy underwent further revision and refinement after the civil disturbances of 1985.

Thus, there was a re-definition of the role of the police in the fight against crime involving the creation of new channels of information and communication with the community and other statutory agencies. As far as Newman was concerned, if the new strategy was successful the effectiveness of the force would be improved in three key areas: first, in dealing with the problem of crime through giving the community and other social agencies the primary responsibility for looking after itself, second, by building the consent of the community through closer police-community contact through the consultative committees and neighborhood watch and third, in the maintenance of public tranquillity through the creation of a more efficient riot-control force, which would have the consent of the community. Central to the latter would be the criminalization of any instance of civil disturbance and targeting this form of crime would be a priority of the Metropolitan Police. Through this strategy, social order in the inner cities would be restored.

The Labour Party, the Police and the Community: Partners Against Crime

The leadership of the Labour Party began to take the issue of crime seriously because of first, its electoral vulnerability to being labeled anti-police and soft on crime and second, the possibility of scoring electoral points as the crime rates officially soared under a law and order government.

The 'loony left' campaign of the media and Conservative Party during the mid-1980s had a considerable impact upon the Labour Party's law and order stance. The result was the emergence of new realism in the attempt to regain lost electoral support. There was a considerable distancing of the national party leadership from any controversial issues that its political opponents could use against it, most notably during the coal dispute of 1984-5 and in relation to minority issues which were re-defined as fringe issues (Thatchell, 1983; Hollingsworth, 1986; Wainwright, 1987; Negrine, 1980).

During this period the Conservatives, the pro-Conservative media and the police pressed Labour on their new-found realism, particularly in relation to law and order. After the 1985 disturbances considerable pressure was exerted upon the party leadership to expel Bernie Grant, Leader of Haringey Council, for his statements after Broadwater Farm erupted. At that year's Conservative Party conference the Prime Minister's key-note speech denounced the Labour Party's anti-police stance. In November 1985 the Police Federation renewed its demands for the Labour Party to deal with those members of the party who were anti-police. In early 1986 the Home Secretary renewed the government's attacks on those anti-police Labour-controlled police authorities who were in conflict with their chief constables.

It was in this period that the leadership of the party began to profess publicly its support for the police, its concern about crime and its apprehension about those members of the party demanding police accountability. Statements by the Labour leadership promised that a future Labour government would give full support to the police and would promote policies to bring about community support for the police in the fight against crime. In May 1986 Neil Kinnock denounced those in his party involved in 'police bashing' and in the same month Sir Kenneth Newman was able to state that the policies of the Labour Party and the Conservative Party on law and order were virtually indistinguishable (Sim *et al.*, 1987: 54-6).

Bolstered by the crime surveys and ideological shift of the new realist criminologists (Taylor, 1981; Lea and Young, 1984; Kinsey, 1984; Jones, McLean and Young, 1986; Kinsey, Lea and Young, 1986) in the run-up to the 1987 election, the party leadership fleetingly confronted the Conservatives on the issue of law and order. Crime prevention was one of the key themes of Labour's 1987 manifesto, which stressed the importance of local authorities and the community, in partnership with the police, spearheading a co-ordinated multi-faceted approach to fight crime. In its critique of the failure of the Conservative government to defeat crime the document harked back to the golden days, before Thatcherism, when the community and the police were at one. Within this critique and proposals the position of the police was enhanced both in relation to the community and other government and voluntary agencies.

As a consequence, the issue of police accountability was downplayed to a commitment to first, give more (unspecified) powers to police authorities, second, abolish magistrate representation and third, create community police councils whose functions were to be similar to the existing consultation committees. As a consequence, during the 1987 election on the issue of police accountability "inter-party conflict was muted by a 'new realism' which seemed to infect all parties" (Reiner, 1989b: 5). That the conflict was muted was an indication of how far the Labour Party had reconstructed its policies to accept once more the dominant ideologies concerning law and order in Britain (Bridges, 1986: 80).

The Victims of Crime

For the government, the police and the Labour Party, the aim of active community participation in crime prevention and multi-agency policing was to make it more difficult to become a victim of crime. As the 1980s progressed, and as a result of the various crime studies, concern with the victim became "a powerful motif" within the criminal justice system (Rock, 1988: 172). In 1987 the Home Office allocated £1.5 million to support previously underfunded victim support schemes and Home Office circular 20/1988 called for the criminal justice agencies to improve the manner in which they dealt with victims. Within this prioritization of victims certain sections of the community came to the fore. The concerns of feminist groups and the police monitoring groups concerned about racial attacks became part of a formal political agenda on crime victims. As a consequence the anxieties of women and Asians in relation to crime became a key concern for all agencies and institutions.

Home Office circular 69/1986 to chief constables offered advice on how the police should treat victims of rape and domestic violence. The police responded by developing specialist training for police officers, recruiting women doctors for forensic examinations, establishing specialist police units, producing publicity on women's safety and setting up rape examination suites. Within these professionalized and medicalized structures there was no necessary place for groups such as "Rape Crisis," "Taboo" and "Women's Aid" (Scott and Dickens, 1989).

After the Home Office reports on the subject of racial attacks in 1981 and 1985 formally acknowledged the nature of the problem the police began to take the issue seriously. In January 1987 Sir Kenneth Newman announced that the Metropolitan Police would be launching a concerted campaign against the "moral and social evil" of racially-motivated attacks. It was no coincidence that this campaign specifically focused on Newham and Ealing where the local police monitoring groups had been vociferous in their criticisms of the police response to racist attacks. Since then the Metropolitan Police in particular has continued to make highly public statements concerning its commitment to responding to those who have been racially attacked. In February 1989 a £900,000 publicity campaign was launched to encourage the reporting of racial attacks and harassment. However, the monitoring groups still point to the discrepancies between the publicity campaigns and the continuing tendency for the police to de-racialize such incidents. As a consequence there is no correspondence between the police's conceptualization of the problem and that of the police monitoring groups (Newham Monitoring Project, 1989; Rose, 1989).

The manner in which these issues have been prioritized has had considerable implications for those radical women's groups involved with the issue of male violence against women and those police monitoring groups involved with the issue of racial terrorism. As a consequence of their response the police have been able to reclaim groups of victims and in doing so have been able to marginalize radical feminist analyses which are premised upon the idea of women being the survivors of male violence, not the victims of violence, and radical black analyses which are premised upon the notion of racial terrorism, not racial harassment. In addition to neutralizing the opponents of the police, the dominant conceptualization of the problem has both legitimized and facilitated corporatist policing strategies.

The overall impact of the emergence of the discourse on community and crime was three-fold for those campaigning for police accountability within the Labour Party. First, it made them vulnerable to the accusation of being anti-police by their political opponents. The practical implications for local authorities who were at the forefront of campaigning for police accountability and fundamentally opposed to such corporatist community policing approaches to crime prevention were serious. Non-cooperation was ideologically and financially damaging, particularly in a climate when local authorities were under constant attack from central government.

Second, it made them vulnerable to those sections of the Labour Party, both locally and nationally, who alleged that an anti-police stance was an electoral liability. Third, they had to confront the issues of crime prevention, the fear of crime and the mobilization of the community to participate actively in a co-ordinated fight against crime. As a consequence, considerable pressure was brought to bear on Labour-controlled local authorities to participate directly in multi-agency crime prevention projects. This pressure resulted in local authorities, such as Manchester, distancing themselves from the controversial police monitoring initiatives. Instead of monitoring the actions of the police, Labour local authorities began to concern themselves with community safety. As a consequence, the concerns of those sections of the community for whom the police were a problem were once more excluded from the political agenda.

Police Accountability into the 1990s

Towards a national police force?

A series of developments in relation to the overall organizational structure of the police had serious consequences for the issue of democratic accountability. A succession of important statements and recommendations were made by senior officers and politicians that provided an indication as to how British policing should develop in the 1990s. The statements and recommendations indicated a final move towards a fundamentally restructured nationalized police-force in some form or another.

In autumn 1988 the Chief Constable of Sussex, Roger Birch, suggested that serious attention should be given to the idea of a regionally differentiated *de facto* national force. Both Sir Peter Imbert and Sir John Wheeler, the chairman of the all-party House of

Commons' Home Affairs Committee, added their support to the idea of existing police functions coming under more nationalized or regionalized control. Wheeler stated that such rationalization would facilitate easier consultation for the Home Secretary. In terms of accountability he suggested that a regional board of directors could be appointed, made up of a financial director from outside the police service together with appointed community representatives. Although the then Home Secretary, David Waddington, effectively rejected the suggestions relating to full nationalization, he supported the idea of further intra-force co-operation through ACPO co-ordination and further rationalization of the police function. In September 1989 the Home Secretary announced his support for Imbert's idea of a national criminal intelligence unit. Further support for the idea came at the Superintendent's Association conference in October when a call was made for the separation of local and national policing functions. After much debate in July 1990, chief police-officers finally agreed in principle to the establishment of a *de facto* national detective force which would be supported by a criminal intelligence network at an estimated cost of at least £60 million.

The impetus for such radical developments stemmed primarily from first, a trenchant fiscal critique of the effectiveness and efficiency of the present policing system and second, the policing implications of the commencement of a single European market in 1992.

Fiscal accountability

The police service, through the unquestioning support of the Conservative government, effectively negotiated demands for democratic accountability. However, this dependency upon central government patronage has had a negative side for the police. In the latter half of the 1980s the government's Financial Management Incentive attempted to increase the financial accountability and performance of the public-service sector. Such Treasury attempts to control public expenditure resulted in close attention being paid to the effectiveness and efficiency of the police (Horton and Smith, 1988: Morgan, 1989).

Furthermore, the House of Commons' Home Affairs Committee, which was also concerned with the monitoring of public expenditure, also confronted the issue of the effectiveness and efficiency of the present policing system. In July 1989 the Chairman of the Committee, Sir John Wheeler, stated that he supported the idea of a drastically reformed policing system. He argued that the police forces in England and Wales should be merged to create between 5 and 10 regional forces because as they stood they were "insufficiently business like." The report of this committee reiterated Wheeler's criticisms. It was asserted that it was necessary to create some form of national police-force if the "glaring deficiencies, incompetent use of resources and blinding incompetence" of the management of the present system were to be overcome *(The Independent,* 26 July 1990).

The possibility of stricter financial accountability came as a shock to a service which has had access to considerable financial resources since the 1979 election. In late 1989 the representative bodies of the police service set up an "Operational Policing Review" to counter the possibility of a possible 'slow down' on expenditure on the police. This review body was highly critical of the government's efficiency drive and objected to the police-service being subjected to marketplace economic criteria. Sir Peter Imbert, Commissioner of the Metropolitan Police, in a manner reminiscent of other public-sector leaders, stated that a "non-profit making, caring public service could not be judged by economic criteria used by ICI and Marks and Spencers" *(The Independent,* 5 March 1990).

The struggles in 1989-90 over resourcing resulted in the Home Secretary being accused of betrayal during the 1990 Police Federation conference. The threat was made that if the government did not respond to the needs of the service the Police Federation would be forced into considering its non-trade-union status. It was within this context of the possibility of relatively strict financial restraints being imposed on the police by the Conservative government that the issue of 1992 began to take on central importance.

1992: The single European market

Whilst fiscal rationalization was dominant in the explanations for such moves, an over-arching justification was given as the supra-national consequences of 1992. Bilateral and multilateral agreements which facilitate cross-border police co-operation are already operational. In December 1989 the Home Secretary signed an agreement, within the forum of the Trevi group, to facilitate closer co-ordination between European police forces in the areas of narcotic controls and counter-terrorism. In addition to these specific concerns, the agreement aimed to bring about increasing co-operation on training, science and technology as well as supporting the idea of establishing a European criminal database. The only thing that Britain was not party to, at the time, was the agreement between France, Germany, Belgium, the Netherlands and Luxembourg allowing communal opening of borders in "hot pursuit" operations after 1991. In May 1990 Britain signed an accord with Italy enabling their respective police forces to confiscate the profits of serious crime.

In addition the meetings of the highly influential Trevi working groups, since their inception in the early 1970s, have tried to harmonize policies on terrorism, drugs, frontier checks, extradition, organized crime and, since 1986, immigration controls. Such moves would be all the more effective if, as is suspected, Britain is pushing for the *Prevention of Terrorism Act* to be the basis for a European Internal Security Act. Effectively this would mean that the tightly-controlled border regulations that have been built up in Britain since 1974 could become the basis for policing the boundaries of Fortress Europe. The aim is to create what official jargon refers to as a "security surplus," as opposed to a "security deficit." This involves constructing a strict external frontier and creating a co-ordinated internal law enforcement and intelligence gathering organization.

The policing implications of the realization of a single European market in 1992 have provided opportunities for the British police to break out of the financial constraints being imposed by the Conservative government. The implications of 1992 have provided an extra lever to counter government criticism whilst also providing the police with access to supra-national funding arrangements. It has been estimated, for example, that a capital outlay of one billion pounds and a significant increase in personnel will be needed to bring about the initial harmonization of the various European policing systems (Weeks, 1990).

The Metropolitan Police: The professional police force for the 1990s

The ramifications of 1992 and the move towards official acceptance of the idea of some form of national force has had significant implications for one force in particular, the Metropolitan Police. One can make sense of the reforms taking place within the Met only through understanding that in any shake-up of policing in Britain this force will take the lead role. As a consequence of the internal debate stimulated by the 1988 Wolff Olins report *A Force for Change,* the *Plus Programme* was launched in April 1989. According to Imbert, this program is intended to be "the hallmark" of professional policing in the 1990s. Internally there was to be both strong management but more flexible and responsive management through the streamlining of the command hierarchies. In addition considerable emphasis was placed on open management and meaningful consultation with all ranks of officers. Imbert's intention was, unlike previous commissioners, to carry the force with him in the implementation of the reforms. Externally a new relationship was to be forged with the community. The *Plus Programme* stressed the idea of providing a professional public service. The Commissioner stated that the police had behaved in an unaccountable manner in the past and emphasized that the force would have to respond to community determination of needs and law and order priorities. Imbert elaborated upon the ideas as the basis of the approach at the 1989 International Police Exhibition and Conference. He stressed that if the Metropolitan Police was to achieve its force goals, the confidence of the community was essential. This could be achieved only by a commitment to openness and a commitment to sharing power and responsibilities with the community.

At the same time as Imbert's professional policing strategy was being unveiled, a series of other statements relating to the future professionalization of the British police was made. In October 1989 the Audit Commission, in an efficiency study into general force training, was highly critical of existing arrangements and put forward the idea of creating centers of excellence. In the same period the above-mentioned House of Commons' Home Affairs Committee was also highly critical of first, the training and career development programs for senior officers and second, the appointments procedure. The Home Office responded immediately by announcing measures for the further professionalization of the top officers through the upgrading of the Senior Command Course and the introduction of a central monitoring training structure. However, a more startling response came in the form of a suggestion by the Home Affairs Committee, and subsequently supported by the Prime Minister, that senior police officers should be in a professionally managed career structure equivalent to that which operates in the military. The idea of a military-style cadre of senior officers sparked off another internal debate similar to one precipitated by the Trenchard reforms in the 1930s.

Implications for police accountability

What is significant in the debates that have taken place about the future of policing in Britain is the lack of discussion of police accountability. To whom will this restructured police force with supra-national functions be accountable? From what can be gleaned from the various statements there seems to be little possibility of the structures of local accountability being enhanced. Sir John Wheeler in his discussions with representatives of the Association of County Councils and the Association of Metropolitan Associations during 1989 and 1990 stated bluntly that as far as he was concerned local control of policing "must go." He advocated the setting up of regional boards of directors which would be made up of a financial director from outside of the police service and community representatives. These boards of directors would be accountable to the Home Secretary. In addition he suggested that a national police policy committee be set up which would consist of the regional chief constables and representatives of the Home Office. When James Sharples, the Chief Constable of Merseyside, was asked about the implications of such moves for police accountability he tersely stated that chief police officers were fully aware of the problematic issue of accountability. However, he would not be drawn on what type of accountability senior officers would favor.

For those groups who are subject to the attention of the police the ramifications of the seeming lack of concern about police accountability for their substantive rights of citizenship are staggering. It should not be forgotten that whilst the debates about the future of British policing were taking place, there were at least 41 official inquiries taking place into controversial incidents involving the police. Central to many of these cases were the experiences of black as well as Irish communities.

Many of the 55 people who made formal complaints against the disbanded West Midlands Serious Crimes Squad were black. The Commission for Racial Equality pressed the Police Complaints Authority to investigate allegations of racial discrimination by members of this squad. The policing of the 'front lines' is still causing controversy in terms of the inadequacy of the means of redress against discriminatory policing. In 1986 the Police Complaints Authority initiated an investigation into the policing of Notting Hill, after a series of acquittals of those who had been charged during 1984-5 with possession of drugs and/or assaulting police officers. All the complainants claimed that the drugs had been planted and that they had been assaulted by police officers, known as the "Black Watch." The result of this investigation, announced in 1990, was that the eighteen complainants were told that there would be no criminal or disciplinary proceedings against any officer. The outcome of the investigation confirmed the worst suspicions of those in the black communities who are cynical about getting justice through the official complaints procedure. Figures released during 1988-9 confirmed the growing trend of those with complaints against the police initiating private prosecutions rather than utilizing the cumbersome and ineffective official procedure. An indication of this shift was demonstrated by the fact that between 1987 and 1989 the total damages awarded against the Metropolitan Police rose from £11,000 to £250,000, with out-of-court settlements by the force increasing from £82,000 to £266,000.

The allegations about police malpractice in Notting Hill were strengthened further by a series of controversies in 1989. In June 1989 Frank Critchlow of the Mangrove Club was acquitted of drug charges despite 66 officers testifying against him during the five-week trial. In December 1989 the Metropolitan Police had £100,000 awarded against them for planting cannabis upon a black man and subjecting him to racial abuse in Notting Hill. In the same month the key prosecution witness in the conviction of Alban Turner for a murder at the 1987 Notting Hill Carnival admitted that he had lied and that the police had paid him to give evidence.

Such complaints and scandals confirmed the allegations and suspicions of those who, since the early 1980s, had campaigned for new structures to be implemented to strengthen the democratic accountability of the police. However, given that such demands had been outlined out by the mid-1980s, what was notable about the above-mentioned incidents in the late 1980s was the absence of political debate or concern. This is not to say that there was not a political context or political implications. But the debate that did take place was located firmly *within* the legal and organizational context of police accountability. Those participating in the debate were the same senior police officers, the respective police organization, Home Office officials and senior government figures who were also at the forefront of the debates about the future of the British police.

There seemed to be a concerted attempt by senior police officers and members of the judiciary to minimize the impact of such scandals and to persuade the public that the very fact that such investigations were taking place was proof that the police were capable of rooting out the rotten apples. More liberal members of the judiciary indicated that the overturning of the Guilford and Winchester convictions was proof that British justice was the finest in the world. Sir Peter Imbert, who was the intelligence officer of the bomb squad responsible for assessing the information in the Guildford case, issued a warning to those who might demand that the police officers involved be held to account for perpetrating such a miscarriage of justice.

> let's not fall into the trap which it seems police are accused of calling into at the end of 1974 of having convinced themselves that those people were guilty of that particular crime. I see a very clear similarity between the atmosphere now and then, let's be careful that we don't make another mistake now (*Guardian*, 24 October 1989).

The Chief Inspector of Constabulary in his annual report for 1989 also defended the police as an institution from being held to account over such incidents when he stated that: "It would be quite wrong to condemn all policing practice on the strength of a few, albeit significant incidents, even though they may have had tragic consequences" (Her Majesty's Inspectorate, 1989). Whilst it was emphasized by all concerned that they had every confidence the internal inquiries would get to the truth of the matter, the judiciary and the police were setting clear limits to any investigations into the miscarriages of justice.

Given this context, it is little wonder that civil libertarians expressed concern about the implications of 1992 for those communities susceptible to non-accountable policing.

They have argued that the advent of a single European market will detrimentally affect those groups already disadvantaged and discriminated against in the present system, that is, third world migrants, political refugees and asylum seekers and established black communities (see Joint Council for the Welfare of Immigrants, 1989; Arnott, 1990; *Spare Rib,* 1990). The supra-national Eurocops will have the key role of policing Fortress Europe and certain groups are, if past experience is anything to go by, vulnerable to their attentions. As Sivanandan (1988: 9) has argued:

> Citizenship may open Europe's borders to blacks and allow them free movement, but racism which cannot tell one black from another, a citizen from an immigrant, an immigrant from a refugee — and classes all immigrants and refugees as terrorists and drug dealers is going to make such movement fraught and fancy.

It is because of this context that the issue of the democratic accountability of the police must once more be placed on the political agenda in the 1990s.

Chapter 16

Crime and Punishment in the United States: Immediate and Long-Term Reforms from a Marxist Perspective

Tony Platt
Institute of Labor and Economic Crisis

Law and Order

As several commentators have noted (Hall *et al.*, 1978; Taylor, 1981; Horton, 1981), there has been in recent years a decisive shift to the right in criminal justice and penal policies in many of the advanced capitalist countries. This shift has been most pronounced and clear-cut in the United States, as evidenced by: the unprecedented growth in the penal population; the rapid deterioration in conditions inside prison; the abandonment of the "rehabilitative ideal" in favor of deterrence and "incapacitation;" the rise to prominence of powerful "law and order" lobbies in the halls of Congress and state legislatures; longer sentences and criminalization of previously lawful behavior; increasing political repression and revocation of "watchdog" legislation with respect to the CIA and FBI; and the dismantling or gutting of federal regulatory agencies which had attempted, albeit in token fashion, to penalize corporate crimes. In sum, repressive policies of "law and order," which not too long ago appeared to be monopolized by extreme right-wing political organizations and alienated petty bourgeois intellectuals, have quickly become the conventional wisdom in the White House, government and academia (Platt and Takagi, 1981; Platt, 1982).

While this shift to the right has been most evident in the United States (which of course is the most powerful capitalist nation in the world), the trend to the right is not limited to one region of the globe, and cannot simply be attributed to the political idiosyncrasies of Reagan. (Actually, many policies associated with Reagan, a conservative Republican, were in place under Carter, a liberal Democrat.) Similar trends have been

* Originally published in *Crime and Social Justice*: 38-45 (Winter, 1982).
Reprinted by permission of Global Options.

reported in England, West Germany, Canada, Australia, New Zealand, Norway and Sweden — countries which, unlike the United States exemplify welfare state policies of social democracy (see *Crime and Social Justice* 15).

It is not the purpose of this paper to describe or analyze this rightward trend in criminal justice and the penal system. This task has been adequately undertaken elsewhere, though we have by no means yet developed a full appreciation of the dynamics of the current crisis. Suffice it to say that the current "penal crisis" is rooted in the larger crisis of capitalism, that the crisis is international in scope (as is the capitalist mode of production), that the rise of the Right in the sphere of "law and order" is an expression of a much more profound reorganization of the political economy, and that we cannot understand the rapid demise of liberalism in criminology without an appreciation of how the imposition of austerity policies in the core capitalist countries is related to profound and complex changes in the world economy (Dixon, 1982; Frank, 1982; Wallerstein, 1982).

What is important for the purposes of this paper is that "law and order" has become a *central* component of the ideological and political repertoire of the Right. The Right (by this term I am referring to a political tendency rather than to a specific set of political interests) has seized upon the issues of "crime in the streets," "law and order" and "terrorism" to legitimate and justify attacks on the political and labor organizations of the working class, on public services, on constitutional rights, on women's right to control their bodies, and on the hard-won legal and political gains made by minorities, immigrants and "guest workers." In the United States and England especially, a rhetorical concern for "street" crime has been used to cloak fundamentally racist policies, resulting in intensified police repression and increased use of imprisonment against minority and immigrant communities. The Right has been successful in exploiting the issue of "law and order" because crime is a very real and serious problem in working class communities. At the same time, the successes of the Right have been greatly facilitated by the failure of the Left to take crime seriously and to generate progressive alternatives to the politics of "law and order."

Fortunately, it is not too late. The Right by no means yet represents a mass popular movement in the United States. Despite concerted efforts by the Reagan administration and its deputies in the state apparatus and mass media to mobilize a *popular* right-wing movement, there is still widespread cynicism about and opposition to the government's policies. Since mid-1979, opinion polls have consistently reported that over two-thirds of the American people oppose U.S. military intervention abroad, and a March, 1982, poll published in *Newsweek* showed 90 percent of those polled were specifically opposed to sending U.S. troops to El Salvador. A more recent nationwide survey by the *Los Angeles Times* (reported in the *San Francisco Chronicle*, 9 August 1982) found that more than a third of the people who voted for Reagan in 1980 would not support him now, largely because they lack confidence in his economic policies.

The Right has been very successful in exploiting people's real concerns about crime to promote its "law and order" policies, but the campaign seems to be wearing thin. The argument that an increase in the severity of punishment is required by seriously escalating crime rates is undermined by the government's own victimization surveys (U.S.

Department of Justice, October 1981), which indicate that the "street" crime rate, though high and serious, remained quite stable throughout the 1970s. A Harris Poll, conducted in the summer of 1982, asked respondents to say what they thought were the greatest problems facing the country: 48 percent cited unemployment, 36 percent cited "fear of a depression," 25 percent cited high interest rates, and 19 percent cited the danger of nuclear war. Only six percent — as compared to 14 percent in the spring of 1982, and 33 percent in the summer of 1981 — thought crime was the most serious problem (*Oakland Tribune*, 22 July 1982).

Heritage of the "New Left"

Beginning in the late 1960s and until late into the 1970s, there was a complex variety of movements and organizations taking up the challenge of prison and police reform and crime control. Sparked by spontaneous prison revolts and by massive police repression in the black community and against the student and anti-war movements, criminal justice became an important political focus for corporate and government reformers (concerned about the "counter-productivity" of unregulated repression), for petty bourgeois liberals (concerned about the abuse of discretion and power by state functionaries) and for working class and progressive activists (concerned about political repression).

By the early 1980s, little remains of these enterprising efforts, except for the technocratic and managerial "reforms" initiated by corporate-liberal professionals associated with the President's Commission on Law Enforcement and the Administration of Justice (1967) and subsequent special commissions and governmental agencies. There have been several critiques and exposés of corporate and petty bourgeois reforms. Here I want to focus on the heritage of the New Left, since the politics and strategy of this movement played no small part in contributing to the overall demise of progressive reforms. Moreover, as we now embark on a new round of progressive activism, it is imperative to summarize and learn from previous experience.

The New Left's approach to criminal justice reflected is overall political immaturity, its petty bourgeois worldview and roots, and its confused approach to strategy and tactics. The "radical" critique of criminal justice was generally moralistic, atheoretical and utopian. Within this framework, there were wild swings from short-term, essentially liberal reforms (for example, civilian review of the police) to dangerous adventures in ultra-leftism (for example, the abolition of prisons). The former were typically co-opted or reduced to inoffensive tokenism, while the latter were debated in small sects or, if translated into radical action, quickly and brutally repressed (as in the case of the SLA). It was only at the height of the prisoners' movement, when there was organized leadership inside prison and links to working class organizations outside prison, that the limits of the Left were momentarily transcended.

Let me give some specific examples of the fundamental weaknesses of the New Left:

- Spontaneous struggles with the police, especially in the black community and on the campuses, led to exposés of the police and various programs to control their repressive practices. The "radical" analysis was quite primitive: it posited that the police were the direct instrumentality of the ruling class, that there were no contradictions or class distinctions within the police ("a cop is a cop is a cop"), and that the police were simply agents of the state (forgetting that they are also employees of the state). The poverty of theory about the police reflected the weaknesses of anti-police practice — glorification of spontaneity, substitution of tactics for strategy and localism. "Community control of the police," which reflected the most radical expression of this movement, was essentially reformist at best because it assumes: 1) a classless "community" in which all elements co-operate for the common good; and 2) that local control of the state could be legislated out of the hands of the ruling class (for an elaboration of this critique, see Institute for the Study of Labor and Economic Crisis, 1982).

• Between 1968 and 1971, the prisons erupted with spontaneous riots, followed by organized militancy. So long as the prison movement was organized internally and had close links to progressive working class organizations outside prison (such as the Black Panther Party), it had vitality and strength, and put forward realistic programs of reform. But after the assassination of George Jackson in San Quentin and Rockefeller's massacre at Attica in 1971, the organized prisoners' movement was brutally repressed, and the domain of "prison reform" became monopolized by petty bourgeois liberals and dogmatic, ultra-left sects.

The New Left approach to prisons was romantic and utopian. Prisoners were regarded as victims of political persecution (thus conveniently liquidating the responsibility of prisoners for their acts of criminal victimization). Rather than take on the very difficult struggle of generating short-term and intermediate reforms, the New Left instead raised the slogan of "tear down the wall," and called for the "rehabilitation of the entire social order" (Prison Action Project, 1975). Anything less than "revolution" was dismissed as tokenism; any reform regarded with suspicion as a diabolical plot by the state to increase repression. And when it came to the question of "rehabilitation," the New Left radicals and petty bourgeois liberals found common ground, uniting in their exposés of the coercive nature of "treatment" and violation of prisoners' civil liberties (e.g. the right to refuse treatment).

The critique of "rehabilitation" was of course useful and played an important role in demystifying the realities of prison life. But rather than fight for an authentic program of prison reform (the prisoners' movement, for example, had put forward very concrete demands concerning education, treatment, job training, etc.), the New Left rejected reforms as a concession to the state, and united with liberals who stressed the primacy of individual rights *vis-à-vis* the state. Thus, books like *Struggle for Justice* and *Radical Nonintervention*, which were written by liberals, were embraced by New Left radicals because the former opposed "rehabilitation" and the latter proposed that the best kinds of reforms were those that do nothing at all. As Cullen and Wozniak (1982) have pointed out, the New Left's critique of reforms made it so much easier for the Right to argue that rehabilitation does not work, and that the goal of prisons should be "punishment" and not "treatment." Objectively, the positions are indistinguishable: the radicals oppose the "crime of treatment," the liberals call for "radical nonintervention," and the conservatives advocate "benign neglect." Consequently, a New Left prison organizer like John Irwin (1980: 238) sounds much like a right-wing crusader when he says that

> the main purpose of imprisonment...should be punishment. We are dishonest and foolish if we do not admit that punishment is basic in our response to crime. This is not a brutish retributive atavism in human beings; it is an essential part of the bargain that we make to live by the rules.... When nothing is done, the rules lose their meaning and persons lose their social commitment.

• The most serious criticism of the New Left was its failure to address the problem of crime in working class communities. In general, the New Left either glossed over "street" crime as an invention of the FBI to divert attention away from corporate crimes or romanticized it as a form of primitive political rebellion (Platt, 1978). But, as we well know from both experience and knowledge, "street" crime is not a fiction, but rather a very real and serious problem, especially in the superexploited sectors of the working class and its reserve army of labor. Moreover, under monopoly capitalism, "street" crime bears almost no resemblance to the social banditry of Sicilian peasants, the pastoral nomads of Central Asia, or even the rural poor of mercantile England (Hobsbawm, 1969). It is only among ultra-leftist sects and the New Left, which have no base of support in working class communities, that "street" crime is practiced or glorified as anticapitalist revolt. The New Left separated the penal and police "questions" from the issue of crime, thus allowing the Right to monopolize the politics of "law and order." This was irresponsible and dangerous, a reflection of the profound alienation of the New Left from the daily conditions of life in working class communities.

It was this failure of the New Left to address the problems of crime and violence (as well as its institutionalized sexism) which prompted the autonomous women's movement to publicize and agitate around the issues of rape, battery and family violence. While the anti-rape and shelter movement, like its counterparts in police and prison reform, has done important educational work in making the "private" world of the family a public concern, it too reproduced the errors of the New Left (glorification of spontaneity, anti-theory, anticommunism, etc.) and became increasingly reformist and opportunist as petty bourgeois feminists seized control of the institutionalized women's movement (Dixon, 1978; Schwendinger and Schwendinger, 1981).

• Finally, when it came to long-term alternatives to criminal justice under capitalism, the New Left had very little to offer other than pie-in-the-sky and pious proclamations about socialism. Crime and criminal justice under socialism were typically addressed in idealist and abstract terms without reference to concrete historical/comparative studies, or to the contradictions of socialist construction in a world capitalist economy. Richard Quinney, a leading entrepreneur in "radial criminology," proposed in 1977 that "what is emerging [in the United States] as capitalist development moves to socialist development is a transformation in social, political and economic life. We are now beginning to create the social theory and practice appropriate to socialist development.... A socialist economy as well as a socialist state is in the making" (Quinney, 1977: 146, 157). Clearly, Quinney either had access to information that was not available to the rest of us or he had simply forgotten to step outside his office and take a look at the real world.

Quinney's mindless statement of faith about socialism was typical of "radical" criminology and did nothing to address people's real questions and concerns about socialist construction. Moreover, it is not enough to explain the persistence of crime and other forms of class relations under socialism as simply a *legacy* of capitalism. Such a view is not only wrong and simple-minded, it is also a lazy way out of tackling very difficult and complex theoretical problems in contemporary Marxism. With respect to both immediate reforms under monopoly capitalism and long-term socialist construction, the New Left has bequeathed us an almost nonexistent program of action and a distorted and reductionist version of Marxism.

Taking Crime Seriously

The rise of the Right and its politics of "law and order" requires us to re-examine the legacy of the New Left, to learn from its failures, and to develop a new praxis which both addresses the need for concrete programs and deepens our theoretical framework. "On crime," writes Bertram Gross (1982: 52, 54), "more than on most matters, the left seems bereft of ideas.... Nothing is clearer than that crime is too important to be left either to the law enforcement establishment or to the repressive right." Gross, of course, is absolutely right. Fortunately, the backruptcy of Reagan's anti-crime program (which is more rhetoric than substance) and the failure of the Right to mobilize a mass right-wing movement in the United States means that it is not too late to develop alternatives to Reaganism.

Already we see the beginning of a lively and healthy debate about a progressive anti-crime program. *Crime and Social Justice* No. 17 (1982) includes some modest proposals by Bertram Gross. In England, an important new book by Ian Taylor (1981) calls for the reconstruction of socialist criminology. In a comment on Taylor's book, Alan Hunt (1982) takes issue with many of Taylor's formulations, but nevertheless recognizes that "Ian Taylor has contributed to winning a wider recognition of the need for the Left to have a real strategy and policy in the arena of law, crime and justice." Herman and Julia Schwendinger have also in recent years (1980, 1981) stressed the importance of linking theory to practical interventions.

Recently, Paul Takagi and I were commissioned by the National Association of Blacks in Criminal Justice to write a policy analysis of "Racism and Imprisonment in the United States in the 1980s" (1982). At the conclusion of our analysis, we developed a set of policy recommendations which I am including below in an edited form. Some of these proposals are short-term reforms which could, with government support, be implemented immediately. Others are long-term proposals and structural reforms which require fundamental changes in the political economy. Though we do not address the tactics and strategy required for implementing these proposals, it should be noted that, given the current climate in Congress and the White House, even the most modest reforms will meet powerful political resistance.

Bring Equal Justice to Bail System

Our review of the literature reveals that there is systematic discrimination against the poor and minorities, who are denied equal access to legal resources, i.e., bail, release on one's own recognizance, private attorney and a trial by jury. The inability to post bail and not having access to legal resources produce more serious convictions and sentencing outcomes (Swigert and Farrell, 1976; Bernstein *et al.*, 1977):

> a) The setting of bail is assumed to be related to the type of offense charged and to guarantee the defendant's appearance in court. In reality, the bail system and the system of "O.R." operate to benefit the privileged and discriminate against the poor. Legislative and constitutional changes are required in order to make the bail system more equitable, namely, on the basis of an individual's income.
>
> b) Bernstein *et al.* (1977) report that judges and prosecutors employ bail, by setting a high amount, to sanction the poor and black. About 40 percent of those detained in jail because they are unable to post bond are ultimately dismissed by the court. The setting of high bail performs the same function for the poor as does concept of preventive detention. As Pfohl (1979) reports, "dangerousness" and "violence" cannot be predicted even by the best psychiatrists, let alone by judges and paroling authorities. Both of these procedures are frequently employed by court personnel on the basis of racist and class stereotypes (Swigert and Farrell, 1976). Similar to the "tissue committee" in hospitals that monitors unnecessary or over-surgery, it is recommended that the state judiciary immediately establish in each local jurisdiction a representative committee to monitor judicial excesses in the area of bail, preventive detention, the denial of private counsel, and so on.

The adoption of these recommendations will immediately impact the congested conditions of local jails, whereby the construction of larger local facilities will not be necessary.

Abolish Mandatory Sentences

Many offenses, especially those defined as violent crimes, presently call for mandatory prison sentences. Violence is a relative term used in selective ways to create public alarm. The reality of violence, when measured in terms of mangled bodies and death, is most serious for the victims of corporate fraud and deception — the victims of unsafe products and dangerous commodities, such as improperly tested drugs that are pushed on the public. Unsafe working conditions and chemical pollution also produce their share of injuries and death. Thus, crimes such as homicides that engender strong societal reaction are punished with the longest terms in prison, but corporate officials are very rarely criminally indicted for their killings.

> All mandatory sentences should be abolished. Incarceration rates are not statistically correlated to the rise in violent crime rates; that is, the present high incarceration rates are not responses to a shift towards more serious, violent crimes. It is this misconception of crime and punishment and the prevailing myth that have stampeded both criminal justice officials and legislators to call for harsher and mandatory penal sentences.

Restore Indeterminate Sentences

Offense and prior record are the major determinants of a prison sentence, and in some states, the basic sentence is enhanced by the circumstances of the offense, such as the use of a weapon, injury to victim and so on. Legislative guidelines are specific in most instances, but there are loopholes that permit the introduction of non-legal factors, e.g. the defendant's employment record, age, race, socio-economic status and clinical reports (a psychiatric evaluation, probation report and similar evaluations of a person's moral character). There is no science in sentencing or paroling. Instead, there is a tendency to make moral judgements of the poor and minorities. If specific legislation can be enacted to control these tendencies, the indeterminate sentence and the concept of a paroling authority are mechanisms far superior to the current trend toward determinate and mandatory sentences.

a) Legislation should be enacted to permit paroling authorities to release an offender immediately from prison, either on parole or to a community-based facility. This authority is needed as a corrective to practices by some courts that unnecessarily sentence offenders to prison.

b) Studies have shown that judges rely on non-legal factors in selecting a sentence from among the range of alternatives. The poor and blacks tend to receive the more severe sentence. Given this reality, legislation is needed to set precise lower and upper limits for specific offenses, including misdemeanors. Punishment guidelines that specify "up to $500 fine or six months in jail" result in the poor and blacks ending up in jail for the maximum term.

c) All indeterminate sentences should be fixed within a narrow range, that is, the indeterminate sentence should not have a broad range such as one year to life. The lower limit of an indeterminate sentence should always be at zero.

Combat Racism in Criminal Justice Professionals

The very large proportion of black males and females in the nation's penal facilities is accounted for by institutionalized racism, specifically the systematic discrimination against the poor and minorities at every step in the criminal justice process — concentration of police in the most oppressed communities, selective prosecution, inequitable use of bail and legal resources, punitive sentencing, etc. These discriminatory practices are even more aggravated during the current long-term economic crisis in which a right-wing "law and order" climate promotes the scapegoating of minorities. Judges and other criminal justice officials are currently under tremendous pressure to impose tougher sentences, to articulate and act upon racist stereotypes concerning the criminality of minorities.

a) Judges and other criminal justice officials need to be informed that crime rates, and, more specifically, violent crime rates, have no relationship to incarceration rates (Nagel, 1977; Thornberry, 1979; Box and Hale, 1982). A concerted effort to re-educate criminal justice officials is especially critical in states where blacks are disproportionately imprisoned compared to whites, namely, Wisconsin, Nebraska, Iowa, Massachusetts, etc.

b) It is recommended that National Institute of Justice funds be earmarked for the continuing re-education of criminal justice officials to address the specific processes of discrimination.

Prosecute Corporate Crime and Racist Violence

Crime is a very serious problem in minority communities. Well over 41 million people are victimized annually by serious "street" crime Blacks, especially those who are unemployed and poor, have the highest rates of criminal victimization (Platt, 1978). While this high level of crime is clearly linked to economic conditions, it is also a reflection of the demoralizing social relations and individualistic ideology that permeate capitalist society. Since most "street" crime is a form of "penny capitalism" that seeks to emulate the predatory practices of big business, we call for vigorous prosecution of corporate and government crime. This is not only a matter of equal justice. Such prosecution is necessary in order to demonstrate that crime does not pay. So long as corporate and government crimes go unpunished, we cannot expect the selective punishment of working class crime to be an effective deterrent.

Similarly, we call for vigorous prosecution of illegal acts of racist violence and terrorism by such organizations as the Ku Klux Klan. The government's current policy can best be described as one of "benign neglect" or, as in the case of the Communist Workers Party in North Carolina, covert complicity. We cannot demand a reduction in crime within minority communities so long as such communities are victimized by unregulated business crime and by racist violence.

Increase Employment to Lower Incarceration Rate

Since unemployment and incarceration rates are tightly linked together, a major solution to the burgeoning penal population is to ameliorate the conditions of unemployment. The appropriation of $2 billion in federal assistance toward construction of state penal facilities should be redirected toward providing needed material and social services for the unemployed. Historical evidence shows that nations which provided benefits for the unemployed during the Great Depression had a much lower penal population than nations which provided minimal benefits (Rusche, 1980).

From the findings on the relationship between unemployment and incarceration rates, it follows that blacks have historically suffered the ravages of unemployment, thereby accounting for their very large proportion in the prison population. Immediate and substantial material and social services need to be provided to the black community, including the redirection of a substantial portion of funds authorized under the *Vocational Education Act* toward an educational program for black youth.

Restore Funding for Community Alternatives to Imprisonment

According to the U.S. Department of Justice, criminal justice expenditures in the U.S. in 1978 totaled over $24 billion, representing an increase of 129 percent from 1971 to 1978. Until recently, there was an effort to use some of this money to provide community-based programs, such as halfway houses, social services and other resources. Though these programs had limited success and were not without problems, they nevertheless provide a more humane alternative to prison, and also provide some minimum employment opportunities to local communities.

We know from an important study, conducted by Fredric Solomon and his colleagues in the 1960s, that community organization and political mobilization can be very successful in reducing black-on-black crime: "as a result of the need for unity, people begin to know their neighbors and their neighbors' problems. A spirit of common concern pervades the community and serves to discourage crimes of violence" (Solomon *et al.*, 1980: 34).

Consequently, we recommend the substantial allocation of criminal justice funds to local community organizations, which are representative and accountable, involved in crime-control programs and other related social services. Citizen patrols, block organizations, community-based halfway houses and other such social services should be supported.

We oppose inhuman conditions in the prisons. We call for an end to overcrowding, to antiquated facilities, and we call for protection against rape and all forms of sexual abuse. Prisoners should have the right to conjugal visits. Prisoners have a basic human right to work for a decent wage, to have an education, to be given proper nutrition and medical care, to be protected from physical and psychological abuse, and to practice constitutionally protected freedoms (speech, religion, etc.).

While the above basic rights can be won through the legislature and legal system, history teaches us that state officials and professional organizations have been either unwilling or unsuccessful in doing so. Therefore, we believe that the key to winning such rights lies in the political organization of prisoners. We support the right of prisoners to form and belong to prisoner unions and political organizations.

Given the history of repressive practices against politically active prisoners (for example, George Jackson) and against prisoner unions, we also oppose arbitrary and unlawful practices (informers, provocateurs, lockups, beatings, etc.) by prison authorities.

In order to successfully oppose such practices, we must fight for the right of working class and progressive political organizations to freely support and co-operate with prisoners' organizations. This is currently subject to mail censorship, literature censorship and visiting restrictions.

Once these basic political rights have been achieved, it would then be possible to agitate for a variety of reforms, such as decent rehabilitation programs, job training, wages for work grievance procedures, and political and religious freedom.

Conclusion

It is time to go beyond a "radical" criminology that simply exposes the horrors of capitalism and the injustices of criminal justice. The fact that progressive intellectuals are now beginning to recognize the necessity for concrete proposals and short-term reforms is generally a healthy sign that we are approaching a degree of political maturity. At the same time, we must guard against the pendulum swinging so far in the other direction that we abandon the long view and become mired in incrementalism.

So I will conclude on a note of caution. True, we need to develop concrete proposals that speak to the real needs of the people and that recognize the urgent need to comprehend the viciousness of the Right. At the same time, it will be very difficult to achieve even the most modest success and reforms because we are currently experiencing in the United States a concerted mobilization of conservative economic and political power, a "reactionary counter-offensive," to use Andre Gunder Frank's term (1982: 1). Or, as Marlene Dixon has put it (1981), "it is the *implosion* of the Empire, it is the very beginning of an era which the people of the United States will begin to see the democratic striped away. They will begin to experience what has been the fate of the colony."

Consequently, we should not have any illusions about the possibility of finding immediate panaceas; nor should we put all our energies into developing the 'perfect' program or debating the correctness of this or that blueprint for change. As the world and its class relations change, so do the viability and practicality of particular reforms or programs. The concrete proposals listed above, which may make sense under current conditions, might very well be tactically and strategically unsound a few years from now. So we should be careful to resist dogmatic debates about who has a monopoly on *the* correct political manifesto. The viability of a particular proposal or set of proposals is not, after all, going to be settled in the academy or by debate in professional journals and conferences. It can only be settled by practice, by concrete interventions in the political arena of class struggle.

Overall, I think it is a positive sign that we are now beginning to address the serious problem of crime and to formulate progressive policy proposals. At the same time we need to do a great deal of difficult theoretical work, to escape from the intellectual straitjacket of "criminology" and use the complex science of Marxism to get beyond muckraking radicalism. And given that Marxism is, after all, a guide to action, our policy proposals and theoretical enterprises must be informed by and tested in practice. These tasks before us, then, pose a considerable challenge which will require stamina and serious determination. But, however difficult this undertaking, it is necessitated by the horrors of Reaganism and the specter of neofascism.

REFERENCES

Bernstein, Ilene Nagel, William R. Kelly and Patricia Doyle. 1977. "Societal Reaction to Deviants: The Case of Criminal Defendants." *American Sociological Review*. October.

Box, Steven and Chris Hale. 1982. "Economic Crisis and the Rising Prisoner Population in England and Wales." *Crime and Social Justice*. 17.

Cullen, Francis and John Wozniak. 1982. "Fighting the Appeal of Repression: Avenues of Progressive Reform." *Crime and Social Justice*. 18.

Dixon, Marlene. 1982. "World Capitalist Crisis and the Rise of the Right." *Contemporary Marxism*. 4.

Dixon, Marlene. 1981. "The Empire Turns Against Its Once Favored Children." *Plain Speaking* June 1-15.

Dixon, Marlene. 1978. *Women in Class Struggle*. San Francisco: Synthesis Publications.

Frank, Andre Gunder. 1982a. "After Reaganomics and Thatcherism, What?" *Contemporary Marxism*. 4.

.... 1982b. "The Political-Economic Crisis and the Shift to the Right." *Crime and Social Justice*. 17.

Gross, Bertram. 1982. "Some anticrime proposals for Progressives." *Crime and Social Justice* 17.

Hall, Stuart Critcher, Tony Jefferson, John Clarke and Brian Roberts. 1978. *Policing the Crisis: Mugging, the State, and Law and Order*. New York: Holmes and Meier.

Hobsbawn, Eric. 1969. *Bandits*. New York: Delacorte.

Horton, John. 1981. "The Rise of the Right: A Global View." *Crime and Social Justice*. 15.

Hunt, Alan. 1982. "Law, Order and Socialism." *Crime and Social Justice*. 18.

Institute for the Study of Labor and Economic Crisis. 1982. *The Iron Fist and the Velvet Glove: An Analysis of the U.S. Police*. San Francisco: Synthesis Publications.

Irwin, John. 1980. *Prisons in Turmoil*. Boston: Little, Brown and Co.

Nagel, William. 1977. "On Behalf of a Moratorium on Prison Construction." *Crime and Delinquency* April.

Pfohl, Stephen J. 1979. "Deciding on Dangerousness: Predictions of Violence as Social Control." *Crime and Social Justice*. 11.

Platt, Tony. 1978. "Street Crime: A View From the Left." *Crime and Social Justice*. 9.

.... 1982. "Managing the Crisis: Austerity and the Penal System." *Contemporary Marxism*. 4.

Platt, Tony and Paul Takagi. 1981. "Law and Order in the 1980s." *Crime and Social Justice*. 15.

Prison Action Project. 1975. "The Struggle Inside." *Crime and Social Justice*. 4.

Quinney, Richard. 1977. *Class, State and Crime*. New York: David McKay.

Rusche, Georg. 1980. "Labor Market and Penal Sanction" in Platt, Tony and Paul Takagi (eds.), *Punishment and Penal Discipline*. Berkeley: Crime and Social Justice Associates.

Schwendinger, Herman and Julia Schwendinger. 1980. "The New Idealism and Penal Living Standards" in Platt, Tony and Paul Takagi (eds.), *Punishment and Penal Discipline*. Berkeley: Crime and Social Justice Associates.

Schwendinger, Julia and Herman Schwendinger. 1981. "Rape, Sexual Inequality and Levels of Violence." *Crime and Social Justice*. 16.

Solomon, Frederic, Walker L. Garrett J. O'Connor and Jacob R. Fishman. 1980. "Civil Rights Activity and Reduction in Crime Among Negroes." *Crime and Social Justice*. 14.

Swigert, Victoria Lynn and Ronald A. Farrell. 1976. *Murder, Inequality and the Law*. Lexington: D.C. Heath.

Takagi, Paul and Tony Platt. 1982. "Racism and Imprisonment in the United States in the 1980s: A Policy Analysis." Report commissioned by the National Association of Blacks in Criminal Justice.

Taylor, Ian. 1981. *Law and Order: Arguments for Socialism*. London: Macmillan.

Thornberry, Terence P. 1979. "Sentencing Disparities in the Juvenile Justice System." *Journal of Criminal Law and Criminology*. 70.

U.S. Department of Justice. 1981. *Criminal Victimization in the U.S.: 1973-79 Trends.* Washington: U.S. Department of Justice (October).

Wallerstein, Immanuel. 1982. "The USA in Today's World." *Contemporary Marxism*. 4.

CHAPTER 17

CRIMINAL JUSTICE RESEARCH: TWO COMPETING FUTURES

CYRIL ROBINSON
SOUTHERN ILLINOIS UNIVERSITY

Abstract: The Western world is at a crossroads. There are clear signs that we have already entered a period as momentous as the transformation from feudalism to capitalism — a time in which our ways of thinking, organizing, marketing, governing, and most important, our ways of relating to each other are undergoing a simultaneous degeneration of the old and generation of the new. There are two world views in battle. To the extent that we realize the portent of this clash, we can make choices that will enable us to lead rather than to merely flow with the current. As one futurist stated, "The most reliable way to anticipate the future is by understanding the present" (Naisbitt, 1982: 2; see also Wallerstein, 1983a: 68).

Although its exact contours are unclear, the future will be more than a prolongation of the present.[1] What I will be suggesting in this article is not a visionary view of some undefined future, but that we should recognize the meaning of the multitude of events around us that are pointing in the same direction.[2] Moreover, the combination of these events and the impact of Reaganomics have resulted in the reconceptualization and reconstitution of the community, developments which provide opportunities to radicalize social relations.

I will first describe the characteristics of these worldviews and then discuss their intellectual and material heritage. Following this, I will examine the general implications of these competing paradigms for criminal justice research, and indicate areas of inquiry and praxis that appear to satisfy this developing model.

* Originally published in *Crime and Social Justice*, No. 23: 101-128 (1985).
Reprinted by permission of Global Options.

Characteristics of Competing Worldviews

By definition, the predominant world-system and corresponding world perspective permeate all aspects of society and thereby create their own reality. Today's society is patriarchal, hierarchical and dominated by values of self-assertion, competition and "winning at any cost," with control and power exercised from above by a privileged elite. It is characterized by an industrial reality: standardization, specialization, synchronization, concentration, maximization[3] and centralization. It is dependent on irreplaceable fossil fuel. Its institutions are big government, the nation-state, the nuclear family, the giant corporation and the factory-style school, accompanied by mass education, mass media and a blind faith in the power and efficiency of machines.

Life is seen as a competitive struggle in which unlimited progress is possible and desirable through technological growth. The pursuit of knowledge is limited to linear thinking: to a person's ability to subdivide problems into their component parts, to study things in isolation (specialization) and to behave in fixed and predictable ways consistent with concepts of scientific testing, thus rejecting what cannot be quantified, needing experts and ignoring folk wisdom. Here, there is an emphasis on evenly-measured linear time concepts that are required by the money economy and that extend back into the past and look indefinitely into the future. Hence, there is dependence on a belief in evolution and progress. Economic motivation is the primary moving force (Toffler, 1980; Capra, 1982; Naisbitt, 1982).[4]

The alternative vision of reality — the "transindustrial society" (Harmon, 1976), *Creating Alternative Futures* (Henderson, 1978), *The Third Wave* (Toffler, 1980), *The Rising Culture* (Capra, 1982), or *Megatrends* (Naisbitt, 1982), however expressed, has the following characteristics: mass production is giving way to individualized markets, fining production to customized consumer need. There is movement from an industrial to an information-dominated society in which a number of Americans will find employment.[5] Accompanying changes will include: decentralization, production to appropriate scale, use of renewable energy sources, de-urbanization, more working for ourselves and less for the marketplace; self-help and networks replacing hierarchies; participatory democracy inching out representative government; small components linked together in temporary, flexible arrangements; an end of giant multinational corporations in favor of mini-companies or co-operatives; and nation-states giving way to transnational agencies or matrices that mesh different kinds of organizations with common interests. States, local communities and neighborhoods will be the focus of power and decision-making.

Synthesis — thinking in whole, related contexts rather than in fragments — will be the logic of the future. The mechanistic view of causality — a search for a single cause — will be replaced by the system of concept feedback in which causality is viewed as a product of chance and necessity (negative and positive feedback) (Toffler, 1980; Naisbitt, 1982). The universe will no longer be seen as a machine made up of a multitude of objects, but perceived as one indivisible, dynamic whole whose parts are interrelated and can be understood only as patterns of a cosmic process. Out of this network of interlocking concepts and models, social organizations will develop. The shift is from concern with objects to concern for relationships (Capra, 1982: 81, 266; and Harmon, 1976: 32-33). Vast changes are predicted at an ever-increasing rate. Older institutions need not necessarily disappear. Rather they will be reformed to fit within niches appropriate to the new value system.

This is the reformist capitalist view of past and future (See "What the Next 50 Years Will Bring," *U.S. News and World Report*, 9 May 1983). How did these changes evolve, both intellectually and materially, and what is the leftist counter view?

The "Third Wave:" Its Intellectual and Material Heritage

Each of the writers to be discussed made a contribution to this new perspective. Each had certain things in common: (1) an enlarged perspective of the analytic unit; (2) the use of both history and theory (a set of general guiding principles) as part of that perspective; (3) a belief in the fusion between scientists and their product; (4) research conceived as a value-laden commitment; and (5) adoption of a holistic view in preference to a mechanistic research framework.

One of the first to question the industrial paradigm, though he did so in a way limited to his own discipline, was Thomas Kuhn in his now classic *The Structure of Scientific Revolutions*, originally published in 1962 and revised in 1970. Kuhn sought to explain the emergence of a new theory or discovery and how "each scientific revolution alters the historical perspective of the community that experiences it" (Kuhn: ix). He attacked the idea that "scientific development" was a "piecemeal process by which these items have been added, singly and in combination, to the ever growing stockpile that constitutes scientific technique and knowledge." This he called the "development-by-accumulation" concept (*ibid.*: 2). After studying the way scientific discovery took place, Kuhn found that the process could more properly be studied by examining the competing theories current in the scientific community of the time, seeking what "gives those opinions the maximum internal coherence and the closest possible fit to nature" (*ibid.*: 3). The scientific community and its beliefs were inevitably intertwined. Scientific revolutions "necessitated the conmunity's rejection of one time-honored scientific theory in favor of another incompatible with it" (*ibid.*: 6). Thus "both normal science and revolutions are...community-based activities" (*ibid.*: 179).

Alvin Gouldner's *The Coming Crisis of Western Sociology* (1970) was a reply to the rejection of sociological theory by the New Left. To Gouldner, "The criticism and transformation of society can be divorced only at our peril from the criticism and transformation of theories about society" (Gouldner: 3). Like Kuhn, Gouldner held that "theory is always rooted in the theorist's experience" (*ibid.*: 8) because "social science is a *part* of the social world as well as the *conception* of it" (*ibid.*: 13, emphasis in original). Sociology must be "seen in its relation to larger historical trends, to the macro-institutional level, and especially to the state...." As researchers and teachers, sociologists operate out of a particular locale, the university, pursuing careers within a "received occupational culture" (*ibid.*: 14).

Gouldner attacked Talcott Parsons' "ideology of convergence and continuity," seeing it as a conservative view of society (*ibid.*: 18). Methodologies rested "on certain domain assumptions concerning *who and what people are*" and that people may be treated and studied as "things." These are not purely technical matters, but are permeated with ideology (*ibid.*: 50-51, emphasis in original). In place of such traditional notions, Gouldner conceives a Reflective Sociology which refuses to "segregate the intimate or personal from the public and collective;" rather than "a bundle of technical skills, it is a conception of how to live and a total praxis" (*ibid.*: 504). A mission and a "passionate commitment" are required to "help men in their struggle to take possession of what is theirs — society and culture" (*ibid.*: 509). This sociology is "based upon an awareness that the academician and university are...themselves active and willing agents in the dehumanizing of this larger world" (*ibid.*: 512).

Although Kuhn's and Gouldner's views have wider implications, they restricted their critiques to their own disciplines. Both were seeking the same thing, a proper analytic perspective. They achieved their objective by expanding earlier parameters. The historian Fernand Braudel opened, or perhaps reopened, a whole new world as one of the foremost advocates of folk culture, or history from the bottom up.[6] This work initially appeared in French in 1967 under the general title *Civilization and Capitalism, 15th-18th Century*. Volume I was translated into English in 1973, and was then revised in 1981 under the title *The Structures of Everyday Life, The Limits of the Possible*. In 1982, Volume II, *The Wheels of Commerce* appeared in English. Volume III, still untranslated, is entitled *Civilization Materielle Economie et Capitalism*. In writing his treatise, Braudel's task was similar to that of our other authors. In his case, he sought to counter the textbook view that "the development of pre-industrial Europe consisted of its gradual progress toward the rational world of the market, the firm, and capitalist investment, until the coming of the Industrial Revolution, which neatly divides human history in two" (1981: 23).

Braudel saw no such even, incremental development. Instead, his observations disclosed a three-tiered, interacting, and dynamic movement that had been apparent since the 15th century: 1) "the mechanisms of production and exchange linked to rural activities, to small shops and workshops, to banks, exchanges, fairs and (of course) markets...the easily observed processes," the "so-called market economy;" 2) lying underneath this market economy was what Braudel named "*material life or material civilization*...this infra-economy, the formal other half of economic activity, the world of self-sufficiency and barter of goods and services within a very small radius;" and 3) "looking up instead of down from the vast plane of the market economy, one finds that active social hierarchies were constructed on top of it: they could manipulate exchange to their advantage and disturb the established order.... Certain groups of privileged actors were engaged in circuits and calculations that ordinary people knew nothing of" (*ibid.*: 23-24).

This tripartite plan became the framework of Braudel's study of "the whole world." He would "write outside the world of theory, or all theories, and...be guided by concrete observation and comparative history alone. Comparative both through time, using the language...of the long term and the dialectic of past/present...." (*ibid.*: 25). The upper and lower levels form an analytic unit:

> The co-existence of the upper and lower levels forces upon the historian an illuminating dialectic. How can one understand the towns without understanding the countryside, money without barter, the varieties of poverty without the varieties of luxury, the white bread of the rich without the black bread of the poor (*ibid.*: 29)?

Immanuel Wallerstein, a follower of Braudel and a leading thinker of the Fernand Braudel Center for the Study of Economies, Historical Systems, and Civilizations, extended the views of these writers to their logical conclusion — a worldview of historical capitalism (Wallerstein, 1974, 1983a). Each of the authors recounts the intellectual meanderings that led them to a larger perspective (Kuhn, 1970: v-ix; Gouldner, 1970: 3-6). In the case of Wallerstein, this quest is of special interest. Far from being self-conscious and fumbling, such statements empirically support the writer's conclusion that individual scientists and the scientific community are interconnected.

Wallerstein started his "conceptual search...with an interest in the social underpinning of political conflict" in his own society. Neither the theories of Marx which saw "all history" as that of class struggle, nor that of Weber, which added the categories of status-group and party, appeared to be satisfactory to Wallerstein (1974: 3).[7] He sought "to place the issues within a larger intellectual context." He found himself examining ever-expanding analytic units. After looking at postcolonial African states for the "appropriate unit of analysis," he turned to "states in the period after formal independence but before they had achieved something that might be termed national integration." Such a concept, however, included Latin America and even the United States. This led him to the history of early modern Europe, and "some implicit notion of stages of development" (*ibid.*: 6).

> Finally, there seemed to be another difficulty. If given societies went through "stages," that is, had a "natural history," what of the world-system itself? Did it not have "stages," or at least a "natural history"?.... It seemed to me it did. It was at this point that I abandoned the idea altogether of taking either the sovereign state or that vaguer concept, the national society, as the unit of analysis. I decided that needier one was a social system and that one could only speak of social change in social systems. The only social system in this scheme was the world-system (*ibid.*: 7).

Wallerstein was then faced with the problem of the empirical manageability of such a project. Social scientists, used to quantification of their research findings, have often chosen to avoid examining the operation of a social system which more easily lends itself to historical narrative than to quantification.

> Thus the quantifiability of data determined the choice of research problems which then determined the conceptual apparatuses with which one defined and handled the empirical data. It should be clear...that this is an inversion of the scientific process. Conceptualization should determine research tools, at least most of the time, and not vice versa (*ibid.*: 8).

Wallerstein's views on commitment and the social relations of the social scientist and his product are very similar to those of Kuhn and Gouldner. "For recounting the past is a social act of the present and affecting the social system of the present" (*ibid.*: 9). His concept of objectivity is very specific to the social system in which it takes place: "Insofar as the system is lopsided, concentrating certain kinds of research activity in the hands of particular groups, the results will be 'biased' in favor of these groups" (*ibid.*: 9-10). Like Gouldner, and perhaps Kuhn, Wallerstein's research has a mission: "It depends on our image of the good society" (*ibid.*: 10).

For our purposes, the essence of Wallerstein's analysis is that instead of viewing the world as a series of independent though loosely linked economies, he sees one world capitalist system. That there are certain core countries (for example, the U.S., Japan, the Soviet Union) to which certain semi-peripheral countries (for example, Italy, Israel, Saudi Arabia, Canada) relate and on which certain peripheral countries (for example, those of Africa, South America and most of the rest of the world) depend in a system of unequal exchange, is less important than the way his ideas fit into the debate on how social scientists are beginning to view their world. The world-systems perspective, in part, arises as a critique of modernization theory which held that nation-states were independent units with inequalities being determined by conditions attributable to these states (Bach, 1980: 290-291, 294). "The meaning of the social whole and its parts follows from this example. Whether we are talking about a world-order or a nation-state, the whole in this instance is nothing more than the sum of its individual parts" (*ibid.*: 291). Wallerstein's perspective is different:

> The key conceptual innovation is that a world-system consists of a set of singular processes.... It is the singularity of the processes which constitutes the world capitalist system and distinguishes it as a social whole.... The implication here is that the "structures" we normally use, to organize our thinking and observation and which are said to form the parts of the whole, are no longer useful as a way *of proceeding* analytically.... For the world-systems perspective, then, the whole consists of a singular process which *forms* and *reforms* the relations that express patterns or structures (Bach, 1980: 294-5, emphasis in original; Wallerstein, 1977: 118, 140).

Popularizing World-System Theory

It was the writers I earlier mentioned (Toffler, 1980; Capra, 1982; Naisbitt, 1982) who brought the insights of these scholars to popular literature. Toffler employs waves as his "grand metaphor," describing the present as consisting of "colliding waves of change" (cf. Capra, 1982: 419; Robinson, 1982). As his main analytic concept, Toffler suggests that the "invisible edge," the splitting apart by the industrial revolution of production and consumption, is what disrupts family, education and work productivity, and is at the bottom of numerous other industrial world problems. Citing Braudel, Toffler classifies the economy into A and B sectors. A sector comprises all unpaid work that people do for themselves. B sector consists of the production of goods or services through market exchange. In First Wave (agricultural) societies, sector A is dominant. In Second Wave (industrial) societies, sector B is dominant. The gap between the producer and consumer is the primary articulating factor of Second Wave civilization. To the extent that this gap narrows, "the entire function, role and power of the market is brought into question" (Toffler: 293).

In Second Wave society, "the very word 'economy' was defined to exclude all forms of work or production not intended for the market," and therefore Sector A has become all but invisible (*ibid.*: 284). This means that the work of the housewife, cleaning and child-rearing, or reconstructing one's own home or community, is seen as outside the economy and therefore as nonproductive. Trends in the economy, however, show that the relationship between production and consumption is shifting toward an economy with Section A characteristics.

Fritjof Capra, like Kuhn a physicist, makes his greatest contribution in rejecting linear "rational" thinking in favor of an analytic process which synthesizes, is holistic, intuitive (see Kuhn, 1970: 175), and in harmony with the natural flow of nature. This takes its inspiration from Chinese culture and Taoist philosophy (*ibid.*: 37). The Cartesian (Descartes) heritage of division between mind and body (I think, therefore I exist) led to the conception of the universe as a mechanistic system, to the separation of psychiatry and medicine into two separate specialties, academia into multiple disciplines and to conceiving analysis as the job of reducing matter into fundamental building blocks. As a result of our social and cultural evolution

> [w]e have modified our environment to such an extent...that we have lost touch with our biological and ecological base more than any other culture and any other civilization in the past (*ibid.*: 42).

One casualty of linear thinking is the loss of the concept of the whole (the trees for the forest). In words reminiscent of Braudel and Gouldner, Capra states:

> Living systems are organized in such a way that they form multi-leveled structures, each level consisting of subsystems which are whole in regard to their parts, and parts with respect to the larger wholes.... All these entities — from molecules to human beings, and on to social systems — can be regarded as wholes in the sense of being integrated structures, and also as parts of larger wholes at higher levels of complexity. In fact, we shall see that parts and wholes in an absolute sense do not exist at all (*ibid.*: 43).

A fragmented view of reality has its analytic casualties. Capra complains that science proceeds with little theory (*ibid.*: 119): though biologists know a great deal about the fragments of the body, they know little about the "phenomenon of healing," of the function of living systems as wholes, their interaction with their environment, the integrative action of the nervous system, or about "how we breathe, regulate our body temperature, digest, or focus our attention" (*ibid.*: 123, 103). Research is restricted to specific etiologies of specific diseases. Technological innovation has replaced the search for why disease occurs (*ibid.*: 129, 130, 151). The same weakness can be found in the social sciences and economics (*ibid.*: 188; Fisk, 1980).

On the other hand, Capra's "new vision of reality" embodies the "systems view" which:

> Looks at the world in terms of relationships and integration. Systems are integrated wholes whose properties cannot be reduced to those of smaller units. Instead of concentrating on basic building blocks or basic substances, the systems approach emphasizes basic principles of organization.... All these natural systems are wholes whose specific structures arise from the interactions and interdependence of their parts. Systems thinking is process thinking; form becomes associated with process, interrelation with interaction, and opposites unified through oscillation.... The behavior of the individual parts can, in fact, be so unique and irregular that it bears no sign of relevance to the order of the whole system. This order is achieved by coordinating activities that do not rigidly constrain the parts but leave room for variation and flexibility, and it is this flexibility that enables living organisms to adapt to new circumstances (*ibid.*: 266-268; Boulding, 1978: 19; for applications of this concept to politics, see Lewis, 1983: 98).

Instead of a pyramid, symbolizing a hierarchy in which orders are transmitted through a rigid system of domination and control, Capra uses the metaphor of a tree in which power flows in both directions, with neither end dominating the other and all levels interacting in independent harmony to support the functioning whole (*ibid.*: 282). Capra asks the same question posed by some of the earlier scholars: "Can there be a science that is not based exclusively on measurement; an understanding of reality that includes quality and experience and yet can be called scientific?" (*ibid.*: 375). Yes, as long as the research satisfies two requisites: "all knowledge must be based on systematic observation, and it must be expressed in terms of self-consistent but limited and approximate models. These requirements — the empirical basis and the process of model building — represent to me the two essential elements of the scientific method" (*ibid.*: 375-376; Harmon, 1976: 95).

As evidence that this new view of reality is already on its way, Capra cites various advances in soft technology in harmony with the environment, such as solar heating, and the ecological, women's, and various citizens' movements, as well as public interest consumer groups. These "are also the sources of emerging counter-economies based on decentralization, cooperative, and ecological harmonious life styles, and involving the bartering of skills and home-produced goods and services" (*ibid.*: 408-410). Like Toffler, Capra notices the phenomenal growth of the non-monetary underground economy (*ibid.*: 411). Such unidirectional movement is also evident in changes in consumer and worker styles, in health practices and in the coming together of unrelated groups for joint action to protect the environment, for the nuclear freeze, or against the bomb (*ibid.*: 413-418).

Naisbitt, not a scientist but a "social forecaster, speaker and adviser to many of America's leading corporations" (book jacket), affirms and complements the observations of Toffler and Capra. His findings are based on an analysis of two million articles from local newspapers about local events during a 12-year period (Naisbitt, 1982: 3). He concludes that what is going on in America today is what is going on locally; that America is a "bottom-up society," because while fads may come from the top down, new trends begin in cities and local communities (*ibid.*: 3). Naisbitt argues that the U.S. has moved from an industrial to an information-based society (*ibid.*: 11-24). He notes that the U.S. has long been in decline as a world leader (*ibid.*: 56). Among other factors, Naisbitt attributes this to "the short-term orientation of American managers" in contrast to that of the Japanese (*ibid.*: 79). Such self-destructive activity results from demands for immediate results, that is, profits and "quantitative measurements of performance" (*ibid.*: 81-83).

He suggests that in reaction against this bureaucratized, centralized and industrialized society there is a movement toward decentralization; that power is leaving the federal government and moving toward cities, towns and neighborhoods; that there is self-help in health care, birth and family living alternatives; that there is self-education, job creation by small business, participatory democracy and the restructuring of corporations, local political initiatives, workers' rights and participation in corporate planning (*ibid.*: 97-187) and the replacement of hierarchical arrangements with networks ("people talking to each other, sharing ideas, information and resources" *ibid.*: 192). Networks represent a symbol and an agent for societal change. There is no hierarchy. Each network is a center; it is egalitarian rather than elitist because every co-worker is a peer. Networks form because hierarchies cannot solve problems and persons begin working outside them (*ibid.*: 197-199). "Today we live in a world of overlapping networks, not just a constellation of networks but a galaxy of networking constellations" (*ibid.*: 205; for the growth of oil co-op networks, for example, see *New York Times*, 28 August 1983: F8; cf. Naroll, 1983). The message sent by these writers from different fields and objectives is clear that our conception of the universe must change from a linear, fragmented, single causation perspective to a systems or ecological approach in which our activities are more in harmony with nature; that our patriarchal, hierarchical, corporate-dominated, hard technocracy world is dooming and doomed (Gorz, 1980: 64); that as scientists we must become engaged in this struggle; and that this vision is not a forecast of a wished-for millenium but is based on a largely unrecognized present. To what extent are the criticisms leveled at other areas relevant to criminal justice research, and how is this provisional future appropriate for criminal justice?

The Current State of Criminal Justice Research

Because the following points have been well expressed elsewhere and these propositions are unimportant to the main thrust of this article, they will be stated rather than elaborated. My critique can be reduced to five propositions which generally parallel what has been said earlier namely that criminal justice research: 1) lacks long-range theory (Willis, 1983: 447; Johnson, 1980; Bayley, 1979: 137; Monkkonin, 1979: 452; Harring, 1976: 54-55; Platt, 1975: 6); 2) is present or future oriented, with little historical depth (Conley, 1980; Hofrichter, 1978); 3) is narrowly utilitarian, that is, researchers have the burden of showing the immediate use to which their research can be put (Quinney, 1973: chapter 3; Platt, 1975; Wallerstein, 1974: 9-10); 4) is unrelated to popular culture and to its use by common people (Capra, 1982: 103; D. Johnson, 1979; Ericson, 1982; Wallerstein, 1974: 10; Takagi, 1982: 41); 5) rarely grapples with important questions of power, preferring to deal with methodological inquiry or quantifiable subsidiary matters (Boulding, 1981: 10; McDonald, 1981); and 6) is technically rather than value-oriented (Gouldner, 1970: 8; Wallerstein, 1974: 10; Platt, 1975: 3). Such results are preordained by denial of funding or access to data for research which challenges establishment ideology (Longmire, 1982: 19).

Overall, these criticisms add up to an industrial view of reality, specialization, fragmentation and domination by methodology, all to the exclusion of value-oriented, committed and passion-directed research (Harmon, 1976: 124). Given that criminal justice research is flawed, what difference does such a view of reality make? There is nothing magical about long-range theory. It is necessary only because it potentially leads to fundamental explanations which in turn generate research that may make a difference in the way people run their lives. Rather than helping people solve their everyday problems, criminal justice research helps to mystify, obfuscate and complicate possible solutions. In a word, its looking constantly at parts serves to hide the whole. In today's world, it is impossible to explain crime by studying crime or the institutions which combat crime. Likewise, it is wrong-headed to study independently the myriad problems that plague us. A list of the "social problems" found in current social problems texts is enlightening: spouse and child abuse, child runaways, divorce, illegitimacy, abortion, aging family members, mental stress, alcoholism, drug abuse, prostitution, single-parent families, teen-age pregnancies, dissatisfaction with work, inadequate health care, mental illness, stress, violence, rape, dissemination of handguns, nuclear arms, pornography, juvenile delinquency, organized crime, environmental problems, overpopulation, poverty, maldistribution of wealth, corporate power, gang warfare, employee and customer theft, incest, suicides, murders and gambling (Hartgen, 1977; Johnson, 1977; Horton and Leslie, 1978; Scarpitti, 1980).

Are the problems on this list in any way related to criminal justice? Are they (and which ones) even a subject for criminal justice research, or are they "properly" the domain of sociology, or one segment of sociology — social problems? Our approach, assuming as criminal justice researchers we are at all interested, is to select one problem and find its cause: the cause of juvenile delinquency, of drug abuse, or of gang warfare. We perceive our society as if it were a doll factory turning out huge percentages of "defective" dolls. As researchers, we sit outside the factory in little individual, separated and sealed houses, one house for fixing defective fingers, another for ears, another for right feet, left feet, hair and so forth. No one deals with the whole doll and certainly few ask what's wrong with the factory. If we do not ask the right questions, we cannot set out in the right direction to find the answers.

Implications of These Paradigms for Criminal Justice Research

Is there anything about our society that is unifying, that must drive us toward a holistic, theory-based view of the crime problem? Whether one is a Marxist or not, social scientists must take into their 'database' the economic history of the country relative to criminogenic behavior. For example, the fact that "business cycles, panics and depressions" are endemic to our economy, that 33 expansions and contractions can be chronicled between 1834 and 1975, gives us some perspective on today's depression (Moore, 1980: 151; Wallerstein, 1980: 5; 1977: 122) and speaks to the instability of life for persons and communities in the United States.

Likewise, it is important to realize that aggregate statistics can hide significantly different lifestyles, economic disparities and geographical shifts in wealth and power. In the post-Civil War period, the U.S. can best be described as a dual economy in which the North and West experienced dynamic growth, while the South lagged behind in a semi-colonial, underskilled and undercapitalized status to be exploited by Northern capital. "The consumption side of this maldevelopment was woefully low incomes and their accompaniment of malnutrition, disease, infant and adult mortality, illiteracy — and a comparatively high endemic violence" (Cohen, 1981: 3).

That picture of wealth-accumulating activity dividing the population in two has not changed, but the areas of the country affected have been almost inverted, thus making enforced mobility a constant of American life. The 1980 census shows that population, economic activity and wealth have shifted from the North to the South and West (Naisbitt, 1982: 207-208; King and Rees, 1982: 28). What has all this to do with crime causation?

> Much of the phenomenon that we call crime is the direct, and much the indirect, consequences of these institutional disruptions and injuries.... The workings of causation may be direct, from social instability to disrupted or disturbed family to individual crime; but they may be indirect, for example, by the formation of "subcultures" within which what is criminal to the encompassing society becomes normal. A fuller understanding of these chains of causation and their meanings and resonances requires a more ambitious exploration across customary disciplinary boundary lines than has been common in either academic or vocational practice (Cohen, 1981: 6-7).

These "megatrends," the mass migrations of peoples, the pauperization of one part of the population and the capitalization of another has the long-term effect of reconstituting and reconceptualizing the community, a point dealt with below. From a practical and conceptual standpoint, the problem is an old one — how to join structure which is a sociological and praxis construct with the individual *in* society (MacGuire, 1984). With reference to criminal justice, we can think in terms of a style of life which reflects low incidence of criminal activity. While there are many theories of human personality development, that of Abraham Maslow is particularly useful. Maslow's work emphasizes normal human fulfillment rather than human pathology. In seeking to learn about the highest potential of human beings, Maslow constructed a hierarchy of human needs. Basic needs include certain physiological needs (food, water, etc.); next, there are safety needs (approval of self and others). Each of these needs can be fulfilled only when the needs lower on the hierarchy have been actualized. Thus, until persons have physical needs satisfied, they cannot be or feel safe and secure; without either physical or security satisfaction, one cannot feel, or have belongingness, or love and so on. Mere fulfillment of physiological needs can maintain but cannot enhance life. The ultimate result of the fulfillment of the entire hierarchy of needs will be the full expression of the individual (Maddi, 1976: 93-102).

Using this "full expression of the individual personality" as a measure of well-being, let us apply our "new reality" analysis to a phenomenon of contemporary society: the latch-key child. That tag has been given to children whose parents, both father and mother, work. Parents either lock them in the house, or if the children are not of school age, they hang a key around their neck. Such unsupervised children are denied Maslow's safety and esteem needs. Their condition leaves them subject to accident, mistreatment from other children and adults, drug abuse, criminal activity, truancy, the temptation to run away and the like. The latch-key child arises from no single cause but from a series of interrelated structural transformations.

Capitalist development in core countries resulted in the changeover from a household to a factory economy. In the feudal period, the home had been the economic unit in which all food, clothing and tools were made by the collaborative work of the family. Under the factory system, the family moved or was moved away from the farm and to the town, so as to be near the factory. There, one or more of the family worked to earn money to buy food. The family, no longer able to produce its own food, was dependent on the employer for its livelihood.[8] More recently, as a result of inflation, increased aspirations in terms of material needs and education for children and the demand for additional workers during the wars, women entered the work force in ever-increasing numbers. Between 1970 and 1980, the percentage of women employed jumped 58 percent, so that by 1982, 43.4 percent of the work force was women (*N.Y. Times Book Review*, 31 October 1982: 2). Of families with children, 5.8 million or 19.1 percent are one-parent families, a high percentage of whom are women in poverty raising children. The effect on black families is particularly grim (*New York Times*, 29 January 1984: 20E). This trend, termed the "feminization of poverty," has the natural result that in the world's wealthiest nation, 21 percent of its children live in poverty (*Wall Street Journal*, 8 August 1983: 1; Ehrenreich and Piven, 1983).[9] Since the U.S. has the highest divorce rate in the world (Naroll, 1983: 357), huge numbers of these become latch-key children. Estimates run from six to seven million (*New York Times*, 14 August 1983: Y21). Few childcare facilities are available, or when available, are beyond the financial resources of most families. The latch-key child may now be disappearing to be replaced by the abused child, as more parents are at home unemployed. With unemployment comes stress, low esteem and hopelessness, easily translated into the anger and violence that makes the U.S. one of the world's highest child abusers (Naroll, 1983: 247, 252). A true "causal" analysis also would have to include Wallerstein's world-system analysis, which sees industrial blue-collar jobs migrating to peripheral, Third World countries in search of cheaper labor, and the replacing of unskilled labor with high technology, "more efficient" machines (Wallerstein, 1977: 136; Aronowitz, 1983: 36).

To attack such problems by counseling individual children or parents for the secondary results of drug or child abuse, truancy, or juvenile delinquency is futile.[10] Synthesizing some of the concepts that have been discussed — community, networking, the interrelationship between the whole and the parts, decentralization, self-help, the importance of social relationships as compared to objects — begins to provide the basis for a coherent direction.

The dialectic of the latch-key child starts with an understanding of the separation of the community from itself. People have become dependent on a series of economic, social and political rituals that for many no longer work. The trends described in this paper represent the individual reactions of millions of people finding new ways to help them lead better lives. As radical researchers, our task is to find the means to understand and encourage these trends — to find the appropriate analytic unit for study and praxis. I propose the "neighborhood," still a nexus that unites individual interdependencies (kinship networks) with cultural, economic and political ties outside that unit (Elias, 1978: 61). Little is known about the internal dynamics of neighborhoods. Studies of migratory currents, economic and market forces impinging on the neighborhood, individual motivations and internal organization, as well as a kind of Wallerstein study of its core-peripheral relations with the outside world, can tell us about how legitimate and illegitimate activities fit together; how social control on the horizontal level (network) or vertical level (outside institutions — police departments and courts) merge, clash, or cancel each other out. Studies detailing the everyday life of people, how they cope with work-a-day problems; the mix of criminal and non-criminal behavior; its integration into the daily work schedule of both the neighborhood dweller and the police officer (D. Johnson, 1979); and how 'crime' blends into neighborhood culture, and is acted upon by the criminal justice system, should provide the road maps necessary to help neighborhoods move in the direction they wish.

THE NEIGHBORHOOD AS A SUBJECT OF ACTIVIST RESEARCH

There are several reasons why leftists should turn their attention to neighborhood communities. Mass politics in the U.S. shows little sign of being a viable means of promoting a socialist direction. In taking this view, Aronowitz (1983: 9-10) suggests that leftists must carve out a "public sphere" within a capitalist private world. This public sphere consists of three prongs: the trade union, the political party and finally alternative institutions — cultural, social and educational — where in the past workers received their education about possibilities of building a new society.

But today, many leftist groups are engaged in instrumental, one-issue struggles. Though these are valuable in themselves, they are basically defensive and contribute little to the building of a public sphere, a task left to a few left-wing journals (*ibid.*: 16-21). Aronowitz poses the same question as André Gorz before him: how to build a socialist society within the interstices of a capitalist one? The common misery of parts of the working class can no longer be thought of as a revolutionary primer (Gorz, 1967: 3). Leftists are beginning, therefore, to address possible alternative outcomes to capitalism, seeing the present crisis as a period of possible transition, and are trying to think through (imagine) strategies leading to a socialist-leaning future (Aronowitz, 1983; Bowles *et al.*, 1983; Ehrenreich, 1983; Wallerstein, 1983a; Wright, 1983).

Perhaps because of their commitment to radical change by mass movement, leftists have generally overlooked the possibility that the expansion of the "public sphere" might come through local community action and development. Leftists have concentrated on changes in structure which would purportedly lead to changes in social relations, rather than believing in the process of building a foundation of better social relations leading to a more equitable structure (Gornick, 1983: 18). Most leftists have tried to find a "better" hierarchical arrangement rather than finding ways to replace hierarchy by other social arrangements. Following Marxist logic, leftists have relied on the "working-class" vanguard, whereas in the U.S., it has been the working class that is most captive by vertical institutions, split by race, sex and false class interests. In other words, leftists hoped to use as the building blocks of revolution the socially dispersed products of capitalism rather than the social and ecological whole — the community from which the workers had been sundered. Now that many of these same workers have been returned as obsolete to the community, it is perhaps time to re-evaluate the potentiality of the community as an agent of social change.[11] Three interrelated structural factors should turn leftists to the community as potential building blocks of a society based on the alternative direction I have outlined: 1) a reconceptualization of the American community; 2) the expansion of the underground economy; and 3) a resurgence of community organizing and networking. Although this article cannot extensively develop these themes, it will emphasize their importance as research directions.

Reconceptualization of the American Community

Reconceptualization of the American community to eliminate its "nonproductive" portion has naturally followed from the reconstitution of the work force, the result of recurrent crises in capital accumulation.[12] By implementing a kind of triage of the population, Reagan's policies have merely given political coherence to this structural event. Triage is a concept developed during World War II to separate the wounded into three groups: those who were not seriously wounded and needed no treatment; those who were seriously wounded but with treatment had a good chance to survive; and those who, regardless of treatment, could not survive. While Democratic Party policies implicitly accepted the fact that there was no productive place in American society for large parts of the minority and female population, they nevertheless sustained that population with welfare, small grants and an assortment of professional services. Reagan policies have taken the next logical step. Recognizing that this segment, together with much of the blue-collar population, has no further productive place in the capitalist community, the elite now in power is in the process of withdrawing this support.[13] This withdrawal is more than a struggle over transfer payments. It represents fundamental change in the way these elites view the American community. It flows from a series of changes in the American industrial landscape, including the increased geographical (ghettoization of Old Cities) — (Gordon, 1978), occupational, and social separation of these groups from other Americans, and a bust and boom phenomenon that cycles beyond the reach of this population (King and Rees, 1982: 28-31). Such a situation is very different from the treatment given blacks as slaves, or women as extensions of their husbands, or immigrants as unwanted foreigners who were polluting Anglo-Saxon purity. In these instances, conflict took clear-cut forms, such as exclusionary legislation or denial of specific rights. Here, there is no attempt at physical exclusion, solely a recognition of a structural condition: persons who are not needed to produce for someone else simply do not economically exist.

The Underground Economy

Where an economic and political organization fails to meet the need of large numbers of people, which accurately describes our present economy, counter-systems evolve to fill that gap and to support more and more people. Braudel has shown that the material life of the people has a historical foundation. Underground material life has expanded under the pressures of a degenerating system.

> The market economy still controls the great mass of transactions *that show up in the statistics*. But...today as in the past...the only *real* capitalism...is multinational.... [I]n the wake of the economic depression following the 1973-4 crisis, we are beginning to see the development of a modern version of the non-market economy: hardly disguised forms of barter, the direct exchange of services, 'moonlighting' as it is called, plus all the various forms of homework and "odd-jobs." This layer of activity, lying below or alongside the market, has reached sufficient proportions to attract the attention of several economists: some have estimated that it may represent 30 or 40 percent of the gross national product, which thus lies outside all official accounting, even in industrialized countries (Braudel, 1981: 23-25, emphasis in original).

Evidence of this kind, of a rich fabric of community activity, suggests that there is an irregular, underground, counter, subterranean, or alternative economy. This is created by the pressure of government rules, regulations and taxes, and by the limited access to the "regular" economic system, consisting of both cash and non-cash exchange as payments for part-time and casual labor, as well as various quasi-legal and illegal transactions. There is a range of reciprocal services, co-ops, swaps and bartering. It "provides employment for those unemployable in the legal economy; employment for those — like the retired who draw social security, or illegal aliens without resident status — whose freedom to work is restricted; and incentive to do additional work for those who would not do it if they were taxed." It deprives the government of billions in tax revenue. The total value of such an economy has been estimated as the equivalent of $1,522.72 for every family of four in the United States (Gutmann, 1977; Simon and Witte, 1982: xii). A more recent estimate is five percent of the $3 trillion GNP, or about $150 billion, of which crime may account for $5 to $10 billion per year (*New York Times*, 23 October 1983: 3: 1). One study showed that one of five Harlem adults gained their incomes from illegal underground sources (Simon and Witte, 1982: 292). As a yard or garage sale, the underground economy is apparent on any street corner, a people's exchange peripheral to the regular market system. From a radical point of view, its significance is to reunite the "producer" with the consumer, a departure from advanced capitalist market relations.

Such an economy has received scant analytic attention.[14] Its structural rationale lies in the occupational and residential restrictions forced on racial and ethnic groups. These restrictions, together with the growth of unions, bureaucracies, specialization and technology, create a potential labor force for the irregular economy. Thus, the irregular economy arises out of three sets of circumstances: 1) the imperfect distribution of goods and services (high prices and lack of proximity to population in these areas); 2) the blocked opportunity structure for low-income and minority groups (Ferman and Ferman, 1973); and 3) the imposition of laws and regulations making huge areas of market activity illegal or legal only with the benediction of government authority (Simon and Witte, 1982: 293).[15]

For a neighborhood, a crucial feature of the irregular economy is that a worker may be better off when employed in the irregular economy but unemployed in the regular economy. Irregular employment, as against regular employment, may provide relief from pressures of work and credit; it often provides a steadier income (as in the case of welfare payments) and therefore a more stable and predictable existence (Ferman and Ferman, 1973; Ferman *et al.*, 1978).

Yet the interrelationships between this economic counter-system and the social and political structure of the community remain unclear.[16] To what extent are new social relationships taking form upon which can be built internal strengths in terms of social control, conflict resolution, joint action, economic self-improvement and, if need be, concerted political action? There seem to be few microanalytic studies of neighborhoods seeking to understand the workings of this irregular political economy. Even the Ferman studies are limited to economic aspects and are less concerned with its social and political consequences.

Community Organizing and Networking

Traditional leftist theory has tended to see and portray power as emanating from two sources: the state, as the instrumental organ of a unified capitalist class, and its opposition, the organized workers led by a vanguard party. Michael Foucault, on the other hand, has taught that "power and micropower relations permeate every structure of a society" (Denzin, 1982: 117). Andre Gorz, too, has rejected the idea of a revolutionary seizure as the way to power, stating instead:

> The only possible line for the movement is to seize, from the present on, those powers which will prepare it to assume the leadership of society and which will permit it in the meantime to control and to plan the development of the society, and to establish certain limiting mechanisms which will restrict or dislocate the power of capital (1967: 8).

Power may be harvested where it is sown. But like any crop, it must be planted in properly irrigated and fertilized soil, and must be carefully tended until it is ripe to be gathered. Community organization has developed slowly under a variety of guises, in some instances the taking of political control, but more often in the form of neighborhood block associations. Sometimes these have been formed for progressive purposes. Often, however, these "defended neighborhoods" (Suttles, 1972) have been organized for purposes leftists would deplore. Nevertheless, the extent of that organization is impressive. In 1977, New York City was estimated to have 3,500 separate block organizations engaged in organizing neighborhood councils, community-based crime prevention, health and mental health, daycare and family counseling facilities (Schwartz, 1979: 9). Another estimate calculated that there were 20,000 volunteer crime fighting groups, with New York City alone purportedly possessing 250 anticrime patrols (Troyer and Dean, 1982). Gross (1982) has collected a number of neighborhood initiatives such as block associations, Guardian Angel groups and the organization of street gangs and drug addicts.

National organizations networking local communities include National People's Action, National Neighbors, the National Association of Neighborhoods, the National Center for Urban Ethnic Affairs and ACORN. Rather than competing with each other, they serve different geographical areas or assert different strategies or philosophies of social and political action (Schwartz, 1979: 11). Other neighborhood groups have combined to sponsor academies to train "neighborhood organizers, environmentalists, feminists, unionists," and have formed Citizens Action, an organization that links political action statewide (*In These Times*, 10-23 August 1983: 2). The movement has its own "information service," *The Neighborhood Works*, a monthly publication reporting on everything from urban gardeners and back-alley garbage recycling to a 10-year report by a university urbanologist on the successes and failures of the Chicago South Shore Bank in financing projects in minority neighborhoods.

Leftists have also made local political gains — political office in Santa Monica and Santa Cruz, California and Burlington, Vermont, with the inevitable Gorz-like question being posed: "Is it mere reformism? If so, is mere reformism acceptable?" (*In These Times*, 1-14 June 1983: 2; Kann, 1983). Harold Washington's victory in Chicago, based on the neighborhood organization of black "nonvoters," together with incumbent black mayors in Detroit, Los Angeles, Philadelphia and Atlanta, provided the urban base for Jesse Jackson's assertion of minority national political power (Herbers, *New York Times Magazine*, 4 September 1983: 22). No clear answer can be given as to where reformism stops and radical change begins, but leftists in power have succeeded in bringing more and different groups into the political process, have considered options foreclosed to the capitalist mind and have the opportunity to educate the populace to a holistic and ecological view of city management.[17] Perhaps the best response was given by the South Shore Bank report mentioned above:

> [T]o the degree that a development institution increases economic literacy, makes clear to citizens what it can and can't do, points out why some lines of development cannot proceed without changes in public policy, and helps think through development strategies, mobilizes resources, and builds models of local community enterprises, to that degree a development institution may contribute to the larger requirements of neighborhood economic and political development (*The Neighborhood Works*, August 1983: 16).

Future Criminal Justice Research Directions

Taking these three strains — the reconstitution and reconceptualization of community, the underground economy and the resources of community organizing and networking, what criminal justice research directions are indicated? Almost every criminal justice concern can be placed under some subhead of social control. As discussed earlier with reference to the latch-key child, capitalist development was accompanied by the passing of control over local "citizens" from the community to the state, thereby imposing on the community new and foreign values. Consistent with the management of masses of people, dominant values became depersonalized and rationalized, replacing the primary relationship of family and community with formal controls, *gesellschaft* over *gemeinschaft* (Suttles, 1972: 29-31; Bender, 1978: 111; Pontell, 1982: 133).

Although formal controls became dominant, they were not extirpated. It is useful to recall traditional means of social control in simpler societies. As one Canadian Native American expressed it, "At that time, long time ago, there was really no wrong to be done...because there was nothing else but survival" (Nielsen, 1982: 2). Toleration in such a society would be ended when the individual's behavior indicated it might seriously affect the group's survival, "whether by causing dissension within the group, by jeopardizing food gathering or by provoking others — spirits or human, who could take offense at the group for the behavior of one of its members" (*ibid.*: 3).

"Respect," propagated by the elders, was an all-encompassing value that led to practices such as sharing food, work, objects and children:

> Wrongdoing occurred when people did not show respect — when they stole someone's horse or wife, when they fought with or tried to harm someone, when they got jealous or are impolite. All these acts, directly or indirectly, affected the survival of the group because they destroyed the harmony and therefore the working effectiveness of the unit (*ibid.*: 6).

Children learned "crime" prevention from engaging in activities with adults, being counseled when they did wrong, being told stories about right conduct, and punishments to people who did wrong (*ibid.*: 9).

In drawing lessons from traditional societies, it is necessary to separate romance from vision and myth from reality. Traditional social scientists have constructed a mythical history of communities based on the view of industrial reality described earlier. Out of modernization theory and the Chicago School of sociology, urbanization, immigration and industrialization emerged as the causes of the conversion of a homogenous, idealized, *gemeinschaft*, rural, relation-based society to an associational one of loyalties to formal, vertical institutions. This was seen as a progressive (in both senses, forward and better), unidirectional and evolutionary movement. Instead of individuals having the totality of their daily transactions in the community, their lives were seen as bifurcated into public-private spheres — communal and noncommunal — where attention to the public or communal sphere was one of "limited liability" (Bender, 1978: 28, 60).

While this picture may have a certain validity when applied to middle-class communities, it is false and simplistic when used for working-class neighborhoods. In such communities,[18] recent research has shown family continuity, a network of supportive kin and non-kin relationships, co-operative living arrangements, barter and reciprocal interchange (Lein, 1984; Bender, 1978: 134-135; Stack 1974). With specific reference to social control, it is generally agreed that formal institutions — courts, police and schools — have been ineffective in maintaining a safe and secure community. In fostering the kind of respect present in traditional societies and in handing down to the next generation a coherent moral code, they have abysmally failed, partly because the description of reality which these institutions provide is totally at variance with what inner-city young people need to survive on city streets (Suttles, 1972: 194-95). In a 1962-65 Chicago study of four adjacent black, Italian, Puerto Rican and Mexican inner-city neighborhoods, it was found that the inability of the police and other formal social control institutions to carry out their law enforcement function effectively transferred that responsibility to local residents, in this case mostly adolescent males (*ibid.*: 190). Youth gangs, with varying success, depending in part on the relationship in each society of the young men to the adult males in their families, maintained relative peace and security in their communities. A crucial factor, as in traditional Indian families, was the amount of intergenerational respect between younger and older members.

Such inner-city organization is not referred to as an exemplary model ("the long-range consequence may have been to help perpetuate the ethnic opposition and mutual distrust that prevailed"), but to counter the once-current idea that inner cities are disorganized vestiges of a former glorious past (*ibid.*: 200). Community today, as in bygone days, represents a place where there is a "cohesion" consisting of a "positive and sentimental attachment to neighbors local establishments and local traditions to the exclusion of other persons, establishments, and traditions," a common sharing of local information and inside "dope," and association with neighborhood-defined groups — schools, churches and athletic teams. Attachments to the community tend to be total for most women and children, sharing a range of whole rather than fragmentary interests with their neighbors. These interests become an end in themselves rather than being merely instrumental to attain other goals (*ibid.*: 1972: 34; Bender, 1978: 8-9). With the permanent sectioning off of large parts of the blue-collar work force, men are increasingly spending large parts of their lives in the community. Leftists can aid in "reconstructing" these neighborhoods by turning "jobs" back into work and in helping to re-form fragments into social relational wholes.

What Can We Do?

"Reconstructing" a neighborhood will require the skills of geographers, anthropologists, urbanologists, economists, social workers and historians, as well as community organizers. It is obvious that criminal justice will have to break out of its limited disciplinary framework. Together these "specialties" are a means of putting reality back together, of thinking whole. Because there are no neighborhoodologists (except those who live there), each of these disciplines will have to contribute to the entirety. In doing so, they will themselves begin to take on some of the qualities of wholeness. By suggesting a "reconstruction" of neighborhoods, I do not mean that social scientists should themselves undertake this reconstruction. As I have tried to show, many neighborhoods are always undergoing transformations. Social scientists would function as resource persons, not experts. Such work would require an ideological commitment to the world perspective point of view, an understanding of the significance of class relations to lower-class political life (Fox-Genovese and Genovese, 1976: 206).

In recent years, many inner-city neighborhoods have been forced to change their strategies for survival. Orthodox political appeals for outside funding and resources, now no longer feasible, were already being rejected in favor of increased reliance on internal political, social and economic resources. Residents in ethnic-based working-class inner-city communities have reacted with various degrees of unity and sophistication to the combination of "benign" neglect and destructive attacks on their way of life. Many inner-city neighborhoods have developed a strategy of survival involving partial or total rejection of "outside" aid, attempting instead to evolve relative self-reliance in funding, expertise and organization. This has meant the increased dependence on the construction of internal institutions, including those dealing with social control.

It is understandable why communities are moving in this direction. Apart from the fact that outside funds are now sparse, heavy reliance on the political process meant accepting "outside" priorities as neighborhood priorities: different ethnic and racial groups in contiguous neighborhoods that should have been co-operating were instead competing for inadequate funds. Yet the values of these groups were often the same: a strong, deeply-rooted and infinite culture bond and a revulsion against formal, bureaucratic, fractured solutions in favor of a holistic, self-reliant approach. Many neighborhoods are now becoming convinced that only they can solve their own problems. They reject umbrella or hierarchical organizations except on the neighborhood's own terms — to the extent that these organizations fit into the neighborhood's strategy. Most important, residents are actively participating in direct action (ensuring their own physical security, cleaning up or even occupying abandoned houses) in preference to intervention by established "service" organizations (National Lawyers Guild Notes, September-October 1983; *The Neighborhood Works*, October 1983: 15).

This result suggests a rejection of orthodox political solutions as a means of neighborhood rejuvenation (Wright, 1983: 99). In its place is a reliance on the neighborhood's own inner resources — an attempt to understand, encourage and strengthen them. In a formal sense, the neighborhood is budding on its own political-economic-social structure, one that has always been there, but has been subjugated in being tied to the vertical, dominant, political bureaucracy. Such a regeneration does not mean cutting off all ties with the "outside" world. But it does mean an understanding of the limited worth and the possible destructive tendencies of these "foreign" agencies where the result of these relations is that the neighborhood is dependent on "outsiders" for growth and survival. The up-down, bureaucratic relationship is in the process of being rejected. Such a development is entirely consistent with prospects of different neighborhoods and communities with the same or similar problems working together.

Communities searching for their identity must begin with an understanding of their own economic, social and political evolution as dependent entities and end with a plan for creating their own defensible neighborhoods (Suttles, 1972).

CONCLUSION

Two competing world views have been described. These views have been historically traced and the point made that they are not merely conceptual quibbles but that they represent alternative presents and futures. What Braudel calls the material life of people is not a mere political leaning, be it left or right, but rather tells about a continuity of material existence worth investigating, not in parts (organized crime, drugs, muggings) but as a historical whole. We need a community justice research problematic in which we study the interpenetration (Wright, 1983) of communal by societal structures and values, how each generates "different networks of social interaction" (Bender, 1978: 61), the competitive beckoning call of success and prestige from local and societal institutions, the pattern of local and national elites and their relative influence, the extent that community economic activities are embedded in the web of community social relations, and how all these influence the problems, possibilities and interplay of formal and informal social control. Now is the time for progressive social scientists to make purposeful, long-term commitments to community struggle. If this kind of holistic systems thinking is correct, those "unique and irregular" parts, inner-city neighborhoods, have every possibility of uniting into a whole that in Wallerstein's words approximates "our image of the good society."

ENDNOTES

1. Futurists may be divided into those like Herman Kahn and Daniel Bell who see the future as essentially an expansion of the goods of postindustrial capitalism to more and more people, and those who see the "transindustrial" society as a "break" with the present but find those tendencies in today's society (Harmon, 1976).
2. Radical writers are beginning to search for alternative futures outside of the "preordained" Marxist paradigm of capitalism, socialism, communism. See especially Wright (1983) and others cited hereafter. This "rethinking" is not limited to radicals. A search of *Books in Print*, *Forthcoming Books in Print* and *Underground Books in Print* reveals that 35 titles include the word "Rethinking."
3. For a particularly good example of maximization see Goldberger (1982), the story of urban growth on Manhattan Island.
4. Harmon (1976: 25-28) lists five "fundamental failures" of the industrial paradigm...it fails: to provide each individual with an opportunity to contribute to society and be affirmed by it in return; to foster a more equitable distribution of power and justice; to foster socially responsible management of the development and application of technology; to provide goals that will enlist the deepest loyalties and commitment of the nation's citizens; and to develop and maintain the habitability of the planet.

5. For a view that "know-how" is the "essential element of the process of production" rather than the Marxian mode of production, see Boulding (1981: 28). A rather romanticized view of the world of the "electric cottage" is found in Toffler (1980); some of the problems of such an "information age" are described in Salmans (1982) and *Multinational Monitor*, March 1984. When I expressed these ideas two years ago in presenting the paper, they were new to most people. Today, the reader probably receives them as given. This itself illustrates the speed with which information, and particularly this conception of society, travels and is accepted. The vast overestimate of the number of Americans capable of being employed in high-technology industries represents the projection of the reconceptualization of the community discussed hereafter.

6. For the development and influence of Braudel's ideas, see Wallerstein (1983b).

7. Wallerstein did not however reject Marx but rather extended his perspective (see note 8). The fact that almost no proper Marxist can today write an article in no matter what field without citing Wallerstein itself testifies to the pervasiveness of world-systems thinking.

8. Each of the article's reviewers, following Wallerstein, properly objected to the incomplete treatment I gave to family transition. Greg Shank summarized this critique as follows:

> The *key* point that gets missed is that the *types* of households have changed, they have not disappeared.... When incorporated into the world-economy, [they] experience objective pauperization — they become part-lifetime proletarian households (historically and presently the quantitatively predominant form of household). These households over a lifetime receive wages from employers beneath the physiological minimum required for its reproduction. They add to it taking on odd jobs, growing food, and receiving gifts from relatives (emphasis in original).

These households are thus thrown into the underground economy, a subject dealt with more extensively below.

9. In a recent quality of life survey of 107 nations, Denmark ranked first and the United States 41st in ratings based on factors including "health and welfare provisions, literacy and education, political participation and stability, the rights of women, economic growth and inflation" (Estes, 1982).

10. The trick is to begin asking the right questions: "Suddenly I understood that questions about the roots of needless hunger had to focus not on the physical limits of the earth, but on the economic and political forces that determine what is planted and who eats. I began to realize that the experts' single-minded focus on greater production as the solution to world hunger was wrongheaded. You could have more food and still more hunger" (Lappe, 1982: 21).

11. Coincidentally, three articles in issue No. 20 of *Crime and Social Justice* have independently come to the same conclusion. As one writer stated: "The decline of the traditional blue-collar working class may mean that they too will be forced to begin developing forms of organization that lead to greater community and interdependence and ultimately to greater unity with the traditionally superexploited proletariat" (Bush, 1982: 45). See also Headley, 1983: 60; Fox, 1983: 69.

12. Advanced capitalism's only conceptualization of work is jobs, that is, working for another. Capitalist organization is increasingly incapable of supplying full employment for the total population (community) (Harmon, 1976: 26; Wallerstein, 1983a: 12). "In 1982, 18.3 million people, almost a fifth of the country's employed workers, worked part time.

From 1970 to 1982, while the percentage of those employed rose 26.5 percent , to 99.5 million from 78.6 million, the number of part time workers rose 57.9 percent to 18.3 million from 11.5 million" *New York Times*, 14 August 1983: 1; September 1983: 1; 4 December 1983: 443; *Dollars and Sense*, October 1983: 3. These statistics substantiate Wallerstein's analysis of the pauperization of the working class (see note 8). In March 1984, the Democratic Party's primary campaign in which Hart's "new ideas" appeal to young urban professionals (the so-called "yuppies") opposed to Mondale's "old guard" posture presented the political manifestation of the ideas discussed in the text. It is quite likely, however, that many of these young professionals, in rejecting Mondale for Hart, were likewise rejecting the "heavy spending" on minorities and the poor associated with Mondale. In terms of community vision, theirs is probably not much different from Reagan's. See *The New York Times*, 18 March 1984: 1, 16, and *In These Times*, 21-27 March 1984: 6-7.

13. An August 1983 study by the Congressional Budget Office indicates that 70 percent of Reagan's budget cuts fall on families making less than $20,000 per year (*Southern Illinoisan*, 25 August 1983: 2). 1981 Census Bureau figures show that 32 million Americans, or 14 percent of the population, live below the poverty line ($8,351 for a family of four), an 8.5 percent increase from 1979. 32 percent of all blacks and 24 percent of all Hispanics live below this level (King and Rees, 1982: 13-14, 24-25). The concept of the safety net is particularly inappropriate to describe these policies. A safety net is arranged by the organizers of a dangerous event to protect their star performers. While such a metaphor does apply to capitalists such as Chrysler and other major corporations saved by government policies, it is inapplicable to those who have been "dropped" because they are no longer considered to be part of the circus.

14. In Europe, on the other hand, studies of the underground economy are quite advanced. See Schiray, 1983; Gut and Schiray, 1983; Schiray, 1983; Gaudin and Schiray, 1983; Corpet *et al.*, 1980 and Sachs *et al.*, 1979.

15. Wallerstein's analysis of the necessity of the working class supplementing wages received from the regular economy with income received from the irregular economy is a more fundamental reason for the irregular economy's existence (see note 8) but that reasoning is not central to the theme of this article (see Wallerstein, 1983a).

16. The economy appears in multiple forms, some of which are merely excrescences on the capitalist beast (the doctor who cheats on income tax, or the antique dealer who pays in cash and, like many small businesses keeps two sets of books, one for the business, and one for the government). Some are extremely harmful, such as the drug business, which for cocaine alone involves billions of dollars, is international in scope and politically corrupting (*New York Times*, 24 October 1982: 1; Simon and Witte, 1982); and much of which exploits marginal workers (King and Rees, 1982: 21). Distinction on the basis of class must be made between this part of the economy and that described by Braudel. The first is dominated by market values while the second is integrated into the social life of the people. It is the task of progressive criminal justice researchers to untangle this web. I appreciate the critique by Jane Adams of this part of the paper.

17. I have discussed here only urban manifestations of this "new reality." There has also been a strong resurgence of community and farmers markets (Sommer, 1980) and the regenerative agriculture movement (see *The New Farm Magazine of Regenerative Agriculture*).

18. The community, as described, represents the political unit. From the criminological perspective, it is the stable family that is important but such a family is not likely without a stable and politically united community. On the "successful" family, see Naroll (1983), especially Chapter 10. Naroll is concerned with moral net theory, a concept generally abandoned by leftists to conservatives.

References

Aronowitz, Stanley. 1983. "Socialism and Beyond: Remaking the American Left, Part Two." *Socialist Review.* 69: 7-42.

Bach, Robert L. 1980. "On the Holism of a World-Systems Perspective" in Hopkins, Terence K. and Immanuel Wallerstein (eds.), *Processes of The World-System.* Beverly Hills: Sage.

Bayley, David. 1979. "Police Function, Structure, and Control in Western Europe and North America: Composition and Historical Studies" in Morris, N. and M. Tonry (eds.), *Crime and Justice, An Annual Review of Research.* Chicago: University of Chicago Press.

Bender, Thomas. 1978. *Community and Social Change in America.* Baltimore: John Hopkins Press.

Boulding, Kenneth. 1978. *Ecodynamics: A New Theory of Societal Evolution.* Beverly Hills: Sage.

.... 1981. *Evolutionary Economics.* Beverly Hills: Sage.

Bowles, Samuel, David M. Gordon and Thomas E. Weisskopf. 1983. *Beyond the Wasteland: A Democratic Alternative to Economic Decline.* New York: Anchor Press/Doubleday.

Braudel, Fernand. 1980. *Civilization and Capitalism, 15th-18th Century. Volume III: Civilization materielle economie et Capitalism, Temps du Monde.* Paris: Armand Colin.

.... 1981. *Civilization and Capitalism, 15th-18th Century, Volume I: The Structures of Everyday Life, The Limits of the Possible.* Translated from the French by Sian Reynolds. London: William Collins and Sons.

.... 1981. *Civilization and Capitalism, 15th-18th Century, Volume II: The Wheels of Commerce.* Translated from the French by Sian Reynolds. London: William Collins and Sons.

Bush, Rod. 1982. "Racism and Changes in the International Division of Labor." *Crime and Social Justice.* 20: 37-49.

Capra, Fritjof. 1982. *The Turning Point: Science, Society and the Rising Culture.* New York: Simon and Schuster.

Cohen, Henry. 1981. "Crime in American History: Toward a General Synthesis." Unpublished paper.

Conley, John. 1980. "Historical Research in Anglo-American Criminal Justice" in Talarico, S. (ed.), *Criminal Justice Research.* Cincinnati: Anderson.

Corpet, Olivier, Jocelyne Gaudin and Michel Schiray. 1980. "l'Autre Moitié: L'Economie Cachée du Secteur Domestique et des Marchés parallels." Paris: Maison des Sciences de l'Homme.

Denzin, Norman K. 1982. "Notes on Criminology and Criminality" in Pepinsky, Harold E. (ed.), *Rethinking Criminology.* Beverly Hills: Sage.

Ehrenreich, Barbara and Frances Fox Piven. 1983. "The Left's Best Hope." *Mother Jones.* (Sept./Oct.) 8: 26-29.